UTTLEY

MANCHESTER
1824

Manchester University Press

To the memory of my parents
and Peter du Sautoy

Also by Denis Judd

BALFOUR AND THE BRITISH EMPIRE

THE VICTORIAN EMPIRE

POSTERS OF WORLD WAR TWO

THE BRITISH RAJ

LIVINGSTONE IN AFRICA

THE LIFE AND TIMES OF GEORGE V

THE HOUSE OF WINDSOR

SOMEONE HAS BLUNDERED: CALAMITIES OF THE BRITISH ARMY
DURING THE VICTORIAN AGE

EDWARD VII

PALMERSTON

THE CRIMEAN WAR

ECLIPSE OF KINGS

RADICAL JOE: A LIFE OF JOSEPH CHAMBERLAIN

THE ADVENTURES OF LONG JOHN SILVER

RETURN TO TREASURE ISLAND

PRINCE PHILIP

LORD READING: A BIOGRAPHY OF RUFUS ISAACS

GEORGE VI

THE EVOLUTION OF THE MODERN COMMONWEALTH (WITH PETER SLINN)

JAWAHARLAL NEHRU

EMPIRE: THE BRITISH IMPERIAL EXPERIENCE FROM 1765 TO THE PRESENT

A BRITISH TALE OF INDIAN AND FOREIGN SERVICE: THE MEMOIRS OF
SIR IAN SCOTT (EDITED AND INTRODUCED BY DENIS JUDD)

FURTHER TALES OF LITTLE GREY RABBIT

THE BOER WAR (WITH KEITH SURRIDGE)

THE LION AND THE TIGER: THE RISE AND FALL OF THE BRITISH RAJ

THE PRIVATE DIARIES OF ALISON UTTLEY (1932–1971): AUTHOR OF LITTLE GREY RABBIT
AND SAM PIG (EDITED BY DENIS JUDD, FOREWORD BY RONALD BLYTHE)

Contributed To

THE QUEEN: A PENGUIN SPECIAL

FOUNDERS OF THE WELFARE STATE

VICTORIAN VALUES: PERSONALITIES AND PERSPECTIVES IN NINETEENTH
CENTURY SOCIETY

MODERN BRITISH HISTORY: METHODS AND PERSPECTIVES

DECADENCE AND DANGER: WRITING, HISTORY AND THE FIN DE SIÈCLE

ALISON UTTLEY

Spinner of Tales

*The authorised biography of
the creator of Little Grey Rabbit*

Denis Judd

Manchester University Press

Manchester and New York

distributed in the United States exclusively by Palgrave Macmillan

This edition first published 2010 by
Manchester University Press
Oxford Road, Manchester M13 9NR, UK
and Room 400, 175 Fifth Avenue, New York, NY 10010, USA
www.manchesteruniversitypress.co.uk

Distributed in the United States exclusively by
Palgrave Macmillan, 175 Fifth Avenue, New York,
NY 10010, USA

Distributed in Canada exclusively by
UBC Press, University of British Columbia, 2029 West Mall,
Vancouver, BC, Canada V6T 1Z2

British Library Cataloguing-in-Publication Data
A catalogue record for this book is available from the British Library

Library of Congress Cataloging-in-Publication Data applied for

ISBN 978 0 7190 8456 0 paperback

First published 1986 by Michael Joseph Ltd
Second edition published 2001 by Sutton Publishing Limited

Extracts from the diary of Alison Uttley
© The Alison Uttley Literary Property Trust 1986

Printed in Great Britain
by Bell & Bain Ltd, Glasgow

CONTENTS

ACKNOWLEDGEMENTS

I am grateful to the large number of people who allowed me to interview them, who sent me information of various sorts, who answered specific questions or helped me in any way. They include: the late Helen Uttley, Peter and Mollie du Sautoy, Lilian King, Joyce Kann, Betty and Richard Fairbairn, Martin Byers, Anthony Tolson, Dr Katherine Watson, Lady Katherine Wigglesworth, Barbara Healey, Peter and Vivienne Plummer of Downs House, Dr Elizabeth French, Warden of Ashburne Hall, Glenise Matheson and her staff of the Rylands University Library Manchester, Mr and Mrs Clay of Castle Top Farm, Dick Frost, Mr and Mrs Lees, Dr Frederick Ratcliffe, Librarian of Cambridge University, Giles de la Mare, Agnes and Frances Stewart, Peggy Channon, Sir Oliver Millar, Lady Howe, Susan Dickinson, Phyllis Hunt, Penny Sibson, Kaye Webb, John Smith, the Reverend Oscar Muspratt, Mrs Stuart Young, Del Anderson, Peter Carter-Ruck, Elizabeth Barrett, Julie Scott-Bayfield, the Kerlan Collection University of Minnesota, Kathleen Luscombe, Mary Athay, Dawn Langley Simmons, Dr Alex Paton, David Davis, Frank Dadswell, David and Jackie Mitchell, Judith Elliot, Katharine Thompson, Sheila Beringer, Muriel Holden, Kathleen Day and Joy Feast.

Jill Fletcher typed the text with her usual efficiency. My mother and father, who first introduced me to Alison Uttley's books, provided enthusiastic support and helped to produce the finished typescript. Alan Brooke, Jennie Davies and Michèle Young, of Michael Joseph, have contributed beyond measure to the publication of the book. I am indebted to the Trustees of the Alison Uttley Literary Property Trust for inviting me to write this authorised biography and for assisting me throughout. My wife and four children accommodated my absorption in Alison and all her works with great forbearance.

There is one debt of gratitude that I can never fully discharge. Peter du Sautoy has been a source of invaluable information and encouragement from start to finish. He has also read every word of the typescript and commented upon it, although any errors that remain are my sole responsibility. I dedicate this book to him with great affection.

Denis Judd
London, 1986.

The author and publisher would like to thank the literary trustees of Walter de la Mare and the Society of Authors as their representative for permission to reproduce 'Solitude'. They would also like to thank the following journals from whose reviews short passages have been quoted: *Altrincham and Sale Guardian, Birmingham Post, Church Times, Country Life, Countryman, Daily Telegraph, Dalesman, Education, Friend, Guardian, Homes and Gardens, Irish Independent, Listener, New Statesman, Observer, Punch, Shields Gazette, Scotsman, Spectator, The Sunday Times, Tablet, The Times, The Times Educational Supplement, The Times Literary Supplement, Vogue* and *Yorkshire Post*.

The author and publisher are also grateful to Granada for permission to quote from *The People's War: Britain 1939–45* by Angus Calder, and to the following publishing houses for permission to quote extracts from Alison Uttley's books: Faber & Faber Ltd (*A Peck of Gold, Wild Honey, Ambush of Young Days, The Country Child, The Button Box, Secret Places, Country Hoard, The Swans Fly Over, Here's a New Day, Cuckoo in June, A Ten O'Clock Scholar, Plowmen's Clocks, Something for Nothing, The Stuff of Dreams* and *High Meadows*); Puffin Books (*Fairy Tales*, foreword by Kathleen Lines); Heinemann (*The Squirrel, the Hare and the Little Grey Rabbit*) and Collins (the foreword to the Little Grey Rabbit series). Messrs Collins and Heinemann also made available letters and documents from their archives.

PICTURE ACKNOWLEDGEMENTS

The author and publisher would like to thank the following for permission to reproduce their photographs in this volume: Peter du Sautoy (1), Mark Gerson (14), Ben Judd (12), Dorothy Judd (3), Joyce Kann (16), Dr Alex Paton (15), Rylands University Library, Manchester (2, 6, 7, 8), Anthony Tolson (4, 5) and Penny Tweedie (18).

ACKNOWLEDGEMENTS FOR THE THIRD EDITION

Mrs. Uttley would have been delighted that this latest edition of her authorised biography should be published by the Press of her old University. I am grateful to Matthew Frost for publishing the book. Many thanks too to Marigold Atkey of David Higham for all her invaluable input. Finally, nobody has worked harder or more generously than Sheila Griffiths, chair of the Ashburne Association, to ensure the book's re-publication.

Denis Judd,
London, 2010

SOURCES AND TERMINOLOGY

The notes on sources are collected, according to chapter, at the end of the book. The vast bulk of these refer to documents made available to me by Peter du Sautoy and other individuals as well as by the Alison Uttley Literary Property Trust and the John Rylands University Library of Manchester. The diaries in particular have been an invaluable source. Mrs Uttley left them to Peter du Sautoy assuming that they would one day enable an authorised biography to be written. Eventually most of these documents, including Alison's unpublished diaries, will be deposited at the John Rylands University Library of Manchester.

Mrs Uttley only began using 'Alison' regularly as her first name in 1929 when she published *The Squirrel, the Hare and the Little Grey Rabbit*. To avoid confusion, she is referred to as Alison throughout the text. Where there are quotations from, or references to, her autobiographical writings, the names she used to describe others – Patty, Mrs Fern, Thomas Frost, and so forth – have been reproduced.

A Spinner of Tales

Like Thursday's child in the old nursery rhyme she loved so much, Alison Uttley had far to go. Her life encompassed more than ninety-one years, from 1884 to 1976. She was born when the great Liberal leader, W.E. Gladstone, was leading his second reforming administration and while the Dervish host was closing in around the besieged and doomed General Gordon at Khartoum. When she died, Margaret Thatcher was an inexperienced leader of the Opposition and still to unleash the 'Thatcherite revolution', and Britain, bereft of its empire and uncertain of its future role, was half-heartedly established as a member of the European Economic Community.

Alison Uttley journeyed far in other ways, not least from her humble origins at Castle Top Farm, high up overlooking the Derwent Valley in Derbyshire, to an enviable status as a profoundly admired writer of rural *belles-lettres*, and a best-selling and greatly loved author of books for children. Even within her chosen profession she voyaged as daringly and excitingly as her creation Penelope in *A Traveller in Time*, moving deftly from the imaginative worlds of *Little Grey Rabbit* and *Sam Pig* to her books of essays – clear-eyed, provocative and nostalgic; from fairy tales to finely fashioned autobiographical works, such as *The Country Child*; from magic and nursery rhyme to studies of place and time, and dreams and space; from two novels for adults to a few plays for children and a host of stories, articles and reviews. She even published a cookery book, *Recipes from an Old Farmhouse*, as well as a history of her adopted county, *Buckinghamshire*.

By any standards, anywhere, at any time, Alison Uttley was richly gifted and prodigiously productive. Raised in rustic simplicity, trained as a scientist, widowed tragically and abruptly before her time, and obliged to earn a living for herself and her son, she achieved the fame she craved and the financial security she needed by the heroic exertion of her chief talent – that of a born writer. She was in her mid-forties when she began to write, bringing to what became her life's work an unquenchable curiosity, a fine mind, a sensitive spirit and an unshakeable resolve. Her appetite for knowledge was unbounded and remained with her to the end of her life.

Mrs Uttley's best-selling status as an author was based on a few, relatively simple, formulae; the vivid recollection of a vanished rural England for the pleasure of the nostalgic and curious reader; the creation of several closely knit and wonderfully described communities of animals, in which the real world was mixed with magic, and in which some danger and suffering was contained by the security and goodwill of the wider community; and the writing of many precise and thoughtful essays that sparkle even brighter with the passing of time.

Her success was, however, achieved at the cost of much pain, for herself and for others, as she relentlessly pursued her objectives. Indeed the writer Penelope Fitzgerald was shrewdly to describe her as 'a self-deluding romantic . . . and a compulsive housekeeper, patching and jam-making in an heroically untidy kitchen . . . it is impossible not to think of her as a sorceress, a storyteller whose tales were produced only at mortal cost'.

Often kindly, thoughtful and loving, a provider of merry company and stimulating friendship, she was, however, also capable of being domineering, scornful, harsh and calculating. Very few were able to measure up to the demands she made of them: her husband committed suicide, her only son lived in some fear of her all his life, her daughter-in-law disliked her intensely, most of her relations were set aside as unworthy. Her friends often found themselves in disfavour and several of her domestic servants were abruptly dismissed.

Even within the world of publishing, she was not always easy to work with and although she almost invariably delivered a highly polished and properly considered typescript, she was a shrewd businesswoman, capable on occasion of digging in her toes very firmly. Alison was moreover fiercely competitive with any other authors who seemed to overshadow her. She bitterly resented suggestions that her animal characters owed something to Beatrix Potter's creations. She developed a deep aversion to Enid Blyton who, by an unhappy quirk of fate, lived not far from her after she settled in Beaconsfield in Buckinghamshire; Alison's diary entries sometimes drip venom when, for instance, she describes at the fishmonger's 'a woman ogling [the shopkeeper], her false teeth, her red lips, her head on one side as she gazed up close to him . . . the Blyton, photographed and boastful!'

She also quarrelled bitterly and persistently with one of her most famous illustrators, Margaret Tempest, who had helped so successfully to create the characters in the Grey Rabbit books. The essence of the disagreement, over who had truly created the characters that inhabit the pages of the *Little Grey Rabbit* books with so much grace and distinction, reflected Alison's own high self-regard and her steely determination to protect her literary and financial interests.

Ironically, or perhaps inevitably, Alison herself could not always come up to her own high standards. She often felt 'unworthy' or 'dull and stupid'; she confessed amazement that her books should sell in such vast quantities, and she was able to recognise the havoc that she could wreak among those she loved through the assertion of her powerful personality. Although she generally managed to keep her guilt at bay, the crushing depressions, psychosomatic ailments and chronic in-securities that beset her bear witness to much internal anguish. She was often very lonely and self-pitying.

Her almost desperate desire to assert her view of the world not only made her a singularly overbearing person, but also led her to eliminate much of what she found unpalatable or inconvenient from her published writings. What she has left behind in *The Country Child*, *Ambush of Young Day*, *The Farm on the Hill* and many other books of autobiography, is the censored version of her life – a sort of Alison in Wonderland. For example, the unwary reader would have no idea that she had a younger brother, Harry – he simply becomes a 'non-person' in Alison's autobiographical works. So powerfully did Mrs Uttley project her version of her life that, hitherto, everyone who has attempted to write about her has swallowed it whole and then obediently regurgitated it.

Fortunately, especially for me as her authorised biographer, Alison had the integrity, or possibly the vanity, of the true artist when she left posterity another account of her life in her unpublished diaries. These run to forty volumes and are packed with the most detailed and intimate information. Although externally Alison's life may seem to have been rather prosaic, the diaries reveal an internal world of great passion, where self-confidence and uncertainty, pride and self-pity, joy and anguish are intermingled. For the first time, therefore, the revelations contained in her diaries make it possible to put Alison's long and triumphant career into accurate perspective, and to write a full and fair account of her life. This process has been aided by the testimony of dozens who knew her well.

Not all of it makes for comfortable reading: there are half-truths and evasions to confront; choices have to be made between Alison's different accounts of events; her intense, jealous and apparently incestuous passion for her son John has to be honestly assessed, and many other vagaries of her behaviour scrutinised.

There also a bewildering number of pardoxes to resolve. Mrs Uttley idealised her country origins, yet was stimulated and excited by the cities and towns she lived in and visited; she was trained as a scientist at Manchester University, but believed in fairies all her life; she was an Edwardian suffragette and read bedtime stories to Ramsay Macdonald's children, yet ended her days as a staunch Conservative; she was intrigued by dreams, even writing a book *The Stuff of Dreams*, but shied away from any deep self-analysis.

Of course, these paradoxes and contradictions, and her confused, passionate and often contrary emotions are simply a part of the whole. In the end, it is perhaps a relief to know that she, too, like most of us, could be mean and rude and selfish, just as she was often charming, warm-hearted and constructive; that she changed her mind, sometimes stuck too resolutely to her guns, was capable of prejudice and sometimes failed to suffer fools gladly. Certainly it makes her a far more interesting person to try to understand, and also goes a long way towards explaining why so much of her writing deals with communities that are able eventually to resolve problems and tensions, and with social structures that are based on reassuringly traditional, mostly rural and seasonal, rhythms and patterns.

This biography of Alison Uttley is in no way meant to diminish her, either as a person or as an artist. Indeed her work is currently under-going an important revival with the televising and relaunching of the *Little Grey Rabbit* books. As the new millennium at last gets under way, it is perhaps comforting that one of the twentieth century's classic stories for children is being given a vigorous new lease of life in this way. The timely reissuing of this authorised biography is all part of a gratifying revival and reappraisal of her work and influence.

As we seek to make sense of the year 2001 and those that follow it, the nostalgic appeal of Alison's writing, deeply rooted in her late-Victorian childhood in rural Derbyshire, may prove an irresistible tonic for the jaded, over-stimulated, computer-zapped imaginations of today's children. It is easy to see why this could be the case, for in these sparkling, sharp, diamond-bright, yet also dreamy, stories there are no soulless tower blocks, no bored and distracted au pairs, no lurking paedophiles, no violent and terrifying videos. Instead there is adventure, magic and good-fellowship; a world where small dangers are encountered, but also successfully navigated, and where, more often than not, well-meaning individuals rally to the cause of the community

– even though they may puzzle, mutter, and scratch their heads before deciding what to do for the best.

Above all, the considerable achievements of Mrs Uttley's authorship were built upon a unique creativity, and upon her capacity to write beautifully. Despite the turmoil and the pain of so much of her private life, these foundations are as solid as the rocky Derbyshire farmland from which Alison sprang so many years ago.

Denis Judd
London, 2001

CHAPTER ONE

The Snow-Baby

I was a snow-baby, a lucky baby, they said,
born just before Christmas, in the great storm

ALISON UTTLEY

Alison Uttley was born on 17 December 1884 at Castle Top Farm, which is set in hilly country on the southern borders of the Derbyshire Peak District.

At her birth the countryside was blanketed with snow, brought in by the north winds that had howled through the great solitary trees that stood in the fields surrounding the farm. Winter had come early, but Alison's parents had taken the sensible precaution of sending in good time for the midwife from the nearby village. Henry Taylor, Alison's father, had harnessed the mare to the spring cart and had driven down the hill and away to where the old nurse, with a sixth sense, was waiting for him with her bag already packed and her medicines ready.

The arrival of the nurse at the farm, wearing her bonnet with a little frilled white cap under it, her cloak and her white apron, was a great relief to Henry Taylor's wife, Hannah. Seventy-seven years later Alison Uttley, at the height of her fame as an author, recreated something of the atmosphere in her diary:

> I feel I am nearly born, a babe at Castle Top in Victorian days, all the fuss and preparation . . . my father unhurried. Snow on the ground, the midwife ready, no doctor, not necessary. My mother must have been nervous, her first child, but she was always brave, and the nurse was such a good, kind little old woman: Mrs Marriott of Lea. She smoked a pipe in real old age, about eighty-five – I saw her.[1]

The nurse quickly and efficiently took charge of the household. She helped the Taylor's servant girl, and Alison's mother, making gruel and giving sips of herbal tea to everyone. Outside the weather got worse:

> The snow came down steadily all night and all the next day and every day. There seemed to be no end to it. Day after day it snowed, and soon the roads were impassable. No cart could go to the villages, for the edge of the road was level with deep drifts, and the gates were snowed under. . . . The house was an island in a sea of whiteness.[2]

Although there was now no chance of getting the doctor through the drifts, even in an emergency, the old nurse reassured everybody. She could manage. There was ample food in the larder, baskets of eggs which could not go to the dealers, butter made from the new milk, cheeses, home-baked bread and a sack of flour, and a side of bacon. The fires were heaped with wood and coal, and water was carried in from the stone troughs each day after Mr Taylor and Willie, the servant boy, had broken the ice with axe-heads. A large copper pan was kept full of hot water for the impending birth.

The baby arrived without, it seems, any undue difficulty. Despite the treacherous weather outside, inside Castle Top Farm there was warmth, and comfort, and joy:

> So I was born in this wild storm, with deep snow on the ground, and cattle shut in their houses, and horses in the stable. I was bathed in spring water heated over the fire, and I was held up to the windows to open my eyes and to look out over the fields at the dazzling whiteness, and to look at the candles in their brass candlesticks, alight to welcome me.[3]

Before the baby could be taken downstairs, an old tradition was observed and the nurse carried her in her long robe up to the attic because 'A new-born child must always be taken up before it goes down, so it will go up in life and not down.'[4]

As well as her mother's milk, the new baby was given cinder tea to drink, made by dropping a red-hot cinder into a cup of water which was then allowed to become lukewarm. Since there was no cradle, the old nurse took the deepest drawer from the polished mahogany chest of drawers and, lining it with blankets, laid the baby in it.

Given the circumstances of her birth, it is not surprising that Alison Uttley's love of Christmas and the winter season shines like a star from the pages of her books and through the many years of her life. The first flowers she saw were snowdrops picked from the orchard for her mother and her first vision of beauty, she believed, was the kissing bunch which hung from a hook on the ceiling on Christmas Day, bright with glass balls and silver bells. The first stars she saw were the winter stars, shining in the sky above the farm. For the rest of her days, Alison Uttley made a ready and passionate association between the anniversary of her birth and the rituals of renewal and of light amid the darkness that are characteristics of Christmastime:

> I was a snow-baby, a lucky baby, they said, born just before Christmas, in the great storm. Snow was part of my life, and it would always attract me and bring magic to me, magic of fairy-tale, and snow crystals and miracles of ice flowers on the windows.[5]

Alison Uttley was christened Alice Jane Taylor. Her family had lived at Castle Top Farm for some two hundred years, working the stony soil as tenant farmers; the land was owned by the Arkwright family from Willersley Castle. Because of the Arkwright passion for organising shooting parties based at Castle Top Farm, the farmhouse was being altered and modernised at the time that Henry Taylor had taken his first wife. The young couple were obliged to live in an adjoining barn while the improvements to the farmhouse were being made, and the damp and makeshift conditions there may well have contributed to Mrs Taylor's death from pneumonia. Eventually Henry Taylor remarried on 12 March 1884, taking as his second wife Hannah Dickens who was eleven years younger than him. Hannah Taylor conceived immediately after her marriage and the couple's first child, the future Alison Uttley, was born a little over nine months later.

Alison Uttley has left a precise and vivid picture of her parents in her autobiographical writings, but in her unpublished diaries and letters she added other, franker details. Henry Taylor, portrayed as Tom Garland in Alison's first book of reminiscence *The Country Child*, was born on 30 June 1842. Writing in her diary on 30 June 1957, Alison Uttley recalled the anniversary of his birth 115 years before: 'My father's birthday, and I think of the little fat child born at Castle Top . . . the youngest of seven. William, John, Selina, Susan, Mary . . . not sure, and he was Henry, the youngest.'[6] Henry Taylor was sturdy, solid and weatherbeaten. He had a frank, open face and beautiful hands. His daughter was to remember, 'I always admired them, although I knew nothing about hands. They were the clever hands of a craftsman, who could mould and carve and finger very small objects as well as large ones. There was nothing clumsy about them and he could take up the most delicate object of flower, feather or ornament and see its beauty.'[7]

Henry Taylor's life's work was his farm and he devoted himself to it with a steady and faithful commitment. There was no great profit to be made from his work, but there was a self-sufficiency to be had and a comfortable standard of living. Six decades later, when she had established herself as a successful and profitable author, Alison looked back on the relative hardship of her childhood, at the difficulty her parents had in finding school fees, at the need to be prudent with resources, and longed to give some of her wealth – she had just received a half-yearly royalty payment of over a thousand pounds – to her father and mother.[8] In contrast to his daughter, Henry Taylor could hardly write at all:

> My father flatly refused to write anything except his own name, and as my mother's initials were the same as his he escaped even this literary effort. He could handle a gun as well as anyone, he could plough a straight furrow, and mow, and build a barn, and break in a colt. He could manage a nervous horse, and doctor sick cattle, but the slim penholder was not his tool. . . . When he sent a message it was a verbal one, that travelled from one to another till it reached its destination.[9]

The only writing Alison saw her father undertake was when he made notes in his pocketbook about the dates of calving and foaling, the sums to be paid for extra labour and so forth. His daughter longed to see and find this book, with its leather back, in which he wrote with infinite care and secrecy with a pencil sharpened to a delicate point. She had, however, to be contented with being shown the frontispiece with its engraving of Furness Abbey, or a table showing the phases of the moon and the signs of the Zodiac. More accessible were the marks cut into the beams of barns as reminders of important farm duties and dates.

Although he refused to worship formally and was critical of the local vicar fawning on rich families, Henry Taylor considered himself to be a member of the Church of England. His daughter was later to assess him more shrewdly: 'He was a mixture of stern Puritan and Pagan, loving God and the Earth, the soil, rocks, springs and grass, caring for earth and tending it . . . [his] wisdom was ancient, the lore of dim ancestors, of earth itself, an intuitive knowledge of herbs and weather and animals.'[10]

An undemonstrative conservative by upbringing and inclination, Henry Taylor was not simply and uncritically content with his lot. To be a tenant farmer meant that he did not own the land that he cherished and his attendance at the rent dinner at the nearby village of Cromford each Lady Day, when he paid his dues, was an annual reminder of his inferior status. He expressed some of this resentment by disapproving of the needless slaughter wreaked by the Squire's shooting parties, which 'moved him to contempt as he described how the poor birds were beaten up and frightened away, half-tame as they were after hand-rearing, and then they were shot by the waiting guns with never a chance to escape'.[11] These shooting parties were in fact something of a disruption to the workmanlike routine at Castle Top Farm. Alison Uttley was to remember how the wealthy visitors ate inside the house while outside the dead pheasants were laid in pairs upon the lawn – each pair a husband and wife to her childish eyes. She also recalled: 'Once getting under the dining room table and listening to the conversation of the rich people . . . and then unfortunately I touched somebody's boot, and a lady called out "There's an animal under the table, and it touched my boot!" And I was dragged out into the kitchen!'[12]

Despite his disinclination to write more than the bare minimum, his lack of interest in books, his stolid patriotism and dislike of change – he was a staunch supporter of Britain during the Boer War and was greatly perturbed by the death of Queen Victoria in the middle of that conflict – Henry Taylor had his creative gifts as well. In addition to his skills with beast and field he was also, according to his daughter, a great storyteller:

> Then he told stories of his childhood. . . . He told how they brewed their own beer in the brew-house, and made their tallow-dips. His grandmother sat in the chimney-corner with a spinning-wheel, and made the very same cloth they had on the table. He told of the horse thief who stole the mare out of the orchard, and how he would have been hanged if they had caught him. . . . He told of the ghost his father met by the gate in the meadow, which never answered, but brought death to the house. Strange, grim stories, which [Alison] would never forget.[13]

Alison's mother, Hannah Taylor, had been born on 15 July 1853. She had been thirty years of age when she had married, a comparatively advanced age for a country bride. Alison was to inherit her large dark eyes, her long nose and her brown hair, while her mouth and chin more resembled her father's. Before her marriage Hannah had worked as a lady's maid and she brought, as did so many other girls who had worked in the houses of their social superiors, a sense of what was proper and a certain good taste to the running of her own household. She paid attention to details, dressing her family with care, and ensuring that the house was furnished in a solid decent style and that the meals were cooked and served with some refinement.

Unlike her husband, Mrs Taylor was a convinced and active Christian. She was evangelical, even puritan, in her views and practices and Alison was later to write that she did not discover the talisman of the Cross as her escape from witches until late in her childhood, 'for we were an evangelical family'.[14]

Under Hannah Taylor's guidance, Alison went regularly to the local Anglican church, usually attending both morning and evening services with her mother. The whole family kept strict observance of the Sabbath when, although there was an abundance of good food, only Sunday books were read – the Bible and *Pilgrim's Progress* – Sunday toys put out – Noah's Ark was a favourite – and only sacred music played.

Alison had a younger brother, christened William Henry and born on 28 September 1887. Known to his family throughout his life as Harry, he was to prove both a joy and a vexation to his sister. Like so many first-born children, Alison felt a sense of displacement and envy at her brother's birth, remembering, more than forty years after the event, 'Harry's birthday. I think of those days, when Father was up the filbert trees, and Harry was born, to the great joy of my father and mother. No wonder I wasn't of much account! I wasn't worth it, I realise that now.'[15]

Although Harry was a useful playmate during Alison's early childhood on her isolated farm, they developed different tastes and interests. Where Alison was bookish, a quick reader like her mother, Harry was more stolid and, like Mr Taylor, not a great reader. Not long after Harry's death in 1964, Alison was shocked to learn from his widow that 'she is turning out Harry's books, all mouldy and black! An author's brother! No wonder we had not much in common, he cared nothing for books.'[16] At various times during her adult life Alison felt irritation at what she saw as Harry's mishandling of Castle Top Farm after he took over its management, was often hurt when he failed to respond appropriately to the various presents she sent him and felt frustration at their lack of common interests. She was able to take some pleasure from the fact that in adulthood Harry came increasingly to resemble their dead father and she recognised by the early 1930s that he was her nearest blood relation; yet her perception of him was overwhelmingly that of a brother who always took and never gave. At Christmastime in 1944 she wrote, with much anguish, in her diary, 'Card from Harry – with best wishes, no love! He behaves as if I were the merest stranger. . . . All his life Harry has been cold and calculating with me, and I kept getting hurt against his hardness.'[17]

Harry's resentments towards his sister are easy to understand. Although he was the longed-for son and heir, Alison soon outstripped him in academic and cultural accomplishment. When he was only sixteen, she left him behind at Castle Top for university and the outside world. Eventually she became a celebrated and wealthy writer while he was saddled with the toil and routine of farm work. In appearance 'a proper old country person', Harry had a view of Castle Top that was quite different, and far less romantic, than that of his sister. In his memory, 'he did all the work', developing a permanent stoop from carrying countless loads of hay to the barns.[18]

During Harry's final illness, Alison made some attempt to bridge the gap between them, chiefly by sending gifts of money to make his life more comfortable. On the day of his funeral, which she did not attend, she felt much remorse, kneeling by herself to pray for her dead brother and writing in her diary, 'Goodbye, Harry. Forgive all my impatience.'[19]

Apart from her immediate family, Alison had few other close relatives. There was an aunt Lizzy who died in 1935 and whom Alison mourned, chiefly because with her died some unknown scandal from her past life: 'Now I shall never know the old secrets, she is the last of her generation, the last link with the past.'[20] There was also a cousin, Sissy, who remembered Alison's birthday unfailingly and responded enthusiastically, even gushingly, to presents of her books. Sissy had a sister, Helen Dickens, whom Alison hardly saw but who visited her towards the end of her life in 1971. It is interesting that, although Alison found Helen Dickens ugly and awkward and loud, she gave her her mother's garnet brooch as a present. Alison had another cousin, Mary. Of these relations, it seems that only Sissy had any close contact with the Taylor family, sometimes staying with them at Castle Top Farm.

Throughout her life Alison Uttley was to look back on her early years at Castle Top with a passionate, sometimes self-indulgent, longing which was an expression of love for her rural environment but more especially for her parents. Although she respected her father's reliability and good sense, and particularly admired his affinity with the countryside, Alison Uttley clearly had a closer relationship with her mother, both physically and emotionally. She would frequently, in later life, mourn on the anniversary of her mother's death, weeping for her courage and reproaching herself that she had not done more for her during her lifetime. She wrote revealingly in her diary for 1934 that her husband's needs had prevented her from being as generous of her time towards her mother as she would have liked, and added: 'Poor little darling, I think she was happy. I loved her so much but could never fit in with her, or show my love.'[21] In general, however, Alison Uttley's writings show a strong feeling of identification and harmony with her mother rather than the opposite. Even when she was in her seventy-eighth year, she would cry out for her mother during nightmares and dreams. Sometimes she called 'Mother' repeatedly, and other times 'Mama'. In her dreams, Alison occasionally relived the physical relationship that had existed between them: 'Last night I dreamed Mother came in and sat down with all her outdoor things on. I kissed her cheek and felt that sweet softness, and a surge of love and happiness. I knew she was dead, but there she was, and I accepted it.'[22]

She could be reduced to tears by playing on the piano, 'Sometimes I feel like a motherless child'. During the Second World War, when her son John was a prisoner in Germany, she dreamed of him lying securely in her own mother's arms.[23] She also remembered the bliss of her mother reading to her and Harry, felt herself sick with longing just to kiss and speak to her parents, and in February 1936, while a storm raged outside her home, remembered how safe and secure she used to feel at Castle Top when the wind howled round the farmhouse.[24]

There is thus no doubt that Alison felt secure in her parents' love, and in particular in the love of her mother. Their relationship was not, however, always smooth. Alison was later to admit in a diary entry that she had stolen and cheated as a child, 'alas I did all those things'. But that if she had made an exhibition of those failings, 'I should have got such a thrashing I shouldn't have survived, I think.'[25] There was also the Dark Passage, a space barely six feet by three under the stairs in the hall:

The darkness was intense. . . . In that Dark Passage, I was sent when I was naughty, and there I stayed immobile, never venturing to sit down or peer into the brightness of the sunny hall, till somebody opened the door and called: 'Alison! Are you good?' Then I answered gladly: 'Yes, I am kite good now.' And I skipped out. I felt better, changed by the purging darkness. . . . I felt it was a just punishment for badness, and I never thought of rebelling against the sentence, but walked meekly into the black hole.[26]

She also recorded a confrontation with her godmother when she was only two years old. It was a battle of wills between two strong-minded females and was settled to the satisfaction of both:

I was reprimanded by my godmother for throwing my little slipper on the floor. She bade me pick it up and bring it to her, and I stared back determined not to obey. This I remember very distinctly. My godmother was a beautiful and clever woman, strong minded, deeply religious. It was most important to her that I be taught obedience at the earliest age, and she pitted her will against mine. Over and over she said to me, in a low but stern voice, 'Bring that slipper to me, baby', and I stood very still, waiting too. At last I stooped down, and covered the offending slipper with my pinafore, and picked it up with the muslin around it. Then, keeping my fingers from touching the leather, I carried it across to her. Without a sound I deposited it on her lap. Happily she was satisfied and I, too, was relieved that I had my own way, and not picked up the slipper. In this very early memory I recollect a feeling of importance in myself.[27]

Certainly Alison developed a strong sense of her own worth during her early years. She even felt inordinately proud of the month of her birth, December, as if she was the creator, not the created.[28] But above all, she felt richly secure in her mother's love:

One of my earliest memories was being held up by my mother to see the stars. She stood at the dining-room window before the shutters were closed, and showed me the starlit winter sky whilst she sang 'Twinkle, twinkle, little star' to me in her high soft voice. I must have been only two at the time. . . . Then I was swung closer to my mother. She fastened the shutters and hid the glittering things which I wanted for myself.[29]

Alison remembered sleeping cosily in an ancient basket lined with a blanket under the rose trees in the inner garden; or, in winter, lying on her day bed which was the settle with a wooden shutter fitted across the front of it to keep her secure: 'I distinctly remember sleeping there, lying tucked up, safe and warm, under the shepherd's plaid, a venerable black and white plaid which was my babyhood coverlet. Overhead hung the bright copper pans, the brass candlesticks, and shining tankards. . . . The ticking of the old clock, the homely crackle of the fire, and the sound of the rocking-chair, are the accompaniments of that early time.'[30]

At bedtime in those early days she was undressed and bathed by the great fire which always burnt with 'such a crackle and spurt of flames': 'My round tub was on the sanded hearth, and I sat in it, full of happiness, holding the slippery soap. My mother told me tales as she bathed me: "The tale of the three pigs", and "The pig that wouldn't go over the stile", and "This is the house that Jack built". Then I was lifted out and dried on a warm towel.'[31]

Her flannel nightgown was slipped over her head and she knelt down on the hearthrug to say her prayers, slowly and reverently, after her mother. But when she had finished she was allowed to lie on the settle and to be covered with the plaid rug in order to surprise her father when he came in from work. Henry Taylor played his part well enough:

> The outer door opened, and then the inner door, and my father entered, sighing with content to get in from the cold and wind of the field.
> 'She's gone to bed, has she? I *am* glad,' he exclaimed.
> My mother would never deceive, even in fun. She answered innocently enough, but with a nod, which fortunately I didn't see, at the couch. 'Isn't it quiet, dear?'
> 'Yes, it's very nice and quiet when she's abed,' replied my father, nodding back to her, and I nearly burst inside my plaid . . .
> 'I'll just sit me down and rest awhile, I'm tired,' my father would continue, and very gingerly he let down his sixteen stone on my tiny frail body.
> Then I sprang up, shrieking with joy and terror, and he exclaimed with astonishment, wondering where I had come from, and how I had lain so still to deceive him. I jumped up and down, with little cries of happiness, for once more I had succeeded in giving him a great surprise.[32]

It is not hard to see why, throughout her life, Alison Uttley continued to feel enriched by her relationship with her parents, so much so that one of her best friends from her later years was to consider that all her happiness was in her childhood.[33] But it was not simply the strength of her affection for her parents that gave Alison Uttley so much of her inspiration as a writer, for beyond them lay the varied stimuli of Castle Top Farm and its surroundings.

CHAPTER TWO

Castle Top Farm

I always felt I was a changeling child.
A bit of fairy got into me at Castle Top.

ALISON UTTLEY, diary, 7 April 1963

Until Alison Uttley was eighteen years old, Castle Top Farm was her permanent home and the centre of her world. Indeed, although she spent the next seventy-three years of her life away from the farm, her spirit and her imagination continued to reside there, causing her to look back with a passionate and unwavering nostalgia. Towards the end of her life an old friend gently summed up her feelings, remarking, 'You have been in exile most of your life, haven't you, Alison?'[1]

Alison Uttley's yearning for Castle Top Farm has many explanations. In part it represents a longing to return to an environment encompassed by the steady love and admiration of her parents. In part it sprang from the desire to recapture a Wordsworthian intensity of feeling for the 'splendour in the grass' and 'glory in the flower'. In part it is a hankering for relief from the prevailing sense of loss which was to characterise much of her life – not merely the loss of long-dead and much loved parents, but also the loss of a way of English rural life that was already doomed at her birth. But it also represents something more; it reflects the profound impact of Alison's childhood experiences, which she was able to recall during her writing career with a Proustian accuracy and sensitivity that was to produce a deeply felt and evocative prose with few rivals of its kind.

The power of Alison Uttley's connection with Castle Top was summed up in an interview for television recorded in 1970, when she was eighty-six years old:

> I think I was a very eager little girl, fearfully in love with everything I saw; and I always loved animals, we had many animals, we had horses and cows and pigs and sheep, and we knew all of them by name, and we were very kind to them, and I looked on them as brothers and sisters almost. . . . And it was a very beautiful spot, it was a well known beauty spot, our old house, and we had lived there for two hundred years. Everything was old-fashioned in the house, and all the furniture was what you would call antique, because it was all very ancient and very beautiful. I have written about it in *The Country Child*, and in lots of books, I always wanted to tell people about my old home, you see.[2]

The recreation of her life at Castle Top Farm is indeed the theme of *The Country Child*, significantly the first book she began to write, although not the first to be published. But Castle Top also dominates *Ambush of Young Days*, which she considered to be her truest piece of auto-biographical writing, as well as *The Farm on the Hill* and the novel *High Meadows*, and is an essential and much loved component in many of her other books of reminiscence and country lore. The deep feeling for her old home revealed in her published work is corroborated elsewhere, particularly in her diaries. She describes the 'bliss' of her childhood and writes of her deep 'longing' for that period of her life. In February 1948 a diary entry reads: 'Writing Christmas tale tonight, for the future. Castle Top so near to me, I feel sick with longing for the past, just to kiss them and speak to them.'³ Later in the year she writes: 'O magical life – how lovely it is! Please God let me keep and remember all the beauty for eternity, I know Mother would have loved it too. I thought of Castle Top vividly tonight, feeling I was my Mother on the hearth-rug looking up to the picture, at C[astle] Top years ago.'⁴ Often, when she experienced beauty in nature or in a book or in music, she felt homesick for Castle Top. She was sometimes conscious of living in an 'oasis in time', that linked her to the memory of her childhood home. Many diary entries contain references to 'dear Castle Top' or 'darling Castle Top'. In June 1933, almost fifty years after her own birth, she remembered: 'My dear father's birthday. I always think sweetly of him, and am full of thoughts of that faraway time. . . . I am so glad I have written of Castle Top, and done my best to give it another life.'⁵

Yet events at the farm during her years of 'exile' often caused her as much pain as pleasure. She resented the fact that her brother Harry, who had bought the freehold with his father in 1924, eventually inherited Castle Top and was upset in April 1936 at the news that he was thinking of selling it. The sale did not take place, but it caused Alison to compare the attitude of her 'selfish' brother with that of her devoted and 'selfless' mother.⁶ A year later, conscious of the decay into which the farm was falling she wrote: 'Again my heart aches, I dare not think of it, it is too vivid. I cannot bear these disasters at my darling Castle Top. I feel I would like to rush there and spend a thousand pounds making it all beautiful once more. . . . What a topsy turvy world it is, there seems to be no permanence in it, like I felt at my home.'⁷ Harry, who in Alison's view never really cared for the farm, eventually sold it early in September 1941.

Both before and after the sale of Castle Top, Alison Uttley felt proprietorial on behalf of her old home and sometimes disturbed by it. In 1938, when she had established herself as a successful author, Alison was upset to learn from her brother that 'people go to Castle Top and ask to look over it, having read *The Country Child* and *Ambush!* I was horror-struck. I always ask to remain unknown.'[8] Since she was not by nature an over-modest author, Alison's expression of distaste reflected her deep and lingering love for the farm, and also her resentment at strangers prying into a past life which she wanted above all to present to them in her own writings, in her own way. The same year, on reading a review of her novel *High Meadows* in the *Daily Telegraph*, she was indignant that Malcolm Muggeridge should have described all the characters in the book as stock types, noting in her diary that they were based on members of her family – particularly, her father and mother.[9] Sixteen years later she confessed that she was not able to look too closely at photographs of her old home, because 'my heart is there'.[10] A year later she was distressed to hear that the farm was deserted and in October 1968 a broadcast of *The Country Child* 'brought tears to my eyes, I remember so vividly my home and parents, the fields, lanes, our road down the hill – the horses straining and all the difficulties my parents faced'.[11]

What was Castle Top Farm like to have exerted so powerful an influence over the imagination of so creative a writer? The farmhouse was originally built on a bedrock of Derbyshire gritstone some seven hundred feet over the Derwent Valley which lay to the south-west. To the north-east hilly pasture land led up to the skyline along which ran an ancient packhorse path, once used by the Romans who had mined lead nearby. There was even speculation that the farm stood upon the site of an ancient Roman fort or perhaps a Saxon camp. Certainly part of the buildings dated from Elizabethan times and the foundations were older still. In April 1961 Alison Uttley was overjoyed when Mrs Clay, then the owner of Castle Top, found a reference to the farm dating back to 1415.[12] Rocks lay near to the surface of the stony soil on the hills, 'and often they thrust their muzzles through, like black monsters. These stones were alive to me, and I kept a wary eye on them lest they should move stealthily after me.'[13]

As a writer, Alison Uttley was to leave a patchwork of vivid recollections of the beautiful countryside around the farm. Once she recalled the taste of the exquisitely pure water she drank from the farm pump and a host of memories crowded in:

> The whole of my childhood, eternal and green, appears before my inward eye, and I live again in the brightly coloured circle of hills where I was born. No matter where I am, I seek unconsciously for resemblances to that beloved spot. A draught of spring water, an uncut hedgerow, a broken wall, these bring back visions so real that I cannot tell in which life I am living, the present, or the crystal-clear past, when as a child I ran with arms outstretched to catch the wind down the well-known grassy hillsides.[14]

She remembered the land so well that, much later in life, she could 'see the contours of the hills, the patterns of the fields, the irregularities of the diverse landscape as plainly as if they were painted before me'. She knew every flower-filled ditch, every leafy hedge-bottom and every daisied bank better than the lines of her own hand. During her earliest years, 'my senses had no distractions from the daily scenes of wood and field and hillside. They became part of me, like the cold air I breathed, and I had no conception of other lands beyond our own farm and its neighbourhood, the countryside which filled the crumpled circle of England displayed before my infant eyes.'[15]

The farmhouse itself, built out of local limestone with gables and mullioned windows, was surrounded by stack-yards, outbuildings, garden, orchard, pigcotes and looked 'like an island of fruitfulness, a small Paradise on a shelf all to itself, with the ground falling or rising on every side. A beech wood swept around the base of the spur, protecting the house from the worst winds, with its great warm trees, and from above the wood the house rose like a fortress.'[16]

As a little girl, Alison would have walked to the main door of the house past a monkey puzzle tree and through a porch which opened out on to a stone flagged hall with the dining-room on the right and a parlour on the left. Immediately off the hall was the farm kitchen, the centre of life for her with its bustle and motion and people passing and repassing to save the longer journey round the house walls. From its large window, she could look out on to the wide fields stretched out on the slope of the hills: 'It was my world, our own farmland.' The kitchen sparkled with bright metals, warming pans, horse brasses, painted china, patterned dishes and polished oak furniture. There was a variety of smells: 'the scent of wood-fire, and sticks in the kindling box . . . the strangely exciting smells of pepper and brine, of herbs and cowdrinks, of newly baked bread and strong tea, and also the animal smells which assailed my quivering nostrils'.[17] The oak dresser was the most important piece of furniture in the kitchen, 'for servant men had eaten their meals at its beeswaxed surface for well over a hundred years, and the ends were scarred with their knives. . . . In the drawers were neat piles of starched linen aprons, and in one drawer my mother kept the family Bible, and the book she was reading aloud.'[18] Once Alison, at the age of six, had found a book called *The Mystery of a Hansom Cab*, which she began to read but which suddenly disappeared when her mother removed it on the grounds that it was 'a naughty frightening book' and not suitable for her. At the end of a ledge on the dresser was an enormous dark-coloured pin cushion, which Alison called the Mother of Pincushions: 'No-one moved it; it squatted like an aged fat porcupine, bristling with giant needles and pins. Even the pins were unique, for many of them had once been darning needles. When a needle's eye was broken, my mother put a little knob of sealing-wax on the end, and made a scarlet-headed pin.'[19]

Upstairs was an assortment of bedrooms, several of them spacious and unaltered from olden days and still called 'chambers' – the apple chamber, the lad's chamber, the wench's chamber, the parlour chamber, the little chamber and the oak chamber, where Mr and Mrs Taylor slept in an enormous four-poster bed and which Alison knew as the 'birth and death room'. There was a water closet upstairs, especially installed for gentlefolk who made up the shooting parties, but the house had no bathroom. Alison's small 'summer' bedroom was in the attic; it had a dormer window overlooking White field and the hills beyond. She could kneel on the windowsill, sometimes writing in a special notebook, looking at the countryside or wondering what to do next. In winter she was allowed to move down to a lower floor and share a partitioned chamber with her brother for warmth. The servant girl was less fortunate, staying in her small attic room the year round and sleeping on a primitive raised platform bed. The room was open to the roof beams and must have been freezing in winter and stifling during the summer.

Although Alison knew every crack and cranny of the house and the particular smell of each room, some parts of it were forbidden to her. The parlour was one such forbidden room, with its faint odour of mildew in the winter and the chintz covers on the chairs and the velvet couch and the piano which drew her like a magnet. Then there was the dining-room, with its mahogany chairs, Chippendale sideboard and a table under which she could retreat when she heard footsteps drawing near. There were various treasures in the cupboards of the dining-room – old tea services, painted mugs, jugs and plates with pictures of huntsmen, goddesses and nymphs. Alison had never time enough to investigate these treasures before she was discovered and hauled back into the kitchen.

Except when exploring the forbidden rooms of the house, Alison remained near to her mother or to the servant girl, following them into the dairy or pantry or brew-house. The dairy had wide yellow earthenware pancheons of milk in a row on the bench, set for cream- and butter-making. There the child Alison rejoiced in 'The sweet smell of milk, the harsh smell of sanded benches, and the icy coldness of the room . . . . The dairy was a secret lovely place, with little dripping sounds, mysterious drops and flops, whilst outside the howling wind shrieked round the North gable.'[20] In the pantry, there stood a great stone jar holding fifty pounds of demerara sugar into which Alison could dip her fingers when she was tall enough to reach. The room was festooned with food – hams swinging from the ceiling, spears of lard-like white candles and a side of bacon hanging behind the door. Underneath the bench, on which stood a large canister of tea and various candles (tallow dips for the servants and tall fluted ones for the silver candlesticks), was Alison's toy box, an old oak chest in which she kept her dolls and bricks and picture books.

Outside, a line of stone barns and stables and sheds sheltered the farmhouse from the great gales of winter. There was a collection of discarded items, romantic Alison thought, in the barn near the house – including old wooden cheese presses, scythes and clubs and a broken spinning wheel. There was the cart shed, where the spring cart was kept and where the swallows used to build. Next to that was the stable, with two stalls for the horses. There was a calf place, an open-roofed coal house which could take twenty tons of coal at a time and, next to it, the brew-house built by Henry Taylor so that he could brew ale – a much cheaper drink in those days than tea. There was also a handsome pigsty with a solid stone roof and floor and four stone troughs. This was where Alison spent a good deal of her time, a corner of the farm which she recalled with special affection towards the end of her life: 'It was the most lovely pigsty you have ever seen! I could write a book about our pigsty, because it was two hundred years old, my father said. It had been there in our ancestors' time; and all round the top of the wall that surrounded the pigsty, it was comfortable for a little girl to walk, all along this, I used to walk all around here, calling to the pigs. The pigs never stopped talking, and I didn't either. I was one with the pigs!'[21]

Alison's vivid imagination was fired by the most ordinary things at Castle Top: there was a little white gate into the kitchen garden, which she thought was the gate through which Adam and Eve were escorted 'into the great outside'. There were also extraordinary events, like the hares dancing: 'They used to come in the top pasture, which is a long way from our house, over a great hill . . . and my father told us, now and then, that he'd watched a hare dance. It did dance, you know, it really danced about. I have seen it dance just like a human being, go round and round. And we were absolutely thrilled; we all ran, if we saw hares dancing, we all ran indoors and told everybody.'[22]

Despite the joy she found in her family, particularly in her mother who read to her from an early age, taught her sewing, showed her a variety of games and pastimes and introduced her to the pleasures and hard labour of housework, Alison's childhood also contained a good deal of unhappiness. For although her mother and father were in general very caring towards her, there were occasions when she felt deprived of parental comfort. Later in life, recognising that she was 'miserable enough as a little child' and aware of 'the little tinkles of sadness in *The Country Child*', she recalled: 'We had no nurse to quell the misery, and my mother was always busy, and unaware of the small ills that afflicted us, which we kept secret in our hearts; but we had a supreme nurse in the earth herself. Nature held out her wide arms and we were comforted. We threw ourselves down on the grass and the warmth of the myriad tiny blades soothed us, and kissed us to health again.'[23]

The capacity to find profound comfort in nature was to remain an important factor in Alison's later life. When as an adult she found herself depressed or beset by difficulty, she frequently found comfort and renewal in the simplest manifestations of nature – in field and flower and tree and bird-song and star and shadow. Sometimes the restoration in her spirits brought about by the contemplation of some beautiful, natural object was remarkably sudden, even precipitate, like the appearance of the sun from behind a fast-moving bank of cloud. It was as if her bouts of sadness were too painful to be borne, and had to be swept away by the romantic forces of nature: 'Yet the grief fled in a twinkling, the sun shone and we recovered and forgot.'[24] Certainly, the natural beauties that crowded in on Castle Top were sovereign against the small childhood griefs. Alison 'used to be frightfully sad when people were cross with me, and lots of little things used to make me very unhappy. But then . . . I had only to run down the slope, drop to the ground, and lie on the soft grass, to be helped to bear all the indignities and insults of childhood from grown-up people.'[25]

These lesser miseries aside, Alison was also prey to many secret fears – some of them with good cause: 'in those early years I escaped miraculously from the hooves of kicking horses, and the horns of a "wild" cow, from falls down the high walls into rocky land below, and my baby brother was saved by my screams from drowning in the deepest trough'.[26] For the most part, though, it was the less tangible fears and fancies that haunted her. Trees, for example, had a strange fascination for her ever since she had lain as a baby in a clothes basket under the apple trees in the orchard, babbling to them and in turn listening to their talk. She thought them 'queer, half-human creatures, alive yet tied to the ground. Lucky they are tied too, for rooted they are safe.' One night she had a terrible nightmare of a company of mighty trees waving their branches like a hundred arms, the green hair of their leaves shaking in the wind, advancing upon the farmhouse apparently determined to destroy it.[27] She always looked on woods as haunted places, filled with life, with spectres and goblins – places of great beauty but also containing unknown, invisible creatures ready to spring.

Nor were these terrors confined to the woods: 'Winged, macabre, two-dimensional, black, they came when the furniture creaked and the window rattled. They were large, and they changed their size, they expanded and contracted like shadows, and they flew. . . . Out of the shadows they prowled, searching for something to eat, something to touch, for a contact with life, which was me.'[28] Going to bed was a particular trial. Alison, candle in hand, kissed her parents and said 'Goodnight, God bless you', listening anxiously for the reply since 'if one of them had omitted the blessing, I should have felt unprotected in the battle to come, the war against outer darkness and those who inhabit it.'[29] In winter, when a fire burned in her bedroom grate, she said her prayers on the hearth rug as close to the protecting flames as she could. Sometimes she opened her eyes in distrust of God, to see if all was safe. Then she leapt into bed. But even here there were terrors to be endured; for as she read, hungrily and intently, 'The goblin spirits, the earth demons, the witches made my hair stand on end, as I clutched the sheets to my chin.'[30] Because Alison believed that the printed word was truth itself, and that each character she read about was present in the room, she felt that the nobler among them 'kept at bay the shadowy ones, they flashed their swords and spoke in clear voices I could hear above the crackle of the fire'. Often, fortunately, 'the wicked were confounded before I shut my eyes in blissful sleep'.[31]

Sometimes, however, the forces of terror and darkness were not so easily defeated. She remembered, as a schoolgirl, reading *A Tale of Two Cities*, so absorbed and terrified that 'my soft dark hair might have turned white in a single night from the agonies I endured'. Hearing footsteps on the stairs, she extinguished her candle, hid her book under her sheets and shut her eyes, exhausted with fear. Her mother entered the room, made up the fire and 'kissed me with a soft butterfly touch of her lips, and whispered "Goodnight, and God bless you", again, and I groaned in reply, thankful for the deliverance from those voices from the French Revolution. She closed the door and the house was quiet again. . . . There was no danger. I pulled the sheet over my head, tight round my ears, and I fell asleep.'[32]

Above the fears that sprang from the pages of the books she was reading, there were other anxieties; there was a dread of wolves so strong that she wondered if it was an inherited fear from earlier generations who had lived in the same well-wooded Derbyshire countryside – more likely, it was another variation on the common female fantasy of the ravening assailant that finds classical expression in the story of Red Riding Hood; there was the fear of goblins and giants and dwarfs lurking, with the wolves, in the woods.

Above all, there was the fear of death. Death was a commonplace on the farm and its surroundings: 'The sight of blood was a reminder.

Death of a pig, death of a running rabbit who darted from the woodstack and met the gun, death of an aged dog, death of a child in the hamlet. . . . Death from a poacher's snare was cruel, and death from a weasel was worse. I heard the human squeal of a rabbit in pain, and I knew the weasel was sucking the blood of my innocent friend . . . the world was not a safe place, and Nature had some tricks to play.'[33]

So deep were her anxieties that, as she was later to write of Susan Garland, a self-portrait and the heroine of *The Country Child*:

> She had always felt life to be insecure. At nine years old death might come at any moment. The religion of the time fostered these feelings, the texts decorating the walls were a preparation for death. Any time, too, the world might come to an end. . . . Each morning she prepared for the worst. She left the house for school feeling she might never see her parents again. . . . She kissed them 'Goodbye' with such deep affection they were quite touched by her devotion, and she cried 'God bless you' so fervently, like a pastor blessing his congregation, running back up the hill to say it if she forgot, that Mrs Garland felt her prayers had not been in vain.[34]

Alison's understandable fear of death was probably heightened by her seeing, at the age of two, the bodies of many beautiful red-gold hens which she loved, 'all bedraggled and torn, lying under the oak tallboy when they were brought in. Someone had taken me to them and told me the story of their death, not realising the impression it would make upon me.' So affected was she by this tragedy, that she developed a deep fear of an elderly neighbour called Mrs Fox, cringing away from her exclaiming, 'Fox eat chuckies', and screaming 'with terror when I was near her. I remember this with horrible distinctness, the fear that she would spring and eat me too, when she kissed me.'[35] A few years later she was horrified when, holding up her hand to the sunlight, she saw the red blood in her fingers: 'I was filled with horror at the sight. To think that I was full of blood – that terrible liquid which lay in a pool when a pig had been killed!'[36]

But Castle Top Farm was also full of life. Each year Alison could watch the calves butting each other with their knobbly, woolly heads; there were newborn lambs to be brought into the kitchen and fed; there was the sight of the newborn piglets squeaking as they jostled for their mother's milk. There were the farm dogs and the horses. Alison recalled the joy of riding on the mare: 'The strong smell of the mare's flesh and skin, the feeling of the coarse hair under my fingers, and the warm body under my kicking legs was rapture. I thought of the Queen of England, and felt mightier than she.'[37] So 'royal' did Alison feel as a child that in February 1932 she dreamed of the five-year-old Princess Elizabeth, the future Queen Elizabeth II, staying at Castle Top Farm.[38]

Beneath Alison in Castle Top's hierarchy were the farm's workpeople. There was Dan, Henry Taylor's farm-hand and chief support. There was an old man, Josiah, whose farm had fallen on hard times and who undertook a variety of odd jobs. He was a great storyteller, grew vegetables in the kitchen garden, made herbal remedies and was particularly gentle and patient when undertaking the veterinary work on the farm. In her early years, Alison was especially fond of Willie Miller, whose 'kindly ways and good manners made him a delightful companion and nurse'. Feeling safe with him, Alison treated him like an elder brother, following him around the farm and asking innumerable questions while he 'gave me satisfactory if incorrect answers on the subjects of Jesus and horses and stars'. Willie was the son of a prosperous farmer who had sent him out to earn his keep, get experience and to learn to rough it; he got up for work at five o'clock every morning in the summer and at half past five in the winter. In addition there was a servant girl, sometimes called Patty and sometimes Becky in Alison's books of reminiscence, who worked mainly with Mrs Taylor in the kitchen and dairy.

Apart from these regular members of the household, there were various other occasional workers: the washerwoman, Mrs Bunting, whose fat legs were encased in elastic-sided boots; the mole-catcher in his moleskin waistcoat and cap; the rat-catcher, bearing his fierce red-eyed ferrets; and the weatherbeaten hedger and ditcher, who wore sacking while he worked. Itinerant traders called at the farm, the pedlar with his basket of knives and scissors, the saucepans on his head and a backpack crammed with ribbons, combs and handkerchiefs. Then there was the oatcake man, Gabriel Thorne, who had lost an arm while seafaring and who courted the servant girl.

For Alison, the most important visitors to the farm were the Irish labourers who came over annually to harvest the hay. Although she was often shy – often 'felt the gaze of strangers' eyes upon me as a burning, piercing fire' and shunned visitors, hiding behind her mother or creeping into a dark corner of the settle – Alison awaited the arrival of the Irish haymakers with great pleasure. The first inkling that they were on their way was the arrival of a dirty letter with the postmark of a faraway village in County Galway. This contained a request for the loan of a sovereign to pay for the Irishmen's passage. There was great excitement on Alison's part and much telling of tales within the family in anticipation of the Irishmen's arrival. Henry Taylor had 'views' on the Irishmen's religion, telling his daughter, 'But you know they worship idols in their religion, the Roman religion. . . . Mr Gladstone wants to give them Home Rule, but what would they do? They'd bring the Pope here in no time!'[39] At this Alison imagined a tall man, as tall as the beech trees, stalking into the country.

The Irish labourers' capacity for hard work, though, was greatly valued. The family all turned out to prepare the Irishmen's lodging place, a cow-house in the old buildings near the stable. They swept it clean with besoms, limewashed the walls and laid down bags of fresh straw for mattresses. A barrel of beer was placed in the corner and the Irishmen ate their meals at two long benches, using old willow-pattern plates with iron spoons. On the wall, Alison's father had put a notice which announced sternly 'no smokeing allowed'. One candle in an iron candlestick fastened to the wall provided the light.

The Irishmen, when they eventually arrived, walking in a line up to the farmhouse, provided Alison with a vivid, romantic and deeply satisfying glimpse of another world. They had a distinctive smell, 'of tobacco twist, corduroy, beer and Ireland. [Alison] called it "the Irishmen's smell", and sniffed it up eagerly with mingled fear and delight.' There was Old Mike and Young Mike, his son, as silent as his father was talkative, and the twins Malachi and Dominick, slim, good-looking, brown-skinned, showing white even teeth when they smiled. Then there was Sheamus, old and dreamy, with a gentle smile and a faraway look. Most important were the mowers, Patrick, Corney and Andy, big, broad-shouldered, red-bearded men, who were Alison's idea of 'brigands, or Assyrians sweeping down on the Israelites'.

On Saturday nights the double doors of the big cart shed were thrown open wide and the Irishmen gave a concert of singing and dancing. Sometimes Alison's father brought out his concertina and played the tunes they sang and Old Mike danced, with a great clatter of heels and swinging of arms, while 'The darkness came down like a blue cloud, bit-bats flew in and out of the pitch-black shed, and screech-owls hooted in the fir trees.'[40] So moved was Alison by the Irishmen, particularly the handsome twins, that as she recalled in a letter written towards the end of her life, she overcame her natural shyness and 'kissed our dirty Irishmen, whom I loved'.[41]

The annual arrival of the Irish haymakers, later and touchingly recorded in the Sam Pig books, was only one of the seasonal rituals and rhythms of life at Castle Top Farm. Although Henry Taylor did not farm a large number of acres, he resisted the temptation to specialise in one particular activity. Castle Top supported horses, sheep, cattle, pigs and poultry. There was an orchard and one field always grew cereal, but the meadows were chiefly devoted to grazing and haymaking. So the patterns of sowing, reaping, harvesting and storing reinforced those of the birth, nurturing and death of farm animals to provide Alison with a solid and reliable calendar by which to progress through her childhood. There were also the rituals of the week. Monday was mostly, but not invariably, washday. Sunday was when Alison went to church with her mother, a day altogether distinct from the rest of the week: 'Everything was different on Sundays and this made a welcome diversion in a simple household. We wore different clothes, we ate from the beautiful old china, we had Sunday books, Sunday games and Sunday music, and we sat in the Sunday rooms. It was a day I loved, when everything ought to go right, when sweet fragrance filled the air, from scent-bottle and pomatum-pot, and chests and drawers were unlocked to bring out the treasures.'[42]

Of the two most clearly marked days in the week, Alison infinitely 'preferred Sunday, with its safety, its music, its stories of angels and miracles, for after all, we were very young, and perhaps an everlasting washday was waiting for us round the corner'.[43]

Although Alison's later life was to contain the turmoil and un-certainty of many 'washdays', the childhood security she derived from a repeating pattern of farm life was further strengthened by other pre-dictable and eagerly awaited annual events. There was spring cleaning and Easter time, summer holidays at Scarborough or Blackpool, Guy Fawkes night (which the family called 'Bonefire' Night) and, above all, Christmastime.

The Taylor family's preparations for Christmas were ample and well-ordered. There were piles of logs outside and twenty tons of coal. Inside, there was an abundance of food and drink:

> Stone jars like those in which the forty thieves hid stood on the pantry floor, filled with white lard, and balls of fat tied up in bladders hung from the hooks. Along the broad shelves round the walls were pots of jam, blackberry and apple, from the woods and orchard. Victoria plum from the trees round house and barn, blackcurrant from the garden. . . . Pickles and spices filled old brown pots decorated with crosses and flowers, like the pitchers and crocks of Will Shakespeare's time. In the little dark wine chamber under the stairs were bottles of elderberry wine, purple, thick, and sweet, and golden cowslip wine, and hot ginger, some of them many years old, waiting for the winter festivities.[44]

A few days before Christmas, Henry Taylor and his farmhand took a billhook and knife and went into the woods to cut branches of red-berried holly; they took 'a bough of mistletoe from the ancient hollow hawthorn which leaned over the wall by the orchard, and thick clumps of dark-berried ivy from the walls'.[45] Inside the farmhouse Mrs Taylor, Alison and the maid worked hard to make the furniture and glasses glow and glitter. They decorated every room, 'from the kitchen, where every lustre jug had its sprig in its mouth . . . through the hall, which was a bower of green, to the two parlours which were festooned and hung with holly and boughs of fir, and ivy berries dipped in red raddle, left over from sheep marking'.[46]

On Christmas Eve fires blazed throughout the house, flames roared up the chimneys and the wind 'came back and tried to get in, howling at the key-holes, but all the shutters were cottered and the doors shut'. From the middle of the kitchen ceiling there hung, glittering with gilt drops and crimson bells, blue glass trumpets, polished red apples and little flags of all nations, the kissing bunch, an important central component of Alison Uttley's Christmases. Her mother climbed on a stool and nailed on the wall the Christmas texts, 'God Bless Our Home' and 'A Happy Christmas and a Bright New Year'. There were games like 'turn the trencher' and then the welcome visit of the wassailers or guisers, as the were called in Derbyshire. The guisers, their faces masked and wearing large false noses, sang their wassailing songs, asked each other riddles and then stamped off into the cold outside.

At last it was time for the child Alison to go to bed, joyfully anticipating the early morning excitement of finding what she had in the Christmas stocking:

> I'd dive down all among the little things. There weren't big things, there were no dull things like pairs of gloves and pairs of stockings or anything, there were little toys. I used to put my hand right down, down, down, pulling the stocking up, down to the very tiptoe, and there we found half a crown, which was gold and silver to us. I know one thing there would be . . . a little china doll . . . they sold them in the village, and I loved them, I thought they were enchanting.[47]

At lunchtime there were the pleasures of the Christmas table:

> The potatoes were balls of snow, the sprouts green as if they had just come from the garden, as indeed they had, for they too had been dug out of the snow not long before. The turkey was brown and crisp . . . the stuffing smelled of summer and the herb garden in the heat of the sun. As for the plum pudding with its spray of red berries and shiny leaves and its hidden sixpence . . . it was the best they had ever tasted. There was no dessert, nor did they need it, for they sipped elderberry wine mixed with sugar and hot water in the old pointed wine-glasses, and cracked the walnuts damp from the trees.[48]

Amidst all this plenty, Alison had once been delighted to find that a Christmas tree had been dug up in secret from the fields outside and brought into the house with real snow on its branches: 'On the top of the tree shone a silver bird, a most astonishing silver glass peacock with a tail of fine feathers, which might have flown in at the window.' Alison was later to record her response to this sight: 'If an angel from heaven had sat on the table she would have been less surprised. She ran to hug everybody, her heart was full.'[49]

Conceived as soon as her parents married, perhaps even on their wedding night, nurtured on her mother's milk, contained by a steady, if not always effusive parental love, well-fed, snugly clothed against the bitter winter weather, her material needs amply catered for and her keen senses devouring the details of the world she inhabited, it is small wonder that Alison Uttley remained deeply, romantically in love with the memory of Castle Top Farm until the end of her life. Nor did the farm's influence end there. It also contributed to her lifelong conviction that she was 'special', a cut above so many others, a feeling at least partly derived from Castle Top's magnificent situation above the Derwent valley. From her fortress-like home, the child Alison could literally look down on the rest of humanity as her birthright.

Despite this, and even at the height of her success as an author, she could sometimes see herself as an imposter, threatened by publicity and what it might reveal about her: 'I must not feel frightened, I always feel I am unworthy – I want to hide, for it is only ME, a little girl at Castle Top.'[50] Sometimes she had doubts of another kind, marvelling at how she could have emerged as so gifted and perceptive a writer from the mundane world of the farmhouse: 'I always felt I was a changeling child. A bit of fairy got into me at Castle Top.'[51]

Her sense that was set apart in some way, singled out as a snow-baby, a much wanted Christmas child, extended itself to her surroundings, investing them with an added intensity, and was to become a characteristic strength of Alison's powerful, recollective writing. She conveys something of this feeling in a diary entry for 1963, prompted by a film shown on television: 'The girl reminds me intensely of myself when a child, such eagerness and seriousness and longing . . . but my life was more romantic, with its fields and woods and rocky hills. . . . Just as vivid a life, and the ghosts, and the appearance as if in a dream that I have.'[52]

Alison's childhood experiences were not, however, confined to the narrow limits of Castle Top, nor was the inspiration of her writing to derive solely from its rocks and green fields and woods. Cromford village stood about two miles from Alison's birthplace, and further afield were the rivers and streams, the wooded valleys and the limestone crags of the Derbyshire countryside.

CHAPTER THREE

The Country Child

There was our own village, with its long street
winding away up the hill, with a tap here and there
for water, and the inhabitants carrying buckets to
their neat stone cottages.

ALISON UTTLEY, *Ambush of Young Days*

Little more than a century before Alison Uttley's birth, Cromford had
been a tiny hamlet set in a hollow beside the River Derwent, graced by a
fifteenth-century bridge, a chapel and a manor house. Above the
wooded Derwent valley rose limestone crags and pine woods, with
High Tor and the Heights of Abraham towering over Matlock Vale.

In 1771, however, Cromford had undergone a startling revolution, for
in that year Richard Arkwright, in partnership with Jedediah Strutt,
built beside the swift waters of the Derwent the world's first successful
water-powered cotton spinning mill. Cromford had been chosen for
this experiment because its remoteness lessened the danger of attacks
upon Arkwright's new technology by cotton spinners enraged by the
threat to their livelihood that machinery posed. The success of
Arkwright's mill at Cromford was one of the first steps towards an
industrial revolution that was to make Britain, for all too brief a time,
the Workshop of the World. Workers were recruited from further afield
to supplement the limited manpower available in Cromford's sparse
agricultural community. Mill hands' houses, shops, an inn and a corn
mill were soon established.

Arkwright seems to have been a progressive employer. His work-
places were certainly not the 'dark satanic mills' of Blake's poem. Each
mill at Cromford had as many windows as the walls could safely
accommodate and the effect was to create light and airy working conditions. The family unit was important to the success of the enterprise and
the solid terraced houses that Arkwright had built out of local gritstone
at Cromford and in nearby villages provided good conditions in which
to live – and to work, for they often had a third storey where the
women and children could engage in spinning and other activities.

There is a well-known portrait of Richard Arkwright painted by
Joseph Wright of Derby. The great man sits, his knees open wide and a
heavy paunch bulging inside his waistcoat. His hands are practical and

square, a working man's hands, and his eyes sharp and perceptive. It was the Arkwright family that owned the freehold of Castle Top Farm at Alison Uttley's birth.

In 1794, in order to service Cromford's modestly developing industry, the canal was opened, stretching from the village to Langley Mill on the Erewash fourteen and a half miles away. The building of the canal had been a difficult task, involving the construction of a narrow tunnel three thousand yards long and two aqueducts. It was to enjoy only a limited period of prosperity before the rapid growth of a national railway system during the first half of the nineteenth century took vital trade away from it. Cromford station was opened in 1860 for the Midland Railway Company and was built to resemble a Swiss chalet because its architect, Sir Joseph Paxton, when viewing the site, was reminded of Switzerland by the river Derwent flowing through its rocky gorges. The opening of the railway, running across the Peaks via Buxton to Manchester, enabled local farmers, like Henry Taylor, to send their produce to markets far away. The milk train was also to carry Alison to her grammar school in Bakewell, not far from the Yorkshire border.

Alison Uttley was later to recall in fine detail 'our own village, with its long street winding away up the hill, with a tap here and there for water, and the inhabitants carrying buckets to their neat stone cottages' and, in old age, to speculate on the derivation of its name.[1] After reading an article on fords in *The Times*, she wrote, 'I think of Cromford, the old ford by the bridge. But what did Crom mean? I don't know at all.' But the next line in her diary is triumphant, '*Crooked* ford. The river curves there.'[2]

The river had a fascination for her. She used often to stand on the bridge looking at the water, as someone who had known her as a child was to recall.[3] She must have been a familiar sight on the bridge, for a local woman who admired her work later wrote, 'I always think of you when I go over the Bridge at Cromford.'[4] Alison has left her own account of the pleasure she derived:

> To stand on a bridge over a river is to get the lyrical impression that one is suspended in air, in a timeless state, looking over the promised land. . . . We went over our bridge at least twice a week . . . yet there was never a crossing when we were not intensely aware of the river below, the bridge arching over it, and our own translation in time and space. . . . When we crossed the bridge on foot we leaned over as long as possible, looking for trout in the clear water, staring at the swallows which darted through the arches like arrows, speeding into the half-moon of light. . . . The bridge lay there, couched like a stone dragon, enjoying itself, basking in the sun, and we knew it as a living thing.[5]

Alison's early contact with Cromford and its bridge was through visiting the village with her father. Henry Taylor drove there once or twice a week, 'calling to order cake for the cattle, sharps and meal, or a truckload of coal or grain from the wharf-yard. . . . He took saddles to be mended, and a list of household wants. He talked to men about ploughshares, and harrows and machinery, about bankrupts and sales.'[6] According to his daughter, these trips to Cromford provided Mr Taylor with his only regular contact with affairs beyond his own domestic sphere:

> He heard all the news of the outside world, emigrations and wars, of Mr Gladstone and Queen Victoria, of the Duke of Devonshire and Lord Salisbury, of Elections and Radicals (whom I confused with radishes for a long time). . . . He talked of the land, of the vagaries of animals, of wind and rain and snow, recalling past deluges and storms when trees were blown down and cattle killed by lightning, and of sudden deaths and deeds of violence, wondering mildly what the world was coming to.[7]

During these first years of her life, Alison was by no means intimately involved with Cromford. Indeed, her acquaintance with the village was chiefly through what she saw from her seat in her father's cart or trap. Perhaps she felt a certain disdain, or at least shyness, for she was later to recall that as she sat in the pony trap, 'I held my head high, proud of my position, waiting for the admiring glances at the pretty dark blue trap.'[8] The picture that emerges from her autobiographical writings is of a rather guarded, self-contained child, sitting 'as stiff as a little ramrod', correctly dressed in serge cloak, hat to match and gloves. But even from her exalted position at her father's side, Alison's eyes missed nothing of what was going on around her: 'The stray cats and dogs, flowers in windows, unknown children, glimpses of dark shop interiors, and steady eyes of slow-moving old men and women, I saw them all.'[9]

Her already startling powers of observation were encouraged by her father who, with his whip, would point out items of interest, 'the bluebells colouring the little wood, pigeons on a roof, a cat stalking a bird, for the journey was important in itself, a survey of the country. He noticed other people's crops, and their gardens, their cattle and horses, and references to this drive would be made during the following week.'[10] Alison became familiar with all the shops of Cromford. The milliner's where only her mother and herself entered, because her father 'flatly refused to meddle with fal-lals. If we were long choosing the ribbon velvet . . . he whistled and rattled with the butt-end of his whip, hurrying us out.'[11] There was the butcher's shop at the top of the hill, where Alison's father discussed the pedigree of the animal before he bought the meat. There was the fine shop of the shoemaker who made her father's best boots, where Alison relished the smell of leather that seemed to seep through the bow window. Inside, she remembered the brass winking in the light of the red flames and the woolwork picture of the sacrifice of Isaac with the knife shining in Abraham's uplifted hand and the sticks on the altar ready for burning. There was Mr Stone, the druggist, who advised the villagers on matters of health because there was no doctor nearby. 'He pulled out the teeth of ploughboys, cured the coughs and earaches of children, and the backaches of old men, and advised on matters of health for man and beast.'[12] He was lugubrious and gaunt and Alison was too frightened to enter his shop by herself. Her father particularly enjoyed talking to Mr Drabble, the head of the grain warehouse, touching on all manner of topics – except grain and corn – 'with long pauses, and wise saws, with sayings and memories interwoven in brightly coloured strands. I did not realise that this intercourse with a man who travelled and saw the world was my father's newspaper, his inn, his communication with the outside world.'[13]

The newspaper shop, however, was where Alison most longed to go. Run by Mr Green, for whom Alison felt a great affection, it was the family's toyshop as well as stationer and general dealer. All Alison's presents for birthdays, Christmas and other festivals came from Mr Green's. She recalled the flutter of excitement when at Christmastime she and her mother walked up the wooden stair to the first-floor parlour which had been transformed into a toyshop.

Mr Green, however, was more than a purveyor of cards, clockwork toys, lace-frilled valentines and butterfly transfers to be pressed on the back of the hand. He was also a 'high-minded man of literary interests, who went to Cambridge each year to attend a course of lectures for working men. His eyes shone with scholarly enthusiasm when he talked to my mother and me about it. We admired him for his passion for learning and for his perseverance and self-denial in saving the money for this jaunt.'[14] He hoped that Alison would accompany him one day to hear a lecture at Matlock Bath, but it was not until a 'great lady who exchanged smiles with me when we met now and then, on her occasional visit to the farmhouse' invited Alison to accompany her that this was made possible. Deeply conscious of the great honour bestowed upon her, Alison rode with her patron, Mrs Shaw, in her dogcart to hear a Mr Marriott, one of the best of the extension lecturers from Cambridge, talk upon the subject of the Italian Renaissance. Alison listened, rapt and bemused, as he spoke of artists whose beautiful names sounded like music to the child – Michelangelo, Leonardo da Vinci, Giorgione. Words meant much to Alison, who ardently collected them: 'Latin, French and English words were stored in niches in my mind, written phonetically on old envelopes, examined in private, unseen by anyone. I liked them and sought them, as I also collected stones and fossils, wild flowers and the natural objects of the world which littered the earth as I knew it. Now I had a new store of jewel-like words, tossed to me by the lecturer who knew not that he was scattering them for me to play with.'[15] She was to remember that 'I was changed to a Renaissance girl, charged with new ideas and thoughts and visions. I was half drunk with new-found beauty, as I wandered up the hill among the wild roses and dandelions.'[16]

Although this inspiring lecture was a unique and greatly treasured delight of Alison's childhood, her regular visits to Cromford church also provided her with cultural and intellectual satisfaction, if in a more modest form. She was a regular churchgoer throughout her life, said her prayers frequently at home and often remembered the anniversary of her First Communion at Cromford on Easter Sunday.[17] She began attending morning service at the age of three, wondering later in life how she managed to walk so far and concluding that 'probably I had a lift on [the serving girl's] back. I remember the ache in my legs as I ran at a short trot by my mother, and the stitch which came in my side as I tried to keep up with her, clinging to her outstretched hand, whilst the bells rang fatalistically, warning us we should be late.'[18] Alison was a devout early churchgoer, shutting her eyes tightly while the words of the service flowed round her. Since she could read before she was five years old, she was able to hold the prayer book in front of her while her mother's fingers pointed out the place where she should be in the text.

Despite her determination to participate fully in the service, Alison found the sermons more difficult to digest. Usually her mother thoughtfully provided her with a lozenge to sustain her and keep her still. She was later to recall that while listening to the sermon, 'One hand clasped my mother's, and I poked a finger through the convenient opening in the kid glove to keep a hold on reality when I was lost in the supernatural. In winter one hand went into her little muff, and stayed there during the sermon, for sermons were long in those days, and all the children walked out except myself, who had nowhere to go.'[19]

In part, Alison's enjoyment of the church services was sensual:

> The smells of church enfolded me, wrapping me in a country incense made up of bear's-grease, lavender, camphor, pomades, macassar oil, kid boots, and, at night, the added smell of paraffin lamps. Evening service had a different odour from morning service, for at the latter the Castle was at church, with sweet fragrance and exotic scents, but at night all sorts and conditions of men were there, packed from the front row to the gallery. I much preferred evening service, for there was a heartiness in the singing which swept me along with it.[20]

The lessons read from the Bible were particularly intriguing for Alison, especially the parables and stories of the Old Testament. When the vicar read of Balaam's ass or of the ravens that carried food to Elijah, Alison fitted the stories into her everyday experiences, seeing Balaam 'in a narrow lane where dog-roses grew, or Elijah sitting at the side of the village brook, whilst ravens crying "Cruk! Cruk!" dropped pieces of bread and meat for him.'[21] But above all she enjoyed hearing about angels, imagining that they appeared in the Top Pasture to the shepherds watching their flocks. They were also ready to help, 'guardians to warn us of mad bulls and wolves in the dark'. Alison also thought that when the angels were disheartened by all the wickedness they saw, 'my passions and tears, they flew back to heaven, their white wings beating as they rose above the apple-blossom in the orchard to the golden throne in the blue sky'.[22] Later in life Alison Uttley was prepared to believe that fairies existed and there is perhaps a link between her intense childhood imaginings of angels beating their wings with an adult wish to see fairies. Both as a child and adult, Alison found pleasure in believing that angels were 'waiting to help, to comfort the widows, and orphans, and the lost children'.[23]

Brought up by a pious mother, the church featured prominently in Alison's childhood, the recurring cycle of its festivals imposing a pattern on the year that coincided with the seasonal rhythms of life at Castle Top Farm. Years afterwards, having learnt to recognise that this was no coincidence and that many of the Christian holy days were originally superimposed on old pagan rituals, November came to acquire a particular meaning for Alison: 'November is secret, and evocative of ghosts; it is silent, and the silence is filled with latent power, sometimes hostile. Because it is a month of change, it has feast days and festivals which are remembered. It is the semi-pagan month wrestling invisibly with Christianity. It is becalmed in its past.'[24] Heralded by All Hallows Eve with its superstitions and its evocation of spirits and sorcery, it includes All Souls' Day on 2 November and goes on to incorporate other saints' days, including St Martin's, St Cecilia's and St Catherine's.

For the child, though, more important than these Christian remembrances was Guy Fawkes Day when her family lighted a fire in the corner of the plough field and danced round it, singing and shouting, roasting potatoes and eating parkin and bonfire toffee. The Taylors burnt no effigy and Guy Fawkes was never spoken of: 'he was a historical personage of whom we were ignorant. It was Bonefire night. It was pronounced thus by my father and the old generation of countrymen as if bones were burnt on that night, and it was not until I heard the village children use a different word, that I realised we had no bones in our fire. They pronounced it Bunfire.'[25]

Apart from festivities like these, there was so little to disturb the routine at Castle Top that even going to the dentist was a special event, 'almost a treat, for I had to beg for permission from my father, who had no money for dentists and thought it was a luxury when there was no toothache'.[26] Occasionally, and only in response to urgent need, the doctor was summoned from his home several miles away in another valley. Often the letter requesting a visit was sent by the servant boy, who could travel more swiftly across the hills and along the field paths than a pony and trap. Since the doctor was difficult to reach, and also expensive, the Taylor family used herbs and traditional remedies, drinking medicine from a little eighteenth-century wineglass bought from the Cromford chemist. Camomile tea was a universal remedy for simple disorders, cut fingers were bound with fresh cobwebs, and earache was treated with a hot boiled onion in a little muslin bag that was bandaged on to the ear. Although the parson and dentist and doctor ministered to some of the spiritual and physical needs of her family, Alison drew a greater and more varied sustenance from her contact with the country people of Cromford and its neighbourhood.

Although she was never taken for a walk for the sake of walking, Alison was sometimes taken visiting by her mother or met interesting people on errands of one kind or another. Sometimes Mrs Taylor took her to see the old nurse who had attended her birth: 'She was witch-like, and I imagined it was part of her natural magic, all of a piece with the strange happenings of the world.' Old women generally reminded Alison of witches and she was shy and awkward in their presence, only too happy to make her escape. When she took hot meals, as an act of charity, to old Mrs Fern, she felt anxious, overcome by the peculiar smell of the cottage, like musk and hot geranium, and 'tried to get out of this Christian duty by hiding and excusing myself'. Mrs Fern could not read and sometimes asked Alison to help her understand her letters in their scrawled, crabbed writing. This was a task which the child often found difficult, and it was left to Mrs Taylor to read the letter when she came Sunday-visiting with food, followed by a reading from the Bible and a prayer.

Alison's mother, indeed, seems to have spent a good deal of her time in evangelical work. She had little luck with Thomas Frost, an unashamed atheist with, as Alison saw him, fierce eyes, shaggy eyebrows and a waggling goatee beard. Alison regarded him as an infidel to be avoided, but her mother could not give him up as a lost soul: '"But Mr Frost, surely you believe in our Lord?" asked my mother, in a gently remonstrating voice, and Mr Frost laughed. She left some scripture books behind her, and, embarrassed and shy, I followed her out of the house.'[27] More capable of salvation than Mr Frost, but also in her own way an outcast, was a young woman whom Alison often saw standing at the door of her mother's thatched cottage, nursing a baby. She had learned through school gossip that the woman was not married, but Alison was too unworldly to understand what this meant: 'She was like the Virgin, and I was sure she was very good, for God to give her a baby without a husband. I lingered, hoping she would speak to me, and when she said "Good morning", I was elated.'[28]

Although the Taylor family were part of a closely knit and interdependent rural community, they seem to have had few close personal friends. There were aunts and uncles and cousins certainly, but in general the members of Alison's immediate family seem to have relied largely upon each other for friendship and support. Perhaps this reflected their status as tenant farmers, beneath the local gentry and freeholding farmers but above their humbler neighbours. There was, however, a close and continuing friendship with the Gregory family of nearby Holloway and with a Harry Douglas whom Alison's mother 'adored'.[29] The self-containment of the Taylors as a family unit is easily understandable within the context of their rural environment; the hard work of Castle Top Farm left little time for leisurely social exchanges, and Cromford and its surroundings provided a solid and unchanging network of undemanding relationships outside the family.

Not all of Alison's contacts with the wider community beyond Castle Top were comfortable. She dreaded her music lessons in the village when every stumble was corrected with a sharp flick on her knuckles. The teacher sat by her side, holding a long wooden knitting needle. '"Tips of your fingers," she cried. "Arch your wrists!" and down came the needle on my bones. Tears ran down my cheeks, and I curled my tongue and licked them up quickly lest she should see. . . . I hated my lessons.'[30] Painful though her lessons were, Alison was able to find comfort at home with her own music – hymns, old melodies and a store of tunes in little booklets advertising Beecham's Pills. Throughout her life, music was to provide her with a deep and enduring source of pleasure and was to sustain her during her periods of profound unhappiness and black depression.

Although Alison disliked her music lessons for the predictable and painful flicks across her knuckles, she was capable of courting discomfort herself for the sake of the *frisson* involved – a fearful pleasure. One such ordeal occurred when she visited the Boggart House – a solitary stone cottage, sinister and ghostly. She approached it timorously because one of the inhabitants, the son of elderly parents, was said to have two noses. Sometimes Alison was obliged to take a basket of food to the lonely cottage and, having knocked at the door, 'always felt afraid, for I wondered whether *he* would come to the door, the pitiful son with his strange deformity'. Once the old woman bade her enter and she did so, seeing the huddled form of the son sitting by the fire, his face hidden.[31]

Contact with the world beyond Castle Top Farm brought other forms of discomfort. One Christmas the local schoolmaster and his wife came to spend the evening with the Taylors. During the conversation, the schoolmaster tried to explain the nothingness of the sky and space. Alison was filled with dismay to find there was no floor to heaven, 'God's throne had nothing to stand upon, and my angels were left homeless, whilst I had nowhere to go when I died.'[32] Another difficulty occurred when a stationmaster once came to tea in the farmhouse kitchen when Alison was very young and, to her intense embarrassment, gave her a kiss: 'It was undignified to be kissed by the Midland Railway, and quickly I wiped off the kiss.'[33]

But it was Alison's contact with the gentry of the neighbourhood that was responsible for some of her most uncomfortable moments as a child. Although she was intrigued by the Babington family, whose ancestral home was at nearby Dethick, and was later to base her success-ful novel *A Traveller in Time* upon the ill-fated Babington plot to rescue Mary, Queen of Scots during the reign of Elizabeth I, the aristocratic self-assurance of the Babingtons – and, indeed, other highborn people – both disturbed and antagonised her. In 1962 she spoke on the telephone to a woman who had been born into the Babington family and 'Her polite, affected voice gave me a shiver of childhood.'[34] Two years later she sat in church in front of 'a woman with a piercing contralto voice. She reminded me of women I do not like. Some I knew in youth with the same . . . strong voices.'[35]

By far her most painful experience with aristocratic women, how-ever, occurred outside Cromford Church one Christmas when she overheard the grand lady characterised as Mrs Drayton in *The Country Child*: '"What a very plain child that Garland child is! Positively ugly," said Mrs Drayton to her husband. Susan gasped and stood still . . . her heart ached and lay heavy in her breast. She didn't mind being called "plain", but "ugly" was like the toad, rough-skinned and venomous.'[36]

The emotional wound inflicted by this casual and cruel remark was to remain with Alison Uttley for the rest of her days. Her friend and illustrator for many years, Katherine Wigglesworth, believes that the incident provided a vital clue to her character: 'The local squire and his wife patronised the Uttleys – Alison bitterly said that she was taught to bob to them as they passed after church, and the squire's wife stopped her and her mother and said, pointing to Alison, "Give her a good education, as her face will never get her a husband." [Alison later recalled], "Katherine, those words gave me an inferiority complex I have never been able to get over. For *years* I felt I was a freak!"'[37] Certainly Alison Uttley maintained an ambivalence towards the high-born for the rest of her life. Although two local landowners, described in her writings as Sir Harry Vane and Gentleman Fairlie, are presented as benign figures, the slights which she and her family suffered when Alison was a child made her open to socialism when she first went to London during the Edwardian age. The ease with which she was to enter into a rich friendship with the Ramsay MacDonalds and her sympathy with many radical causes during the early part of her life may well flow from these early discomforts. So too may the snobbery of which she was capable, and the condescension she sometimes showed towards others less successful than herself after she had become a well-known and prosperous author.

Despite her comparatively lowly status, Alison was clearly an exceptionally sensitive and able child. She was to be rewarded by achieving remarkable success at school, a success which was to lift her from the homely surroundings of Castle Top and Cromford and set her on the path to fame.

CHAPTER FOUR

Lea Board School, 1892–97

I struggled home through the dark wood alone,
and goblins haunted my steps. I told my mother I
would not go to school, I did not like it.

ALISON UTTLEY, *A Ten O'Clock Scholar*

At the age of seven, Alison Uttley went to her first school. The question
of her formal education had for some time troubled her parents since
Cromford village school, and Lea school on the outskirts of the hamlet
of Holloway, were both, in their different ways, difficult to get to. If
Alison was sent to Cromford School, she would have to walk daily by
the side of the Derwent with its fast flowing and potentially treacherous
waters. If she was sent to Lea School, which was in a valley separated
from Castle Top Farm by a long hill and dense woods, the walk would
be lonely and two miles long each way. The dauntingly long walk to
either of these schools was the reason why Alison's formal education
began as late as it did, for a younger child would have had great
difficulty in covering anything up to four miles a day. In the end, Mr
and Mrs Taylor chose Lea Board School, despite its greater distance
from the farm, for the excellent reason that its headmaster 'was famous
in our district for his strictness and discipline, and for his learning. He
had letters after his name, which impressed everyone; he was a lecturer
and a musician.'[1]

The headmaster, Mr Allen, was indeed a remarkable man – progressive, a little eccentric, with a flair for geology and the violin – whose
reputation for strictness and good sense was deserved. He had shown
considerable understanding of the difficulties of Alison's journey when
her mother had gone to see him to explain the problem. Mr Allen and
Mrs Taylor soon came to an arrangement that was designed to make the
long walk to and from school less challenging. If Alison arrived at
school drenched through, then she should be dried by the fire and go to
the schoolmaster's house for hot cocoa in the middle of the morning.
She was allowed to take her dinner with her and eat it in the schoolroom
by herself. She might go for her music lessons in the next village during
school hours and on winter nights she could take a lantern and leave
school before the other children to begin her long walk home. In return
for these concessions, Mr Allen insisted that she should never be late for

school, pointing out that he caned all latecomers and that any absences must be due only to illness, not to bad weather.

Alison was much excited at the prospect of school, glad of the opportunity of meeting other girls and boys and hoping (rather optimistically) that in addition to the basic lessons in the three 'Rs' she would also learn Latin and French.

She began school on 4 April 1892. She wore a brown checked woollen frock with a tight bodice which was fastened from neck to ankle by large bone buttons with steel centres. She carried her dinner in a little blue linen bag and a pencil 'poppet', a container which was apparently of great age. Her mother accompanied her.

The walk took Alison through countryside whose inhabitants were 'strange' to her and she felt cut off from her home once it was 'hidden from sight behind the great hill, which stretched away in the distance with its trees and rocky fields'. There was also the 'uncharted wood which had no path except the one I used'.[2]

As she and her mother followed the road which curved around the base of the hill, Mrs Taylor gave her a list of do's and don'ts for when she arrived at school: 'I must wear a hat when I played, I mustn't sit on the cold stones, I must come straight home, and she would send a servant to meet me in the wood for the first few days.'[3] While Mrs Taylor, Polonius-like and perhaps a little anxious herself, exhorted Alison to good behaviour in her new environment, they walked through the wood, skirted Smedley's woollen mill at the hamlet of Holloway, and passed not far from Nightingale's lead smelting works – owned by the family that had produced the famous local heroine, Florence Nightingale.

Alison was both impressed and pleased as she went through the big gate with its stone balls on the gateposts and up a flight of broad steps which led to the playground. The school, she thought, had a certain importance with its long church windows and heavy door. Shrubberies sheltered it, and its flowerbeds were full of roses and pansies and sweet peas, stretching up to the dark walls. The schoolmaster had a pretty gabled house nearby. There was also a small infant school, a chapel and the minister's house – a community in themselves.

Lea School had been built some thirty years before and served the three villages of Lea, Dethick and Holloway. Although nearer to Holloway than Lea, it owed its name to the original dame school established at Lea village in 1808 which Alison's father had attended. The buildings which Alison first saw had been improved in 1888, when it became a school catering for all ages. There were about seventy children in the two schools.

Having kissed her mother goodbye, she followed the schoolmistress into the infant school. There she sat on some low wooden steps in a gallery, threaded coloured paper into mats and counted beads on to an abacus. Curiously, Alison Uttley has left different versions of her reception by her fellow pupils in her autobiographical writings. In *A Ten O'Clock Scholar* no reaction is recorded to her arrival. In fact, she finds the experience very dull.[4] In *Ambush of Young Days* there is a far more dramatic description of her reception: 'All my senses were assailed at once, and I was a wild animal caught in a trap as I realised I was alone, cut off from my mother, left in a noisy horde of children who all stared at me and whispered. I looked back at them with frightened eyes, inhaling the odour of the strange place, the coke stove, the chalk, the teacher and children, sweet-sour, harsh and acrid smells surrounded me.'[5] In *The Country Child* Susan Garland is positively tormented by the village children, laughing and pointing at her:

> 'What's your father?' they sang, swaying and swinging in a row, and pushing against her. 'I don't know,' said Susan, hesitating. It was the first time she had thought of this. In her little world there were no trades.
> 'Where do you come from?' they jeered, louder and louder as they rocked with laughter at her simplicity.[6]

She was also, apparently, mocked for the old-fashioned, brown checked woollen frock she wore; one that her mother had, it seems, dug out of an oak chest and which Alison had at first protested against, weeping at its ugliness and its horrible buttons:

> 'Aye, what a figure of fun. Where did you get that frock?' they gibed.
> She had loathed her dress, but now she held it tightly with one hand. It came from her own home, and was part of her. She had been called a 'figure of fun'. She stood with her back against the wall, and a crowd of jeering girls jostled her. One pulled her hair with a mischievous tug, one opened her satchel and looked at her sandwiches, and one, the most shameless, put her tongue out at her. A little boy of her own age ran up rudely and kissed her. . . . Susan took out her handkerchief and rubbed her cheek as the cries and gibes rose higher. She stood like a frightened rabbit, her face white, her eyes big with horror. 'Mother' she whispered to her heart, and the school bell rang.[7]

Clearly Alison felt uncomfortable on her first day at school. She was unable to answer properly the preliminary questions that her teacher asked her:

> 'When were you born?' she continued.
> 'On a Saturday, mam,' I replied. It was my sad fate. 'Saturday's Child has far to go', and I hoped no-one would find out about it. However the mistress had asked me, and doubtless she wished to know whether I was 'Full of Grace or Fair of Face'.

She gave a little laugh and did not write down my reply.
'When is your birthday, child?' she asked.
'A week before Christmas, mam,' said I. She closed the book and
sent me to my place, and I realised I had not made the correct replies.[8]

In the tiny infant school, even Alison's scholarly skills were a disadvantage. When the writing lesson began and she opened her pencil
poppet and drew out her quill pen, 'The mistress gave a little cry. . . .
She took it away and went to the desk. The two teachers whispered
together and looked at me. It was an unfortunate beginning, and I hung
my head with shame. . . . No pens were used by little children; I must
bring a slate pencil next time, said the teacher.'[9] Even after she had been
given a slate, Alison could not clean it because she lacked the piece of
damp sponge necessary. She watched a boy spit upon his slate, then rub
it with his cuff. Disdaining such vulgarity she licked a portion of hers,
refusing to spit and then rubbed it clean with her frock.

When they did sums, however, she found them far easier than those
she had done with her mother and rattled off the answers to the
admiration of the other children. When a book was passed along the line
for reading, Alison skimmed through the easy story while every other
child struggled with the words.

Next day she was promoted to the larger schoolroom, where fifty
children had lessons in the long open room. Small classes of children,
each with a pupil teacher, sat along the room and in the centre sat the
headmaster at his desk 'engrossed in his writing, yet all-seeing, like
God'. At Mr Allen's side was a cane with which he pointed at any pupil
to whom he wished to speak. The cane was also used for corporal
punishment. Late arrivals got one stroke of the cane unless they came
armed with a good excuse. In her time, though not for being late,
Alison 'had many a stroke from that cane for talking. I had blisters on
my palms, which I showed proudly. I deserved the punishment for I
whispered stories of servants and riches at home, of a dog and horses
which had supernatural gifts, and then I was sent to the desk.'[10]

Although she was 'enchanted by school' when once she had settled in,
for some time Alison tried hard to avoid being sent at all, even feigning
illness. She gives various reasons for this reluctance: that her first day at
school was dull, which clearly it was not, although it was both
humiliating and alarming; that she was afraid of being late and that she
would be caned as a consequence; that she detested the effort of being
punctual and restrained when she had been previously free to roam as
she pleased; that she was afraid of the lonely wood through which she
had to walk and of its supernatural denizens.[11]

Of all the justifications for her early school phobia, Alison's fear of
her long daily walk, part of it through the dark and threatening wood, is

the most commonly reiterated in her writings. In winter, when darkness came early, she held up her hand and asked if she could go home before the other children. She has left several vivid descriptions of this journey that she made in her round woollen hat with a pheasant feather in the ribbon, a matching plaid cloak over her shoulders, and carrying a small tin lantern in her hand:

> I set off home, running for the first mile, for it was downhill and easy. Then I passed a mill and walked up a steep field where calves grazed. I came to the wood, and I stopped at the big gate to light the candle in my lantern. I shut the gate softly so that 'they' would not hear. The trees were alive and awake, they were waiting for me. They whispered together, they shook their skinny arms and tried to catch my cloak, but I held the lantern out and faced them with it. . . . It was a rustling wood of invisible creatures, with rocks which hid prehistoric man, with Dinosaurs who came to walk and to see a little girl powerless before their claws and their eyes.[12]

Although at the end of each winter journey through the dark wood her mother was waiting for her, peering down the hill, Alison never lost her fear of her daily walk. Throughout her writings, and in various interviews, she speculated as to the root of her anxiety: 'Every step of that wood was haunted. I always walked on tiptoe so that the creatures – "they" – couldn't catch me. I don't know who "they" were; men partly, I thought a man might carry me off. I always walked on the soil between the stones. I had a feeling I must never make a noise in the wood, and never chink with my little iron heels.'[13]

As well as employing various rituals to ward off the threatening denizens of the wood and never voicing her fears lest 'they' should know of them, Alison resorted to another device. She sometimes used to entice other children to walk with her, telling them stories as a reward. It was a formative experience in the development of a born spinner of tales: 'I used to bribe children, I think that was my first story-telling. I used to bribe children with the promise of a story, and I told lots of stories, made them up as I just went along. And as long as I went on talking, they didn't notice anything, and followed me. I always felt there was a witchery about that place.'[14]

Why did the wood which, after all, she could see every day from her home on the farm, arouse such fears in the child Alison? Partly it allowed her youthful fantasies full play; demons and dinosaurs and wolves and goblins are commonplace in childish, fearful imaginings. Girls may also feel deep unspoken anxieties about men lurking in dark places, ready to attack and perhaps rape them. In Alison Uttley's case, there is perhaps something else. Having spent the first seven years of her life in daily and intimate contact with her parents at Castle Top, to venture beyond the physical bounds of their protection and love aroused in her deep anxieties about separation and loneliness and even a neurotic fear of death: 'Each morning she prepared for the worst. She left the house for school feeling she might never see her parents again.'

Despite her dread of her walk through the lonely wood, Alison greatly enjoyed her years at Lea School. She had an unquenchable thirst for knowledge, something that was to characterise her throughout her life: 'Lessons enchanted me, and I was eager for more learning as I listened to other classes going on at the same time. . . . I picked up crumbs of learning which were scattered in that big room and I learned poems and even French words when a pupil teacher had a private lesson near me.'[15]

Her enthusiasm owed much to inspiring and caring teachers. On her first day in the big school she noticed a serious young teacher with dark curls and a pale, sweet face. This teacher, called 'Miss Patty' in *Ambush of Young Days*, drew Alison into the group which was clustering round her when she saw the new girl hanging about on the fringe alone. Alison 'fell in love with her at that moment, for when I was lonely she had spoken to me. . . . I felt I would gladly die for her. She was the first stranger in my life who inspired me with devotion, a childish adoration for the good and beautiful, for I was sure she was as good as she was lovely.'[16] It is perhaps significant, in view of the deep early impression made upon Alison by this young teacher, that the heroine of her largely autobiographical novel *High Meadows* is called Patty Verity. Patty was thus a name which enabled Alison to identify with the young teacher who filled her with such adoration, and Verity conjures up images of truthfulness and sincerity. Once she had completed her university education, Alison herself was to become a young teacher.

At Lea School, apart from the three female pupil teachers and a young master who taught the big boys football and gymnastics, there was Mr Allen. A Cornishman by birth, the headmaster had red hair and fierce blue eyes. He had large bony hands, and was tall and slim in build. He was the dominating force in the school and his dynamic teaching was to have a profound impact upon the seven-year-old Alison:

> The best lessons which I never forgot were those given by the headmaster on Geology. He stood in front of a double class, his blue eyes blazing with excitement as he told us about the age of the earth, discovered from rocks, of the great forests which later made the Coal Age, of the Ice Age, when our land was covered with ice, of the great animals which roamed the earth. We sat, entranced, longing for more as we followed his footsteps into the past. . . . I was stirred to my heart . . . and I started off on my own to experiment. Now my collection of stones took on a new interest. The life with which I had endowed the rocks was manifest and true.[17]

It is easy to see how Mr Allen's inspired teaching was instrumental in promoting Alison Uttley's deep and lifelong interest in science. The headmaster was also a good musician with an accurate ear and during singing lessons he accompanied his pupils on the violin. Sometimes they sang 'Rule Britannia', which puzzled Alison, 'for I had no idea at that time I was a Briton'. Much of the learning, however, was by rote; they chanted weights and measures and learned to recite 'The Charge of the Light Brigade'. Alison found the reading books dull and resented that she was obliged to read the same stories over and over again. One innovation, however, came when Mr Allen introduced a school news-paper on the American model and Alison was delighted to read the story of Rip Van Winkle 'which I believed implicitly, and pondered over for years. I longed to go to America, to the Catskill Mountains where such things happened.'[18]

There were outdoor activities too – drill, when the girls carried wands and the boys lifted dumbbells. Alison felt some jealousy for the boys, who were allowed to have school gardens where they worked on fine afternoons while the girls struggled over their sewing. Strangely, the geography lessons were also reserved for boys but she managed to overhear a good deal of what was going on and learned, to her surprise, that England was an island and not just what she could see with her own eyes.

School lessons were encompassed by a framework derived from the Christian religion. School started with prayers and a hymn and then the pupils recited the creed and the Ten Commandments. Sometimes they wrote out the Lord's Prayer on their slates. They also learned various psalms and proverbs, and recited an alphabet of texts which pleased Alison immensely: 'A. Ask and it shall be given to you. B. Blessed are the peacemakers. C. Consider the lilies of the field.'

At playtime, Alison learned traditional folk songs from her fellow pupils. The girls, as girls are wont to do, played in their own small section of the playground where they danced and mimed ancient ditties like 'I wrote a letter to my love' and 'Oats and beans and barley grows'. The first singing game Alison learned at school was the May song, 'Here we go gathering Nuts in May'. In springtime the girls skipped, using more rhymes and incantations. Then the skipping season ended, for no apparent reason, and it was time for battledore and shuttlecock. There were days with mystic rituals which surprised her, like April Fool's Day and Royal Oak Day, in memory of King Charles II hiding in the oak tree during the Civil War. There was apple bobbing on All Hallows' Eve and on Pancake Day they ran races.

By the standards of many modern schools, Lea Board School was cramped and overcrowded with small groups of children pursuing different lessons in the same room. Yet Alison Uttley remained, to the end of her life, 'glad I went to a little village school in those early days, and learned about the rocks and the fossils and the masses of dark stone in the woods'.[19] Half a century after the event, she was happy to be reminded by an old friend, Ethel Gregory, of the times they had spent at Lea School,[20] though she became irritated by the frequent, and as she saw it, tedious letters sent her by another, male, ex-pupil.[21] She responded warmly in August 1963 to a letter written to her by the then head of Lea School, though she confessed she could not help him about the dates of the school: 'I wrote to him, and the children, speaking of my schooldays. I wanted to learn French, Latin, Algebra, Chemistry, and Astronomy. . . . I liked mental arithmetic and Geology.'[22]

Alison's success at Lea School was not based simply upon her application and upon her natural intelligence. She had received a flying start through her mother's teaching at Castle Top Farm. Mrs Taylor 'sang or recited poetry every day', making it later Alison's 'favourite reading . . . it coloured my life before I even knew the alphabet'.[23] Alison's early lessons were also given to her by her mother, 'who taught me to read, write and do easy sums. I began with an old alphabet-book with large letters and queerly dressed people in the illustrations.

> A was an Archer who shot at a frog,
> B was a Butcher who had a great dog.'[24]

At the age of four she went straight to books; old leather-covered children's books, some fifty or sixty years old, and spelled her way through *The Ladder to Learning*, reading the tales aloud, helped by her mother. It was the beginning of a life of voracious reading. At the age of seven or eight she heard long books read aloud, for during the winter months her mother read to her father until nine o'clock at night. In the bedroom above theirs, Alison could hear scraps of wonderful books, *John Halifax, Gentleman*, *Adam Bede* and *The Mill on The Floss*. From the age of eight she listened while her mother read most of Dickens, although sometimes she heard her father say, 'you've missed something' and saw her mother give him a frown and a nod, indicating that she had omitted something not suitable for a child's ears.

During her first years at Lea School, Alison also absorbed a wide variety of literary and other stimuli from an unexpected source. In a letter written in 1961, as an autobiographical memoir, she admitted that when she was a child 'we were poor, farming did not pay even in those early days, and it got worse. We had a standby, we took in "visitors", like other farms, and they helped very much. The house was large, and we took one or two families, of professional people, and clergy, of people whom we liked, who came again and again, every year, until the children were adult, they came with a nanny, and books and high spirits.'[25]

This confession of a poverty which found some relief in the annual taking in of paying guests is generally absent from Alison Uttley's published writing. Her pride and her tendency to romanticise her childhood at Castle Top Farm doubtless explains the omission. She was to claim, in the private letter quoted above, that:

> I never felt jealous of the riches I saw, I accepted the strangers, shy at first, and then glad, for often they had marvellous books, all new, and I used to creep in the drawing room when they were out and read surreptitiously. I read Stevenson, Barrie and Kipling this way, in stealthy sips, and I put down the books and flew when the dog gave warning of the return of the visitors. Some brought serious books on philosophy, for the owners were from universities, lecturers and professors, and I dipped into these. I read a good deal of astronomy at one time. . . . I had my first French lesson from a French governess who came to stay with us with two children, – a lovely time. I asked her words, and wrote them down. Latin too. I was only about eight. Some children brought piles of music, Mozart and Beethoven, and I used to play it when they were out. I read easily, and loved it. In fact I had a great deal of pleasure in these contacts, when I was a shabby little girl and there was seldom any snobbery. I think they were envious of my life in such a lovely place with all the freedom and the animals. The house itself was like a magnet, it drew us all close to it, in an occult way.[26]

As she reached the end of her time at Lea School, it is clear that Alison Uttley was both highly intelligent and, given her circumstances, well-educated. But her parents were too poor to send her to the appropriate secondary school. Lady Manners School at Bakewell, however, was a nearby grammar school which admitted a few scholarship children annually from the Cromford area. Mr Allen had no hesitation in recommending to Mr and Mrs Taylor that their daughter, one of his brightest pupils, should be entered for the examination at this relatively prestigious school.

CHAPTER FIVE

The Grammar School Girl, 1897–1903

> I remember using a test tube; I thought it was
> a *marvellous* thing.
>
> ALISON UTTLEY, 'The Book Programme',
> 23 December1975

In May 1897 Alison boarded the train at Cromford station bound for Bakewell to take the entrance examination at Lady Manners School. Wearing a blue dress and a grey alpaca cloak and gloves, with her Sunday hat in her hand, Alison travelled with a group of boys from Lea School. She seems to have been the only girl from the school taking the entrance examination and beside her fellow pupils with their stiff white collars and plastered-down hair, stolid and clumsy, she felt herself to be a high-spirited young colt amongst a group of cattle.

Alison was well-aware of the urgent need to win a County Scholarship. As we have seen, money was short for the Taylor family at Castle Top. Not merely did Mr and Mrs Taylor take in paying guests, but the annual holiday at Blackpool or Scarborough 'was talked of for months, with money put aside for the purpose, small savings and windfalls'.[1] Indications of her parents' need to exercise prudence in financial matters are scattered throughout Alison Uttley's writing, albeit discreetly. One of several examples can be found in *The Country Child*, when Susan Garland brings a chattering crowd of girls home to see her Easter egg and her mother takes her by the shoulders and asks her severely, 'whatever do you mean by bringing all those girls home with you? . . . Don't you see that they must all be fed?'[2]

Conscious of the importance of the entrance examination, Alison had prepared for the great day almost ritually. The night before she had bathed in front of the kitchen fire, washing herself with Pears soap and shivering a little at the chilly blast which for a while came through the back door. Next morning, sent on her way with the confident good wishes of her family and the farm workers, she had left the farm in a milk cart like a young Amazon going to do battle for honour and reward.

In the event, the entrance examination seemed like a disaster to Alison. Once at Lady Manners School, the children were ushered in by an impatient supervisor who seemed annoyed at having to attend school on a Saturday. There was an unpleasantly strong odour of gas, leaking from jets in the ceiling. The examination room seemed bare and hostile, without pictures or flowers. The teacher who superintended the examination snapped out short, sharp commands at the children, making them feel even more ill at ease. Alison was particularly upset when he collected all their private notebooks as a precaution against cheating. Not only was she resentful of the implication that she might cheat but she also felt that her little notebook, packed with information, would somehow guarantee her good luck.

That Alison was so disconcerted by the atmosphere during her entrance examination perhaps indicates how much she wanted to succeed. She seems to have been put somewhat off her stroke, for she did not do well enough to be awarded a scholarship. Her reaction to this unwelcome news, declaring that she did not care and resolving to continue her education by herself, was typical of a tendency throughout her life to minimise, at least in public, disappointments and defeats.

As it turned out, she had done well enough in her entrance examination, for a little later the family received a letter informing them that she was to have a scholarship after all as the parents of the last boy on the list of successful candidates had rejected it. Despite her family's rejoicing and the bountiful present of a shilling from her father, Alison had a mixed reaction to her good fortune. Her pride in her academic competence made her feel that she was receiving another child's leavings. Nonetheless she had now been awarded a Derbyshire County Council Scholarship, one of twelve to be allotted to Lady Manners School.

Alice Jane Taylor's name was entered on the school roll on 13 September 1897. Lady Manners School had been established in 1636 by Lady Grace Manners as a free school for poor boys of the district. From small beginnings, the school was eventually housed in a new building in Bath Gardens in Bakewell in 1895. Most of the money for its re-establishment had come from the trust money from the Manners estate, but Derbyshire County Council made a grant of six hundred pounds on the condition that it should be used as a technical school in the evening and that girls should be admitted as pupils as well as boys. The fees were two pounds a term. When Alison joined the school, it had been in use for barely a year and still smelled distinctly of newly cut stone and fresh paint.

The Taylor family had made much of preparing Alison for her new experience. There had been an expedition to Derby on cheap rail tickets to buy woollen material for her cloak. Mr Taylor had bought her a pencil box with a picture of Queen Victoria at her Diamond Jubilee on the lid. Her mother gave her a silver brooch with her name printed in golden letters.

Alison's journey to Lady Manners School entailed an early morning drive to Cromford station to catch the milk train to Bakewell. Because she had been awarded a scholarship, she also received:

> . . . a red leather season ticket with my name written inside, and I passed it round for all to examine. It cost nothing at all, it was part of the scholarship, and we were deeply impressed. Nobody had ever seen one before, for we were not train travellers except for the weekly market, or a visit to the county town. . . . Now I was going to school by train, with books in a leather satchel and a purse with nothing in it and a season ticket. I had to be punctual, I was now part of the wide world of mechanically minded people who went by train, and not a dilly-dally child, who dawdled among rabbits and pheasants and flowers along the country lanes.[3]

Each morning Alison got up reluctantly for school at seven o'clock, washing in cold water in her bedroom. The household had already been astir since half past five. It was essential that she was ready when the milk cart left, since 'I had to remember that I was of less importance than a churn of milk, and if I were only a minute late, I should be left behind to run all the way to the station. If I missed the train, there was no other for two and a half hours.'[4] At a quarter past seven she ate her breakfast which consisted of a round of toast and beef dripping, crisp and hot and sprinkled with salt. If she did not finish her breakfast, she had to take it with her and eat it in the cart. Nor was she allowed to throw it away once she had left the farm, for that would be a waste. Once she threw away a 'bad-smelling' crust, but later returned guiltily to retrieve it. As she ate her toast and dripping, her father and the farm workers bustled about preparing the bright, shiny milk churns. When she heard the cartwheels scrunching on the cobbles, she rose from the table murmuring, 'For what we have received, the Lord make us truly thankful', knowing that the train was already on its way to Cromford from the county town. She pulled on her black boots, which had been polished the night before and were now warming in front of the fire, and laced them up; then she put on her tartan tam-o-shanter adorned with a pheasant's feather and in which one day Alison vainly hoped to wear a cairngorm, clipped the silver clasp of her cloak and was ready to go. She fled to the cart, having kissed her parents goodbye and called to them, 'God bless you.'

Once she was seated in the cart, with a thick rug pulled over her knees, she felt like a queen on her throne and was able to appreciate the special qualities of the early morning air as the servant boy led the horse down the steep stony road and through the gates to the high road which took them to the station. Sometimes, as the cart swung from side to side down the sharp descent, Alison felt nervous that they might overturn. But the servant boy drove 'like Jehu', seldom using the whip for that was not allowed. Occasionally they had a race to catch the train and Alison would alight, relieved, at the station and nod to the pony gratefully (although not, apparently, to the servant boy) and hurry on to the platform, eager to see the sights.

The train arrived at 7.50 a.m. The guard of Alison's train 'was a kindly man, with a little grey beard and blue eyes. He wore a buttonhole all through the spring, summer and autumn months, a rosebud, a carnation or a geranium. He was the uncle of one of the schoolgirls, and we admired him for his good manners and attention to us.'[5] The children bound for Bakewell had reserved third class carriages, one for the boys and one for the girls. 'The train was clean, the windows shone, and the brass handles were polished. We felt an immense pride in it as if we owned it, and we gave extra little rubs to keep the brass clean.' As the train stopped at each station, more girls would enter the carriage and they all settled down to finish their homework, to compare answers and to hear each other recite French or Latin exercises. They carried bottles of ink in little leather-covered safety cases and worked on their knees when the train stopped at the stations.

Good behaviour was expected, in keeping with the efficiency, cleanliness and sparkle of the Midland Railway. The schoolgirls were expected to wear their gloves, to keep quiet and generally to behave with decorum. To put their heads out of the carriage windows was forbidden, lest decapitation should result. Alison, however, could not resist the temptation: 'One direful day of high wind I disobeyed, not in a tunnel but in the lush meadowland where the river Wye flowed. My summer straw hat was torn away, and I had to go to school hatless. I was severely reprimanded before the whole school, punished and a note sent to my mother. "Bad behaviour on the train" said my report later, and a cloud hung about me.'[6]

In winter the porter brought iron hot water bottles, freshly filled, for them to warm their feet on. At night they sat in the waiting room at Bakewell station, reading storybooks and toasting themselves before a blazing fire which another porter willingly stoked for them. In spring and summer, in Alison Uttley's memory, the girls carried bunches of flowers which they had picked in the land near the station: forget-me-nots in spring and a variety of wild flowers in summer. The train left Bakewell station at 5.15 each evening and Alison felt that she and her fellow pupils were 'proud to be passengers returning, and when the train came into the station we again felt a blissful content with travelling by train'.[7] Seventy years later Alison noted with some sadness in her diary the closing of Bakewell station.[8]

Once they alighted at Bakewell, the schoolchildren had to cross the mediaeval bridge into the town. As she did so, Alison 'had a feeling of exaltation as they walked there, with the river underneath, but beyond the bridge I was caught in a net of conflicting emotions, of Latin prose with its difficulties, of French which had many mistakes, of a speech in Shakespeare which I had not learned. The train had gone on, and I was left to face school.'[9]

Alison Uttley always retained a strong affection for Bakewell, remembering the bridge into the old town as 'enchanting' and relieved to hear, in 1970, that the town was 'just as beautiful and happy, and the school very good'.[10] She was also to remember, however, that conditions at the school were often cramped.

When she first arrived at Lady Manners School she felt considerable unease. The majority of pupils were fee-paying and tended to look down on the scholarship pupils. Alison was conscious of her humbler clothes and her lack of a fashionable hairstyle. The masters also looked rather forbidding, striding by in their gowns and mortarboards like great black crows. Nor did she have all the equipment she was expected to bring and, once back at Castle Top Farm, presented her mother with various items which she needed – to be told that they would be bought whenever they could be afforded. Alison's first meeting with the headmaster, Mr Mansford, increased her early feelings of insecurity and disorientation. Mansford was a Cambridge graduate who had recently come north from a school in London and tended to look down upon the scholarship children, viewing Alison as a mere farmer's daughter. Not that Alison had any real grounds for feeling inferior. She was tall for her age, with long dark hair, fine eyes and graceful hands. Many years later she took great pleasure from being told that at school she was 'a beautiful strong girl'.[11] Eventually she became so anxious to assert her presence that in school photographs she held a hand to her face in order to be noticed.[12]

Nor had she any reason to be ashamed of her academic accomplishments, although at first there were many difficulties in adjusting to the standards expected at the school. Latin was a particular trial, especially since the headmaster, with his sardonic tongue, taught it. Alison's unease with Mr Mansford made her fearful of asking him for explanations lest he should ridicule her and once she was almost reduced, while struggling with her homework, to go down to the Cromford chemist who was the only Latin scholar in the village, to ask his help.[13] She was, however, determined to master the subject and found some inspiration in her struggle by reflecting that the Romans who had worked the nearby lead mines had actually spoken Latin. Nearly seventy years later she was to remember the pain and pleasure of learning Latin: 'Odes of Horace have come, to remind me of youth and my struggles in the attic window as I translated. Vitae summa brevis. Ah, it makes my heart ache for all the shortness of life.'[14]

Although Latin was a compulsory subject and, at least early on, an ordeal for Alison, she later saw it as an invaluable preparation for the art of writing. The prose of Cicero, the verse of Virgil, Ovid and Horace, despite the difficulties of the language, gave her 'an appreciation of words and a realisation of choice offered to us'.[15] Alison also made, perhaps predictably and over-romantically, a link between the study of Latin and her childhood experiences at Castle Top Farm: 'Latin was . . . the ancient language of the earth, the tongue of trees, and we read legends I never forgot. Somebody gave me a copy of *Smith's Smaller Classical Dictionary*, and the stories of the gods and heroes became my daily reading, with the Bible for company. The dryads lived in our trees, I had always known, the water nymphs in our river and in the springs, the fauns in the woods, and Pan himself in the pastures. The world was peopled by the figures of mythology, and I accepted them as true.'[16]

Despite her later fame as a writer and the fact that she won a Silver Medal for English in 1901, Alison did not enjoy the subject much, finding it 'too easy and dull, except for Shakespeare's plays which I learned by heart'.[17] Certainly, she found the writing of English essays a dispiriting ordeal: 'All my ideas of being a writer were shattered by the essays and their structure as I was taught in my youth. Our essays were a test of good handwriting and an absence of blots. I could attain the former by exerting the greatest care over forming each individual letter, with loops unfilled with ink, but smudges and blots always were a hazard.[18]

Her parents' contribution of 'sermon' paper from a high-class stationer in Matlock still left the problem of the watered-down ink that she was obliged to use for economy. Even her new Waverley pen couldn't guarantee her against the perils of the ink bottle with its 'thick sediment . . . to be brought up on the tip of the nib by the unwary writer'.[19] Alison Uttley remembered that 'my words never came to life. I could not use my own experiences, the pithy talk of the countrymen I knew, the tales I heard, the awareness of earth, of woods and fields, which were the kernel of the life around me. There was no spark of inspiration, I was cut off by the inky smudge which took possession.'[20]

One of the problems was that she was not confident enough to experiment. Nor was this encouraged at Lady Manners School:

'Nobody could write even a humble essay without some idea of the subject, and my attempts were dull with no gleam of light or fancy because I was afraid to wander from the beaten track of conformity. Individuality was not encouraged. No essays were set on country subjects, and we were all country children. Essays were read aloud by the teacher who would pounce on anything that gave a chance for sarcasm. The girl who compared the moon to an incandescent light, in the evening sky, was mocked at before the whole class.'[21]

Once Alison was asked to write an essay on 'The Novel' and although she was an avid reader 'for pure pleasure . . . like a drug addict', this task led her to a near-disaster. Dickens and George Eliot were familiar enough from Mrs Taylor's evening readings at Castle Top, but she saw these – not altogether accurately – as 'homely household books about country people', whereas novels were something different, even wicked, in her reckoning. She went ahead and wrote her essay, with imaginative flights of fancy about various novels, including books of family life and what she called dramatic novels, such as *Treasure Island*. Then she ventured on to novels of passion, 'where passion had the old meaning of the word, hot-tempered clashes, and wild feuds. Scott was in this list, but unluckily I gave the names of two authors whose names I had heard, but whose books I had not even seen, so I did not know their titles. Thomas Hardy and Grant Allen, and I added Marie Corelli with some misgiving.'[22]

This essay was neatly written on sermon paper and quite devoid of blots. Nonetheless the headmaster, arriving 'white-faced and bitter-tongued to the class', scolded all his pupils for their rubbish:

> 'What did I know of novels of passion, he demanded? What could a schoolgirl know of passion? What had I read of Hardy, or Grant Allen, or Marie Corelli?'
> 'Nothing, sir,' I murmured truthfully.
> 'What did you mean by passion?'
> I was too frightened to reply. He was in such a passion himself that I was intimidated and scared out of my wits. . . . I was a passionate child who should curb her hasty words, I was often told, but I did not discuss this with the master. I was mocked at and scorned and degraded by the man's tongue. In adult life one never has the humiliations and agonies of childhood. . . . I never wrote an essay at school with any ease after this, I said as little as possible, and only in exterior examinations could I do well.[23]

Even in science, at which Alison was later to excel, there were early humiliations. Shortly after entering Lady Manners School, Alison produced an essay on 'The Atom', writing that 'The Atom is the smallest particle of matter. It can never be divided.' The science master proceeded to hold her up to ridicule before the whole class:

'Who is this girl?' he asked, as he flicked my paper with impatient hand, 'Who dares to make such an assertion? How does she know the atom can never be split? Is she omniscient? The atom has not been split, so far, but nobody knows what discoveries may be made in the future.'

He tossed my paper back at me and swung away in scorn, with his black gown flying behind him, and I , withered and unhappy, stored this dictum in my mind. 'Nobody knows what discoveries may be made in the future.'[24]

Quite apart from the difficulties she encountered with various teachers and in various subjects, Alison also found it a trial to do her homework properly. One of the problems was that she used the kitchen table at Castle Top Farm for her work, 'with the cloth, the plates and cups pushed back to make room'. Her family and farm workers walked back and forth through the kitchen carrying cans of milk, doors were left open to the wild winds, the lamp flared or candles blew out in the draught. Once her elbow was accidentally nudged, throwing a long streak of ink upon the white paper. Occasionally a cow's hair would find its way into her inkpot. Nor could Alison integrate the experiences of her bustling home with the tasks her school had set for homework: 'Tales of horses, cattle, revival meetings, circuses and robberies went on regardless of my presence, and I gazed dreamily at the kind homely faces around me as I struggled to find the words to describe a Shakespearian character, when the live characters out of the past were already there. Phoebe and William, Audrey and Touchstone were playing their parts, and Bottom the Weaver was whittling the sticks, and I had only an inkling of the truth of time itself, time past and time present mingled there.'[25]

Despite these difficulties, and her problems in adjusting to the new routine of school, Alison worked extremely hard. She was later to recall that she had read too much as a child, so much so that when she suffered an attack of measles, she nearly lost the use of her weakened eyes.

There were compensations, however. Despite the painful raps on the knuckles she had received from her village piano teacher, Alison cherished a deep love of music. At Lady Manners School she exchanged her village music teacher for the school music master. So successfully did he teach her harmony and the principles of composition on the piano, thus deepening and extending her understanding of music, that she was at one time tempted to study music after school.[26] The music master also taught them from the Harrow Song Book: 'We sang "Gaudeamus Igitur" and "Forty Years On" and "The Lorelei".' She was delighted by her private piano lessons: 'Now I played Beethoven and Weber, Chopin and Bach . . . the master told me of their lives and their works, he told me stories of the music and operas, and he gave me

music to read that was important and satisfying instead of the
sweetmeat scraps I had enjoyed.'[27]

These deeply satisfying lessons at Lady Manners School confirmed in
Alison the natural music she felt she had absorbed during her country
upbringing:

> It was my background, wherever I went, for it was in my mind,
> music running as an accompaniment to walking and talking, to
> breathing and doing – living tunes unheard were ever present, with no
> dimension of scale or interval. In winter the icicles sang as they hung
> from the eaves of the farm buildings or clung with firm grips of their
> sturdy feet to the water troughs and pumps. The trees sang
> throughout the year, changing their song from sweet soughing to a
> mighty roar. . . . There was a time, after reading Thomas Hardy's
> *The Woodlanders*, when we went out with eyes shut and tried to
> discover each tree by the music it made as the wind played in the
> branches.[28]

Alison also developed a keen interest in sport. In 1901 she won the
Challenge Cup for sport and in the following year she came first in both
the high jump and the long jump. She also fell in love with cricket and,
remarkably for those days, played in the school cricket team and was
judged to be the best fielder. She never lost her passion for the game and
later in life followed the sport intently, once even aspiring to become
cricket correspondent for the *Manchester Guardian*.

But it was in science and mathematics that Alison achieved her
greatest triumphs. She had been immediately excited by the science
facilities, modest as they were by present standards, at Lady Manners
School. She was enthralled as she inhaled the smell of sulphurated
hydrogen in the chemistry laboratory and became increasingly excited
by physics. She was later to recall the excellent teaching of her physics
master, Mr Halgate, and to remember that the boys had to stand on one
side of the laboratory and the girls, in their long skirts, on the other. She
also remembered first 'using a test tube; I thought it was a <u>marvellous</u>
thing!'[29]

Towards the end of her life, after she had achieved international fame,
Alison Uttley rationalised the apparent paradox of her feelings for
nature, magic and mystery and her lifelong devotion to science: 'My
subject is physics, the poetic science. There is too much applied science
nowadays. Everything has life. If there is one thing science teaches you,
it is that. Once you have grasped the structure of the atom, you realise
that everything is alive, even metals, minerals, so-called inanimate
objects; so you see, even Sam Pig and Grey Rabbit are alive, in their
own fashion. Life is a many-sided thing.[30]

She left Lady Manners School in July 1903, when she was eighteen and a half years old. She had by then achieved considerable success. Her name occurred frequently in the school magazine, the *Peacock*, and she had won numerous commendations in the Headmaster's Report. School prizes abounded; the Natural Science Prize in 1899 and 1900, the Scripture Prize, the Silver Medal for Mathematics, and for English in 1901, and in 1902 the Silver Medals for Chemistry and Physics. In 1903 she was acclaimed Dux of the school.

Alison capped this remarkable school career by winning a Major County Scholarship from Derbyshire to Owens College in Manchester, then part of the federal Victoria University. She could not have managed to go to Manchester without this crucial financial support: 'I went in for a scholarship. I was very keen on mathematics. We were very well taught. We did advanced mathematics, not just algebra and trigonometry. We did spherical geometry and things; I was very keen, and I went in for a scholarship, and I was top in physics.'[31]

The winning of the scholarship was not without its hazards. She had to travel to Derby for the examination and was there confronted with an experiment in their big empty laboratory. She drew the illustration on paper as to how the experiment should be conducted, showing the correct circuits. The examiner, wandering by, was apparently 'amazed' at this diagram and gave her some apparatus to conduct the experiment practically. A problem arose immediately, for at Lady Manners School there had been no electricity in the laboratory except when the pupils had made it by simple experiment:

'Where is the electricity?' I asked, staring about me. There was no sign of the small batteries we used in simple work. He pointed to a couple of brass terminals on the wall. They were tiny things with no wires, no visible circuits for electricity.
'Where is the electricity?' I asked again, and he showed me how to connect up with a blank wall. This was astonishing, for not even water came from a wall in my kind of life. . . . This was my first introduction to the generation of electricity, and the examiner enjoyed telling the wonders of town electricity to a country girl.
I performed my experiment to my own satisfaction and it worked, to my amazement. It was an enlightening experience, this transformation from theory to practice, and the flow of the 'fluid', the energy, fulfilled my dreams. Everything went smoothly. I put in resistances, and I made a Wheatstone Bridge.[32]

Alison Uttley's discovery of the new world of electricity flowing from a mains supply symbolised her position in 1903. The daughter of an unlettered tenant farmer, educated in village and small-town schools, she was now to make one of the greatest leaps in her life, from the homely surroundings of northern Derbyshire to the great city of Manchester with its recently established and expanding university.

CHAPTER SIX

Manchester University, 1903–6

We talk of the status of woman kind
Of suffrage, and greatness of human mind.
Equality, love, but we always find
'Argument'.

A[LICE] J[ANE] T[AYLOR]
Yggdrasill the student magazine of
Ashburne House, 1906

Manchester was the first great city that Alison had visited. She was at first a little overawed by its size, as well as being fascinated by its trams and by the abundance of electric lighting. After the clean rural air of northern Derbyshire she was to find the murk and fog of Manchester a trial. Nor did she ever completely reconcile herself to the dirt and litter which she came to associate with certain parts of the city.

There is no doubt, however, that she greatly enjoyed her three years there, particularly the excitement and stimulation of studying at its university. Although Manchester University was a natural choice for Alison because it was the nearest to her home, it was also appropriate in possessing one of the most distinguished schools of physics and mathematical science in the country. When Alison arrived at Manchester, the Professor of Experimental Physics was J. J. Thomson, the founder of the Cavendish Laboratory at Cambridge which was involved in atomic research. Thomson's pupil, Rutherford, who was later to succeed him as professor, was also working with him on the nature of the atom. It was ironical that the schoolgirl who had been derided by her teacher for assuming that the atom could never be divided was to study for her degree under the two scientists whose work resulted in the splitting of the atom.

For a year, Alison belonged to Owens College. But in 1904 the Act of Incorporation of Owens College with the Victoria University of Manchester was passed.[1] Alison was one of a very small group of students reading physics for the degree of Bachelor of Science. When she graduated in 1906 she was only one out of four students so to do. She was not, as is sometimes claimed, the first female student to obtain a physics honours degree at Manchester: 'I was the second girl to take honours physics. I was the first to work for it from the start, but a graduate B.Sc. returned and took the third year of the examination to be the first.'[2]

Throughout her time at Manchester University, Alison stayed at Ashburne House in Victoria Park off the Oxford Road. Ashburne House had been opened on 27 January 1900, as a residential college for the growing number of young women coming up to the university.[3] At the start there were only nine residents, but the numbers grew steadily during the early 1900s. In 1901 a further wing was added and in 1906 a small house in Denison Road was taken and opened under the name of Ashburne Lodge. There is still an Ashburne Hall in Manchester, but it is not the one in which Alison Uttley resided as a student. In 1910 the community moved to new premises on the Fallowfield estate – to a fine building designed by Percy Worthington. Some students had been accommodated since 1908 in the nearby grand house, The Oaks, which had been generously offered to the university for just one half of its market value by the Behrens family. The two units now became known as Ashburne Hall. The old Ashburne House became Egerton Hall, for Church of England theology students at the university. New buildings and the purchase of houses like the original Lees and Ward Halls followed, until by 1932 Ashburne Hall was complete.[4]

The original Ashburne House, the residential hall where Alison stayed as a student, has now been destroyed.[5] It is nonetheless possible to imagine its atmosphere while standing amid the discreet yet solid buildings and the pleasant surroundings of the present day Ashburne Hall.

Alison's chief problem on arriving at Ashburne House was one of adjustment. Her Major County Scholarship, though essential, was a confirmation of her relative poverty: 'Money was always scarce, and I do not know how [my parents] managed for me to go to College. . . . There were fares and clothes, and books to buy – it must have been a struggle.' The Warden, Helen Stephen, seemed unsympathetic, and she believed that she had not been given such a good room as the other girls and had thinner blankets on her bed.[6] Certainly, in her early days at Ashburne she sent her laundry home in order to save money.[7] This had other advantages: 'When my laundry was returned to me in College days there was a delicious smell, for everything carried the cold air and smells of herbs and flowers and grass';[8] also the basket always contained 'a half crown tucked in a pair of stockings, and a few cakes and apples.' Alison must, at any rate at first, have felt uneasy to be among so many students from rich families. At the same time this experience introduced her to a hitherto unknown world, the world of female privilege, of college servants and of chaperones.[9] Alison's natural sensitivity to her generally inferior social and financial status at Ashburne House was doubtless one of the main reasons why in her will she bequeathed a third of the future income from her literary property, after her son's death, to Ashburne Hall for students in need.[10] In keeping with this gesture, an Alison Uttley bursary was established in 1984 for the personal benefit of students in residence at Ashburne Hall who required financial help.

If Alison felt some early unease at Ashburne House, it soon evaporated. She was to look back with great pleasure upon her time there, in 1970 telling Mrs Barbara Lees, the Warden, to 'Give my love to Ashburne!' She remembered staff and fellow students with equal affection. Among the staff for whom she had a high regard was Miss Hilda B. Oakeley, who was Warden of Ashburne House from 1905 to 1907. Dr Oakeley was a lecturer in philosophy at the university and her culture and sensitivity made her a great success both as Warden and as Tutor to women students. Alison Uttley remembered 'dear Miss Oakeley, with her quiet voice and brilliant mind . . . her sweet nature and gracious presence had a strong influence for good'. Sixty-five years later, after she had been awarded the Honorary Degree of Doctor of Letters by Manchester, Alison recalled her as 'a darling woman of great perception, we loved and admired her'.[11] In 1943 Alison sent Miss Oakeley a copy of her book *Country Hoard* and received an affectionate letter four pages long, full of comments on the book and summing it up as '*very* refreshing'.[12] A few years later Dr Oakeley sent Alison 'A most loving letter' and 'a Metaphysical article which I simply cannot understand, bless her, she over-rates my brain'.[13] One of the reasons why Alison had such a high regard for Dr Oakeley was that, as a distinguished philosopher, she was interested in the same concepts of space and time that fascinated Alison, sending the manuscript of a book on the subject to Faber (one of Alison's main publishers) in 1947.

Among other staff at Ashburne House were Miss Hughes and Miss Ada Conway whom Mrs Barbara Lees, then Warden of Ashburne Hall, recalled in a letter written to Alison in April 1970. There was also Miss Maude Parkin, later Mrs Grant, the Vice-Warden under Miss Oakeley who, 'with her deep-set laughing eyes and serious mind, was the spirit of modern life, and brought colour into the students' lives with her Russian books, her pictures and her music'. Alison met her at an Ashburne Hall reunion in July 1938, finding her: 'Rather stout, although she was always largely made, her eyes bright and speaking, her smile sweet, just the same as she called me "Alice Taylor", and swept away the years, so that I was the slim young girl who had worked at Meteorology and she was the lovely Vice-Warden in her blue silk frock and red roses.'[14]

The staff at Ashburne House during Alison Uttley's time there expected high standards of their girls. Even in 1937, when Alison was travelling by train to a reunion at Ashburne Hall, she noted with evident pleasure a girl with 'non coloured straight hair parted and short, bright red cheeks, bright eyes, such a contrast from the other girls – an Ashburnian'.[15] On her subsequent arrival at Ashburne Hall Alison saw a play, sitting beside a member of the staff – Miss Conway – and noting 'a lovely young heroine with bare legs and thighs and back – rather a shock for Miss Conway'.[16] In 1970 Alison heard with disapproval of 'the queer hard girls who now, in the last three years, go to the college'.[17]

The deportment of young women at Ashburne Hall in the 1970s was clearly different from that of their predecessors in the Edwardian Age. Yet many of their private and public preoccupations must have been similar and the women's libbers of the 1970s were preceded by the suffragettes of the early 1900s. Manchester was closely identified with the women's movement during the early years of the century. Mrs Swanwick and Mrs Pankhurst were prominent in the public life of the city and Christabel Pankhurst was a graduate of the university. The girls of Ashburne House debated the issue of the female franchise with the same animation which they brought to the discussion of books and plays and music. It must have been an enlightening experience for Alison to have been in daily contact with so many proper and serious and merry and intelligent young women. Sometimes discussions took place at Cocoa Parties, where the stimulant was conversation rather than the drink or drugs of later generations. Many years afterwards a fellow student was to ask Alison whether she had 'still got a browny-green mug bearing the inscription, "Lost Time Never Returns!" I used to think it a cynical thing to bring to a Cocoa Party!'[18]

From early editions of Ashburne House's student magazine *Yggdrasill*, it is possible to reconstruct the atmosphere during Alison Uttley's time there. For the Michaelmas term of 1903 there were twenty-seven students in residence, of which only two were first year students. One of these was Alice Taylor reading physics honours and the other Gwladys Llewellyn reading for classics honours. Gwladys Llewellyn was to become one of Alison's greatest and most long-lived friends. Always referred to by Alison as 'GL', Gwladys Llewellyn was a talented artist; she produced the cover for the autumn 1903 edition of *Yggdrasill*, a watercolour painting of the foliage and fruit of a horsechestnut tree (not of the more appropriate Yggdrasil, the ash tree of Scandinavian mythology). The handwritten pages of the magazine compared Westfield College in London ('until quite recently surrounded by comparatively open country') with Ashburne House. They also carried a spoof advertisement for 'Clarkson's Pink Parties for Pale People. This elegant preparation . . . produces a soft rosy glow. . . . An efficacious remedy for Depression, Overwork, Worry, Headache, Debility, Anxiety, Extreme Exhaustion, Neurasthenia.'[19] It is perhaps significant in view of Alison's subsequent fondness for Scottie dogs as pets that the magazine also carried a picture of the house dog 'Thistle, the Scottie'.

A year later *Yggdrasill* remained indebted to 'G. Llewellyn for illustrations to her interesting suggestions to Ashburnians'. It also recorded that A. Taylor had become Joint Librarian, and was serving, with Gwladys Llewellyn, on the Committee for Debating and Social Evenings. In connection with Alison's responsibilities towards the latter the magazine stated, rather enigmatically, 'Though Cocoa-fights are no unusual thing in Ashburne House, still never before this year was one held on Halloween.' The magazine also included an article on 'Heroines of Eighteenth-Century Fiction', and describes the work of the three women's houses of the Bermondsey Settlement.

The issue produced for the Lent term of 1906 included some '*Hallmarked Proverbs*' collected by A.J.T[aylor] and C.M. Watson. The proverbs are mostly innocent and charming pieces of Ashburne House lore:

> Half a loaf is better than no bread,
> A third class is better than swelled head.
> A stitch in time, saves nine,
> A lamp turned off, saves fine.
> You cannot make a silk purse out of a sow's ear;
> You cannot make a mag-contributor out of a First-Year.[20]

In the same edition of the magazine a poem appears, giving a light-hearted impression of the discussions and arguments that went on in Ashburne House. Bearing the initials A.J.T., it is Alison's first published work in anything other than her grammar school magazine:

> At Ashburne there is a society
> Which has rapidly gained notoriety.
> Its name I can state with propriety –
> 'Argument.'

> We meet after lunch on a Saturday
> With tea and sweet cakes we're a party gay,
> Instead of chit-chatting as students may.
> 'Argument.'

> We talk of the meetings Political,
> And all of us soon are so critical
> Our speeches become analytical.
> 'Argument.'

'The signs of our age *are* synthetical.'
'Do *you* call Walt Whitman poetical?'
'My theory is not hypothetical.'
'Argument.'

We talk of the status of woman kind
Of suffrage, and greatness of human
mind.
Equality, love, but we always find
'Argument.'

If we began all our talks at the break of day
They'd continue till after the sun's last ray.
As we get into bed, the last word we say –
'Argument.'[21]

Alison was to remember various friends from her student days later in life. Among them was Helen Eden and in 1946 she was delighted to receive 'a lovely letter' from Helen 'saying how much she admires my work'.[22] In 1953 Alison was saddened to hear of the death of a great friend, G. Thomas. 'I think of her long ago . . . when we were bosom friends, and she was not a Communist.'[23]

Of far greater significance to Alison, however, was the friendship she developed with a young woman, Gertrude Uttley, who entered Asburne House in the autumn of 1905 to read for a classics honours degree. Although Alison was by that time in the third year of the physics honours course, the intimate atmosphere of Ashburne House allowed the two young women to become friends. Gertrude, at first, flourished at the university, winning the joint prize for Junior Honours Greek in 1906, before suffering a breakdown and withdrawing from her course. It is interesting that Alison's other great friend at Ashburne House, G.L., won a university scholarship and was awarded the Latin prize in the summer of 1906. Alison, in contrast, won no prize or university scholarship during her time at Ashburne House. Her friendship with Gertrude Uttley was, however, to shape her future in a far more dramatic way than the winning of prizes.

Gertrude introduced her to her brother James, who was a graduate in civil engineering and with whom she thought that Alison at least had a scientific training in common. The Uttley family lived nearby at Bowdon on the outskirts of Manchester. James and Alison were eventually to marry in 1911. During her time at Manchester University, however, Alison, like so many of her female friends, seems to have had little to do with young men. The conventions of the age were certainly strict and the staff of Asburne House kept a watchful eye on their charges, yet it is strange that a young woman in her late teens and early twenties seems to have passed her university career without any emotional involvement with the opposite sex. One of her friends did arrange a meeting between Alison and her brother 'for tea at Parkers', but nothing seems to have come of it.[24]

One explanation of Alison's nun-like deportment at university may be found in her passionate commitment to her academic work. But her studies in mathematics and physics were never simply academic pursuits. She appreciated then, as she was to do throughout her life, the aesthetic qualities of scientific work: 'I used instruments that fascinated me by their beauty – the electroscopes and galvanometers, the diffraction grating (the best in the world), telescopes and optical instruments. Radium had been discovered, and men talked of Madame Curie and her wonderful work. The lecture gallery was full of men, a darkened room, and we sat entranced to see a faint living glow of uranium earths, radium and fluorescent bodies.'[25]

She was to recall in later life 'the lab, with its polished benches, and their exquisite smoothness. . . . Such delight, in contrast to the noise of Manchester, another world.'[26] She found light to be the most mysterious and provoking of subjects, and believed that music was connected with mathematical equations. Once she was horrified while watching a television programme at the building of nuclear power stations in fields, but then 'thought of God's presence in those works. I used to feel this in the engineering work I visited. I feel God is there, in great machines as well as in Nature. God on the Moon, as well as on Earth.'[27]

For the most part at Manchester she 'was filled with excitement of discovery and conjecture on the new theories of Physics':

> Metals were no longer stable, lead was disintegrating and the world was changing atomically with new discoveries. Each month there was a symposium when papers were read on research work. I fell in love with Mathematics and Physics, and I thought of nothing else. The Mathematics Professor made his subject alive and scintillating, to match the Physics. We studied the speed of Sirius and we experimented with light in outer space, and distant stars. I read many ancient books, to give fresh insight. The marvels of the rainbow and the speed of light, the distance of stars in light years, the spectra of stars, all were explored in that great city, which was so inspiring. . . . Matter was alive, it was filled with energy, and atoms were swinging in their orbits, while we tried to measure their speed and find out properties. Every day there was news of some discovery, and men came to do research in the network of underground rooms.[28]

As part of her degree course, Alison was required to write a paper on a piece of research. The subject she chose was 'The Ionisation of the Atmosphere'. She recalled this as 'the first book I ever wrote, to be

printed. . . . It amuses me to think of it, and the fuss there is now about
the fallout of radioactivity. They used to find quite a lot even then, and I
stood on a roof and took readings with an instrument.'[29]

A problem arose, however, over the requirement that she should study
engineering as part of her course. Since she was one of the first two
women to study physics at Manchester, it was unclear what she should
wear while in close contact with machinery. In those more decorous
days, it was unacceptable that a girl should wear trousers. Skirts, on the
other hand, might catch in the moving parts of machinery, causing her to
be injured. The solution to this dilemma came when Alison was introduced to a 'tall and very good looking man . . . he was awfully interested
in meteorology, and he wanted a little nucleus of people to start this new
subject, and I was chosen to go with them.'[30]

Alison's saviour was Professor Sir George Simpson, who was a gifted
teacher and with whom Alison was more than a little in love: 'How I
loved Meteorology and Mr Simpson! He was so inspiring and enthusiastic. I still feel that fire burning within me, the fire of life.'[31] It was for
Professor Simpson that Alison wrote her paper on the rate of ionisation in
the atmosphere. Sixty years later she noticed his obituary in *The Times*: 'I
feel very sad. I used to adore . . . G.C. Simpson, who taught me and
danced with me.'[32]

Another Manchester academic with whom Alison was to develop a
much closer and warmer relationship was Professor Alexander. Samuel
Alexander, born in Australia and Jewish in origin, was Professor of
Philosophy at Manchester for thirty-one years. Not only was he a
distinguished scholar but, as a generous and progressive administrator,
was one of the chief founders and friends of Ashburne House. His
remarkable, even eccentric, appearance instantly appealed to Alison's
own sense of the dramatic and the romantic:

> No-one ever created more interest than did Professor Alexander whose
> simple progression through a town caused as much comment as the
> passage of a Hebrew prophet would have done. For he closely re-
> sembled one's idea of Isaiah or Elijah as he walked serenely and
> unconcernedly along the pavements of Oxford Road, Manchester. . . .
> In my own college days I saw him first in the quadrangle, with his
> straggly, golden-brown beard, his bright brown eyes, his heavy build
> and his lively manner, and, as is the way of youth, I thought he was
> very, very old. He must have been about forty-five. I never spoke, I had
> no occasion, for I was reading Honours Physics, and my way was to the
> Physics laboratories, and he was the famous Professor of Philosophy.[33]

Alison continued to admire Professor Alexander from afar. She eagerly
listened to anecdotes of his wit and wisdom and wished that she could go
to his lectures. She noticed that when he spoke to students at Ashburne

House, he doffed his large round felt hat. Everywhere admiring glances followed him. When she took her own degree, he spoke a few words on the subject of physics and the universe and shook her hand with a look of recognition. Interestingly, Alison 'felt that I knew him, secretly, we shared a private intimacy of space and time, for he was reputed to be intensely interested in the new physical theories of radio-active waves and of light'. She also met him now and then at functions where she was a guest, and remembered that he smiled at her and thought he knew her and she was content.[34] The rich and satisfying friendship that later developed between Alison and Professor Alexander was indeed to be based chiefly on their mutual interests in concepts of space and time – also, in the power of dreams. It is probable that the kindly, bachelor professor appealed to Alison in other ways too. Alexander has been described as 'sexless', and their relationship thus avoided the predictable entanglements of male and female while at the same time presenting Alison with the learned, understanding father figure for which, despite her own father's solid qualities, she must have yearned.[35] It is significant that later in life she formed an equally deep attachment, and on very similar terms, with Walter de la Mare.

Although she was to claim towards the end of her life that at Manchester 'I didn't care a button about English, and I couldn't bother to go down and do this dull English subject, it was much more exciting to do the scientific work',[36] this simply does not seem to have been true. She herself recalled on another occasion, 'I wasted a lot of time at college, that is, I did many things not connected with my work, dipping into other subjects and joining all the societies that I could.'[37] She read widely, sometimes encouraged by her college tutors who lent her books by Meredith and Turgenev. So impressed was she by Turgenev's limpidity of style, 'like spring water', that she decided that if ever she wrote seriously she would choose to write like him 'with no knowledge of the difficulty of obtaining such simplicity'.[38] For the moment, however, Alison's literary efforts were confined to the pages of *Yggdrasill*.

She also went often to the Manchester City Art Gallery. She was already deeply devoted to music by the time she went to university, but felt that her 'real musical education came later when we went each week to the Hallé concerts, to hear that incomparable orchestra play under the baton of Sir Hamilton Harty. . . . Strauss, Stravinsky, Constant Lambert gave us the excitement of a brilliant new artist, a painter, a new poet, a star in the sky. Hamilton Harty we adored, and the years lived with this weekly festival of music were some of the best of life, when we met so much music and fell under its spell.'[39]

Alison's passion for music and her growing interest in the significance of dreams were to be compounded into an unusual incident while she was at university. She was twenty years of age and had been invited to a Hallé concert by a student at the Manchester Royal College of Music. The pianist Wilhelm Backhaus was playing. Unfortunately Alison was taken ill before the concert and had to stay in bed, nursing a high temperature. She fell asleep and dreamed the music, leaning over and reading the score as Backhaus played. She awoke and remembered it:

> Late that night my friend returned and she came to my bedroom in Hall to talk about the concert and to show me the programme. Before she could tell me I interrupted with my dream. I gave her the air of the first few bars, the time, the key, which I had seen, the feeling of the first movement, the surge and flow. I had dreamed this correctly. She was astonished, for she knew I was quite ignorant of the music Backhaus played. . . . I should add that in real life at that time I was deeply interested in music and I used to read music scores as one reads a book, but how seldom I ever had the chance! In this dream the music was the *real* music of the pianist, but usually the music is dream music of no earthly source.[40]

The intellectual excitement and stimulation of working for her honours degree at Manchester University heightened her sensibilities and led to much vivid dreaming. During her first year at Ashburne House she had a precognitive dream which led to an embarrassing incident. She was sitting one morning at breakfast amongst second and third year students of classics, English and history, when 'these older and wiser students, who were women of the world to me in every way, began to discuss Sappho. I always listened to their interesting talk, and it was there I first heard of G.K. Chesterton and Swinburne . . . and Shaw.'[41] Normally respectful of her senior fellow students, Alison felt emboldened:

> On this occasion I joined in, for I had dreamed of Sappho the night before. The name sprang to my memory with that shock of recognition and remembrance which I knew only too well. I had seen her in a dream, I had heard her lovely name, and watched her stand by a river with some others, and I had heard her voice. Sappho! I did not know who she was, except that I had dreamed of her. A storm broke about me, a surprising tumult, as I dared to mention this. How could a science student from the country have even heard of the immortal Sappho? I had made it up, they said. . . . Their natural disbelief silenced me, I could not argue against the opposition, and I was held to ridicule as spectacled eyes stared coldly at me.[42]

Other precognitive dreams followed. Once she dreamed very clearly of an experiment which she had never seen and the next day she was privately overjoyed to see the experiment performed in the lecture theatre. Alison's love of cricket while at university ('often I stole away with a packet of sandwiches to sit at Old Trafford on the sixpenny side to see the County matches') led her into friendship with a cricketing chemistry honours student of whom she dreamed that he had failed his degree before this unpleasant result was actually revealed.[43] She also dreamed of equations which were presented to her for solution the next day in class. Once she was able to surprise Professor Lamb, one of her mathematics tutors and according to her 'a genius', with a dream solution to a complicated piece of mathematics. One male student and herself were the only ones to get it right and she 'felt guilty to receive applause from the class and a surprised smile from that incomparable mathematician for something which came out of his own mysterious infinity, where he was so much at home.'[44]

Alison struggled to explain these remarkable precognitive dreams. She was prepared to acknowledge that sometimes the brain goes on working at a difficult problem, providing a clear answer in the morning. But in the case of her solution to Professor Lamb's equation, she had not even understood what she had done. 'It was outside me, uninfluenced by me, quite unknown, a picture in my dream mind of the problem on the blackboard.' At this stage of her life she felt she had a dream every night which contained some slight foreknowledge. Alison pressed her enquiries further:

> I consulted a philosophy student at the Hall about the oddness of seeing ahead in dreams, and she wisely told me it was common enough, that perhaps it was a form of thought-transference. This seemed to shift the responsibility. It was she who spoke of the theory that the mind creates a physical world, that we ourselves, through our senses, make this visible and tangible world. This was another outlook, for I thought of a universe of forces and waves, the electromagnetic and mathematical world. Then again, far away, there was the world of fairy and magic and beauty, which still existed for me.[45]

Equally remarkable was the dream she had a day or two before her final examinations, when she dreamed she saw one of the papers and read a question which was very clearly printed. On the morning of the examination, she opened her physics paper and 'the dream question was the first. I had the old shock of recognition, the queer jolt that always makes me feel sick for a moment, as if I had indeed travelled too rapidly through time. Then, deliberately, as if to mock at the dream, to show my independence, I missed it out.'[46] Though admirable morally, this act of self-denial almost certainly had serious consequences for her. She found the paper difficult and did badly in it. She was finally awarded only a third-class honours degree in physics, an odd result, considering her enthusiasm and commitment as a science student. After the examination was over, Dr Simpson himself came to ask her about this question which was the only one he had set and which was on the subject of meteorology, and Alison confessed her preknowledge of it. She herself later believed that she had 'thrown away my chance of doing well through sheer perversity'.[47]

Having obtained her degree, Alison had now to decide what to do next. Despite her third-class award, she would have liked to have gone on to work for the M.Sc. But 'there was a fee of five pounds for graduation, and I couldn't afford such a large sum.'[48] In the end, Alison decided to train as a teacher. Ashburne House had connections with the Ladies' Training College at Cambridge – an article on it, with a picture, was featured in the *Yggdrasill* that had been published at the end of the Lent Term in 1904. Alison's application, together with that of her friend G.L., was accepted and in the autumn of 1907 she began studying for the Certificate in the Theory and Practice of Teaching.

CHAPTER SEVEN

Going South: Cambridge and London, 1906–11

Cambridge also was a delight. . . . I had never been south I had never seen such architecture.
It took a long time for me to get used to the London children, and the streets. . . but I loved the art galleries, the museums, the operas, the theatres and I went so often that I was reprimanded.

ALISON UTTLEY to Peter du Sautoy, 4 October 1961

The Ladies' Training College at Cambridge was apparently 'Rather select, with its title of Ladies, to distinguish it from the big training college at Homerton for teachers.'[1] Not untypically, Alison Uttley has left different, sometimes conflicting accounts of her time at the college which was paid for 'by a small scholarship'. In *The Button Box*, published in 1968, she claims that the majority of students were graduates of Newnham and Girton Colleges at Cambridge. Seven years earlier, trying to recall essential autobiographical details for a prospective life, she wrote, 'It was for graduates, chiefly of Oxford and Cambridge, but one came from Durham, and there were Indian and Russian girls there, and two from Dublin.'[2] In *The Button Box* the head of the college, who lectured on education and philosophy, is described as Miss Hughes. Elsewhere she is described as 'a well-known head, Eleanor Powell' who was 'very strict'.[3]

Alison was delighted at the teaching she received at Cambridge: 'I had essays to write each week, upon subjects which were congenial, and critical discussions followed. This was the first time in my life I had had any good tuition in the art of writing. I was praised and encouraged, and helped. I explored the life of Rousseau, of Erasmus, and Colet, and a schoolman named Melanchthon. The Renaissance became real after years of enquiry.'[4]

She found it almost as stimulating to work at Cambridge as to take a degree in English, an interesting confession for one apparently so deeply committed to science. More than that, after Manchester 'with its rain and darkness, but its passion for learning', Cambridge seemed to her to be 'a city of light'. The antiquity and beauty of the buildings delighted her, 'I had never been south I had never seen such architecture.'[5] She was later to write that:

The classical bridges at Cambridge are poems in stone, and the water they span is so tranquil that these lovely bridges have no affinity with their medieval cousins which I know so well. . . . Clare Bridge . . . is one of the most beautiful bridges in the world, with its three smooth arches, in semi-circles which make complete circles with the reflections, with its stone spheres, delicate balustrades and carved panels above the cutwaters . . . after the country bridges of the north . . . its symmetry seemed part of the scientific work which was going on at the Cavendish laboratory.[6]

In 1966, in her early eighties, she recalled with great pleasure her time at Cambridge with her 'first vision of beauty, of houses and river and architecture, and the arts'.[7] A year later, listening to a service in King's College Chapel on the radio, 'the feeling of Cambridge came vividly to me. How I enjoyed it! It was rapture to be at College there.'[8] Despite this recollection of rapture, socially her experience of Cambridge seems to have been mixed. She recalled that 'I was often snubbed at the college where I worked because I was a scientist – it was very classical, I did not count. I felt rather unhappy at times.'[9] But mostly it was the good times that her memory conjured up for her: 'It all came back to me – racing fast down the narrow lanes to get back in time for dinner. Going to the Union for debates. To tea at the house of [a] Physics man and his wife. Seeing the Cavendish lab.'[10]

As well as the aesthetic pleasure derived from living in Cambridge for a year, Alison's literary aspirations were properly nurtured. She felt that she had been positively led to explore literature and writing as never before claiming – inaccurately in the light of her experiences at Manchester: 'For the first time I was drawn to literature, but I was still bound by strong ties to science. I was told that these two loves were antagonistic, but I did not believe this. Science and literature could go hand in hand, each showing one side of life.'[11] To prove her point, 'I worked harder to show that science is not divorced from literature, and I enjoyed my essays. I got high marks from a visiting don, who lectured on philosophy . . . I loved writing for him. I felt he was akin, and the other women lecturers were too stiffly conscious of their own cult of Latin and Greek.'[12]

Overall the critical climate was temperate, in contrast to Lady Manners School: 'The essays were not scorned, and there was no sarcasm.' There was a good reference library at her college and she 'enjoyed writing in my little room overlooking Fenners' – the university's cricket ground. But on balance she felt more at home in the world of science and recalled visiting the Cavendish laboratory 'where a friend was a research student, working on cloud formation. This was worth all the writing, I felt, to be in at the exploration of the sky.'[13]

Her year at Cambridge was clearly a broadening experience for Alison. It helped her take a small, but significant step towards the world of literature and writing. Years later she was delighted to hear that her college head 'had been very proud of my books and had given them to friends. So I felt vindicated.'[14] Science, however, was the subject that she was able to teach. Her Cambridge period ended triumphantly when 'a discerning don got me a very good post in London'.[15] In September she went to the capital to take up her position as Junior Science Mistress at the London County Council Secondary School in Fulham.

When Alison moved down to London, she lived first at 164 Engadine Street, Southfields, SW. Wimbledon Common was nearby and she made this her 'daily pilgrimage to keep a memory of the country in my mind and to help me forget the welter of houses around me'. She was intrigued to learn that the poet Swinburne came up the hill from Putney every morning about twelve o'clock, but shocked to learn that the object of his walk was an inn on the edge of the common. She was determined to get a sight of him, however, and loitered on Putney Heath, wishing that he had walked to get inspiration rather than drink. Then shortly after twelve o'clock, he came: 'A small man with a reddish ragged little beard, and piercing blue eyes. I gazed at him with admiration for his poetry, and some surprise that he was an ordinary mortal. His big felt hat hid the long yellow hair, now turning grey. His clothes were shabby and loose and poor. I had expected him to wear a blue cloak and flaming clothes, and I thought his feet would not even touch the ground. He would float along, immortal, always young.'[16]

Perhaps Alison ought to have spent less time lying in wait for great, if shabby, poets walking on the common. She had some difficulty in adjusting to her first teaching job: 'I was a country girl in strange surroundings. I had never been in a large school, for we were only about 150 in [Lady Manners School].' It took her a long while to get used to the ways of London children and she disliked the discipline of the school, the meetings and the peremptory ringing of bells.[17] Eventually she became a successful teacher, even taking some English lessons, though not before the headmistress had told her that she was spending too much time gallivanting about London. Perhaps the criticisms were more serious, for Alison was later to recall being scrutinised by the LCC Schools' Inspector: 'I was teaching the girls biology – it was about animals – and I was making noises to show them, and we were all laughing. When he came in it went very quiet. He told me to continue the lesson, but within a few minutes we were tittering again. When he went out the headmistress apologised to me, and said I could stay after all.'[18]

There is another indication that Alison, during her time as a teacher, sometimes strayed from the highest professional standards. In 1968 she received a 'lovely letter from a girl who knew me at Fulham, Marie Street. . . . She remembered me walking with her, both of us late for school, and now [I] remember it.'[19] Not that Alison had any real reason for dawdling to school. She was for her times a successful and fortunate young woman, earning £120 a year to begin with and increments thereafter of ten pounds per annum.[20] She paid rent of fifteen shillings a week for a small, high bedsitter at 6 Cheyne Row in Chelsea. There she 'had a gas ring and cooked my breakfast, and had dinner at night, of all the food I wanted for one shilling and sixpence. The charwoman kept the flat clean, I made my bed and tidied up. . . . I went on top of a bus to the school at Fulham. Thrilled by the bus, by World's End and Chelsea.'[21] She did not meet the ghost that was said to haunt the flat and was further comforted when the oak chest and table reminded her of home. When she later wrote *A Traveller in Time*, she gave Cheyne Row as the address of the novel's heroine, Penelope.

After two years she moved to a larger studio flat in Cheyne Walk, of which she has left a number of descriptions. From the window she could see the tall chimneys of Lots Road Power Station by the River Thames. Appropriately, she viewed it with an artist's eye: 'There the colour was blue, a sparkling dazzling blue in the morning when the wide river glittered in the early sun, and the dust motes in the air of my undusted studio made lines of black and gold, till night when street lamps were lighted and the river turned a strange deep blue with layers of azure mists lying over it. The colour was intensified for me because I had seen a Whistler-like picture of Lots Road Power Station and its chimneys in this blue twilight of London.'[22]

Alison was excited to discover that the writer Katherine Mansfield had rented the same flat a few weeks before she had arrived. However 'Nobody mentioned her, she seemed to be unknown, but I was too shy to look for her. She was an immortal with the secret of writing.'[23] There is no doubt that Alison had already identified with Katherine Mansfield, admiring her awareness of the life of inanimate things. For a while she became determined to work at being a writer too: 'I began to write in little penny notebooks descriptions of people I saw in the 'bus, in the train, in shops, notes in faint pencil which were soon obliterated and lost. Katherine Mansfield wrote of her childhood and I would write of mine, a very different life from hers.'[24] Nothing was to come of this ambition until 1928. Alison was to draw further satisfaction from her tenuous connections with Katherine Mansfield when, as a married woman, she stayed at Bandol in France where the famous writer had lived for a time.

Apart from such inspiration, Alison found 'a magic in London', hungrily, almost greedily, sampling the wide cultural feast the capital offered her. She 'adored' the museums, the opera and the art galleries: 'I fell in love with the new art, the post-impressionists, Van Gogh's chair, Gauguin, Cézanne, as well as Sisley and Monet. Augustus John lived in Chelsea, and I saw him nearly every day in his black hat; I went to his exhibitions in the King's Road. Colours were revealed which had never been seen before, I thought. . . . The mastery over light was now supreme. Light had been rediscovered.'[25]

The ballet became a particular passion. She was entranced by the Russian Ballet and fell in love with Pavlova 'whom I went to see on every occasion, for she was an immortal come to earth for a short visit. I saw. . . Nijinksy fly through the air as the Fire Bird. . . . The dancers were the poetry of motion: the wind blowing, the lightning flashing, the day dying, all was shown to humanity.'[26]

Exhilarated as Alison was by the cultural stimulation of London, she also found it necessary to make comparisons with the Derbyshire countryside of her childhood. Sometimes these comparisons are apt, but often they are forced – perhaps reflecting her desire to manipulate and mould her new environment into a copy of the old and familiar world of Castle Top. Thus she recognised how different the Thames was from the Derwent, yet saw the two rivers as 'relations'. London revealed itself to her as 'a country town', and Chelsea was 'the village as it had been three hundred years ago': 'I saw this London with country eyes and understanding. I saw the shapes of trees, the spring flowers and fresh leaves, I saw the parks like fields, the palaces like great country houses, the Serpentine like a duck pond in our lands, the art galleries with their treasures, the Victoria and Albert Museum with many objects similar to those in my home. I saw horses, and sheep, and cats and dogs, and pigeons.'[27]

On one occasion she asserted the priorities of the countryside over those of the city by stopping the traffic in Hyde Park to allow some ducks to cross the road in safety. Generally she was eager to return to see her parents. Once she was sitting back happily in her compartment as the train sped north from St Pancras Station, thinking of all her new experiences in London and looking forward to a springtime welcome home, when an old lady sitting opposite her asked her whether she was 'saved'. Despite her protestations that she was sure she was saved, Alison was eventually obliged to kneel on the dusty carriage floor in her light dress, saying the Lord's Prayer as the train rocked with speed, and indignant that the old lady had not respected her privacy. Another time, after being ill, she journeyed north from London on a golden autumn day. When she arrived home she found she 'had forgotten the intensity of the beauty, because I had seen it every year of my life, and it was part of me. I had been unaware of its value. Then I came home. . . . The scents of the lane in autumn intoxicated me, I was a wild animal returned to its country, as I sniffed at the odours of leaves and moss, of trees and soil, of water and rocks.'[28]

But for all the occasional bouts of longing for Castle Top, Alison found the deepest satisfaction from her four years in London. Among other things, there was the chance to make contact, however fleeting, with the famous. Once she peeped through 'a great half-open door on Chelsea embankment and . . . watched Epstein carving his great masterpiece, the memorial to Oscar Wilde for the Père Lachaise Cemetery in Paris. . . . I had the excitement of a few words about it.'[29] On another occasion she saw the young Winston Churchill, then Home Secretary in the Liberal government, at St Pancras Station and half a century later, on the occasion of his death, remembered his red hair.[30]

Her years in London were marked by her close friendship with another rising star of Edwardian politics, Ramsay MacDonald, and especially with his family. Alison had become interested in politics at Manchester, 'not the gentle Conservatism of my parents and friends, but in something romantic called "Socialism", which caused alarm.'[31] A socialist speaker whom Alison had met, hearing that she was soon to go to London where she knew nobody, gave her an introduction to the Ramsay MacDonalds. Alison was encouraged to take up the introduction at least in part because Margaret MacDonald was the great-niece of Lord Kelvin, the eminent physicist.

Alison arrived in London 'longing' to know more about the 'societies for the study of socialism – the Fabian Society, whose star was George Bernard Shaw, and the Independent Labour Party, the famous "I.L.P." to which the Ramsay MacDonalds belonged.'[32]

She made her way rather nervously to the MacDonalds' flat in Lincolns Inn Fields, which she naïvely expected to be amid green fields in the centre of London. She shyly entered a large room where many people were talking and laughing, but was immediately calmed by seeing a print of the 'Happy Warrior' by Watts on the wall. Since she had a copy of this picture at home, she felt that it was like a welcome from a friend. She soon had a welcome of a far more personal and heartfelt nature:

> My hostess came forward at once, guessing who was the stranger who came timidly into her room. Margaret MacDonald took my hands and held them in a firm grasp. She looked at me intently. I was completely conquered by her charm and her penetrating gaze of love. Ramsay MacDonald joined her, and made me welcome as I never had been accepted before. I might have been a long lost young sister who had arrived from the darkness into the light. He introduced me to

people and looked after me, and I listened to the political conversation around me. I was introduced not as a Socialist but as a young scientist who had come to London.[33]

For Alison, the gauche outsider from northern England, the warmth of the MacDonalds' welcome was irresistible. A deep and sensitive friendship sprang up between them instantly. Within a day or two she had been invited to supper to meet the MacDonalds' four children and when they were tucked up in bed, told them 'a tale, and talked of my country life, of dogs and horses, sheep and piglings, while they listened wide-eyed and smiling'.[34] Not merely did her friendship with the MacDonalds give her her first regular adult experience of telling tales to young children, it also provided her with a chance of meeting some of the great figures of early twentieth-century socialism. These included 'John Burns, Keir Hardie, a darling old man, and Snowden and his wife, Margaret Bondfield.'[35] At supper one evening she much enjoyed the conversation of the Labour Prime Minister of Australia and she warmly admired Mary Macarthur, a campaigner 'for women in shops and factories who had long hours and small pay'.[36] She was once startled when a Spanish anarchist was introduced to her at the MacDonalds' and wondered whether she could ask him if he had really thrown a bomb, but since he looked so peaceful she asked 'some simple question' and got on well with him. Once she went to a huge meeting at the Albert Hall where Jean Jaurès, the French socialist, 'spoke in impassioned French, which stirred that vast audience to a kind of frenzy'.[37]

Ramsay and Margaret MacDonald dealt tactfully with Alison; they 'kept away from politics, assuming that I was chiefly a scientist, or a story teller. . . . I was no tub-thumper or speaker.' As it happened, they had no need to proselytise since Alison was 'fascinated by Socialism' and ready to discuss the problems of constructing a socialist state with them.[38] She asked many questions about poverty in London and the work of women. As she travelled about the city, she kept a lookout for barefooted little children whom she imagined could be seen on every street corner: 'I saw only one or two who had no shoes and stockings; but some children ran wild in the streets, as if they had no parents or homes.'[39] Although Alison accepted 'the tenets of Socialism' she 'was doubtful of its working'. Once, travelling back from a weekend at the MacDonalds' country cottage at Chesham in Buckinghamshire, she asked her travelling companion, Philip Snowden, how he would get men to do the ugly and dirty work in a socialist state. When he replied that the highest wages would be paid to such workers, she was doubtful, feeling that perhaps they would be able to bank so much money that they would prefer to take their ease.[40] Many years later, Alison was to recognise that 'now I belong to the possessors. . . . I could never be a Communist, I like possessions too much.'[41]

During the years of her close friendship with the MacDonalds, however, Alison became clearly committed to socialist and Liberal causes. The confidence and idealism of her new friends was a major factor in this commitment and, in general, her association with so many socialist pioneers enabled her to become more at ease socially: 'I forgot my shyness and my ignorance of politics and I talked with ease to strangers, discovering their values and ideas. I should have been lonely in London except for this stimulating gathering of people. I met many people, who were never condescending or pompous.'[42] She went to meetings at schools, distributed pamphlets, visited many societies and small gatherings 'of intimacy and delight for me'. The weeks went past 'with concerts and ballet in the evenings, and politics and speechmaking at the weekends. During the days I taught . . . and I was laughingly called "the little Communist".'[43] Of the MacDonalds, she also remembered, 'I went on platforms with them, and collected money.'[44] She was deeply impressed by Margaret MacDonald's connection with Lord Kelvin whose celebrated work on thermodynamics led Alison, as she was so often to do throughout her life, to make a logically tenuous link between separate influences: 'So mine was a fiery way – but it always gave me a great sympathy with the Labour Party.'[45] This sympathy did not prevent her from voting Conservative for the second half of her life.

Her keen political interests during the Edwardian age encouraged her to participate in the campaign for 'Votes for Women': 'I walked in the suffrage processions, but we thought of it as Romantic and Historical, as we walked with pretty blue and green and purple scarves in London, and people cheered us. I felt so proud and happy.'[46]

Throughout her life, Alison Uttley was to remember her friendship with the MacDonalds with a special affection, often speaking of their kindness.[47] In 1934 she expressed her continuing admiration for Ramsay MacDonald, then leader of the National Government: 'A most stirring speech from the Prime Minister at the Lord Mayor's banquet, brave, courageous, inspiring; referring to this country's efforts for peace, for a reduction in armaments, for international help.'[48]

Alison's friendship with the MacDonalds ended rather abruptly, though with no ill will on either side. This may have been partly due to the death of Margaret MacDonald, for whose sympathy and kindness Alison felt so much gratitude. Margaret's youngest child, David, had died of diphtheria at the age of five and his mother 'never recovered from the shock. She seemed to bear up, but her heart was affected, and after some months she too died at the age of forty one.'[49] The death of Margaret removed one of Alison's chief reasons for her continuing contact with the family. Many years later she was to reproach herself with having withdrawn: 'Oh why did I not continue with the MacDonalds, I just left them, and I loved them so much.'[50]

In her published writings, Alison gives a poignant description of her feelings on leaving London in 1911: 'I felt as if I had left behind a part of my heart. I went to live in the depths of the country, where there was no talk of Socialism. I had torn myself away from London, feeling as if it were a beloved country village, where I had had many pleasures and friends. My communism was after all a simple country affair, mixed with nursery rhymes, and songs my mother had taught me. Life had gone full circle.'[51]

The year 1911 did indeed mark a turning point in Alison's life. For she left her job, her friends and the rich cultural and intellectual stimulation of the capital to go to live, as a newly married woman, with James Uttley.

CHAPTER EIGHT

Marriage and Motherhood, 1911–14

I was very happy, but my husband was often ill, and mentally troubled. He had none of the stability of country people, I think he found it in me.

ALISON UTTLEY to Peter du Sautoy, 4 October 1961

It is clear that James Uttley and Alison were strongly attracted to each other. Once James's sister Gertrude had played her key role in introducing them while Alison was at Ashbourne house,[1] the relationship developed through meetings, reading parties in the Lake District and letter writing. They became engaged when she was teaching in London.[2] There is very little in Alison Uttley's writings about such contact, except for one entry in her diary: 'Epstein died today. I think of that day long ago when James and I met him in his Chelsea Studio.'[3] She was, however, to look back to the last two years of her engagement, 1910 and 1911, as 'her happiest' in the capital.[4]

Both James and Alison had much to be happy about.[5] She was slim and striking in appearance, her figure enhanced by the long skirts of Edwardian fashion. She favoured blouses buttoned to the neck. She often wore her thick dark hair up in those days and parted in the middle. Although her features were by no means classically beautiful, her brown eyes were fine and animated and it was only the hint of hardness about her mouth that gave pause for thought. She was, above all, vivacious and intelligent, interested in all manner of topics from household dust to space dust. She was not shy about asserting her views which she expressed in the plain, measured tones of North Derbyshire, though finding the accent of the mining areas 'ugly'. Sometimes, indeed, she was thought to be overassertive in her opinions and by temperament. She was certainly bubbling with enthusiasm for a wide variety of ideas and causes, had absorbed as much as she could of London's culture and had an apparently secure and satisfying professional life stretching before her.

James Uttley was rather short in height, certainly no taller than Alison. He was of slight build, with rather delicate features and hair that was already beginning to recede at the temples. He seems to have tended

to shyness in public and it is interesting that in Uttley family photographs, unlike his siblings or his mother but like Alison, he chose to look
away from the camera. James had been educated at Sedbergh public
school and had then gone on to take a first-class honours degree in
engineering at Manchester University. His family background was a
great deal different from that of Alison. The Uttleys were Liberal in their
politics and sceptics in religion, though their formal religious adherence
was Low Anglican. George Harry Uttley, the head of the family, once
came downstairs and announced to the family, 'I've thrown it all over-
board.' Later he was so delighted that James had stopped going to
church that 'he leant back in his chair and literally kicked his heels with
pleasure'.[6] Despite his degree in engineering, James was passionately
interested in literature, especially poetry. Together, he and Alison must
have seemed prototypes of the New Man and New Woman,
well-educated, progressive and forthright, whose appearance so troubled
Edwardian traditionalists.

   Although the pair became engaged within two years of her arriving in
London, it was not possible for them to marry straight away. In common
with many young couples in those days, they simply did not have the means
to marry. Alison was obliged to stay on teaching 'for some time as we had
not enough money to get married. . . he got £100 a year only. So we
waited, and I had my fill of operas and art galleries, a most happy time.'[7] In
part, however, Alison was relieved not to be rushed into marriage: 'I did not
very much want the domestic life, so I did not mind, and all the time I was
really a student, learning whenever I could.'[8] But she also dreamed, literally
and with clear Freudian phallic symbolism, about the time when they would
be married, recalling later in her widowhood: 'There was a darling letter to
me from James, when I told him that I had dreamed we were married, and
we lived in a tulip, our house in the flower, and we climbed the stalk to get to
it. How mad he must have thought I was! I found lovely, sweet letters from
him, the darling one.'[9]

   During this prolonged waiting period, their exchange of letters continued crucial to the relationship. In the early years of her widowhood,
Alison came across thousands of love letters in a chest. Although she
burned most of them, it was with great sadness: 'How glorious they were!
They brought such pain and ecstacy and misery I felt I would die as I
read them. Death seemed desirable, I felt again the pangs of love of long
ago, the loveliness of London and our meetings. . . . One telegram told
me he had two hundred less twenty five [pounds] and if he had had two
hundred we could have been married!'[10]

   James and Alison were at last married on 10 August 1911. The
wedding did not take place within the Anglican Church: 'Then I got
married (in London at the Ethical Church, for my husband was an

unbeliever . . . to my mother's dismay).[11] There is no record of where they spent their honeymoon, but their financial circumstances in 1911 would not have permitted an expensive foreign excursion. As a consequence of her marriage, Alison gave up her job as a teacher. Despite her enthusiasm for science and her obvious, if somewhat unorthodox talents as a teacher, she was never to hold a salaried position again – an admittedly conventional act of self-denial for the times, but one which exacted a heavy toll over the next twenty years. Her extraordinary talents and energies could not be satisfied by domesticity or even by motherhood. Before she established herself as a successful author, it is plain that she expressed her discontent by becoming an overcontrolling and over-assertive wife and mother.

Not that she was a meek and retiring bride. Her relationship with her Uttley in-laws was unsatisfactory from the beginning, and was to continue to be the source of much pain to her, and them, throughout her life. The Uttleys, in their turn, were a complicated family, holding strong views and expressing them forcibly.

George Harry Uttley and his wife Katherine had produced five children, Emily, Alice, James, Gertrude and George. Emily was the first to be born in 1878, followed by Alice in 1881. Then came James in 1883, Gertrude in 1884 and George in 1887. Katherine Uttley was to die in 1923 and George Harry Uttley in 1926. There seems to have been no contact whatsoever between the Uttleys and Alison's parents. The explanation for this is not difficult to find for the Uttleys, with their comparative wealth, high educational and intellectual standards and their sparkle and wit, would have seemed like creatures from another planet to Mr and Mrs Taylor.

Alison's father-in-law was an entrepreneur, who worked his way up in the cotton trade. He bought and sold cotton companies, mostly for a reasonable profit, and arranged for imported cotton to be spun and converted into textiles. Once he sent a ship to Carolina to buy raw cotton. He also imported raw cloth and had it printed and re-exported, often to India. As is often the way with entrepreneurs, his success in business was reflected in the family house; when things were good a large house was rented, when times were harder, the family moved to a smaller house. When Alison married James in 1911, the Uttley family lived in some affluence in a pleasant house at Bowdon. The Uttleys' fortunes were firmly based in the cotton-dominated economy of Manchester, where the traditions of free trade and Liberalism were strong.

Katherine Uttley was welcoming, homely and much loved, though that did not prevent Alison being sometimes at odds with her.[12] Mr Uttley was of middling height and sported a white, walrus moustache, behind which his features were clear and sharp and his gaze straight.

When Alison first got to know him, he dressed in some style, sometimes posing for photographs in a frock coat and winged collar and straw boater, at other times in the more relaxed tweed suit, soft hat and spats of the Edwardian country gentleman. His wife had a pleasant open face, often wore her greying hair up and exuded an air of reliability and good sense. Of the two, she seems to have been the steadier, while her husband played the cotton trade with all its attendant risks, threw over religion and expressed various unorthodox views. Perhaps his somewhat capricious behaviour had its roots in early insecurity, for his father had died when he was only thirteen and he had had to make his own way in the world.

There was apparently 'a nervous streak' in the Uttleys. Much anxiety was expressed and wet feet were fussed over amid fears of impending illness.[13] Emily, the oldest child, seems to have been a worrier and Alison, on hearing of her death on Christmas Day 1943, wrote 'Poor Emily, she has had such a sad life, always depressed, always wanting more.'[14] She added, however, that 'She was the best of them, devoted to James. . . . I hoped to see her again.'[15] Despite Alison's fond recollections of Emily on hearing of her death, their relationship contained much coldness and antagonism. Emily, her husband Alfred Byers and their children came to dread the visits that Alison made to them 'in the early days before she had become an author' when she 'wiped the floor' with Emily.[16] Emily's youngest son, Martin Byers, was to remember 'She did not enjoy Alison's visits. . . . My mother was a cultured, intelligent and gentle person who found Alison opinionated and inclined to treat views, which she did not share, with scorn.'[17]

The coldness between Alison and the second Uttley child, Alice Katherine, seems to have been more in the nature of a clash between equals. There was certainly a considerable rivalry between the two. On hearing of her death in May 1956, Alison wrote 'poor Alice K, so proud and haughty and so unkind to me always. I have no feelings for her.'[18] Although Alison's perceptions of Alice Uttley were sufficient in themselves to have been responsible for the coldness between them, it is possible that their shared first Christian name caused some resentment. After her marriage Alison, not having yet assumed the first name under which she was to become a famous author, became Alice Uttley. There were therefore two Alice Uttleys in the family. A way was found round this problem by calling one Alice K and the other Alice T, after her maiden name of Taylor. Alison, with her extraordinary sense of self and her tendency to pride, may well have resented this even though, awkward as it was, it was not a problem of long-standing – Alice K was soon to become Mrs Tolson. It is clear that she sometimes toyed with calling herself Alison before she adopted it on the publication of her first book in 1929.[19]

Apart from James, Alison's closest connection inside the family was with Gertrude. Indeed, there was something of the triangular in the relationship. After all, Gertrude had not only introduced James to Alison, but she had shared a year with her at Ashburne House. Of the five Uttley children, however, Gertrude and James had been the closest friends, sharing an intense interest in books, poetry and radical politics – both were early Fabians. The love affair that developed between Alison and James disrupted that close sibling relationship. The two women, therefore, had mixed feelings about each other. Gertrude apparently 'enjoyed Alison a lot' whereas Alison felt some hostility and rivalry towards Gertrude, writing dismissively sixty-five years after they first met, 'I never liked her or her sister [Alice]. Too giggly and silly.'[20] Gertrude was the blue stocking of the Uttley family, bespectacled and serious in family photographs, and many years after they first met, Alison was to dismiss her as 'a Rationalist and a follower of Bertrand Russell'.[21] There is a photograph of the two together, taken in 1910: amid trees and rocks, Alison sits demure and neat, Gertrude barefooted, less formal, surrounded by picnic baskets, cups, maps and books.

As is apparent, Alison's feelings about her in-laws were mostly hostile. She seems to have felt that they were condescending towards her, a 'show off family' and that 'they looked down on her'.[22] She once complained bitterly of 'the snobbery descending to George Harry Uttley and his girls'.[23] Perhaps the elder Uttleys, to an outsider like Alison, seemed to be patronising her and putting on airs.[24] For her part, although grateful for the diamond ring that her father-in-law gave her, Alison reacted with a self-protective and haughty disdain. Resenting their scrutiny and self-confidence, she in turn became overbearing and intolerant, a pattern established shortly after she met them when she looked at their shelves and remarked, 'Oh, the usual books.' It is remembered within the family that she insulted her future parents-in-law before her marriage and showed little affection towards them after it, maintaining a detached attitude towards the family.[25] She was later to write 'how wise to cut away from the Uttleys after James died. That same spirit pervades them all. No simplicity, no real love, no religion.'[26] Perhaps if Alison had been warmer and more giving towards the Uttleys from the start, they would later have supported her as fully as she wanted – especially during her widowhood.

In the years following her marriage, however, Alison had more pressing preoccupations than relations with her Uttley in-laws. She and James went first to live at the Old Vicarage, a seventeenth-century house on the corner of King Street and Drury Lane in Knutsford, Cheshire. James and Alison had found the house together:

It was a whitewashed seventeenth-century house with panelled sitting rooms, and oak shutters to cover the windows and keep out the cold. There were cupboards in the thickness of the walls, and tiny cupboards over the beds to hold a book and candlestick. A beautiful staircase with newels at each turn, went from the cellars to the big attic, which had once been the council chamber for the town. . . . In the daytime it was gay and bright and lively, the cobbled streets of the old town echoed with footsteps, with the whistling of boys and the clatter of horses' hooves at 'The Angel'. On May Day there was a May Queen, and the procession moved through the streets under my windows.[27]

Part of the charm of this house for Alison doubtless lay in the fact that it had been featured in Mrs Gaskell's novel *Cranford* as the house where Peter lived. It is curious, but perhaps no more than an explanation of why choices are made, that Alison had moved from a Chelsea flat that had once been inhabited by Katherine Mansfield to a house that Mrs Gaskell had known. Alison was to remember the Old Vicarage as 'our little fairy house. . . I liked the long room, orange tulips at one end, the cosy chairs, the ceiling moulded and beamed. The narrow windows, and the lovely picture of snow, with trees. I wanted to look and look at that and [the] blue shadows, *cold* shadowed snow, the tiny pink glow on the trees.'[28]

Ever alert to an atmosphere, the 'secret life' of the apparently inanimate, the Old Vicarage aroused fears in her not unlike those she experienced when walking as a child through the dark wood from school: 'I was always apprehensive . . . and I stepped softly at night with my lighted candle, looking behind me to see who was following. Somebody lived in the cellars, I imagined, and when it was dark they came out and glided up the shallow staircase.'[29]

The cellar, surprisingly the first Alison had seen in her life, continued to haunt her:

These underground caves were unknown in my country life. The houses had the living rock for foundations upon which the stone structure was built. . . . Who would have guessed how sinister the cellars would have looked in a cataract of moonlight? What kind of face might appear against the window glass of the door to the garden? A 'face of crumpled linen' might easily look in. What might lurk in those underground rooms, what spectre from the house's ancient past when the Cranford ladies had knocked on that very door? Who might step lightly up the flight of stairs, appearing round the corner where the staircase turned at right angles? What ghost from another century would walk there?[30]

Alison's discomforts were not merely due to ghostly imaginings. She was deeply hurt by being cut socially by a Mrs Watt, 'She couldn't bear us, and was pointedly rude, which used to make me sad.'[31] Twenty years later, when Alison had achieved some success as an author, she revisited Knutsford, calling on her once next-door neighbour and seeing her 'little Old Vicarage . . . looking rather bedraggled in the damp air'.[32] On this occasion, Mrs Watt 'bought a bunch of violets for "one who had given her great pleasure". She had dimples in her cheeks and looked a dear.'[33] This incident is a trifle puzzling – either Alison had exaggerated Mrs Watt's hostility or the latter was snobbishly prepared to forget her dislike in the light of Alison's literary success.

The only account of the quality of Alison's early years of married life is to be found in her private diaries. Admitting later to herself that 'I have inherited domesticity',[34] she seems to have been happy enough at first to assume the conventional housewifely responsibilites. Although not always as efficient a household manager as she liked to think, throughout her life she threw herself into a variety of domestic chores with a good deal of vigour:

> She *was* a practical person, certainly in gardening and also to some extent in cooking, though I must say towards the end of her life, her standards fell a little bit. But still, she was a practical person, and she was interested as we know from her books, in all aspects of housework and looking after a household and her guests and so on. She washed the sheets and things like that, which normally people don't do nowadays, in towns anyhow; and I was struck by the amount of work she did, Spring cleaning and that sort of thing. That was very important to her.[35]

She and James seem also to have been very much in love. Looking back, she was to regret that her son John might miss the 'rapture and beauty of young love'.[36] Twenty years later, looking through her dead husband's papers, she found not only a yellow curl cut from her baby son's hair but also 'little notes from me. Somehow my own notes to J touch my heart more than his to me, mine are so young and trusting and innocent – poor child.'[37]

James and Alison had many interests in common, apart from their scientific educations. Poetry gave them both particular pleasure and Alison was to remember 'how well James used to read and share poetry with me. He was a poet in mind.'[38] The poetry of Robert Bridges seems to have been a particular favourite. There were also foreign holidays, most of them in France.

There was, however, one shadow which fell dark and menacing across Alison's relationship with her husband. James Uttley was prone to periods of acute self-doubt and depression. She was later to write of this period of her life: 'I was very happy, but my husband was often ill, and mentally troubled. He had none of the stability of country people, I think he found it in me, I have a sheaf of poems he wrote to me, for I was always happy, with little things.[39]

Even allowing for Alison's capacity to delude herself, James Uttley was often a disturbed and uncertain man. His nephew, Anthony Tolson, has remembered that James seemed puzzled as to how to relate to him as a child, trying to be pleasant but not knowing how best to make contact.[40] One of James's nieces, Dr Katherine Watson, re-members him as a very jolly and kind uncle but also recalls, still with a sense of shock, his taking the icing sugar saved on the side of her plate at a children's party and eating it, saying as a joke, 'I see you don't like icing.'[41]

It is perhaps significant that shortly before the birth of his son John in 1914, James abruptly resigned his engineering job. Although, as we shall see, James found little satisfaction in his work, to take such a step at that time seems particularly irresponsible, even self-destructive. The couple were living at Didsbury at the time, and Alison reacted with a mixture of despair and bitterness:

> There in that boredom and 'in the hands of fate' feeling, the future so terribly unknown, for James had resigned his job, and had to get another, we had to leave our little house, my baby would be born in a few months, I was sick and ill and Manchester's heavy atmosphere pressed on me. I felt I had no friends there, Castle Top was far away, the Uttleys took no notice, not realising our awful difficulties. Their thought was on Alice K's marriage, on Gertrude, on Emily and her maids and the birth of Martin, so from them we had no help. God! How despised and rejected I was. Yet I was sustained by the thought of the coming life, bringing hope.[42]

James and Alison's son was born on 12 September 1914, five weeks after the outbreak of the First World War. For whatever reason, and Alison's preoccupations with her husband's uncertain situation may have played a part, the baby was underweight: 'I think of the tiny baby, only 4½lbs, and the anxieties of people, but I always felt confident and at peace and happy, aware of a source of strength and courage which indeed was needed at that time.'[43] Over thirty years later, Alison was to recall 'Oh darling John, what a happy day for me that you were born, in 1914.'[44] The baby was christened John Corin Taylor Uttley. Alison now had both a husband and a son, but the relationship that was to develop between mother and child was to prove, for all the joy and content that it brought, ultimately one of great pain and tragedy.

CHAPTER NINE

Frustrated Housewife and Aspiring Author, 1914–28

I [was] always the optimist, James the pessimist. I don't know
how I kept up my heart. I worked very hard. . . . Why I didn't
injure my health I don't know, saving on meals, living so
frugally. . . . Yet James urged me always to do without, and to
keep strict accounts to a penny.

ALISON UTTLEY, diary, 22 September 1954

For all her sense of being a superior young woman, Alison Uttley's life
during the First World War put her on a par with millions of other
wives and mothers. Like so many of his contemporaries, James Uttley
served with the British Army in France. He was commissioned into the
Royal Engineers and spent a good deal of the war away from his wife
and young son. Years after the war was over and James himself dead,
Alison was reminded in various small ways of her husband's involvement in the conflict: in 1935 her son John, involved in his school's
Officer Training Corps, asked for 'Daddy's old spurs'; she found a bag
of First World War ammunition in 1938; and when, in 1940, John was
himself an officer in the British Army, she dug out his father's old Sam
Browne belt after he had lost his own.[1]

The great happiness and fulfilment that Alison had felt with the birth
of her son were partly dissipated by her husband's absence at the front.
The pain of parting, and the uncertainties that followed it, were to haunt
her later in life. In 1933, deeply moved by Noel Coward's *Cavalcade*, she
recalled 'the war, and parting. "If you were the only girl in the world". I
cried a little during the war, the futility, but one goes on, it was
magnificent.'[2] She recalled losing her heart to a bridge across the river
Hodder in Yorkshire, looking down 'suspended between two worlds,
while across the seas the Great War was raging'.[3] In 1964 a television
programme, 'Fifty Years', looking back to the outbreak of the war,
took her back to 'James, and the First World War, and all the pain and
excitement and bliss'.[4] Apart from Alison sending James various home
comforts (including, in the memory of a friend, Sanatogen wine), their
only communication at that time was through letters. Three years after

James's eventual death in 1930, Alison was reminded poignantly of this interchange:

> A strange thing. I took W. de la Mare's Motley from the shelf, and read some poems. Suddenly I came across a tiny photograph of soldiers, and I hunted again and found a letter from James, an exquisitely beautiful little love letter. I turned to the beginning of the book. June 29th 1918 . . . I had the letter a few days later, and slipped it in the book and there it has lain till now. He speaks of our great love, and our joy in John, and our sweet life together. It is like a voice coming out of space. Beloved, darling, I do love you always.[5]

Alison and John spent much of the war in a lonely cottage in a remote part of South Wales. It was here that Alison first became enchanted by the poetry of Walter de la Mare, who was in those days only 'a vague but romantic name' to her. She nailed a copy of one of his poems 'Arabia' to the wall of the cottage:

> Every day and several times a day as I went about my household duties, I read it. I was very lonely, cut off from libraries and from people I knew, my husband was in France, my beloved home far away, and this poem was a light shining in the Welsh wilderness. I sang the poem to my little son. It was the first poem he heard except nursery rhymes, and his first words were the chiming endings of the lines. He filled in the gaps as I paused, comprehending nothing except the music of the poem, because he was not two years old.[6]

But not all Alison's comforts during this trying period were as rarefied. She also found more solid support in her small son. The predictably deep and close relationship of mother and only child was intensified by their dependence upon each other during the lonely years of the First World War. A quarter of a century later, she discovered in her son 'such goodness and sweetness and bravery and love [that] my heart aches for him. He is still the little child I knew, the one who cheered me with loving arms when James was at the front. I recall too vividly. I get back with such poignance it hurts.'[7]

Towards the end of the war, Alison and John left the cottage in Wales and moved back to Cheshire to live with the Uttleys at their house, 'Southborne', near Hale. This was a period of great unhappiness for Alison. Many years later, walking along a road in Hale:

> . . . the feeling of long ago when I walked there came on me. I used to feel 'lost' in the world, nobody wanted me, I had quarrelled with Castle Top – I don't know why – Southborne was hateful, as I was on sufferance with J at the war, Alice K and her husband came in each day in luxury clothes, snubbed me, snubbed John, and Mrs and Mr Uttley seemed infatuated with their success in life, their dinner parties and the invitations, and all the time the war went on and I felt lost, no home,

no-one to love me, no money, no place even where I could cry. I know what it is to be [an] outcast, and I was that fifteen years ago, it's as clear as today.[8]

Even allowing for Alison's deep-seated and sometimes unreasonable resentments at her Uttley in-laws, and her capacity for self-pity, she does seem to have had some excuse for these feelings of isolation. That she regarded herself as having quarrelled with Castle Top is remarkable in itself and may reflect the struggle she had in the early years of her marriage to reconcile the conflicting demands of her husband and his relations with those of her own parents back in Derbyshire. Certainly, it is odd that she and John did not live with them for at least part of the Great War. Nor does it seem that they resumed close relations once the war was over, though Alison and John visited them. It is almost as if, having provided Alison with Castle Top and the background that was to inspire so much of her successful writing, they were no longer needed, discarded like supports that have outlived their usefulness. There is hardly mention of their deaths in Alison's writings, although Mr Taylor died at Castle Top Farm on 29 March 1926 and Mrs Taylor at the Almshouses at Matlock Green on 13 September 1930.

Thrown back on the Uttleys, Alison had to endure a time of some unhappiness. She was subsequently to tell close friends about her trials while living at 'Southborne': of how she was sent shopping by the Uttleys, did it uneconomically and was criticised; how she found their house cold, in all senses; how she felt that every mouthful that she and John ate was watched.[9] For all these discomforts and humiliations, and there is no need to doubt that Alison felt them, she was more fortunate than hundreds of thousands of young women in Britain – her husband survived the war. But although James was not even wounded in the conflict, he returned having endured the fearful stresses of the war on the Western Front. He had been prone to depression and self-doubt before the war broke out; all that he had experienced in France was to further undermine his emotional and mental stability.

Unlike so many other reunited couples, James and Alison at least found a home fit for a hero and his family to live in. Although they lived briefly in a house at Clitheroe in Lancashire, eventually, towards the end of 1918, James and Alison bought Downs House at Bowdon near Altrincham in Cheshire.

Downs House was to be Alison's home until, eight years widowed, she moved to Beaconsfield in 1938. The choice of Downs House must have seemed like an act of liberation for Alison and a pledge of her future happiness. Her husband had returned, she could be rid of her in-laws and she and James and John could start to build together the family life that had been so abruptly and cruelly interrupted by the Great War. Certainly their decision to buy the house was quickly made:

> At the end of the war we returned to Cheshire and chose a house in a few minutes, with no hesitation. When I unlocked the door of this ivy-covered early Victorian red brick house, I immediately felt happy. There was an air of welcome in the empty rooms. I pushed open each door, and the place was filled with warmth and goodness. Up the steep stairs to the attics I went to see the four rooms with the crooked ceilings and tiny windows, and again there was a warmth which had nothing to do with the sunshine, for the house faced north-west and was cold.[10]

Alison's writing contains several detailed accounts of Downs House. She particularly liked the fact that it had several cellars, as the ground floor was an integral part of the house. There were windows looking on to the garden, which was light and bright even if rather small. The steep stair had a plain wooden staircase with a narrow handrail. Below, in the cellar, the lofty larder was icy cold, whitewashed and dim, with a great stone table standing in the centre and hooks fixed to the ceiling above it for hanging game. The floor of the larder was made of old uneven bricks, that were once a week swilled with water which drained away through a grid. In this room the butter stayed frozen and the food kept fresher than any place Alison ever knew. The wash-cellar she found a happy, cheerful place with its blazing fire under the copper every Monday morning, its clothes' baskets and little rubber mangle, its glimpses of blackbirds on the lawn and roses on the old white rosebush.[11]

Downs House had been built in 1851 as part of a property development in the wake of the opening of the Manchester South Junction and Altrincham Railway Company. The fact that the builder who had constructed it lived in it himself shows its quality. Apart from the cellars, the other rooms were very substantial, with solid door furniture and ample sash windows. Several of the rooms had high ceilings and the large front sitting-room had a bay window. Alison and James's bedroom was a square, spacious room with an attractive fireplace. Through the sash window it was possible to look out on to the garden with an apple tree that Alison grew greatly to love and a high brick wall at the back. The apple tree is still there and so is the high wall, shielding from view some industrial chimneys which Alison liked to represent as being further away than they actually are. Gardens were always to be immensely important for Alison and this one, which seemed to trap the heat in summer, was rewarding to tend. Looking over the garden wall there is a vista of Victorian villas and from the sitting-room window it is easy to see the church across the road.[12]

It is not surprising that Alison who had led a rather unsettled existence during the war, living in several places 'often in ugly rooms',[13] should have jumped at Downs House: '"Let's buy it," we said at once, forgetting everything. . . the house itself seemed to call us, and in this house we found serenity and peace. I began to write there, in the largest of the attics, with pointed window and beamed ceiling.'[14]

This over-romanticised and warm recollection of Downs House, written twenty years after the purchase was made, is essentially false. For it was not only 'serenity and peace' that Alison and James found there, but also conflict, frustration and, ultimately, death. Even in her own account of the house there are absurd contradictions, as when, four lines after writing 'no ghosts lived in this pretty Victorian house', she notes that the door at the top of the stair 'could be locked and bolted to keep the ghosts safe'.[15]

This is not to deny that Alison found much happiness while she lived there or to belittle the loving and constructive quality of her relationship with her husband. She and James clearly had a passionate, if sometimes stormy and potentially destructive marriage. Her pet name for him was Little Bimbo and he called her Mimbles, a form of endearment she also liked her son to use. They had much in common: their son John, their interest in politics and current affairs, their holidays together, art and literature – above all poetry. The deep significance of poetry as a link between Alison and James is indicated by her reaction, two years after his death, to the reading on the radio of a poem by Robert Bridges, 'I will not let thee go': 'I turned it off. Oh James, darling, darling, darling. It was *our* poem, and you *have* let me go. Did you forget the stars, the moon, the flowers? I *cannot* let thee go.'[16]

Yet Alison was also conscious of the problems that beset her marriage. Typically, however, she put the blame for these difficulties upon others, in this case James. She presents a clear picture of 'the worries of poor James haunted by failure',[17] and of the problems that threatened to engulf him in his career as a civil engineer: 'He found the work too difficult, he was very sensitive, and he had to repel bribes, and men whose thought was only money. He cared nothing for money, and helped all the poor labourers and felt sympathy for the poverty stricken people. He was too sensitive for an engineer, and he had a nervous breakdown.'[18]

As is common in close relationships, Alison desperately wanted James to be as much like her as possible: an attitude typified when once she returned with him to her home at Castle Top and, taking him through the dark wood that had so terrorised her as a child, 'was filled with an unreasoning anger against him because he walked calmly and noisily over the rough and smooth places alike',[19] whereas she stepped as silently and carefully as ever.

She was also later to revel in self-pity, once imagining, as she re-read hundreds of old letters that had passed between her and James, that the fault had been all on his side:

> Some touched my heart deeply, but I felt that James's letters were very dull, often, and often censorious, urging me to duty, full of politics and H.G. Wells and Socialism. I strove to keep up, and fairy and magic and joy kept coming in. I [was] always the optimist, James the pessimist. I don't know how I kept up my heart. I worked very hard, and did many things, and I saved pennies, and lived on the minimum. Why I didn't injure my health I don't know, saving on meals, living so frugally. No wonder my mother said I was thin and ill when I got home. Yet James urged me always to do without, and to keep strict accounts to a penny, and always my letters brimmed with devotion.[20]

It is difficult to imagine Alison, with her strong character and her capacity to browbeat and overawe, as the timorous wife worn to a shadow by her husband's strictures. Martin Byers, James's nephew, remembers a very different relationship when he was staying at Downs House not long before James's death: 'I remember him coming home in the evening with a briefcase containing work which he intended to do after supper. My recollection is that he was prevented from getting down to his work because of constant nagging interruptions by Alison, possibly about money.'[21] Although they were not poor, money does seem to have been a problem for them. James's failure to settle without misgivings into his career doubtless held him back from promotion. Any private income they might have hoped for from Sugdens, the family firm, failed to materialise in the depressed economic situation of the inter-war years. Alison earned no money herself. They seem not to have been able to afford a car during this time either. Perhaps James found it essential, then, to encourage a housewifely prudence in Alison, a pressure to which she would not have submitted tamely. Being essentially thrifty herself, she must have resented his strictures and accused him in turn of not providing his family with sufficient money. There is little doubt, therefore, that she indulged in special pleading and came to see herself as the innocent victim of financial deprivation.

Alison's capacity to deny her own aggressive and destructive feelings is nowhere better illustrated than in her relations with her son John. That which developed between them was of such intensity, even passion, that John stood scant chance of attaining a mature and successful manhood. It is not clear why the marriage produced no more children.

In the event, Alison came to see her son as a very special only child and concentrated upon him the full power of her maternal longing and expectation, leaving him emotionally maimed, like a young tree scorched by devouring flames. Her tendency to concentrate so much of her love, and so many of her demands, upon John, was doubtless encouraged by their enforced isolation together during the Great War.

Alison remembered John's early years with great affection and longing: 'How I thank God for John, that adorable babyhood, the little boy I took for walks.'[22] Thirty-three years after, she had 'a vivid dream of John, a baby of five years old, most poignant and extraordinary'.[23] Together, John and Alison made a 'baby squeak', a communication of mutual love and affection in which they were still indulging in John's twentieth year.[24] In some practical ways, Alison was clearly a very coping and competent mother. She knitted many of John's baby clothes, sometimes reworking his father's sock wool, and ensured that his material needs were well catered for.[25] John had toys: she came across his old golliwog in 1954. He was read to, played with, encouraged to join the Scouts and to take up sport, particularly cricket.[26]

John was an exceptionally good-looking little boy, with clearcut features and an open, trusting, almost wistful gaze. He grew up into a remarkably handsome man. Yet beneath this attractive and well-groomed exterior, there was much pain and uncertainty. Despite her passionate love for John – perhaps, even, because of it – Alison was an overcontrolling, demanding and sometimes unreasonable mother. In part, this was the product of her failure to come to terms with the warring elements within her own personality. In part, it may have sprung from the frustrations of her modest housewifely role. But she was also conscious of wanting to stamp her own mark upon her only child, to stop him becoming one of the Uttleys, whom she collectively despised and resented and whom she thought devoid of love and finer feeling.[27]

Alison dominated John in various ways. When he was two years old, he was tied to the leg of the table while his mother busied herself in another part of the house.[28] He was also sometimes denied food as a punishment and locked by himself in a room.[29] Even when there were no acts of positive cruelty, Alison remained an enormously powerful mother. Martin Byers remembers an incident at Downs House during the early 1920s which illustrates this and also shows Alison's housewifely inefficiency, or her determination to disrupt John's play with his cousin, or both:

> John and I were playing cricket . . . when the kitchen window was thrust open and Alison called out 'John, will you go to the shops and bring me a pound of butter?' John dropped his bat, looked at me

resignedly, and we set off for Altrincham, a walk of about a quarter of a mile, I suppose. On our return with the butter, we resumed our game, which was shortly interrupted again by an order to fetch a pound of sugar. John's look of resignation was even stronger, but he made no protest, and we repeated our journey to the shops. . . . I never thought Alison lovable or charming . . . she dominated John all his life.[30]

At the age of nine, John was sent to Yarlet Hall Preparatory School for Boys in Stone, Staffordshire. The Uttley family at large favoured this school and, apart from John, his Byers and Tolson cousins also went there. Separated abruptly from his parents, John apparently 'loathed' Yarlet Hall,[31] which has been described by one of his cousins as 'a school for the rather dim sons of Midlands businessmen'.[32]

Sending John away to school at that tender age cannot have been easy for Alison, in view of her close relationship with him. Since it was apparently an Uttley tradition to send sons there, it is possible that she viewed the move as in John's best interests, but also as a deprivation deriving from her husband and his family. It is also conceivable that James Uttley was relieved to see the intense relationship between his wife and his son disrupted by Yarlet Hall. Not that James can be described in any way as an unloving father. His own relationship with John seems to have been one of great affection and fellowship. He shared many of his interests, particularly in sport, with his son. Later on, when John was at public school, father and son seem to have sometimes established a mutually supportive alliance against the dominating tendencies of Alison. That John was desperately unhappy to leave his parents for prep school is illustrated by a letter he wrote at nine years old, 'I am John and . . . I like best to cuddle my Mummy and Daddy.'[33]

With John away at prep school for so much of the time, family holidays assumed a special significance. Many years later, Alison was to recall holidays at 'Tenby, and James and John and all the happy days'.[34] And they must have found much happiness at Arles. In 1932, listening to the music of Bizet's suite 'L'Arlesienne' on the radio, Alison wrote in her diary, 'I *feel* that story very intensely – the parents, the boy – Arles, and its glory. Provence swept over me. I would like to write short stories like those.'[35]

France moved Alison deeply. Over thirty years later a postcard 'brought nostalgic memories of little French towns, where I used to loiter. They are timeless, in a changing world, for France has not changed as England has.'[36] It was as an adult on holiday in France that her artist's eye at last saw the colours in shadows: 'I remember staring dumbfounded at the shadows of a palm-tree on a beach in the South of

France. The shadows lay on the stones rich purple, like a petunia. Once again, we were driving in the Pyrenees, in the heights, and suddenly we went round a corner and a line of mountains appeared, shining in the late sunshine. One mountain was the colour of violet, another was as red as a rose, and a third was azure blue. I wished to ask the Frenchmen who were with us if they saw the same shades, but I was too shy.'[37]

Back in England, such exalted moments were rare in Alison's domesticated life. Consequently, the links she still possessed with her youth and the intellectual stimulation of Manchester and London became increasingly precious to her. One was Gwladys Llewellyn, her friend from Ashburne House and Cambridge days. GL was a teacher at the Royal Grammar School at Clitheroe in Lancashire where she was to become head. She was John's godmother, concerned, thoughtful and never forgetting his birthday. The other was Lily Meagher, whom Alison had met while teaching and who was to remain faithful and supportive until her death in 1960. Lily Meagher, always referred to as LM in Alison's diaries, was delicate-looking, rather prim but beautiful. A devout Roman Catholic, she remained a spinster living with her sister Lucy. Alison, occasionally aware of her own shortcomings, described her as 'a saint always'.[38] Although at times Alison was to find fault with both LM and GL, these two acquaintances from her early years, though apparently (and probably by design) never meeting each other, remained her staunchest and most faithful friends. But neither friends nor family alone were enough. Alison needed creative occupation, and it was in the late 1920s that she first resumed her London habit of jotting down short descriptions – this time, of places she had seen, particularly when travelling in France with James 'who was totally unaware of my desire to write'.[39] Although she was conscious of wanting to construct a book, she was not ready: 'The words would not settle themselves in any pattern, I had not found my style. It was too soon. I knew I wanted to write of the country as I saw it with all its beauty and serenity, from within.'[40]

In 1928, Alison did publish her first article in the August edition of *Homes and Gardens*. The article was entitled 'What Should Children Read?' It was signed, rather bleakly, 'A.J. Uttley' and consisted of some four hundred words. It began: 'The children of to-day are provided with abundant literature of an ephemeral sort, but it is as well to see that their reading matter includes also a good selection of what may be called the classics.'[41]

Having delivered herself of this schoolmarmish and cautionary judgement, Alison went on to extol the virtues of a variety of classic children's books, many of them those she had herself enjoyed as a child. Apart from *Swiss Family Robinson*, *The Wind in the Willows* and *Puck of*

Pook's Hill, Alison also recommended *Black Beauty*, 'well-nigh forgotten by this generation', and an adaptation of Homer's *Odyssey*. Fairy stories made a predictable appearance in her list and so, less predictably, did Hugh Lofting's *Doctor Dolittle* series. The list ends with *Little Women*, *Tom Brown's Schooldays* and *Westward Ho!* She showed her sensitivity to the power of good illustrations for children by complimenting those in Ernest Seton's *Pacing Mustang*, which were 'full of imagination. Little footprints of bird and beast run round the margins, and feathers flutter down pages.' She concluded, rather earnestly, 'It cannot be too strongly emphasised that good reading should begin early.' Oddly, towards the end of her life, Alison denied all memory of this article.[42] Although it can be seen as a first, small step, in itself, the article was of little weight. Far more important was the fact that Alison, sitting at a desk under the pointed window of her attic room at Downs House, was beginning to write the books that would establish her as one of the best-known of twentieth-century children's writers.

CHAPTER TEN

The Making of
'The Country Child' and
Little Grey Rabbit, 1929–30

> I think of lovely days, James and John and I . . .
> feasting, laughing, dancing round the table when
> my Squirrel, Hare and LGR was taken.
>
> ALISON UTTLEY, diary, 3 September 1938

Alison Uttley has left various accounts as to how she first became a writer. As with so much in her life, her testimony is not coherent. There are flat contradictions, some glossing over of the truth, assertions which are not in accordance with the facts and a little special pleading. One thing, however, is clear. She possessed from an early age a deep, almost desperate need to express herself. This was part of her drive to assert her powerful personality and, later, to recreate the vanished world of her childhood, showing her readers precious or extraordinary things they might otherwise have missed:

> I began to make up stories when I was a little child, as soon as I could hold a pencil, for all the world of strange objects was filled with life. I made words on paper, in crooked letters. There was no paper for me, but I tore open envelopes and wrote on the inside. My first story consisted of six words. I had been driven by my parents to the village a few miles away, and I nursed my wooden doll. I showed her the rushing river, the old bridge over it, the horses and a donkey, and the smithy. I told this adventure to whoever would listen, strangers and all.[1]

This first story was written when she was aged two. When she was four, she wrote a little poem which began:

> The wind doth blow,
> The cock doth crow,
> Cockadoodle do,
> So early in the morning.[2]

Although she continued to make up stories of 'mouse and cock and cat and dog', she seems to have abandoned her spontaneous writing when she went to the village school. She still wrote the occasional poem in secret but showed them to nobody, fearing both laughter and praise. She was later to claim disingenuously, 'All my early life I wanted to write, but I had no notebook and my scraps of paper blew away or got burnt.'[3] As we have seen, her experiences at grammar school were discouraging, since she found herself obliged to check the creative impulse in her essay writing for fear of the sarcasm of her teachers.

One early confirmation of her potential capacity to write came when, on a seaside holiday, Mrs Taylor decided to take Alison and Harry to a phrenologist on the beach. Having passed his fingers through Alison's short dark hair, touching her skull and talking quietly, 'He wrote down his observations in a paper-backed book and at the end he gave his prediction of the child's future. I should be a writer, he said, and my mother smiled gently. It was a high flight of fancy, and nobody took it seriously, but sometime, somehow, it might happen.'[4]

Although at Manchester University Alison's overriding commitment was to science, she had toyed with the idea of taking an arts course afterwards. Her year in Cambridge proved a watershed because of the encouragement and sound training she received in the art of writing. With her fear of ridicule lifted from her, she began to write the occasional sketch. But her work was cautious, even predictable: 'Always I wrote of village life, for this was familiar to me, and the fashionable life of the towns had no attractions.'[5]

One of her chief difficulties in beginning to write was to find 'a subject in a world packed with treasures like Pandora's Box'. Although she had told stories to her son John from an early age, just as she had previously entranced Ramsay MacDonald's children with her country tales, she felt compelled to write for adults too – to evoke the beauties of the rural world which haunted her, but which she mistakenly thought would not appeal to potential readers:

> I thought of country stories told by my father, concerning people dead a hundred years, yet fresh as if still alive. . . . Nobody was dead, nothing had dissolved, all things lived in an eternity between two worlds, a fair land where they walked and did their daily work among animals and birds and beasts.
> Thoughts were alive and green-growing, and I wanted to tell about them to a world with different ideas, to people who had forgotten the essence of beauty which fills this planet.[6]

Nor was the choice of subject matter the only obstacle. When she had attempted to write as a young woman at her old home in Derbyshire, the words would not come. Alison lacked the confidence to express in writing the thoughts and images which teemed in her brain. Towards the end of her life she was to give a curious explanation of her difficult transformation from scientist to author:

> I never thought of writing a book: I didn't know anybody who had written a book, I didn't realise they *were* written, I thought they were created, in a way. Then, later on, I wanted to write, but I never knew how to set about it. Once I sat with pencil and paper in a bedroom at my old home, determined to write the feelings that flooded my mind before I went away. I could not do it. I don't think I ever realised one could write a book until I saw a typewriter, and that cheered me up.[7]

When she had established herself as a successful and prolific author, Alison Uttley was fond of claiming that she was obliged to turn to writing after the death of her husband in 1930. In the sense that it became an essential source of income for her during those years, this is accurate enough. But the truth is that two events, the first in 1927 and the second in 1928, started her upon her career as an author. While at Manchester University, she had much admired Samuel Alexander, the professor in philosophy. In 1927 she met Professor Alexander at a small exhibition of painting in Altrincham. This chance meeting was a turning point in her life:

> He came up to me, smiling, and I was agreeably flattered and touched that he had remembered me.
> 'You were a student at the university,' said he. 'I remember you. And what are you doing now?'
> I said, rather diffidently, that I was married. It was a poor excuse.
> He looked rather surprised. 'But what are you writing? Have you written anything lately?'
> It was my turn to be surprised. It was the desire of my heart to write, to invent, to do some creative work, but not a word had I produced. I stammered that I was thinking of writing something, and he listened intently and said he hoped that I would write some more poetry.[8]

Ironically, Professor Alexander had confused Alison with another student with the same maiden name of Taylor. The mistake, however, proved to be an inspiration: 'I determined I would write. I made up my mind that instant that I, too, would write something for him.'[9]

Towards the end of 1928 Alison attended the opening of an arts and crafts exhibition in Manchester over which Samuel Alexander presided as master of ceremonies. After he had made his speech, Alison approached him shyly with a basket of 'the most beautiful fruit I could buy in our small town'. Professor Alexander was overjoyed and was later to write to Alison that the gesture had been 'charming and dear. . . . I wish I had some fruit of my brains to send you to show my gratitude. But they are barren rascals at present.'[10] It is interesting that at the exhibition where Alison presented the fruit to Professor

Alexander, she first saw and admired the art of C.F. Tunnicliffe, who was later to provide the beautiful illustrations for so many of her books of essays.

The second significant event which prompted Alison to write was the departure of her son John for Sedbergh public school in 1928. She later recorded, 'My small son was going away to school and I had nobody to listen to my tales which always came into my mind.'[11] And her diary confesses, 'I was feeling rather lonely, and my son had gone to school.'[12] There is nothing unusual about a mother feeling loneliness when her son goes away to boarding school, but John was a veteran of preparatory school. Perhaps Alison felt that his public school, Sedbergh in North Yorkshire, was more remote. Perhaps her relationship with her husband was at an unsatisfactory stage, making John's presence more precious to her than ever before. At any rate, by 1928 she was struggling to write her first book.

The process of writing was to become richly rewarding for Alison at an emotional and personal level. She had been toying for some time with an attempt to recreate her memories of her country childhood and it is clear that this was the basis of *The Country Child*, the first manuscript she put her hand to although only her third book to be published. It was in this recreation of her life at Castle Top that she found the greatest fulfilment: 'I found a strange excitement and happiness in writing. I entered a world which existed in my mind, and I brought it to light. Everything I had ever done was vivid and clear, waiting to be remembered, hidden on shelves in my brain. I could catch the evasive scent of lavender fields and juniper hills, of kitchens and drains and a pigsty by the dining-room, and a cow-house by the door.'[13]

She has left a vivid picture of herself in the attic room at Downs House:

> It was very quiet, all sounds were dulled up there, and I looked around with pleasure. In a gable, like a doll's house in the large attic, was a tiny pointed window and below it stood an old Pembroke table from my child-days, banished there. It looked enticing, this small intimate little room within a room. I fetched pen and paper, and sat down to write. I drew round me a cloak of silence, and within its shelter I worked. I told of my country home, for I was filled with longing to write of that place before I forgot the spell that bound me to it.[14]

Alison was caught up in the web of time remembered, 'just as Proust returned to his childhood drawn there by the taste of a brioche in a cup of tea [sic]. Hours passed like minutes as I secretly wrote. It was not memory but a return in time, and I was exhausted when at last I went downstairs.'[15] Believing that 'I have a sacred fire burning in my heart',[16]

Alison prised open wider the lid of Pandora's Box. Although she was always to remain reticent about much of her private life, particularly her marriage and her relationship with her son, she was aware, as she delved into the past, that 'all things escape, the good and the bad, the sweet and the sour, and as these thoughts floated out visibly in the air, they all had virtue for me, they were aspects of a world which I could capture and put in books'.[17]

She never regretted the sometimes cathartic discomforts that were an intrinsic part of her extraordinary powers of recollection:

> Remembrances from this store spring to life with such startling vividness that I experience a shock, almost a pain, as if the pangs of rebirth tore something within me, but the pleasure of recall is exquisite, the pain is mingled with joy.
>
> Sometimes the change – that is the translation into the past – is only for a fraction of a second, and I have grasped nothing to carry away with me before I am back in my ordinary consciousness. I try to get 'over there' again, but I cannot get rid of the clogging 'Now'. I am bound in the present, and nothing I can do will take me into that region of another world and time. I feel I have lost some precious experience forever.
>
> Suddenly, with no preparation or conscious willing on my part, it comes again, time doubles upon itself in a loop, and I am in the past. These sudden reversals are brought about by slight touches which I can trace backwards after the experience when I seek the origin. The scent of new walnuts, the sharp whinny of a horse, the sunlight slanting on a tree. . . . The whole scene reappears before me. The figures of my mother and father come alive and talk gravely to one another. I, a very small child, stand near, listening, feeling like a child, experiencing child sensations, piercing joys and sadnesses, breathing the warm air, feeling the sharp edge of my starched pinafore frill around my neck, smelling the many odours which pervaded a room long ago.[18]

These moments of 'translation' and their setting down on paper were partly an aesthetic experience, partly a reparation for her later neglect of her parents, partly a compensation for the difficulties of her marriage and partly a proselytisation – 'I always wanted to tell people about my old home, you see.'[19] It was also part of Alison Uttley's conviction that to be a writer 'one must have something to say about those "ordinary things", a new vision to bring to the reader so that he too can find pleasure which had escaped him'.[20]

Alison felt great misgivings about showing the manuscript of *The Country Child* to her husband. 'I finished the book, I cut it shorter, I copied it out on a borrowed typewriter which I could hardly use, and I kept it secret for the old fear of mockery was strong. I was justified, for unwillingly I was prevailed to show the copy.'[21] Having got Alison to show him the typescript, James Uttley was apparently very discouraging: 'even the beginning was scorned as "not the way to write a book". It was too simple, too childish even to read.'[22] James, no doubt troubled and depressed for other reasons and perhaps feeling some rivalry of Alison, is also alleged to have thrown *The Country Child* across the room and to have derided it as 'rubbish'.[23]

Before this traumatic rejection, Alison had let her friend Lily Meagher into her secret. Here the response was quite different: 'I first showed LM the manuscript of The C Child, the first to see it, and she liked it, and then we timidly showed it to James, who didn't at all like it. Shall I ever forget? She encouraged me with my writing.'[24] James's rejection was, however, more powerful than LM's encouragement: 'I threw it in a drawer and forgot about it for some months.'[25]

While the typescript of *The Country Child* lay in a drawer at Downs House, Alison achieved her first breakthrough as a writer. She has given her own account of the book's conception after John's departure for Sedburgh school had removed her chief justification for composing tales: 'Every day on our walks, in England, Wales and France, I told stories of hares and weasels, wolves and foxes, each one different and new. I was compelled by a strong urge to write down a tale and send it to him. This was my first little book, *The Squirrel, the Hare and the Little Grey Rabbit*.'[26]

Although this book, which was published in 1929, is generally believed to be the first that Alison Uttley wrote, it is not quite as straightforward as that. She had already, in her own words, 'been working at "The Country Child" in secret for some months'.[27] There was also a little book entitled *Mrs Nimble and Mr Bumble: a Tale of the Tiniest House in the World*. Published in 1944 by Francis James publishing company of London and sharing its hard covers with a story by Herbert McKay entitled *This Duck and That Duck*, it had possibly seen the light of day some time before. After the Second World War, Alison presented a copy of this to her friend and publisher at Faber, Peter du Sautoy, writing on the title page, 'My first book???', and adding a note, 'My dear Peter, Here is the mysterious little book. I have no recollections of its charms.'[28] This story may well have been a very early product of Alison Uttley's pen and the creation of a character called Mrs Nimble – very like the pet name of Mimble by which her husband called her – may indicate that it was written before James's death. It is a straightforward tale, with none of the rich country lore and fine drawing of character which characterise the Grey Rabbit or the Sam Pig books.

In view of the significance of the publication of *The Squirrel, the Hare and the Little Grey Rabbit* for Alison's writing career, it is instructive to examine how it was accepted for publication. Alison remembered that it was she who took the initiative: 'The little book, which I sent to several publishers, was accepted by Messrs Heinemann.'[29] The facts seem more complicated than that. According to Heinemann, on 28 January 1929 they received the book and a covering letter from Alison saying, 'the illustrations will be important, Beatrix Potter made such charming ones'. Alison recommended an artist called Dorothy Hutton, but three weeks later Heinemann asked her to see some illustrations by Margaret Tempest.[30] The publishers were therefore instrumental in bringing Alison and Margaret Tempest together in an experimental partnership. Alison may have resented the rejection of her own suggestion for an illustrator. She may also have been resentful that the terms offered by Heinemann implied that her work was less valuable than Margaret Tempest's: she was paid ten pounds outright, and the latter fifteen pounds outright. These terms did not vary for the first four Little Grey Rabbit books, all published by Heinemann.

Certainly Alison was to remain extraordinarily sensitive as to whether she or Margaret Tempest had been the foremost creator of the host of animals, Little Grey Rabbit, Hare, Squirrel, Moldy Warp, Fuzzypeg and many more who, within a short time, were to become world famous. When the publication of the books was taken over by Collins in 1934, author and illustrator had an equal share in the copyright and in the ensuing royalties. This did not prevent a good deal of subsequent bickering, particularly when the stories were broadcast and Alison claimed, with some logic though little charity, that the purely verbal images presented over the radio entitled her to a greater share of the proceeds. As late as 1971 she was incensed when Margaret Tempest asserted in an article that she had created the characters visually and Alison 'orally'.[31] In her view, she had played by far the most important part by conjuring up the characters which Margaret Tempest later illustrated. This extreme sensitivity throughout a lengthy and profitable partnership may have its roots in Alison's feeling that, at the outset, Heinemann had treated her as second fiddle.

Within Alison's immediate family circle, the news of the contract was greeted with great joy: 'I think of lovely days, James and John and I . . . feasting, laughing, dancing round the table when my Squirrel, Hare and LGR was taken.'[32]

Although Alison later liked to give the impression that all her stories flowed freely and unceasingly from her pen, the writing of *The Squirrel, the Hare and the Little Grey Rabbit* was evidently hard work. The first paragraph beginning with the immortal words 'A long time ago there lived in a little house on the edge of a wood, a Hare, a Squirrel, and a little Grey Rabbit' was followed, in the original manuscript, by four lines of considerable confusion and crossings out. Even in the opening sentence, the word squirrel is spelt wrongly – with two L's – none of the characters has a capital letter in front of their name and the disposition of commas is a little eccentric. In this first, tortured paragraph, the hare is first of all allotted 'very fine whiskers', Squirrel wears 'a brown dress the colour of beech leaves in autumn' and has 'a tail of which she was very proud'.[33] Each of these descriptions has been crossed out. Thereafter the writing becomes much freer and the number of alterations sharply declines. The original manuscript lacks a title and it is clear from examination of the manuscripts of subsequent Grey Rabbit tales that Alison had some difficulty in fixing on a final title. There is much crossing out of original titles and sometimes the publishers have been obliged to suggest the final version.

The opening words of the story, emerging from that first, tangled, handwritten paragraph, were to set the character and the style of the whole series of Grey Rabbit books:

> A long time ago there lived in a little house on the edge of a wood, a Hare, a Squirrel, and a little Grey Rabbit.
> The Hare, who wore a blue coat on weekdays and a red coat on Sundays, was a conceited fellow.
> The Squirrel, who wore a brown dress on weekdays, and a yellow dress on Sundays, was proud.[34]

Towards the end of her life, Alison Uttley was to explain why she had created so many animal characters and, in particular, those in the Little Grey Rabbit books:

> I write much more about animals. I think they have such a raw deal, and I think they are very faithful and very, very patient. In the Little Grey Rabbit books, Grey Rabbit is supposed to be rather a good little person, not too good, but quite fun, and the head of the family. Hare, as every child who writes is pleased to tell me, Hare is bold and rather bad, but all the little boys like Hare. Squirrel is very conceited; I brought up that trait in little girls, who are very often rather like that. In these little books, I always try to give some specially English touch of country life, which might be forgotten.[35]

It is clear that the three main characters of the Grey Rabbit books also reflect different aspects of Alison's own personality, with its combination of love of home and home-making, her pride in her intellectual capacity and her achievements as an author, and her strong sense of her own worth. Although it is easiest to identify her with Little Grey Rabbit, both of them warmly valuing domesticity, there is no denying that Alison Uttley was also capable of conceit, condescension and selfishness.

The characters and their friends also inhabit a rural world very like the one that Alison associated with her own childhood and wished to create for the new generations of her readers. Later editions of the Grey Rabbit books carried a foreword, which told readers:

> Of course you must understand that Grey Rabbit's home had no electric light or gas, and even the candles were made from pith of rushes dipped in wax from the wild bees' nests, which Squirrel found. Water there was in plenty, but it did not come from a tap. It flowed from a spring outside, which rose up from the ground, and went to a brook. . . . Tea did not come from India, but from a little herb known very well to country people, who once dried it and used it in their country homes. Bread was baked from wheat ears, ground fine. . . . The doormats were plaited rushes, like country-made mats, and cushions were stuffed with wool gathered from the hedges where sheep pushed through the thorns. . . . The country ways of Grey Rabbit were the country ways known to the author.[36]

What was the inspiration for these famous fictional characters? Alison was insistent that they were not simply 'humans dressed as animals', and once, infuriated, replied to a 'crass' reader who made that assumption, 'saying the characters were chosen imaginatively, creations of my own, and not based on children, nor epitomes "of a wondering child" . . . I spent the rest of the day thinking of it'.[37] She was able to identify closely with animals, watching deer in a park in January 1932 and trying 'to feel like one of those little wild creatures, to imagine its thoughts'.

In 1969, interviewed for 'Woman's Hour', she gave a fuller explanation of the creation of her animals' characters in the books:

> I set down three animals about the same size. I was used to Sq[uirrel], to rabbits which played on our lawn and Hare in the top pasture. Not based on real people. Why do children love them? Because I believe in them. Mine aren't made up, they're real. . . . I don't sit down to write a story, they come. . . . I was born in a place of beauty. Animals [are] more important than man. I talked to all the animals. I don't want to go back. I could live in the middle of London, and I would still feel the country.[38]

She was to defend herself further in her book of essays, *A Ten O'Clock Scholar*, saying, 'I am often accused of allowing human attributes to animals. . . . Animals are not allowed by modern conceptions of animal behaviour to have any feelings that even remotely resemble those of the conquering tribe called Mankind.'[39] Alison Uttley rejected this modern view of animals, preferring the model of Aesop's Fables where animals and birds behave like Man to point a moral, and denied that there was no such thing as a jealous or inquisitive animal. She also argued that in her stories about animals she used names in order to distinguish one from another. Towards the end of the essay, she asserted her views with great force and feeling:

> Animals are mysteries, a race apart. . . . They are too noble to be humanised in story and fable, they are too great for our small civilisations, and yet only by a humanisation shall we know them and learn to love them.
> To humanise is to attempt to bring animals and nature itself into our lives, a way known to ancient man, who felt that the rocks and earth were alive and full of power and living substance. . . .
> Far from the machine age, the animals are older and wiser than we in the best sense of the word, inhabitants of earth alongside humanity, struggling to survive, yet waging no wars, and using no poisons, as they struggle on through life to silent death.[40]

These views are a further expression of Alison Uttley's belief that, 'Everything has life. . . . Once you have grasped the structure of the atom, you realise that everything is alive, even metals, minerals, so-called inanimate objects; so you see, even Sam Pig and Grey Rabbit are alive, in their own fashion.'[41] Certainly she was always to feel a profoundly proprietorial attachment to her animal creations. She was careful to insist that the personalities of the characters she had established should be maintained throughout the Grey Rabbit series, telling the illustrator of the later books, Katherine Wigglesworth, that in *Little Grey Rabbit Goes to the North Pole* Grey Rabbit must not be shown to be falling down a crevice in 'an unladylike way'.[42]

The Squirrel, the Hare and the Little Grey Rabbit was published in the neat, squarish format that came to characterise the series. Its hard front cover had a modest two-tone illustration of the three chief characters and inside it ran to one hundred and eleven pages with twenty-nine colour illustrations. The book establishes, apart from the three protagonists, several of the other characters that were to become a feature of the series, Milkman Hedgehog, Postman Robin, Wise Owl and the weasels.

Alison Uttley was particularly sensitive to suggestions that she had drawn on other authors for her inspiration. Certainly her menacing weasels have something in common with the Wild Wooders, the potentially revolutionary proletariat of *The Wind in the Willows*. There are also obvious similarities with the Beatrix Potter books. Both sets of animals wear early twentieth-century clothes and in Alison's first book Grey Rabbit, like Squirrel Nutkin, loses her tail. Throughout her life, Alison was capable of fury when the comparison was made, tearing up a review from the *Scotsman* in May 1969 which had suggested that her books were 'an imitation of Beatrix Potter'.[43] She also indignantly rejected the suggestion that she was 'a Victorian writer'.[44] She felt particular rivalry towards certain women authors of children's books and she was to develop a positive dislike of Enid Blyton, whom she met during her Beaconsfield years.

It is interesting that the first Little Grey Rabbit book appeared with the author's name shown as 'Alison Uttley'. Subsequently Alison was to claim, on several occasions, that she only adopted the name Alison after her husband's death and on the publication of *The Country Child* in 1931.[45] In fact, two Little Grey Rabbit stories were published before James's death. Nor is there any validity in Alison's claim that she finally rejected her first name of Alice in order to avoid confusion with her sister-in-law, since by 1929 the latter had been married for almost a decade and was known as Alice Tolson. We have seen that at various times after her own marriage in 1911 and especially when with her in-laws, she adopted the name Alison in order to maintain a separate identity from Alice Uttley. But it seems very likely that she decided to publish her first book as 'Alison' Uttley chiefly because she liked the sound of the name, perhaps feeling it had more of a romantic quality than Alice. At any rate, she chose to be known thereafter, both in public and in private, as Alison Uttley.

It is odd, in view of the subsequent appeal and success of the Little Grey Rabbit books, that the first few titles published by Heinemann aroused little interest or reaction. Alison herself confessed that she was 'surprised' to be asked to write a second story. This book, *How Little Grey Rabbit Got Back Her Tail*, was published in 1930. It is essentially a sequel to the first book in the series and deals with Grey Rabbit's successful quest to recover her tail. No new animal characters make an appearance, although there are three rather stereotyped human characters, Mrs Bunting, Mrs Snowball and the blacksmith, who all try to prevent Squirrel dragging away a jangling shop bell.

How Little Grey Rabbit Got Back Her Tail was written, like its predecessor, in ink on lined notepaper rather like that found in a school exercise book. It is very similar in style to the first Grey Rabbit book, but with fewer crossings out – certainly, on its early pages. The name of her mole character, though, was to pose problems. Soon to be famous as Moldy Warp, in the manuscript he appears as 'Mouldy Warp', 'Moody Worp' and 'Moody Warp'. It is perhaps odd that Alison should have forgotten so quickly the traditional Derbyshire name for a mole that she had known as a child, moldy worp. The title of the story is written clearly on the first page of the manuscript in Alison's own hand, although it appears, rather oddly, as '*How Grey Rabbit Got Her Tail*'.[46] The text is a little over four thousand words in length and Margaret Tempest's beautiful illustrations glow upon the pages, even though the animal characters occasionally look like stuffed exhibits. The cover is in the same two-tone plain format as the first story.

It was perhaps difficult for contemporaries to anticipate the cumulative power and appeal of these tales, with their homely characters, scraps of country lore and their occasional brushes with violence and pain. It was easier once the series had established itself as a best seller, to sum up the appeal of Little Grey Rabbit and her friends:

> Possibly the magic of the books is that their stories about country people to a certain extent reflect Alison's own country childhood. . . . The settings are isolated, the characters are very dependent on each other for all their amusements and entertainments, their news; they have a fantastic child appeal because of this type of community. Basically, of course, she was writing the books for her little boy, and therefore wanted to tell him in a childlike way the things she had enjoyed herself as a child, what had given her pleasure.[47]

Towards the end of her life, Alison described what she set out to achieve in these and all her books for children:

> A story for children, however fanciful, should have truth in the background. There should be a solid foundation for the thistledown tale. . . . In each story I hide something, a legend, a proverb, scraps of wisdom which I heard when I was a child. Morality should be implicit. The world of the child should be a safe world, with good prevailing over evil. . . . The writers of children's books have to exercise care . . . a feeling of security should be built up. . . . So I take the children . . . into a land without real fear – although there are small fears which are surmounted.[48]

By the end of 1929, with one Little Grey Rabbit book published and the second written, Alison must have looked at the future with some hope. Within a year, however, she was to undergo the greatest trauma of her life.

CHAPTER ELEVEN

Tragedy, 1930

Mummy thinks this letter is hopeless . . . she is
going to call me a bald old man because of what I
said just now. I don't feel old; I feel quite young
and skittish.

JAMES UTTLEY to John Uttley, 1 June 1930

My family held the view that James was allowed
no peace at home, that he was driven to drown
himself through worrying about money and constant nagging by Alison.

MARTIN BYERS, 22 September 1984

On 18 September 1930, James Uttley drowned himself in the river
Mersey. He was the civil engineer in charge of constructing a new bridge
over the river at Northenden for the Manchester Corporation.[1] He was
forty-seven years old.

The inquest into James's death, held at Sale on 29 September 1930,
returned a verdict of 'suicide while of unsound mind'. James had been
missing since 1.45 p.m. on 18 September and the inquest was able to
reconstruct both his movements and his mood before that time. Several
witnesses testified to James's mood of depression and anxiety. William
Law, a chainman employed at the work on the new bridge, was a crucial
witness:

> On September 18 Mr Uttley seemed to be abnormal and depressed. He
> told witness [William Law] to do work that was already being done,
> and asked strange questions as to what time the men went to dinner.
> Witness took Mr Uttley his lunch, and when he returned later he was
> counting money. About 12.45 p.m. witness saw him on the bridge for
> the last time, and at 3.00 a search was made, but he could not be
> found.[2]

James had appeared inexplicably upset to his assistant engineer, R.T.
Wyllie, who had been working with him on a daily basis since February of
that year. According to Wyllie, 'The work had suffered damage from
floods, which had meant delay, but there was nothing to unduly upset or
worry Mr Uttley.' The witness had noticed, however, that when James
had returned from his summer holiday in France, his manner had been

'very strange, and once he apologised because he could not concentrate his thoughts'.[3]

A labourer working on the bridge had seen James go down to the water's edge alongside the dam. Later the body was seen in the river, near the bank, by a fourteen year old boy and a police constable had recovered it, later telling the coroner, 'The clothing was not disturbed, and in the pockets were an engineer's diary with Mr Uttley's name and address, and eleven shillings and eightpence ha'penny in cash.' The coroner was 'in no doubt that Mr Uttley had thrown himself into the river'. James had arranged his own death with some forethought, even, in a bizarre way, some consideration, for he left a note in his office for Alison, saying, 'I am drowning myself in the Mersey below the bridge' and making a careful reference to his will and other relevant matters.[4]

James's suicide was the single greatest tragedy of Alison's life. For many years afterwards she was to mourn his death, on his birthday and on the anniversaries of their marriage and of the day he had killed himself. Her feelings of loss and regret were at their most powerful during the next few years. Perhaps inevitably, in view of her complete failure to acknowledge her share of responsibility for the difficulties during their marriage, she continued to express puzzlement as to why her husband had killed himself. Two and a half years after his death she visited his grave:

> . . . which had a brown bowl and four pink and white tulips from an unknown, perhaps from George [Uttley]. It was very neat and quiet and I had a little prayer. I always feel he moves as I approach and half raises himself. 'I am so glad to see you darling.' O Bimbo, why did you do it? You had a lover, and a sweet son, a house, a private income, a job, everything one would wish.[5]

As she tended to do in her reminiscences of her childhood at Castle Top, Alison continued to look back on her marriage with considerable nostalgia, almost eliminating from her memory the conflict and disharmony that had characterised it as much as the love and warmth. On the day King George V was buried, 28 January 1936, she wrote in her diary, 'so ends a great King . . . twenty-five years, the middle portion of my life, marriage, war, John's birth, our houses and life, J's death, our struggles . . . I thank God for it'.[6]

Alison was not the only one posthumously to extol the virtues of her marriage. Although in private many of her Uttley in-laws believed that Alison's nagging and controlling tendencies had helped to drive James to his death, in public they closed ranks. At the inquest, George Uttley, James's younger brother, said that the dead man's 'married life had been very happy, and as far as he [George] knew, he had no financial troubles'. George added, however, that James 'was a man who did not like to acknowledge any weakness, was very conscientious and took things seriously'.[7]

In the three months before he killed himself, James's emotions had swung between a manic elation and deep despair. On 1 June he had written a merry and optimistic letter to his son, then at Sedbergh public school. Perhaps the jolly tone of the letter was an attempt to cheer John up, for, as a fellow pupil at the school later recounted, 'he had not been happy there. He had short legs and found the running we had to do there very trying. He was not athletic, but he had plenty of courage. I found him a bit aggressive at school, which, no doubt, owed something to his insecurity, of which, at the time, I was unaware.'[8]

Even if James had felt some guilt for John's unhappiness at Sedbergh, which was his old school and had been chosen on that account, the letter reveals a loving and fond relationship between father and son. It also shows something of James's relationship with Alison:

> My dear old chap,
>   We were delighted with last Monday's cricket letter from you, some champion batsman, Jones, eh!
>   Mummy and I have had one evening's tennis this week, at Arcot; it was great fun and, although I whacked the Mimbles, serving with great effect and celerity, yet she put up a good fight on the second set, and got three games. Between ourselves, a bit stoutish for tennis.
>   She has threatened me with you; I am prepared to fight for dear life against the all-conquering Jones; I bet you a 2d ice that I win, Championship of Angleterre, best of three sets.[9]

James then spoke with great optimism of the French holiday he was planning for the family. He had 'visited the good Cook's this week, and discussed times and tides and Paris hotels, for once I struck an intelligent man'. He hoped that they would all get some good tennis by the side of the Mediterranean. The itinerary included several days in Avignon, from where they could visit by bus the old Roman remains at Nîmes and Arles. From there they were to move on to Cavalaire, 'bathing, tennis, perhaps a trip to Monte Carlo – only the Mimble is a doubtful party at Monte Carlo; she might try to break the bank, and we might depart sadly homeward, begging our way across France'.[10]

James and Alison planned to visit John at a Sedbergh open day at the end of the month. James referred to this at the end of his letter to John, makes a wry allusion to Alison and ends on a distinctly upbeat note:

> Cheerio old chap; it seems a long time till June the 28th; I hope you have lots of fun before then and will have completed your first thousand – not runs, wickets of course.

Mummy thinks this letter is hopeless; it is full of silly jokes; she is going to call me a bald old man because of what I said just now.

I don't feel old; I feel quite young and skittish and ready to take on that fellow Jones at anything.

Your very loving,
Daddy[11]

As well as containing a happy anticipation of a family holiday, the letter from James refers cheerfully to his work which, as we know from Alison's accounts, he often found troubling: 'I am going off this afternoon on an Engineering Geology trip into Derbyshire – Wyllie is coming with me, and a little boy called Dreyfus, a pupil at the Town Hall, who is my assistant nowadays on the Road and Bridge. He is a nice chap and very useful in respect of an Austin 7.'[12]

Within a month, however, James's zest had evaporated and he had sought a consultation with his cousin, Dr Harry Cooper, 'for his nerves and depression'. As a witness at the inquest into James's death, Dr Cooper told the court that he had: 'advised him to take a six months' rest, advice which a specialist confirmed. Mr Uttley went on holiday to France, and witness did not see him again. He was suffering from neurasthenia, which might affect the brain; he was run down, which made his work a big effort, and he was losing his sleep and power of concentration. There was no doubt his mind was unhinged at the time.'[13] James felt he was 'a badly broken reed'.

For many years, Alison was to try to convince herself, in a variety of ways, that she bore no responsibility for James's death. She frequently expressed her surprise that he could have done such a terrible thing; she remembered the travails of his work and that he did not like a fellow engineer called Kent.[14] She even wrote in her diary that if he had been called 'Jamie' instead of James, this would have helped him in his difficulties.[15] She also recalled on several occasions his 'agonies', even consoling herself during trying times that James was not there 'to be agonised'.[16]

It is probably indicative of Alison's feelings of guilt and remorse that she subsequently steadfastly refused to acknowledge the nature of James's death and avoided, as far as she could, ever referring to it. When she was interviewed as a successful author, she did sometimes refer to her husband's 'dying', or even to his 'sudden death', but mainly as a – misleading – explanation of her need to write. John, too, remained reticent about his father's suicide. A fellow pupil at Sedbergh remembers: 'The whole thing was very hush-hush. . . . John never once, to my recollection, made any reference to his father, nor do I ever remember Alison mentioning him, except once . . . when she made some passing remark.'[17]

In view of the close relationship that had existed between father and son, James's suicide must have dealt John a crushing blow. The tragedy occurred only six days after his sixteenth birthday – a bizarre piece of timing which Alison later resented keenly and which might suggest, at least symbolically, that ultimately the birth of the only son had led to the father's usurpation and death. The suicide of a parent often provokes, consciously or unconsciously, a feeling of guilt on the part of the surviving offspring. At some level, John must have asked himself why his apparently doting father had chosen to leave him so dramatically and irrevocably. The suffering and shame that John felt as a result of his father's suicide almost certainly helped to turn him into an insecure and often depressed young man. Although Alison, as we shall see, undoubtedly played a major part in this unhappy process, James's death may well have started the rot. Certainly, the lively, happy boy shown in earlier family photographs became increasingly wary and morose, developing the nervous habit of suddenly looking over one shoulder as if on his guard.

The Uttley family at large were naturally deeply troubled by James's death. They tended, however, to put the blame upon Alison. Martin Byers remembers his mother Emily's 'distress at hearing the news by 'phone. She was told that a note had been found in James's office. . . . The note stated that he had gone into the river below the bridge, and contained some statement to the effect that his death would mean one less mouth to feed.'[18] The Byers family believed that a relative shortage of money was one of the causes of friction between James and Alison. Martin Byers recalls Alison's 'habit of lamenting that they (the Uttleys) could never afford to do something or other which my family (who were far from rich) were able to do. I think that this trait was prompted by a feeling of regret, tinged, perhaps, by self-pity, rather than by jealousy.'[19] Certainly, Martin Byers had been a witness to domestic conflict between the two: 'James was a very patient, kind and gentle man, so he listened, and did not protest at the interruptions.' The Byers family as a whole 'held the view that James was allowed no peace at home, that he was driven to drown himself through worrying about money and constant nagging by Alison'.[20] It is evident that Alison's in-laws saw her as a dominating and demanding wife, who had hounded her frail and emotionally unstable husband to his death.

In the aftermath of James's death Alison felt haunted by the prospect of poverty. John's school fees had to be paid for and she had to provide enough money to maintain herself and him in reasonable comfort. She later wrote of this time, 'I remember considering ways of livelihood – to let rooms, or to have a little school.'[21]

The truth of the matter was that James had left Alison well provided for – at least in theory. He had drawn up his will in November 1926, appointing Alison and his brother-in-law Harold Armfield as joint executors. His estate was to be divided between Alison and John: Alison receiving four fifths and John a fifth, which was to be held in trust until he reached the age of twenty-five.[22]

The estate itself, according to the official valuation, was a substantial one. James had bought shares in a number of concerns including Crosse and Blackwell, the Union Commercial Investment Company and Abford Estates; he had purchased £200 of Victory Bonds and a small number of National Savings Certificates. The overall value of these holdings after his death was £1526. 1*s*. 11*d*. – some £200 more than their combined original purchase price. In addition, James owned 6150 shares in Lawrence Sugden's, had £1057. 16*s*. invested with the Halifax Building Society, Life Insurance worth £500, over £133 in the bank and Downs House – valued at £750. The net value of the estate, allowing for the paying off of debts of £165. 10*s*. 5*d*., was £5960. 13*s*. 9*d*.[23] Estate duty was levied at nearly £300, but this still left a very substantial residue, four fifths of it immediately at Alison's disposal.

The problem was that the great economic depression of the early 1930s made it impossible to realise these assets profitably. As share prices tumbled and firms went bankrupt, it appeared folly to sell investments at a greatly undervalued price. Some companies ceased paying dividends altogether. Alison was thus caught in a financial trap. She tried to sell a thousand of her Sugden shares through the good offices of George Uttley and Harold Armfield (Gertrude's husband), even indicating that she was prepared to drop the asking price from fifteen shillings to ten shillings per share 'in view of the loss last year and the present state of trade'.[24] Nothing came of this or other attempts, something she bitterly resented. She continued to feel that George Uttley, who managed Sugden's, was responsible for her inability to sell her shares and, moreover, that he ought to have bought her out as a gesture of family good will.

Alison clearly felt great anxiety in these circumstances. Inhibited from selling her investments, without any certain prospect of receiving dividends and denied James's salary, she was obliged to draw on her small capital. John's school fees were a particular problem. In November 1930 the governors of Sedbergh, hard-pressed by 'claims for extra help at the present time', were unable to increase John's scholarship by more than twenty pounds. Alison wrote an urgent letter to George Uttley, saying that she would have to find £120 per year instead of the fifty pounds she had expected.[25] George, recognising himself as John's only surviving godfather, told Harold Armfield that 'of course I am prepared to help but I can't do it all'.[26]

In the event, very little financial help seems to have been provided by

George Uttley and James's five hundred pounds life insurance policy was rapidly devoured by the estate duty, the funeral expenses and the raising of an eighty pound loan. Alison was obliged to take in two female teachers from the local high school as 'paying guests at £2 per week each'.[27] She doubtless felt this to be an indignity. Certainly, she remained convinced that her Uttley in-laws had given her insufficient support. In June 1931 she wrote angrily to Harold Armfield, 'I cannot understand why you have not written re. the division of the estate. I think it is extremely unkind of you to give me no help at all in my difficulties.'[28] A few years later she wrote to him bluntly, presenting some of her problems:

> As co-trustee for John, you ought to know that the investment settled on him appears to be a failure. The Union Commercial Investment Trust has paid no dividend since 1931, – it should pay £34 a year, – we have had nothing.
>
> It was valued, you may remember, at £129% at James's death, and now it has dropped to £35%, – a loss to us of nearly £400. I have recently made enquiries about it & find it very bad. The stockbroker says it ought to be sold or we may lose every penny.
>
> It is a thousand pities it was not sold in 1930, or invested in trustee stock for John. . . . This is the third failure on the list.[29]

Alison, surrounded by her fundamentally disapproving in-laws, may well have had intimations of these future difficulties at James's funeral. She was to receive, however, comfort and hope from an unexpected source:

> At the funeral, when I felt lost in a nether world of blackness and horror, as I stood by the open grave, I looked up and saw Professor Alexander standing a short distance away in the cemetery. His big, wide-awake hat, his flowing Ulster, his brown, kind eyes gave me a flood of hope and courage. He was the only alive person in the midst of death. I went across and kissed him. Never did a hand stretched to the drowning help as he helped me at that moment. Strength came at once to my heart.[30]

Immediately after the funeral, Professor Alexander wrote Alison a loving and supportive letter, telling her:

> I cannot tell you how sorry I am for what has happened – sorry for the loss of a good life, & sorry for you that you lose your life-companion and have to bear such grief. You have always shown me such affectionate kindness that I could not do less than stand by you today; but it is a satisfaction to me to think that my presence was comforting to you. . . . Fortitude (which I know you have) will bring you help . . .

you will count me among the friends who care for you. Do
not answer this letter, but believe me.

Yours affectionately,
S. Alexander[31]

The encouragement of Professor Alexander, who also gave her some
financial help, was crucial to the fulfilment of Alison's writing plans.
Perhaps the death of James, who had dismissed *The Country Child* as
'rubbish', was an unexpected liberation. At any rate, she felt that
'Strength came at once into my heart and in the sorrowful days that
followed when I replanned my life, I decided to write in earnest.'[32]

CHAPTER TWELVE

Living Alone, 1931–33

Things are desperately low now I have to draw on
capital, and I must earn some money to carry on.
Besides I am only really happy when I am writing,
so I will try to begin tonight.

ALISON UTTLEY, diary, 20 January 1933

The years following James's death provided Alison with the greatest
challenges of her life. She had to make the difficult adjustment of living
alone, as well as trying to reconcile herself to the uncomfortable fact of
her husband's suicide. This was a painful process, but a necessary one.
At the same time, she had to be both mother and father to her son
John, whose private education was a heavy extra financial burden.
Making ends meet, while often struggling with a feeling of poverty,
became one of Alison's over-riding preoccupations during these years.
While she sought to rearrange her private life, she also tried desperately
to establish herself as a successful writer. The urgency with which she
approached this objective is an indication of her need to assert her
talents as well as that of earning badly needed money for herself and
her son. The breakthrough that she achieved in 1931 with the
publication of *The Country Child* was thus of tremendous significance
for her. The warm reception for this deeply felt, autobiographical
book and the feeling that she had 'arrived' in a modest way as an
author may have encouraged Alison to begin keeping a diary from
January 1932. Her diaries, written in blue ink within solid hardback
volumes, provide an extraordinarily detailed and intimate record of her
life until the end of 1971.

One of the ways in which Alison dealt with the pain of James's
suicide was to visit his grave and to try to communicate with him. She
gained some reassurance from these visits:

My darling's birthday. I took flowers, snowdrops, violets and scarlet
anemones to his grave. It was all very still, and I could hear him speak
to me. 'Little Bimbo, I love you. I'm all right, dear', and I told him
too that we are 'going on', loving him always. . . . I put a few
snowdrops from my drawing room bunch among his, to tell him
about the room, the sounds and the secrets and the feel of the writing
table; and I brought back a few violets which had lain on his cross.[1]

At other times she consoled herself that the cemetery 'felt so peaceful, and I realised how happy are the dead. The grave was beautiful.'[2] And again: 'I went into the Cemetery, thinking very sadly "He, poor darling, will be there, always there." The grave was so nice, the atmosphere of the graveyard was soothing and beautiful. I had a prayer for him and a little talk to him and came away.'[3]

For all these attempts to reassure herself that James was happy and that she need thus feel no guilt, she was at various times overcome by the pain of what had happened. At a church service on Whit Sunday in 1932 she found the words '"the quick and the dead", most tragic, so that I felt a shiver of horror'.[4] Each anniversary of her husband's suicide was particularly painful and at various times she was overcome with fright at the memory of the tragedy.[5]

She dreamt often and vividly about her dead husband. Several times during the months of April and May 1933, she dreamt that she was on holiday with James in France, or sitting on the sand beside him, trying to explain to other people that although he looked very much alive, even 'jolly', he was really dead.[6] On another occasion she dreamt that James was singing to her, 'You are the one I love the best.'[7]

Sometimes her dreams had an alarming physical quality, involving a close triangular relationship between mother, father and son. In these dream sequences, John is close to his parents as they have direct and loving contact, rather like a voyeur or even a substitute lover and husband:

> John and I with James in the middle sitting on a wall at Castle Top in hot sunshine. James's sleeves rolled up. I leaned across and laid my face on his bare arm. I saw the veins, the hairs shining, the ruddy healthy colour and I kissed it, and smelled the smell of his dear flesh. I knew suddenly that Death shadowed him. 'You won't do it, darling, will you?' I asked, and he laughed aloud and kissed us both. 'As if I would, when I have my two dears,' said he. Alas! I awoke and lay with aching heart, puzzled and grief-stricken.[8]

A year later she had another vivid and explicit dream: 'James sitting low down by a table, I leaned over and he drew me down to his arms and kissed me. Our lips clung as if he were drinking life, – there we clung in a long passionate beautiful kiss, never moving. John I knew was near, but I did not see him, although I wondered what he thought. I woke happy with the feeling of the kiss on my lips.'[9]

Despite the inner torment which these, and many other, dreams revealed, Alison gradually recovered her zest for life and expressed a growing optimism. Characteristically, her intimate communion with nature was instrumental in this process of recovery. A significant turning point was reached a little more than a year after James's suicide, when she walked through the winter landscape of a nearby park, later noting in her diary that 'There is nothing more lovely than a grove of silver birches in Winter. The company, the intimately talking company of rose-silver trunks, slender and straight, with tiny delicate twigs, so fine that beyond them all a massive beech trunk shines out through the mist of all those boughs, like a green and grey light from beyond.'[10] Trees had always been of great importance in Alison's life; she readily recognised their living, almost human, qualities and could feel physically comforted by them:

> I leaned against my oak tree, and had a little prayer. I felt its affection and its strength. I put my lips to a warm red bud of a lime tree, it seemed humanly alive. It was so lovely in the winter sunshine. Nature seemed to speak to me. There was a smell of growth . . . which filled me with happiness. This is the first day I have felt that vitality and joy of living which I possess so intensely. It seemed to wake up with the sun in the wood.[11]

After this healing contact with nature, Alison's diaries are full of the most beautiful descriptions of the countryside near her home at Higher Downs:

> The willows are the liveliest soft green, a dreamy love-in-the-mist kind of green, the beeches a rich brown with their many pointed buds, only a few of which are out yet. Oaks are ruddy with bud clusters, and I noticed the ash, its tips pointing upward to the blue sky, its trunk with long parallelograms like lattice work. Alders have little green fans, like those old-fashioned hand fans which decorated Victorian parlours.[12]

As a result she often writes that she feels 'jolly and young' or 'rapturously happy, adoring the world . . . the world of the sun and shade, of trees and flowers'.[13] At other times she is so happy that she feels immortal. She gives thanks to God for her son, for roses in her garden, for books, for music, for any number of small but important pleasures. On bonfire night in 1932 she felt inspired: 'Blue lights and fountains fall from the sky, sudden flickers and bangs, shouts of children, and hisses of fire. . . . Little Bimbo sitting in her chair, listening to Jack Payne's band, her foot beating time, her face smiling – absurd infant!'[14]

On 15 December 1932, two days before her birthday, she returned from buying some coloured candles at Woolworth's in high spirits: 'The piano on the wireless is playing a tripping Russian air . . . and I declare the canary has awakened and is dancing in the cage. . . . Again the music ripples like a magic stream which runs uphill and down, and the little shuffles begin again. Oh Life! Isn't it fun! I terribly love life, and the feeling of wildness that surges through me.'[15]

Two weeks later she was to declare, as she looked back over the dying year, 'I am so thankful for this spot in a spinning world, in the great stretch of ether.'[16] Even the rejection, and there were many during these years, of a piece she wrote called 'The Renaissance' in February 1933, produced a spirited response: 'It would make me despair if I were not an optimist, or rather a "Don't care-er". I have had so many ups and downs, so I just think of the solid rock of the earth down below and the bright stars up above, and our atomic struggling here, and nothing matters, at least such small things as this.'[17]

With John away at Sedbergh school, however, Alison often felt great loneliness and sometimes became deeply depressed. Although she had always been an active person, she now began to fill her life almost to bursting with a large number of interests and pastimes. Apart from her ever increasing commitment to writing, she was an enthusiastic, though sometimes erratic, gardener. She enjoyed shopping expeditions and the tracking down of bargains, and found much comfort in the cheapness and 'gaiety' of the displays at her local Woolworth's. She watched cricket at Old Trafford whenever she could and read hungrily and comprehensively, mostly borrowing her books from the Boots' library. She went to exhibitions, fêtes, sales of work and public lectures. She found the theatre too expensive for all but the rarest of visits. Although she went more frequently to the cinema, she agonised in May 1932 over the admission fee of one shilling and sixpence, considering it far too much to pay, but ultimately surrendered to her impulse and bought a ticket.[18] The radio was a great solace and she listened with enthusiasm to talks on a wide variety of subjects. She found a particular and lasting satisfaction in the broadcasts of classical music. She responded passionately to the works of many composers, although Brahms was a particular favourite, and felt that 'music can give me an exhilaration and exquisite happiness beyond anything else, beyond poetry, beyond human love. They played Lady Greensleeves this afternoon, and I cried, it made my heart ache, not with happiness, but with the forgotten things.'[19]

Sometimes she was comforted by old memories. In January 1933, having been ill in bed with influenza for a fortnight, nursed by 'John who slips in and out, smiling', she wrote in her diary: 'Lately I have slept well, and when awake, I have had a seraphic feeling of happiness, a sensation of bliss which I connect with lying in the Parlour Bedroom at C. Top, years ago, when I arrived and was cosseted after a stormy term or difficulties in lodgings.'[20]

Formal religion was another rich source of contentment, even though she exercised a critical vigilance when it came to sermons. In October 1932 she attended morning service and later wrote 'the quietness of the service helped me. Sometimes I pray, sometimes I dream, or a lovely word catches my attention and I feel exhilarated and happy. Today it was the shadow of God's wings, and for long I thought of the rest in the shadow of those great feathery wings stretched across Space.'[21]

She also derived reassurance from the stars, particularly from her favourite constellation, Orion. She would often search the night skies anxiously for it: 'There was a slip of a moon, like a horn, a thin curved hunting horn, or a fingernail, or the horn of a celestial cow, dropped in that blue and gold field. Nowhere could I see my star. Then suddenly I saw it, in the S[outh] W[est], quite near the lovely moon. Ten black rooks flew across, just missing the moon. I knew I had seen perfection; it was one of those moments, always to be remembered.'[22]

Alison took comfort in the observance of superstitions that were part of her upbringing and whose familiarity was reassuring. She often bowed three times to the new moon to bring her luck. On 1 December 1932 she 'welcomed the new month, the month I love, with a kiss'.[23] The month of April was also a favourite, to be welcomed lovingly, 'Lovely darling April has come. I ran down to open the door to let her in yesterday.'[24]

Alison's superstitions had their roots deep in her country childhood. But they also reflected her desperate need to propitiate various gods and to make the future secure for herself and her son, a future she saw as threatened by their chronic shortage of ready money. She felt panic at the prospect, despite her early experience as the child of parents who had struggled to make a bare living. Her diaries brim with self-pity and with graphic illustrations of her impoverished state. She was 'thrilled' to be given some free oranges by a greengrocer, once she would not buy Brussels sprouts because she thought the price too dear and she considered chocolate biscuits to be an extravagance.

She likened herself to Cinderella, denied herself a birthday cake on 17 December 1932 and agonised in June of that year over whether to buy a new frock for a visit to her publisher.[25] Once while shopping she was left with fivepence ha'penny and was determined to make it last, buying some cheese and saving the remaining twopence for her Sunday newspaper, the *Observer*. When visiting her friends the Coopers, she felt herself to be poor and a nobody, at the same time vowing that she would succeed as an author despite everything.[26] On one occasion she made herself ill with worry over a missing one pound note. Despite the pleasure she derived from the radio, she felt despair in March 1933 when presented with a bill of twenty-nine shillings, the year's rental.

Alison's experiences made her conscious that she could now vividly imagine the sorrows of the very poor.[27] Her diaries contain several examples of her desperate attempts to find extra money. As well as taking in lodgers, she went to Manchester to sell the gold bracelet James had given her as his wedding present and a valuable diamond, and in December 1933, she advertised her services as a tutor. Nor could she derive security from the thought of the investments she had inherited. Abford Estates failed in March 1933. In June she learnt that the Halifax Building Society was reducing its dividend and in July that Crosse and Blackwell had made further losses. It is hardly surprising that when sums of money arrived unexpectedly, she was apt to weep with relief.

One such windfall came at the end of John's school career when, on top of winning his rugby colours and the Sterling verse prize for sonnets, he carried off the Kitchener Scholarship to Cambridge University. Its £110 meant that she could now manage to continue her son's education without help from anyone – not that such assistance seems to have been forthcoming.[28]

Her parents were dead and she only saw her brother Harry once during these years. Her in-laws gave her some financial support, but it was minimal and mostly resented. She continued to harbour a long-lasting grudge against George Uttley, then managing director of Sugden's, for his refusal to buy or dispose of her shares and later bitterly resented that he was paid a pension by the firm. Gertrude sent her ten shillings in March 1933 and twelve shillings in November of that year, donations that Alison would have liked to have rejected angrily but which she prudently kept. It is clear that she saw James Uttley's sisters, particularly Gertrude and Emily, as unsympathetic towards her, even critical. In October 1932 she resented the fact that Gertrude had sent her 'a cruel letter, accusing me of lack of courage, hurting me terribly'.[29] Alison felt the accusation to be quite untrue, insisting that she had started again and had begun to rediscover her joy in living. She came to resent and dread Emily's visits, once interrupting her assertion that it was a very good thing for John to help Alison with the housework by replying: 'That's what some people say – "It is excellent for you not to have to pay income tax, and delightful that you don't have my worry with servants. It is a good thing for your boy to do housework all the holidays, and good training that neither of you can have any new clothes or go to the theatre. It is very healthy to have no meat, and so on." I get sick of this.'[30]

The only Uttley relative with whom Alison unfailingly felt comfortable was Aunt Lizzie. She enjoyed her occasional visits to this aunt of her dead husband and in August 1932 accepted an invitation for a meal there, conscious that it was made out of the kindness of Aunt Lizzie's heart: 'Let us invite Alice and John, it will save them a Sunday Dinner.'[31]

Estranged from most of her relatives in the early 1930s, Alison increasingly came to depend on John for emotional satisfaction, imbuing their relationship with a physical, even romantic quality which was sometimes very embarrassing for him. It is impossible not to feel great compassion for Alison, swept along by her emotions. Her diaries, however, leave no doubts that the relationship between mother and son verged on the incestuous. In January 1932, when John was aged seventeen and in his penultimate year at Sedbergh, Alison described bringing him breakfast in bed: 'He sits or rather leans against the pillows with his head on the top rail. . . . His top button is undone, his sleeves up, and he contentedly nibbles the toast. . . . A crumpled blue collar and a soiled handkerchief are on the chest of drawers. He glances at me, with whimsical twitches of his mouth, and loving amused eyes.'[32] The next morning, before John had to leave to go back to school, Alison and he 'had a charming chat in bed this morning, and I lay in his arms and told him my dreams'.[33]

When in September of that year John left for his final year at Sedbergh, Alison wrote a detailed description of their last evening and morning together before his departure: 'I felt like a child in a story. We played cards, I boiled the copper kettle and made tea and we laughed and played together. Today we rushed about all morning, and John went. We had a great hug and kiss in my bedroom, bless him. At the station he was shy and diffident, peeping over the heads of three other fellows. I felt lost and lonely . . . and then came sadly home.'[34]

When she visited him at Sedbergh two months later, she went with John to his study: '"A kiss," I demand when the door is shut, and John kisses me softly lest the boys should hear.'[35]

So intensely did Alison love John that she was soon obliged to recognise the growing ambiguity of her feelings for him. In May 1933 she saw John 'off from the gate, after long clinging kisses, when he reminded me of James. Then I gardened for over three hours, *hard*.'[36] Seven months later Alison recorded in her diary: 'Last night I dreamed James came into my room . . . and said "I have changed my things all ready, darling", and kissed me. The sweetness of the kiss woke me up, such a loving kiss. I feel as if James and John were one nowadays.'[37]

It must have been immensely difficult for John to be the object of so much adoration, let alone to have been perceived as indistinguishable from his dead father. Yet he seems to have connived in some measure, writing Alison affectionate letters to 'no ordinary Mimbles', regularly sending her Valentine cards, bringing her breakfast in bed and helping her with the housework and, on the last night before he went up to Cambridge in 1933, sitting in the living-room in Downs House 'in James's old suit, his face half smiling with amusement, his eyebrows dark lines'.[38]

It is clear that in the immediate aftermath of James's suicide, the relationship between Alison and John deepened into one of extraordinary, clinging love. Although both may have found considerable satisfaction in their intimacy, John was to develop into a young man who was uncertain how to relate to other women and who felt that he owed his first loyalties to his needy and over-demanding mother.

It is interesting that, although Alison flirted so dangerously with her son's affections, she remained extraordinarily prudish in matters of sex. She was shocked when the wife of one of her friends in Cheshire, Professor Carney, struck out for an independent emotional life, calling her 'a horrible wife'. She was very disapproving of young girls wearing make-up or experimenting in their relationships. Later in life she was to confess that the life style of Rebecca West, H.G. Wells's mistress, 'frightened' her. She often put aside books, particularly novels, as being 'over-sexed and horrible'.[39] In 1970 she regretted that she was living in an 'over-sexed world'.

With one or two exceptions, the circle in which she moved at this time offered few threats to her sense of what was proper. Her closest friends remained GL and LM, both spinsters and both warm and encouraging. Alison took great pleasure from their visits and from going to stay with them. She seems to have enjoyed herself most with GL, finding her 'wonderful' and describing her as 'fresh and lovely', though she equally looked forward to the visits of LM, preparing her room with care and providing her with good food and a warm welcome. She often refers to LM as tastefully dressed, beautiful to look at and great fun, although her friendship with GL seems to have included more robust merriment as well as more uncertainty. Both were at a distance, however, and lacking easy access to them, Alison devoted a lot of attention on a daily basis to her Scottie dog, Hamish.

She also seems to have visited friendly neighbours a good deal. Amongst local friends were the Cooper and Kessler families, Professor and Mrs Carney, Lorna Johnson and a Miss Hackforth. These relationships were not always easy ones. Alison dismissed Lorna Johnson as inconsequential and frequently found Miss Hackforth's idealism a trial. Although she recognised the latter's kind intentions towards her, she once refused to walk with her on the grounds that it was too much like a formal school crocodile, privately dismissed her interests as 'arid' and sometimes took great pleasure in shocking her. Even the Cooper family she criticised for their atheism.

Interestingly, she took considerable pleasure from the friendship of two titled women, Lady Crossley and Lady Boyd-Dawkins. Of the two, she enjoyed the company of Lady Boyd-Dawkins the most. Lady Crossley, from the family that manufactured Crossley cars, sometimes talked to her helpfully about her financial affairs. But Alison also had criticisms of her: that she hurried her during games of patience and that she was particularly assertive and awkward when they went together to watch cricket at Old Trafford. Lady Crossley, however, had her uses. She gave Alison lifts in her car, particularly when they went together to watch cricket, and, after Alison had spent ten days in London in the late summer of 1933, lent her money to enable her to pay off the small debts she had incurred there.

Despite her financial worries, Alison did not deny herself holidays during these years. She sometimes stayed with GL at Clitheroe, ventured further afield to the beautiful town of Ledbury and during both 1932 and 1933 spent several days in London, where she not only visited publishers but also spent a good deal of her time seeing the sights and visiting the art galleries, museums and shops. At home she did most of her shopping in Altrincham, sometimes travelling to Manchester. She felt that Manchester was still a dirty and oppressive city, with 'scum-covered canals', and she occasionally commented unfavourably upon the Jewish shopkeepers with whom she did business there.

Politically, Alison seems to have moved away from the vague socialism of her earlier years and certainly away from the more rigorous variety that her husband had supported. Although she was sympathetic towards the millions of those thrown out of work by 'the great depression', she had become generally more ambivalent in her political attitudes. She was once astonished to find that Miss Hackforth thought her 'a staunch Conservative and a Church woman . . . I who am the greatest vacillator in all things'.[40] As the two women walked, Alison clearly resented the fact that the conversation prevented her from fully appreciating the beauties of the trees and fields. A month later, she was asked by the earnest Miss Hackforth whether she was interested in humanity: '*No*, said I, I don't care if it's wiped out – I hoped that would shock her. She *did* look amazed. Confound it, but she isn't as bad as Emily. These Liberals with their Nonconformist consciences bore me stiff.'[41]

Alison reserved a good deal of her venom on political matters for Emily, resenting her pacifist views and putting them down to the 'malevolent' influence of the *Manchester Guardian*. If Alison had any political position of any consequence during these years, it was the straightforward and robust one of the committed Patriot. It was this attitude which enabled her to approve of Ramsay MacDonald's agreement of 1931 to lead a National Government to deal with the financial crisis which faced the nation.

If Alison showed little sustained interest in political developments, she had at last immersed herself in her writing, keeping steadily to her resolution 'to write in earnest' and producing at an almost feverish rate during the early 1930s. In 1931, the year after James's death, she achieved her greatest success to date with the publication of *The Country Child*. Despite her husband's scorn when she had first shown him the manuscript, Alison had clung to her belief that the book had value. It was, however, sent to several publishers before Faber finally made her an offer for it. She was to confess three years after its publication that at one stage she thought it would never be taken by any publisher,[42] but that to have the book published was 'once my heart's desire'.[43]

The Country Child is essentially a book of fond autobiographical reminiscence. The country child is Alison herself, presented as Susan Garland. The choice of the family name Garland itself is significant, with its implication of floral, garlanded achievement and its incorporation of the word 'land' within it. There is much naïvety as well as great beauty in the writing, and although painful episodes are described, they are all too often glossed over by the bright-eyed and pervasive optimism of the child, Susan. Occasional false notes are struck, as in the naming of the nearby villages of Raddle and Dangle. Despite these blemishes, the book is ultimately a triumph; nostalgic, whimsical and sufficiently honest to captivate the reader.

Reviewers certainly reacted favourably to it, even though a few misgivings were expressed. *The Times Literary Supplement* described the book as 'a series of loosely-connected chapters, any of which might stand alone', but went on to state that 'Mrs Uttley writes simply and clearly; and it is pleasant to follow her through all the rooms of the old farmhouse.' The reviewer felt, though, that 'with all this, we never live inside her mind'. The review concludes by saying, however, that 'Mrs Uttley has written a pleasant book of an unusual kind.'[44] The *Manchester Guardian* told its readers that 'Should you desire release for a blessed hour or two from the brain-racking consideration of Five (or fifty) Year Plans . . . then hasten to get hold of, or preferably buy, "The Country Child", sink into its atmosphere, and savour its charms . . . Mrs Uttley in her little masterpiece, has passed on to us a deep yearning for that peace.'[45] *The Times Educational Supplement* compared her writing with that of Laura Ingalls Wilder and the *Evening News* said, 'Mrs Uttley writes with knowledge and with deep affection, and to those who care for good writing, married to quiet ways and rural life, her book can be warmly recommended.'[46] *Time and Tide* agreed that 'Mrs Uttley writes well, and she knows the country through and through. The book possesses charm and atmosphere and, what is much more important, it contains an element of humour. It is rather a pity that Mrs Uttley did not allow her humour more scope.'[47]

The success of *The Country Child* gave Alison the confidence to persevere with her writing plans. It brought her a modest measure of fame and she was pleased when her hairdresser expressed her pleasure at perming the hair of 'a real author'. Apart from being one of her best-loved and most profitable books, *The Country Child* gave Alison an invaluable base at Faber. A year after the publication of *The Country Child* Faber published her second book for them, *Moonshine and Magic*. Alison eagerly anticipated the publication of this book of fairy tales and was delighted by the illustrations by Will Townsend. The arrival of the advance copies of the book at Downs House on 15 September 1932 was an occasion for great celebration:

> Joy! Moonshine and Magic came. The big parcel lay in the hall. John met me as I came from Manchester to carry my things and tell me the news. We undid the knots, eager and thrilled, on the drawing room couch. Bright colours peeped out from the brown, and we cried 'Oh! Oh! How lovely!' Such a gay charming book. I love it, the cover, the size, the coloured pictures, and my own dear stories. I read them again and adored them.[48]

The next day a cheque arrived for *Moonshine and Magic* as well as proofs of the illustrations for *The Story of Fuzzypeg the Hedgehog*, which was to be published later that year – the last of the Little Grey Rabbit stories to be brought out by Heinemann. On 17 September Alison and John went into Manchester to celebrate their good fortune and to spend a little of the money: 'We rushed off to M/C, and went to the Rylands Library – a gem in dark Manchester. Silence, books, marvellous jewelled books, illuminations, manuscripts, and all those alcoves with chairs and tables ready for the students. A marvel of a place, a secret heart in the busy street. I bought "The Bridge" in honour of "Moonshine and Magic".'[49]

Moonshine and Magic was very favourably received. The magazine *Everyman* thought the stories 'deliciously entertaining'.[50] The *Listener* commented that 'Alison Uttley has achieved a simplicity without sentimentality which is so difficult to obtain when writing for young children',[51] and the *Manchester Guardian* thought that the book showed 'she has the rare gift of writing imaginative stories in simple prose, that retains its dignity and never stoops to conquer the child's mind'.[52] The *New Statesman* found the tales 'Full of charm and whimsicality',[53] though the *Spectator* added a cautionary note, remarking that 'some of the stories are rather slight; but the best of them are exactly what they should be'.[54]

The success of the book brought an interviewer from the *Manchester Evening News* to Alison's door, 'a dark young man' who flattered her by making a comparison between herself with her physics degree and

Lewis Carroll, the mathematician turned children's author. When the article appeared on 28 October 1932, however, Alison was enraged by its tone:

> A most impertinent and patronising article. . . . All day I have felt sick at being called 'a kindly woman who lives in a house in the Higher Downs'. . . . I wrote a wrathful letter to the paper, but that doesn't help . . . I must brave it out. One ought to keep as clear of newspapers as of the law. I felt so unhappy that I thought I must leave here and go to London where one is not questioned and stared at.[55]

A few weeks after the favourable reception of *Moonlight and Magic*, Heinemann published *The Story of Fuzzypeg the Hedgehog*. Alison had hoped that this, the fourth Little Grey Rabbit tale, would meet with success and 'put some more butter on my bread!' Compared with *The Country Child* and *Moonshine and Magic* this book, once more illustrated by Margaret Tempest, seems to have evoked little interest. One of the few favourable reviews appeared in the Christmas edition of the *Bookman*, even though Alison must have been irritated by what she would have perceived as an unflattering comparison: 'The delightful fashion set many years ago by Miss Beatrix Potter . . . is being most ably followed by Alison Uttley and Margaret Tempest. . . . Certainly no nursery should be without a copy of this dainty little volume.'[56]

Alison had put a lot of her energies and hopes into this book. She had worked hard to get the manuscript right, altering it quite heavily, and had only fixed on the final title after an unsuccessful draft title which began 'Hedgehog and ?'[57] Heinemann had published the third of the Little Grey Rabbit books, *The Great Adventure of Hare* a year earlier. Alison had insisted that Dwye Evans should publish *The Great Adventure of Hare* before the Fuzzypeg book because, in her view, it followed on from *How Little Grey Rabbit Got Back Her Tail*. So anxious had she been to facilitate the publication of *The Great Adventure of Hare* that she had agreed to an alteration in the text to clear up the apparent problem of the fox misreading a label: 'Hare cannot tell a lie, and call it scent! That's the difficulty.'[58] In what had become a familiar pattern, Alison's original title for this book, 'Hare Goes a-Journeying', was again dispensed with before publication.

But for all the energy and imagination which went into production of these four Little Grey Rabbit volumes, Heinemann felt they were not worth persevering with. One reason for this was Margaret Tempest's demand for a larger fee for future illustrations. Heinemann recall that 'there had been some small difficulty with Margaret Tempest over her financial remuneration for the drawings'.[59] Alison certainly felt that her illustrator's intransigence had dealt the series a fatal blow: 'M.T. refused to do new pictures for Heinemann, and wrote a very rude letter, which finished it off.'[60] This early misfortune may well have laid the foundation for Alison's belief that Margaret was a difficult partner with whom to do business. At the same time Heinemann, in her view, were not free from blame for the series' demise and four decades later she wrote, a little unfairly, 'It is strange they always start a series and let it dwindle away as they did with the Grey Rabbit books forty years ago.'[61]

The Heinemann decision to end the series was a serious blow for Alison. A further setback came when Faber, in December 1932, rejected her book *The Secret Spring*. Alison had sent this off with high hopes on 29 November 1932, but when she visited London early in December she entered the publisher's offices in Russell Square 'feeling rather nervous'. Her description of her meeting with Richard de la Mare shows how insecure she felt and how difficult it was for her to take rejection:

> Waited in the little room, and then shown into R. de la Mare's room. He came forward, staring very hard, pale, thin, with moustache, slightly aggressive and distinctly curious about me. 'I'm sorry to say that our reader's report is not favourable.' I felt more contemptuous than disappointed. I *know* it is good. . . . I kept cheerful and laughed, told him of John, asked his baby's name. She is called 'Tillie' and some strange long name. He promised to read the book 'if I have time'. I really felt rather sick about it. I went to the National Gallery and had a chat with the lovely old people there, who told me they had a thousand times worse things to contend with.[62]

Interestingly, after Alison had sent off *The Secret Spring* to another publisher and had it rejected in February 1933, her comment was that she did not care, and that 'It wasn't terribly good.' Faber's opinion that her manuscript was not worthy of publication rankled, however, and for some time she harboured considerable resentment against Richard de la Mare: 'I don't like R. de la Mare, he is weak and uncertain, and irritable, too young and inexperienced for his job. I shan't go there again, I didn't like it.'[63] She even wished, in her pain, for 'a heavenly dart' to be directed at Faber. In view of her long and highly successful association with Faber, Alison's early irritation with the firm, and in particular her misgivings about Richard de la Mare, are ironic. But they are also very revealing and clearly illustrate how ill-established she felt herself to be as a writer by the end of 1932.

In January of 1933 Alison was determined to write as much and as widely as possible. On 20 January, the day John left for the Easter term at Sedbergh, she recorded her writing plans in her diary:

> This term I want to write two or three 'stories', to sketch out an animal book on the lines of 'The Wind in the Willows', to try to start a

novel, and to put into order the 'little pigs' book, besides writing for My Magazine and the other children's papers. I must do some work each day. Things are desperately low now I have to draw on capital, and I must earn some money to carry on. Besides I am only really happy when I am writing, so I will try to begin tonight.[64]

Alison's commitment to her self-imposed schedule was remarkable. First writing a manuscript on lined paper, she would then leave it for a while before rereading it critically and deciding what to alter. 'It is fresh to me, and I see the faults. I rewrite, always cutting or changing. This is something I enjoy very much. This is the real writing of the story. I make a pattern for my own pleasure . . . the result must be a satisfaction to one's inmost desires, one's secret life.'[65] She would then type up the final version. She wrote at all times of the day and often in the evening, although she sometimes admitted that she felt 'dull and stupid'. She still felt fundamentally unsure of her talents, wishing in February 1933 that she could write as well as H.E. Bates. By October of that year she had set herself the demanding task of writing four stories each week. For most of 1933, however, she faced consistent rejection from publishers and even from the children's magazines *New World* and *My Magazine*. Her anxieties about placing her work successfully were greatly increased by the news, at the end of October 1933, that *My Magazine* was closing down.

Alison produced a very large number of stories and articles during 1933, including: 'Susan does Homework', 'Cinnamon', 'Toady Lion', 'Shadow School', 'The Renaissance', 'Silver Tea', 'Jezebel', 'Midsummer Fair', 'Votes for Women – a sketch', 'The Baby Clinic', 'Lace in the Wood', 'The Little White Ass' and 'The Hedgehog and the Cornfield'.

She reacted to the numerous rejections of most of these pieces with her usual mixture of defiance and self-criticism. She agreed that her story 'The Baby Clinic' was 'stupid stuff', and confessed in the summer of 1933 that 'I tried to write last night, but the result wasn't *magic*, not as I want it to be.'[66] She achieved some successes, however. 'Mrs Nimble' was accepted for publication, *New World* magazine took 'A Cock and Bull Story' and 'Peter Pan', and *Blackie's Annual* published 'The Hedgehog and the Cornfield'.

Her greatest trial, however, was in trying to place her first Tim Rabbit story. Eventually published in 1937 by Faber under the title of *The Adventures of No Ordinary Rabbit*, the book was to be reprinted many times and to lead to the publication of four more Tim Rabbit stories. As a creation of Alison Uttley's imagination, Tim Rabbit has much in common with the even more successful and popular Sam Pig. Like Sam, Tim Rabbit is apt to tear his trousers on brambles and to get into various scrapes and adventures, invariably returning to a cosy cottage through whose open door wafts the comforting smell of baking and other homely scents.

Originally entitled 'No Other Rabbit', the typescript made over a dozen journeys to London publishers and back during 1933. So well-travelled did Tim Rabbit become that Alison felt sorry for the 'poor little chap, his legs are so tired running up and down'.[67] Perhaps her greatest disappointment came when William Collins rejected the book at the end of November 1933. Collins's reasons for declining the Tim Rabbit story, however, arose partly out of Alison's most significant success of 1933. With Heinemann no longer willing to publish the Little Grey Rabbit tales, Alison and Margaret Tempest had agreed to find another publisher. 'Someone suggested' to Alison that she should send *Squirrel Goes Skating* to Collins. This was a particularly happy choice since William Collins and his wife were already Grey Rabbit enthusiasts; this knowledge may also have encouraged Alison to try this publisher. At any rate, she received the news of Collins's decision with enormous relief: 'A jolly beginning, for there was a letter from Mr Collins, the publisher, telling me how much he likes the GR books, and saying he will continue publication. I felt on air, elated, happy, and I read the new Squirrel story and found it entrancing, one of the best.'[68]

Encouraged by this warm response, Alison had offered her Tim Rabbit typescript to William Collins who eventually wrote back courteously saying that he thought to publish the book would only jeopardise the success of the Little Grey Rabbit series.[69] Despite this tactical setback, the publishing relationship that developed between Alison and William Collins was to be one of the great bastions in a writing career about to gather an irresistible momentum.

CHAPTER THIRTEEN

Making Progress, 1934–36

> Sometimes I think 'Why write? Why work?', but
> then I feel dissatisfied. I *must* go on and produce
> and use my talents which have been hidden all
> these years.
>
> ALISON UTTLEY, diary, 15 August 1936

Alison Uttley wrote on the inside cover of her diary for 1934 'I will look
unto the everlasting hills from whence cometh my strength.' During the
next three years she was to display a remarkable resilience, coping with
the many difficulties of her private life and displaying an unquenchable
determination to establish herself still more securely as an author.

Her diaries for this period contain comparatively few references to her
dead husband. She dreamed much less of James, was less beset by
anguish and expressed fewer regrets over the tragedy of his death. On St
Valentine's Day 1934 she recalled that during the night she had dreamed
of him: 'he was kissing me in an empty room, quickly embracing me
before anybody came in. I reminded him he was dead, but he said he
didn't care, and he hurried on with his lovely warm human passionate
kisses. I glanced round, fearful lest anyone should see him but I suppose
he was invisible to others. Bless him.'[1]

Sometimes incidents prompted painful recollections of her husband's
suicide. She once wept after a radio reading of the death of Socrates; the
news of the death of the King of the Belgians on 19 February 1934 made
her identify with the grief of his queen, '"this time last week we were
doing this or that", she thinks'; a year later she was to feel a sharp pang
on seeing a 'suicidal Jew' in Manchester.[2] At other times she was put in
touch with the pleasures and complications of her married life in various
ways. In August 1934 she finished reading *Sons and Lovers*, noting that it
was 'too rambling and not quite "true" enough for me' and remarking,
interestingly, that the mother was 'too harsh' with the father.[3] She
mourned the death of her husband's Aunt Lizzie as the loss of 'another
link with James, for she admired and loved him and always spoke so
nicely of him'.[4] She also identified, tenderly and warmly, with the
feelings of her mother on her wedding day, fifty years before: 'Last
night I thought of my little sweet mother . . . how pretty she must have
been, and how simple and wide-eyed, and timid and brave, and how she

prayed to God to help her do the right, and be a blessing. It was so real, I could feel it.'[5]

On what would have been her Silver Wedding day in August 1936, she 'tried not to think of it, for such things bring pain, but I looked at James's photograph and saw the extreme delicacy and sensitiveness of his face, too frail for this world's turmoil'.[6] A month later, in what was perhaps a symbolic act of putting the past behind her and pressing on unencumbered by grief and doubt, she burnt 'thousands of love-letters, for I must not keep them . . . it was best to burn them, but it made me very very sad '.[7]

Alison's feelings for her son John retained much of their intensity, although she became a little less demanding of his time and attention. But she still felt lonely and depressed when he went back to Cambridge or when, towards the end of 1935, he went on a trip to Canada. The voyage to Canada provided John with a female friend, causing Alison to note tartly in her diary on 3 January 1936, 'John is out tonight, gone to see Miss Henderson, whom he met on the boat. La! La!' [8]

The relationship between mother and son remained an exceptionally close one. She fretted when there was too long a gap between the letters he sent her and confided a good deal in him, particularly asking for his advice and approval over her writing. She needed him to help her with the housework she either found too difficult herself, or which was not done by the succession of domestic servants she employed during these years. The quick turnover may have had something to do with the rate of pay, or perhaps these women recognised a hard taskmaster when they saw one. John seems to have given his help in the house without too much complaint and it was left to Alison to lament in June 1935 that perhaps he had only achieved a second-class result in his tripos examinations at Cambridge because he had done too much housework.[9] Certainly, John seems to have fulfilled a role that teetered between that of son, home help, husband and man servant. There is one piece of film showing him and his mother together and, although it was taken much later in their lives, for the 1975 BBC television programme *Alison Uttley and Little Grey Rabbit*, it is very revealing. The programme shows John, balding, good-looking, rather formal, ushering a group of visiting schoolchildren into Alison's presence at her house in Beaconsfield with a butler-like gravity. Other footage in this film shows him nervously pushing tobacco into his pipe, fiddling with his hands and looking at copies of the first Little Grey Rabbit books, commenting monosyllabically in a rather muffled voice, 'Yes' or, 'Fox'.[10]

The formality of John's public demeanour in his mother's presence was in inverse ratio to the deep feelings expressed in their personal relationship. He brought her breakfast in bed, often complimented her on her appearance (once telling her as they 'scurried off to Manchester, I in my new blue felt hat. "You look hot-stuff"')[11] and frequently went with her to social engagements near their home in Cheshire. On one visit to Lady Boyd-Dawkins, Alison and John were asked whom they knew: 'we said "Nobody. We are apart. We don't want to know people, it is much more fun."'[12] At no time were mother and son more companionable than at Christmas. On Christmas Day 1935, although Alison had earlier been ill, they managed to make a merry show, both cooking, preparing the room, giving each other presents and singing carols together:

> The drawing room is gay with the holly, decorated by John after I went to bed last night, and the mistletoe surrounding the lamp is the prettiest bunch I have ever seen. . . . John has been a marvel in this illness of mine, helping me and cheering me. I write it down, this special Christmas of 1935. At night we sang carols . . . a lovely time, I only humming, my throat was sore, J singing with a deep rich voice.[13]

Alison found parting from John especially difficult, describing him leaving for Cambridge in October 1934 thus: 'We had our little prayer, most beautiful and helpful, and a great kiss as he left the house. When the train went, I came sadly home, dawdling through Altrincham, loath to reach the lonely house. All day I struggled slowly and glumly.'[14] Kissing remained important for them, Alison recounting that on her birthday in 1934 'I worked hard, dusting and sweeping, and got John's breakfast, and then, when he called, went up for a birthday kiss. How happy I feel with him here!'[15] Sometimes such warm physical contact was embarrassing to them both, and when Alison saw John off on his voyage to Canada in August 1935, she confessed later 'I wanted to kiss him goodbye [in his cabin] but was shy, so we only kissed hurriedly on the dock, with many dockers passing.'[16]

Despite Alison's disappointment with John's upper second-class honours degree and her fear that this would limit him in his school teaching career to second-rate schools, he seems to have been successful enough at Cambridge. He won a two guinea prize for his academic work in November 1934 and in the summer of 1935 won his oar for rowing. Alison visited him several times at the university which was also, in a more modest way, her own; she enjoyed the physical beauty of the place and found the service in King's College Chapel 'beautiful, magical, ancient'. She had felt, six months after John went up to Cambridge, that he was rather disappointed with his life there. This feeling is not borne out by the testimony of one of John's best friends at Cambridge, Dick Frost. Frost, who had been at Sedbergh with John, persuaded him and another old school friend, Sam Cope, to join the artillery branch of the Cambridge University Officer Training Corps, where they had 'a lot of fun together'. Although Dick Frost considered that John enjoyed his time at Cambridge, he was also aware of his friend's lack of maturity and poise:

> I began to notice his social gawkiness and basic shyness and insecurity. He was never very good at beer drinking, and had an embarrassing habit of being sick in cinemas and other public places. An incident when we were in camp at Hythe sticks in my mind. Someone had stuck a French Letter on a bayonet, and John innocently wanted to know what on earth it was. He never seemed to have any girlfriends.[17]

John made several good friends at Cambridge, including two young men, Geoffrey Healey and David Paine. Alison met both, particularly liking the latter's 'serious face'. The connection with David Paine was to be of great significance to both their lives, for, a decade later, John was to marry David's sister, Helen. Helen Paine visited her brother at St John's, Cambridge and met John there. John also spent some summer holidays at the Paine's home in Guernsey. John 'grew to love Helen' during these years, according to the latter's sister, but 'she didn't return his love'.[18] No mention of this appears in Alison's diaries.

When John was close to graduating in the spring of 1936, both he and Alison became occupied with his future career. Schoolmastering was the most obvious profession to enter but Alison proved much more choosy than John, even snobbish, over the most appropriate school, advising him not to take a post at Newcastle Grammar School in the 'ugly industrial North'. She was also increasingly aware of the tensions that beset John, remarking as he punted her along the Cam that he 'looked rather anxious. He doesn't take life easily enough, he strains at things and is too conscious.'[19]

With John away at Cambridge, Alison contrived to keep herself busy with the host of activities she had so sensibly cultivated during the early years of her bereavement. Nonetheless she was sometimes overcome with depression, particularly when she was ill (she suffered the common cold badly) or worried by her relative lack of money. She continued often to feel lonely and abandoned, although she was mostly able to reconcile herself to her situation. Once, in October 1936, she was able to take comfort in the thought that she had a house full of her own books for company. In practical terms, Alison's periods of solitude were essential to her development as a writer, enabling her to reassess and reorder her internal world. Her diaries contain several, almost lyrical, descriptions of her life alone:

Pale milky sky with a white moon. Black boughs of pear trees with
fresh buds already forming. Light on the yellow chimneys and red
brick of a distant house. In my room the wireless plays Liszt, a
lightning ripple of notes. My tea tray with the flowered teaset, and the
important hot water jug, stands waiting on the chest of drawers,
beside a vase of incomparable anemones, a bowl of oranges and
bananas and John's photograph.

   On the mantlepiece more anemones . . . and John's grey jug of
violets. The photograph of Castle Top. The funny laughing picture of
John, his silver cups, the box of matches, and blue china treasures
from Castle Top's double-bedded room. Above them the St Francis
picture, and the adoration of Richard II. A medicine bottle and glass,
and a box of tablets – a full complement.[20]

A few months later, while a great wind howled around the house on St
Crispin's Day, she wrote: 'It was delightful to touch the piano again. I
didn't go for my usual walk, but sat by the fire *enjoying* life. A great fire,
a cosy chair, roses in the vases, my knitting, Hamish by my side. I felt
carefree, a curious feeling which I only get in winter, – as if I were on an
island.'[21] She also drew great comfort from her bed, often having her
breakfast there, and once writing joyously in her diary, 'Bed last night
was exquisite; cosy, warm, the nicest place on earth! I lay enjoying it!'[22]
Despite these pleasures, she was conscious of her difficulties in recon-
ciling the comfortable lost world of her childhood with the harsh
demands of her widowhood, once remarking when the manuscript of
her book *Cuckoo Cherry-Tree* was returned from a publisher with the
criticism that it was too old for children and too young for grown-ups,
'How true! That is my fault. I live a fairy tale, in-between life, dangling
myself on the rail between the flowery fields of childhood and the arid
plains of grown-ups.'[23]

   One of Alison's chief adult preoccupations continued to be the pro-
vision of enough money for herself and her son. During the mid-1930s
there was a clear, though not spectacular, improvement in her financial
position. This was derived almost entirely from her growing success as
an author, a fact which strengthened her already steadfast determination
to succeed. The dividing line between relative prosperity and penury
was still a narrow one. Alison frequently felt short of money. Once she
borrowed two pounds from her friend GL; she also borrowed money
from Lady Crossley and for Christmas 1935 was grateful to receive a
cheque from Lady Boyd-Dawkins to help her pay for the festivities.[24]
She was sometimes worried over how to pay doctors' bills, or how to
continue to support John at Cambridge. During 1936 she appeared in
person before the Altrincham Council and successfully got the rates on
Downs House reduced. A month later she was delighted to get eleven
pounds back from the Inland Revenue. She often felt deprived of

material comforts, once staring in W.H. Smith's with 'longing eyes at Lawrence's letters, two shillings and sixpence. I have only one shilling and sixpence left to finish the week.' She still shopped carefully, weighing up her purchases and delighting in bargains.

Her investments began, during these years, to pay small dividends. Although her shares in Crosse and Blackwell and Lewis's Bank produced nothing in 1934, a year later she was overjoyed to receive an eight pound dividend from Lewis's. She also received small dividends from U.C. Stores and from Liverpool Council, though Sugdens seems to have paid nothing. By the end of 1936 she had some four hundred pounds in the Halifax Building Society. Of far greater significance, however, were the sums of money, in advances and royalty payments, that now began to arrive from her publishers. She was delighted to be able to pay fifteen pounds into the bank in April 1935 and in August of that year reacted joyously to her largest royalty cheque to date:

> I took a letter from the box and opened it as I went into the garden for breakfast. Imagine my amazement when I saw a cheque for seventy seven pounds from Fabers, mostly for *Moonshine and Magic*, that darling book! Oh joy and thankfulness, and I didn't forget to thank God. I want to buy John a blazer, and for myself a picture of a Van Gogh's, and I shall pay my bills and get straight. I bought a 4d ice to celebrate.[25]

Her growing financial success, however, did not liberate Alison from feeling both insecurity and envy. She sometimes felt herself to be snubbed by what she described as the 'rich women of Bowdon', she was hurt when she imagined that Lady Crossley condescended towards her and once she declared herself 'sickened' by the snobbery of the local Sixty club.[26]

Yet she in turn was capable of snobbery: she was appalled by the 'ugly surburban women' she encountered in a cinema café and recalled, after visiting her friend Maude at Timperley, that 'I sat in her "lounge" for about ten minutes before she appeared – I was amazed at the ugliness. Silver wallpaper(!) with all her pictures and trashy watercolours – a really common room, half-nude girls holding bowls, a tall vase with imitation tulips. . . . Maude's bedroom was rather appalling with its satin quilt and the common look overall.'[27]

Ironically, Alison was particularly sensitive to being patronised or pitied by her Uttley in-laws. Before the visit of her sister-in-law Alice Tolson in October 1935, she prepared thoroughly: 'the brass and copper shining everywhere, a big fire. I dressed in my very best blue dress – for I determined I would not look the shabby down-and-out relation whom she despises.'[28] The following night, however, Alison could not sleep for jealously of Alice's clothes and also for the number of friends of whom she boasted. Her relationship with Gertrude remained distant and cold. She believed that her sister-in-law was plotting behind her back, trying to undermine her friendship with the Holt family, and on Christmas Eve reacted with a singular lack of seasonal charity on hearing that Gertrude's daughter Katherine 'has *not* won any schol[arship]! I am glad, they need snubbing by Fate, they think they are so brilliant, and they can afford to pay. It will be a blow to G's pride, she was quite certain she would get one, so were the others of the family.'[29] Her dislike for her brother-in-law, George Uttley, was unabated and once, on meeting him coming from James's grave, she cut him dead. In all these ways, Alison seems to have been determined to rid herself of what she saw as the Uttley incubus. Reviewing the past year on New Year's Eve 1936, Alison took stock of her relationship with her in-laws:

> I've not cared about the Uttley family. I felt I have cast off their shackles, which have fettered me for over 20 years, – no visit to Emily this Christmas, no writing to George, no annoying Gertrude's long letter, except a few words, ignoring her hints and her curiosities. Only through escape can I find myself and become myself once more, living in flowers and trees and dreams, in my writing, in nice ordinary people, unselfconscious and without belittlement.[30]

Her brother Harry and his wife Frances were, on any analysis, examples of these 'ordinary people' with whom apparently Alison wished to associate more. In fact, her relationship with her brother continued to be distant. She resented his move to St Anne's in Lancashire, in the autumn of 1934, mourning that this broke the last link between her and Castle Top. Her ambivalent feelings towards her brother are illustrated by an unexpected call he made upon her in the summer of 1936. Although Alison was 'pleased to see him, and brought him into lunch', she was shocked when he thought there was no harm in the new owner of Castle Top putting up bungalows in the White Field and when they eventually talked of her books, she noted rather resentfully that the news of them 'astonished him, although he thought I was making a pile of money! They all think books bring in lots of money!'[31]

All in all, Alison got through the visit creditably enough, though in general she did not like people to drop in on her. It is interesting that, apart from GL and LM, Alison visited friends far more than she invited them to her own home. There is no doubt that she made an interesting and lively guest, ready to express her views on any issue, perceptive, cultured, intelligent and quick to communicate some of the intensity and passion that characterised her. But she also seems to have been reluctant, perhaps through financial constraints, to have returned the hospitality of her neighbours. This was partly because, as she confessed, she did not mind 'her housework, as long as I haven't to dress well and entertain'.[32] But it may also have been due to the need to preserve the space and time essential to her writing and her private well being: 'I enjoy my writing and revising, I like my gay lunches and teas, and the big fires, and Hamish and the canary are sweet companions. I like my embroidery, too, I find it quite exciting; and then the thoughts of darling John.'[33]

One visitor for whom Alison always made space was Professor Alexander. His visits had a very special quality for her from when he kissed her delicately on arrival, sometimes complimenting her by saying that she looked 'a mere nineteen'. He always treated her to a wonderfully varied discourse and he interested himself in her writing, being instrumental in the summer of 1936 in persuading her to accept the illustrations for *Candlelight Tales*. In the autumn of that year Alison was even toying with the idea of going with him on a holiday to Burford in the Cotswolds.[34]

Absorbed as she was with her modest circle of friends, her son, her writing and her struggle to earn an adequate income, Alison kept a keen eye on international and domestic politics. Once she was able to have a 'jolly chat' on the subject of Communism with her neighbour, Harry Cooper, but in general she was quick to ascribe all manner of ills to the Soviet system. Typical of her feeling was her anger in the spring of 1936 at being awakened on Sunday morning at 8.00 a.m. by 'two men putting the roof on a house nearby! Oh Bolshevism! All the neighbours must have been swearing at being wakened up. . . . These people can never be quiet.'[35] Like so many of her contemporaries, however, Alison refused to see the menace of the newly established Nazi regime in Germany, commenting in February 1934 that Miss Hackforth thought she was joking 'when I state my point of view, approval of Nazism'.[36] On New Year's Eve 1936 she wrote of John holding the book *Inside Europe* and saying '"I'll tell you Hitler's four aims," says he, and we laugh, for we are in a giggling mood, because I have been looking at him, and trying to make him look at me.'[37] Alison was also resistant to internationalism, praying in August 1935 that Britain would keep out of the Abyssinian crisis and a few months later, on being told by the speaker at a missionary bazaar that the black man was her brother, 'looked round and knew that even the white man isn't our brother'.[38]

Increasingly, Alison expressed her horror at the prospect of war. She declared herself a pacifist like Quintin Hogg, but also supported Winston Churchill's call for rearmament on the basis that this would keep Britain free and independent. Her love of her country was often couched during these years in passionate, almost religious terms. No

doubt part of her reaction to the deepening international crisis was fear
that her son John would be called up if war broke out, and possibly
killed. Her perception of Britain was, however, over-romantic. On
holiday in Devon in 1934 she recorded a 'divinely lovely' day 'the
loveliest day in the world' and wrote in her diary: '"God save the King"
plays the band. England is safe, and rich, and happy. All evil is forgotten in the beauty of the day.'[39]

Alison's affection for the British monarchy was put under some
pressure by the dramatic events of 1936, the year when three kings sat
on the British throne. She was greatly moved by the death of King
George V in January, writing in her diary:

> 'The King's life is drawing peacefully to its close,' said the wireless a
> few minutes ago – and all the hearts of the country and Empire are
> aching. . . . I knew, I felt it – and oh I feel as grieved as if it were my
> own father. It brings my father's death to me. . . . It is so sudden, we
> feel bowed down under the grief of it. Never before have I felt like
> this over royalty – Queen Victoria, I was a child, confused and
> frightened, [for] King Edward I was a young eager woman, just
> engaged, and now I am getting old, and I feel the devastation and grief
> of our King's death.[40]

Her involvement in the death of George V was particularly intense, not
only because it stirred up uncomfortable memories of her own father's
death (to which she hardly ever referred) but also perhaps that of her
husband. She declared herself 'filled with grief, very lonely, the grief of
all England seems to float over the land'.[41] In December of the same
year Alison expressed a not dissimilar anxiety over the abdication crisis:
'today's papers are full of a great crisis, not referred to by name in the
D[aily] T[elegraph], which is most discreet, but people say it is the affair
of the King and Mrs Simpson. With wars in Spain and Germany and
Italy rearming and threatening, and Russia counter-arming, and sending
Communists all over the world, and now comes this blow to
England!'[42]

On the day the king abdicated, Alison wrote censoriously: 'I realise
that he will never know happiness, he has renounced all for that awful
woman, and she will never give him joy, and he will feel longing for his
home, his castles, the royal parks, the wonderful traditions he has cut
away.'[43] She also confessed, 'We feel bewildered, people talk of nothing
else. I felt more cheered as I saw the pictures of the new Queen and the
jolly children. For happiness on the throne, a united family, will make a
great difference to England.'[44]

Despite the trials of Alison's private life and her disquiet over various
public events, these years saw her make steady progress in her quest to
establish herself as a well-known writer. She devoted herself to her

writing with an energy which it is difficult to recreate fifty years later. Ideas tumbled out of her, her imagination darted here and there, and her waking hours seemed to be dominated by the physical task of writing or mulling over ideas for books and articles.

She drew her inspiration from many sources, eagerly noting a rhyming game about Queen Anne that GL told her of, willing herself to think of the beautiful hilly countryside at Lea near her old home as she began to work over the plot for her novel *High Meadows* and dreaming in March 1935 of an Elizabethan house which was later to be incorporated into her novel *A Traveller in Time*. She jotted down conversations heard at cricket matches or on trains and prided herself on an extraordinarily sensitive perception: 'Last night I was wakened by a little strange thumping sound – it was some rose petals falling from a vase on the mantelpiece. I sat up and grinned at myself in the glass. What a light sleeper! A princess!'[45]

She took great pleasure in correcting the proofs of her books, remarking as she posted off *Wise Owl's Story* and *Little Grey Rabbit's Party* that they were full of good jokes and that she had 'gurgled' as she wrote them. She also noted that the writing of *Little Grey Rabbit's Party* had taken only five days. The scale of her writing activities is summed up in her diary for 15 January 1935:

> Resolutions & Review of Work.
> 1. I must write one fairy tale a week to add to my collection, which I want to send out in the spring.
> 2. Once a month, send a tale to the NW.
> 3. Once a week, write a story or sketch for a book of country tales.
> 4. Each day write about six pages of the novel, revise and rewrite and revise again.[46]

From August 1934 she was thinking of a plot for a novel based on her childhood experiences. The book was eventually to be published in 1938 as *High Meadows*. Alison struggled for many months to produce a satisfactory plot, complaining at the end of August 1934 that although she had written the first pages of the novel, she couldn't keep the gamekeeper out of them.[47] Fifteen months later she confessed herself still unsatisfied with what she had written: 'It is nearly midnight. I have been sorting out chapters, trying to fit my crossword of a novel. I don't know what to think of it – there is so little plot, yet many books have no plots. However, I have made some kind of form – if I had nothing to do but write I would finish it.'[48]

In February 1934 Alison was pleased to receive a 'charming letter' from Richard de la Mare, saying, 'I wonder when you are going to write a successor to The Country Child? I do wish you would think about it, and see if you can't plan another book!'[49] Despite the success of *The Country Child*, Alison, as we have seen, had earlier expressed some misgivings about writing a new autobiographical book after what she considered to have been a prying and unfavourable interview with her published by the *Manchester Evening News* in the autumn of 1932. Throughout her life she retained an ambivalence towards revealing the personal details of her life, particularly those concerning the years of her marriage. Even in the rich and varied autobiographical accounts of her childhood, comparatively few painful or discreditable episodes are recalled and, overall, she is in complete control of the narrative, presenting the material as she thinks fit. Nevertheless, setting aside the anxieties she felt over exposing herself to public scrutiny, she had been thinking about at a 'new intimate book' on and off since October 1932.[50] This was later to emerge as the autobiographical *Ambush of Young Days*.

Indeed, it is clear that between 1932 and 1935 she was working on several manuscripts of an autobiographical nature. She sent a manuscript entitled *Winged Chariot* to Collins in February 1934 and a little later sent out the manuscripts of stories called *Blue Ribbons* and *Cuckoo Cherry-Tree*. These manuscripts were rejected by various publishers. In August 1934 *Winged Chariot* was rejected by an agent with the suggestion that it should be rewritten as a novel. A few days later *Cuckoo Cherry-Tree* returned again from a publisher, causing Alison to bemoan the fact that she had had no luck with her 'two Castle Top books'.[51]

Amid all this uncertainty and failure, a clear invitation from Faber to write a successor to *The Country Child* was a great stimulus to Alison's confidence. She began to work on the book, provisionally entitled *Give Us This Day*, in August 1935. It took her only one month to write the first draft of the text. She was delighted when Faber accepted it towards the end of December 1935, offering her a thirty pound advance against royalties. In Alison's view, she 'began to write it properly and retype and arrange on Oct. 26 and finished it on Nov. 12th, in 18 days! A record of hard work. So all my childhood games and fancies, the fields and woods of dear Castle Top, my father and his stories, my mother and her sweetness, will be told to the world.'[52] A fortnight later Alison was busy at work revising the text, finding it 'charming'. Before the book was published in the spring of 1937, the original title was dropped and *Ambush of Young Days* substituted after John had found the words in a sonnet of Shakespeare's.[53]

Although *Ambush of Young Days* was accepted so quickly, Alison continued to face a good many disappointments and rejections during these years. The manuscript of *Cuckoo Cherry-Tree* went back and forth to publishers, almost rivalling the peripatetic career of *The Adventures of No Ordinary Rabbit*.

She also continued to produce a flood of stories, including 'The Star' story, 'Twenty-Four Tailors', 'The Lion and the Unicorn', 'The Apple Tree', 'The Pussy Cat', 'The North Wind Doth Blow', 'Dickory Dock', 'Over the Hills and Far Away', 'The Fairy Ship', 'The Dress and the Pincushion', 'Wee Willie Winkie' and 'The Crooked Man'. Only a relatively small proportion of these stories were accepted, her most consistent patron being the magazine *New World*. The typical fee Alison received for one of these stories was two guineas.

Alison reacted to the many rejections she received at this time with her usual mixture of deep disappointment and defiance. When Gollancz returned *Winged Chariot* in February 1934, she expressed a feeling of hopelessness, writing in her diary that it was not the reviews of her books she dreaded but rejections from publishers. The return of *Blue Ribbons* and *Cuckoo Cherry-Tree* in the spring of 1934 left her feeling devastated. 'Talk about depressions – I felt pretty sick.'[54] When *Cuckoo Cherry-Tree* returned again in December 1934, she declared that all her incentive had gone and that she should burn her manuscripts and instead devote herself to reading books.[55] A little after this rejection she complained mournfully that she had had nothing save her Little Grey Rabbit books accepted for three years. In the August of the following year she again felt despairing and wondered why she should even continue writing: 'Sometimes I think "Why write? Why work?", but then I feel dissatisfied. I *must* go on and produce and use my talents which have been hidden all these years.'[56]

Fortunately, she was to receive considerable encouragement from her publishers during this time. William Collins was a great admirer of her work and often told her how much he wanted her to write another book for the firm. Mrs Collins was also a devoted supporter and there is no doubt that Alison felt a strong sense of loyalty to the firm as a result. She met William Collins for the first time in June 1934, writing, 'He is a dark haired young man who reminded me of Harry when he was young. Diffident, and charming and gay and careless, I liked him very much.'[57] Among the suggestions which Mr Collins put to her at this meeting was that she should write 'a story to fit in with some illustrations he had. Also asked me to write a long animal book, about a dog or something.' More specifically, she was invited to produce a book for the Christmas of 1937 and to write a book for older children, rather like *Anne of Green Gables*.

William Collins made her feel even more valued when he invited her to a publishing party at the Carlton in March 1936, and in the autumn of that year asked her to be a judge in an essay competition sponsored by Collins. Alison felt 'most flattered, and as I dressed I felt elated at the unexpected excitements of an author's life'.[58] But although her friend the publisher Eleanor Graham had told her in March 1934 that she would get recognition in time, she was extremely sensitive to supposed slights. She was deeply offended when Heinemann offered her only five pounds a book when they reprinted the first four Little Grey Rabbit books, although she was obliged to accept the terms. She was still inclined to recommend her books to libraries and felt that the staff of the Altrincham bookshop were contemptuous of her work when they failed to stock it. Even William Collins incurred her displeasure when he declined to publish a book of nursery rhymes she had submitted to him.

The irony is that on analysis Alison's publishing achievements during these three years were remarkable. Five books were published: *Squirrel Goes Skating* in 1934, and *Wise Owl's Story* and *The Adventures of Peter and Judy in Bunnyland* during 1935; *Candlelight Tales* was accepted by Faber in the spring of 1936 and published six months later, at about the same time as the appearance of *Little Grey Rabbit's Party*.

The Little Grey Rabbit books were warmly received, *Vogue* commenting 'Children will love *Wise Owl's Story*' and *Time and Tide* produced a little poem as its review of *Little Grey Rabbit's Party*, which ended with the words 'Buy Soon'.[59] The homely characters contained in the books were evidently well on the way to becoming cult figures within the world of children's books. One indication of this was a picture of Squirrel and Little Grey Rabbit as handmade woollen toys, carried in the *Lady* magazine and accompanied by the words 'Little Grey Rabbit and Squirrel, familiar characters in the famous "Little Grey Rabbit" books, are now on the market as hand-made woollen toys.'[60] In contrast to the undeniable success of these books, the more humble and pedestrian *The Adventures of Peter and Judy in Bunnyland* seems to have made no impact whatsoever.

This cannot be said of Alison's book of fairy stories, *Candlelight Tales*. *John O'London's Weekly*, having stated that 'There must be few nurseries unacquainted with Little Grey Rabbit; one of the neatest, gentlest and most attractive creatures who wears frocks and coats in addition to fur', went on to describe the 'first lovely story' of *Candlelight Tales*.[61] *The Sunday Times* remarked that 'The tales have a twist that is very gay' and *Country Life* considered that 'The treatment is original and charming, and the book thoroughly enjoyable.' *Time and Tide* had some misgivings but ended its review by saying, 'It must be repeated that most children will enjoy these pleasantly written tales, and mothers and nurses will seize eagerly upon that rarity – a good book to be read out of, to and from.'

Apart from the generally favourable critical reactions to her books, Alison had several other concrete proofs of their success. *The Country Child* was chosen to be the Junior Book Club Book of the Month for

February 1934; Amherst College, Massachusetts, wrote for permission to quote from the same book in July 1934; and early in 1935 Alison heard that Nelson were issuing *The Country Child* as a one and sixpenny Classic and paying her a twenty-one guinea fee. She persisted during these years in expressing amazement, both at the numbers of books sold and at the amount of royalties she received. Oddly, perhaps, *Moonshine and Magic* continued to sell more copies than *The Country Child*. The Little Grey Rabbit books were already beginning to sell in their thousands and, during October 1936, Collins told Alison that the books were selling approximately a thousand a month. The first four Little Grey Rabbit books were translated into Swedish and into Spanish. In August 1935 Alison heard that *Moonshine and Magic* had been sold to the American publishers Whitman for a hundred pounds.

She also managed during these years to make a breakthrough into radio broadcasting. In August 1934 she heard that the first four Little Grey Rabbit books were to be broadcast by the BBC and in March 1935 four stories, including 'Wee Willie Winkie', were accepted by the corporation. Her 'Snowman' story was accepted in December 1935 and her greatest triumph came in February 1936 when the BBC accepted five of her Tim Rabbit tales. After the consistent rejection of *The Adventures of No Ordinary Rabbit* by a whole variety of publishers, Alison saw this as 'a feather in my cap and a cheque in my pocket. I was delighted.'[62] Hearing her own stories on radio, although deeply pleasurable, was not always easy and she recounted in August 1935 her struggle to listen to 'The Lion and the Unicorn' on London Regional Radio: 'I crouched on the floor, turning and pressing feverishly, and got it, but I had to hold the knob all the time. The tale sounded delightful I thought.'[63]

Although the broadcasting of the Little Grey Rabbit tales was eventually to exacerbate the friction between Alison and Margaret Tempest over which took precedence, text or illustrations, during the mid-1930s their relationship seems generally to have been a satisfactory one. Alison was gratified to learn that Margaret Tempest thought the jokes in *Little Grey Rabbit's Party* were 'brilliant' and she in turn thought that the illustrations for *The Knot Squirrel Tied* were 'the best ever'. But there was an undercurrent of criticism and rivalry, generated for the most part by Alison. She found the illustrations for *Wise Owl's Story* 'quite good, one or two excellent. Owl looks a nice creature, but there aren't enough of him.'[64] In April 1936 Alison proposed to Collins a book on the lines of the Babar stories and wanted them to be illustrated not by Margaret Tempest but by an acquaintance of hers, Miss Hall, writing of her, 'She *is* clever, much cleverer than M. Tempest. I hope her final results will be good, that Mr C will like them.'[65] Three weeks later William Collins rejected both the pictures and the idea of a Babar book.[66] Alison clearly felt a pervading unease with Margaret Tempest, a discomfort that was in part based on a personal incompatibility. In October 1936, during one of her trips to London, she recounted calling on her most famous illustrator in Chelsea: 'She was just the same, her cold voice, her pale eyelashes and her cold eyes, and her school marm manner. I was glad to get away.'[67]

As her writing career progressed satisfactorily, despite its various disappointments, Alison turned her mind more to the prospect of moving from Bowdon. She often found the environment which she inhabited physically distasteful, declaring herself 'sick' of Manchester, finding Altrincham 'filthy', wishing to escape from the 'monkey house of Bowdon', and once returning from a trip to Manchester commenting that the city had been 'full of dirt and lots of Jewesses with red lips'. She had various dreams of a 'heavenly new house' or of a 'lovely future' elsewhere. One benefit of moving, in her view, would be to escape her Uttley in-laws forever. In July 1936 she got Downs House valued for a thousand pounds, although she considered its true market value to be £1150. Two weeks later, while on holiday in Devon, she fell in love with a house and for a while seriously considered buying it. She discussed her plans for moving closely with John, and during October 1936 recorded an important house-hunting journey they made together to Buckinghamshire: 'Met John at Marylebone . . . went off happily together, laughing and gay, to Beaconsfield. A glorious day, sun shining, the woods golden, the houses charming. We fell in love with several, and felt that we should like to live there.'[68]

Nearly two years were to elapse, however, before the move to Beaconsfield took place.

CHAPTER FOURTEEN

Wanting To Move, 1937–38

I am not well, I am on edge, frightened, hunted, feeling like a wild
little creature with a pack of dogs after me, and the dogs are these
Bowdon women with their brown faces and hats and clothes and
affected voices and supercilious stares.

ALISON UTTLEY, diary, 10 February 1937

Alison Uttley seems to have staying power, and is likely to go on
and increase her reputation and is therefore worth sticking to.

GEOFFREY FABER, April 1937

In September 1938 Alison moved south, to Beaconsfield in
Buckinghamshire. She was to live there for the rest of her life. Born a
northerner, she had hitherto, apart from her temporary stays in
Cambridge, London and Wales, always lived in the north of England.
The move to a prosperous, suburban area like Beaconsfield, within easy
striking distance of London, was therefore an event of the greatest
significance to her. She justified it as providing her with an escape from
what she saw as the squalor and narrow-mindedness of her northern
habitat. But her move was also a symbol of great potency, the affirmation
that her success as a writer, and the relative prosperity that this had
brought, enabled her to move to what she considered to be more affluent
and sophisticated surroundings.

Not that she was free from money worries during these years. She often
felt impoverished, almost destitute. During January 1937 she bemoaned
the fact that she had only thirteen shillings and fivepence left in the bank
and a few days later, waiting in vain for a royalty cheque from Faber, she
took her last ten shilling note from its hiding place.[1] In March she broke
her spectacles and feeling herself unable to pay the repair bill of six
shillings, bought a cheap substitute pair for one shilling from
Woolworth's. She expressed great anxiety during the summer of 1937
over the condition of John's car: she was afraid it would break down and
that she would therefore have to pay the fare for the long train journey
that this entailed. At the end of 1937 she admitted, rather guiltily, that
she hadn't paid her health insurance for a year and at the beginning of
1938, despite the undeniable turn for the better that her financial affairs
had taken, convinced herself that she couldn't afford to buy a bunch of

daffodils at one shilling and sixpence.[2] She also expressed considerable jealousy at all the money which she imagined that Beatrix Potter had made from her children's books.

In reality, her anxieties over her financial position were groundless. Rather they reflect a feeling that there would never be enough money for her needs – a feeling stretching back to her childhood. It is also true that she often had very little money in hand, but the reason for this was that she had invested quite large amounts elsewhere. When in the summer of 1938 she was on the point of buying the new house at Beaconsfield, she revealed that she had £1100 invested with the Halifax Building Society and £550 invested with Lewis's.[3] She received a payment from her investment in War Loans, as well as other dividends. She had, moreover, been greatly cheered by a share certificate issued by Sugdens in July 1937, which showed that she and John had £3588 between them.[4] Alison declared this to be a 'fortune', but it did not purge her from feelings of guilt when she bought an astrakhan muff a few months later, or prevent her delight with a book token for seven shillings and sixpence received from her friend GL for her birthday that year.[5] Although she was able to invest some of her money in Woolworth's, in February 1937 she had written to the Financial Editor of the *Observer*, asking for advice about her shares and signing herself 'Perplexed'.[6] Apart from her healthy and growing investments, her income from writing increased substantially during these years. Her books with Faber continued to earn steadily, she was paid for various magazine articles and BBC programmes, and the success of her Little Grey Rabbit books meant that in March 1937 she was delighted to find a 'fat cheque stuck in the door'.

Perhaps because she was in fact so much more secure financially, she was able to admit to feeling depressed more often. She also developed a larger number of illnesses and ailments than in the previous few years. For much of 1937 she had a very painful knee, which only yielded slowly to the ministrations of osteopaths and masseurs. As with the common cold, Alison suffered this temporary disability badly. She also admitted a distaste for the man who was massaging her knee, 'I noticed his greasy hair, and felt a bit squeamish.'[7] She once felt very sorry for herself when she squeezed some toothpaste painfully into her eye, and in the spring of 1938 she injured her jaw, displacing some of the small cartilages in the joint. In view of the pleasure she derived from eating, this injury was very frustrating for her and she waited impatiently for her jaw to mend.

Far more frequent than her physical disabilities were her depressions. Sometimes she was overwhelmed with sadness when she received what she thought of as disappointing royalties, or when manuscripts of hers were sent back by publishers or the editors of magazines. Compared with the six previous years, she suffered very little in the way of rejection, but she was depressed when the BBC rejected her *Cock and Bull* tales in July 1937 and was distressed when Collins declined the manuscript of 'Thackers', eventually to be published as *A Traveller in Time*, in October 1938.[8] Sometimes she merely felt a hopeless frustration, writing in her diary for July 1937, 'What a task is a book but you have to do [it] quite alone. And I get so little profit. £30 for Ambush, which was months and months of work. No fame, no money, no notice taken, but I feel happy when I am writing, and it helps me along. How lovely to get encouragement!'[9] Sometimes she wore herself out with anxiety over how her books would be received and was only able to sleep 'a healing sleep' in February 1937 when she realised that her book *Ambush of Young Days* had been mostly welcomed by the critics, about one of whom she wrote, 'Bless him! He has cheered a lonely one.'[10]

Her deepest fits of depression occurred when she felt, as she was so often to do, alone and abandoned. Typical of such episodes was the entry in her diary for 31 July 1937: 'Such worry and anxiety, – no letter from John all day. I wept in bed last night for a long time, and again tears fell this morning. I felt deserted and forgotten. However, I pulled myself together, and carried on, did the housework slowly, and then typed on and off for hours.'[11]

On this occasion Alison comforted herself with thoughts of the characters she was writing about in her novel *High Meadows*, 'I keep thinking of Gabriel and Jim and Patty Verity, of the flowers and beauty, and those fields come to my mind with intense reality.'[12]

A month later she felt an almost physical need for the comfort provided by her mother:

> All day I was living in the past thinking of mother, and her wonderful courage and splendid character, her unselfishness, and great over-whelming love, love which would have faced death for any of us, I felt very sad and lonely and wanted her back again. And I felt that James had somehow faded from my thoughts, and mother has taken his place, and she is the one I have always loved more than all the world. Then I wept for her and felt very lonely. Then I thought how pleased she would be that we have carried on, that John has been to Cambridge, and got his degree, that I have written books praising her. And she would have been glad that I have given pleasure to so many little children. I think how she adored and worshipped children.[13]

It is true that James seems to have faded into the background of her conscious and unconscious thoughts. She remembered, naturally, the anniversaries of his birth, death and their marriage. She recalled, too, how he would have 'exploded' at a provocative remark made by her friend, Harry Cooper. But she also sometimes expressed a deep love for him and was able to feel how much he had loved her in return. Once on his birthday she wrote, 'I love him always, poor child, tossed by the world, – yet with so many blessings, I cannot understand why he didn't face life, and battle on. When I think of the trials and difficulties, a million times worse than any of his, of my parents, and my own difficulties too. It must have been his father's fault.'[14]

She continued to feel supported and contained by the love of those who had been closest to her, in July 1938 reading 'letters from Mother and James and John, and felt again the great love they have all poured upon me. How happy I should be remembering their affection & this adoration!'[15]

Of this triumvirate of intimates, only John remained. They continued, from time to time, to express their love with great physical intensity: 'We had a long loving kiss before he went';[16] 'John has just gone. . . . We had our prayer, beautiful and comforting, for which I am profoundly thankful. It is wonderful, this bond between us. Then we kissed, long passionate kisses of mother & son, and I thought of James, and thanked God for John left to comfort me.'[17]

Alison watched anxiously over John. Sometimes her watchfulness had a selfish quality to it, as when in February 1937 she insisted that he would not be happy in a teaching post at 'a great aristocratic school. . . . I knocked it on the head, because I don't think he would be happy, even if I could spare him, and I should be too lonely and desperate without him.'[18] In October 1937 she flatly forbade him to apply for a job in Montreal.

John applied for and failed to get several posts during 1937 and it wasn't until November of that year that he was offered the job of history master at St Laurence's College at Ramsgate. When John left in January 1938 to take up this position, Alison 'couldn't sleep last night, thinking of his going, & then I dreamt a wild dream of being all alone in the world, with no roots, no home, a kind of lost dream, I wandering in a great city'.[19] Less than two weeks after John took up his new post, Alison was troubled to receive an unhappy letter from him, saying, 'He isn't happy, the work is too hard, he says he is exhausted and in a state of collapse. . . . The school he doesn't like, the staff cliques . . . and the feeling too religious, – altogether he is rather sick with it. I feel anxious lest he overdoes himself struggling against odds . . . poor darling, I think of him all the time.'[20] The difficulties John had in adjusting to his first permanent teaching post were an early warning sign of the far more serious problems to emerge later in his schoolmastering career. Despite his undoubted cleverness and sensitivity, his essential lack of self-confidence was to prove a grievous handicap before the sometimes unfriendly scrutiny of his pupils.

John seems to have had no girlfriends during these years. He had some loyal men friends, but Alison did not always approve of these, dismissing one – Healey – as 'too common' and 'flashy'. In material terms, John was well-cared for. He drove his own car and in October 1938 was able to buy his first brand new one. His view of the outside world seems to have been an uneasy mixture of conservatism and idealism. During the summer of 1937 he went, as he had done in previous years, to help at the Duke of York's camp, an annual gathering initiated by King George VI before his accession to the throne and designed to bring together working class and middle class boys in harmony and co-operation. Later in the summer, John went to assist at a camp for the unemployed in Yorkshire.[21] But when in 1938 he visited Austria after the Anschluss, he told his mother that he frequently used the greeting 'Heil Hitler!' and drove his car around with both the Union Jack and the German Swastika adorning it. When he travelled a little later into France, he naïvely left the swastika on his car and seems to have been mildly surprised when it was torn off one night.

Alison's contact with her relations remained fundamentally unsatisfactory. She resented the refusal of Frances, Harry's wife, to give her the old musical box that she cherished from Castle Top Farm. She once dreamed of fleeing in anguish from Gertrude's house, and closed the door after a visit by Emily with the thought 'It is like entertaining an icicle, her frozen face, her hard unkind criticisms of people.' Perhaps she best summed up her feelings in January 1938: 'Really I am blessed with the most wretched relations.'

Apart from preoccupations with her writing career and with her son, Alison kept up the whirlwind of activity that had become necessary to her. The diaries reveal in the most minute detail how she lived, and some of the incidents she recalled are both revealing and touching. She confessed how once she was deeply embarrassed at being obliged to stand in her combinations in a shop while she was trying on some corsets; at another time she was complimented on her rosy complexion, but ruefully admitted in her diary that it had been only the effect of rouge; in December 1937, in preparation for Christmas and her birthday, she made and iced five large cakes and then realised that she had overprovided; two months later she was thrown into a panic by the realisation that she had not paid her insurance stamps. She often regretted the fact that she led a topsy turvy sort of life, with none of the permanence that she associated with Castle Top; and once Dr Johnson's dictum that 'We shall get no letters in the grave', snatched at her heart.[22]

She continued to scrutinise and feel critical of a succession of domestic

1. The sixteen-year-old Alison, in what she described as 'a proud pose', *c.* 1900. She was already a bright 'scholarship girl' at a local grammar school.

2. The newly married Henry and Hannah Taylor, in 1884. Alison was born nine months after her parents' wedding.

3. Alison's beloved childhood home, Castle Top Farm, Derbyshire, photographed in 1985, but still much as it was at her birth in 1884.

4. The Uttley family photographed at Bowdon in Cheshire in 1911. Back row: Alison, James and Alice Uttley. Middle row: Mr G.H. Uttley, Mrs Uttley, Gertrude Uttley. George Uttley is seated at the front. Alison looks somewhat ill at ease in this gathering.

5. Gertrude Uttley and Alison enjoying a picnic amid the beauty of Patterdale. Alison seems more formal and less relaxed than her friend.

6. Professor Samuel Alexander, who Alison much admired while a student at
Manchester University, and who was to encourage her to begin writing.

7. The Manchester physics set poses rather stiffly in the Coupland Building. Alison (front row, second from the left) was one of the very few female students of physics.

8. Alison photographed by her fiancé, James Uttley, on Wimbledon Common just before the First World War. Books seem as necessary as picnic utensils to the young couple.

9. James Uttley, about to take a 'spin' in a hired plane, soon after the end of the First World War.

10. Alison and her beloved son, John, share a joyous moment while on a family camping holiday at Tenby during the early 1920s.

11. John and James within their tent while camping at Tenby.

12. Thackers, Alison's substantial house in Beaconsfield, Buckinghamshire. Bought in 1938 with the income from her increasingly successful writing, it was to be her home until her death in 1976. Thackers was the original title of her novel eventually published as *A Traveller in Time*.

13. John Uttley and his bride, Helen Paine, on their wedding day in April 1947. Alison and Helen were to have a stormy relationship, partly due to their competition for John's affections.

14. Walter de la Mare. Alison developed a warm friendship with him, much admiring his writing, and enjoying their conversations. She was greatly upset at his death in 1956, confessing that she 'adored him'.

15. Margaret Tempest, whose illustrations were crucial to the success of the *Little Grey Rabbit* books. Alison was eventually estranged from her, after numerous publishing disagreements over who had really created *Little Grey Rabbit* and company.

16. A delighted Alison, after being made an honorary Doctor of Letters at her old university, Manchester, in 1970.

17. The elderly Alison posing serenely as the successful writer and grande dame of letters. Her best-selling, autobiographical work, *The Country Child*, is on her lap.
Inset: Alison's gravestone (18) stands in stark and moving simplicity in the pretty churchyard at Penn in Buckinghamshire.

helps, although both a Mrs Jackson and a Mrs Johnson seem to have given satisfaction during 1937. The non-appearance of a cleaning woman, however, often had the effect of throwing Alison into a panic. Once she complained that she must now carry out the spring cleaning when she really wanted to write and on another occasion found that her knee suddenly hurt when she was left alone to cope with the house-work. Perhaps because she loved gardening so much herself, she was particularly critical of the various gardeners she employed. In June 1937 she expressed horror at the slowness with which an old man was weeding, and even the move south to Beaconsfield brought no im-provement, since in November of 1938 she was shocked at how 'slackly' her gardener was working.[23]

Her intimate and mutually supportive friendships with GL and LM flourished. Both gave her steadfast encouragement and advice over her writing. GL frequently helped her in the house, while LM and she often breakfasted together upstairs when her friend came to visit her. All three friends were, during Alison's widowhood, women without male partners and there was one incident during August 1937 which illus-trated in a bizarre fashion how much LM regretted her single state: 'She put on the wedding garment, of pale blue satin, and walked about with the train on the grass, very charming, she looked so young, and quite pretty.'[24]

Alison sometimes imagined that her aristocratic friend, Lady Cross-ley, had turned against her, but was then reassured to be sent tokens of reconciliation like a fish pie and a bunch of lavender in September 1937. Among her friends at Bowdon, she seems to have become particularly close to Winnie Armitage, who clearly valued her so much that just prior to Alison's move to Beaconsfield she told her she was 'potty' to leave all her friends. Eleanor Graham continued to be a close friend in the world of publishing, someone to whom Alison could go for advice and comfort. Alison felt very attracted to her, once writing, 'How vivid and exciting she is. I felt so happy with her.'[25]

Her close relationship with Professor Alexander was brought to a tragic close by his death during September 1938. Until the last, their relationship was one of great and mutual affection. Alison saw him as a substitute parent or husband, remarking in February 1937 that his tender hands made her think of her mother; three months later she kissed him three times when they parted, feeling that it was like leaving her own father, or James.[26] During the spring and summer of 1938 Professor Alexander knew that he was dying. He spoke of his im-pending death to Alison and she felt that Hitler's barbarous treatment of the Jews was casting this black and deadly shadow over him. Alexander was mortified at the prospect of Alison moving to Beaconsfield, particularly since he was so near to death, and in September 1938 wrote her a pathetic valedictory letter, starting in ink and continuing in a very shaky pencil script:

> My dear Mrs Uttley,
>   I fear I cannot face meeting you with John tomorrow, and it is a bitter disappointment – I shall only break down. But I've only one thing to say – to thank you profoundly for the blessing your friendship has brought me. I hope you are going to be very happy in your new home, and John too. God bless you my dear.
>   Yours most affectionately,
>   S. Alexander[27]

It is perhaps significant, in view of the strong bond of mutual affection between them, that Professor Alexander declined and died precisely during the months in which Alison was preparing to move away from Bowdon. His death came exactly two days before Alison moved to Beaconsfield. By a strange quirk of fate it was also the date upon which Alison's mother had died. Coincidentally, although perhaps Alison played a part in willing it, a substitute friend for Professor Alexander was near at hand. During November 1937 Alison met Walter de la Mare, a writer whose works she had long loved. She met him at *The Sunday Times* book exhibition in London, noting that he was 'smiling and very charming, so that I quite loved him, as I do Professor Alexander'.[28] Alison's friendship with Walter de la Mare was to flourish after her move to Beaconsfield, when she was often able to call on him and he on her. De la Mare, like Professor Alexander, provided her with a close platonic relationship. He was also to provide her with considerable intellectual stimulation, particularly sharing her interest in dreams and in the nature of time.

During these years Alison continued unperturbed by her own religious and political ambivalence. She was apt to deplore the hypocrisy of practised religion, but at the same time was shocked by what she saw as a sneering at religion in a performance of the play *Murder in the Cathedral*.[29] She was shocked to notice in the autumn of 1937 the contrast provided by the rich of Harrogate and the poor of Leeds, but she was later to describe a plumber who worked at her house as a 'wretched slum creature'. In February 1938 she felt obliged to say to a decrepit and dirty old man to whom she had given a cup of tea and who wanted to pay less income tax, that he should pay a 'share to England'; two months later she was upset that the Chancellor's budget had raised income tax by sixpence.[30]

As the crisis caused by Hitler's aggressive foreign policy deepened in Europe, she decided that she was an 'Isolationist' – rather as she tended to be in her private life. She saw the activity of the Left Book Club as a vehicle for Communist propaganda, yet once declared that she felt 'rather communistic' when she heard the Russian revolution denounced. Her first instincts remained patriotic: she was delighted when Neville Chamberlain became Prime Minister in June 1937 and bitterly resented her friend Mr Armitage criticising 'the mess' the British had made in India, Egypt and Palestine. The development of the Czech crisis over the German claim to the Sudetenland in the summer and autumn of 1938 preoccupied her greatly. On 23 September she wrote in her diary 'War seems imminent. Hitler and Chamberlain did not meet today. In England people are reviling Chamberlain. It seems as if there is no escape. . . . It will be the end of all things. I must not think of it, it is a nightmare.'[31] A week later she reacted, like so many of her fellow citizens, with joy to the signing of the Munich agreement: 'Thank God. The news has swept over the world. No war. All the terror and foreboding of a terrible slaughter past. . . . I stood outside tonight and saw ten searchlights, flashing across. . . . Our prayers are now answered, millions are saved. I felt dazed and tired, not knowing where I was. . . . I feel so thankful, so happy, so joyful that my darling John is safe.'[32]

Alison's writing flourished during these years. In January 1937 she set down her plans for the immediate future:

I must write a new GR book for the future, GR and the Robin perhaps, or maybe GR and the Speckledy Hen.
I must retype the 4 Pig stories, and send them to the BBC.
I must finish the Patty,Verity.
I must try to write another country book, on people I have known, country types and places.[33]

In what was now becoming a familiar pattern, Alison did not merely fulfil these aims but exceeded them. Her production of stories fell, but only because she was engaged in working on a substantial number of books. Nonetheless, she managed to produce 'The Bird of Time', 'The Cobbler's Shop', 'The Jack in the Box' and 'Jack Frost and the Snowman'. The BBC took four stories of the little pigs, although, as we have seen, they rejected her *Cock and Bull* tales. This rejection depressed her and she also felt, during July 1937, that nobody was listening to the stories of the little pigs. She remained extremely sensitive to what she perceived as public disinterest in her work. She was upset to hear that Faber had actually lost money on the publication of *Candlelight Tales*, and continued to be disheartened by the occasionally disappointing royalties she received, on personal as well as financial grounds. Like so many authors, she remained extraordinarily touchy over whether local bookshops stocked her works, declaring after hearing that the nearby W.H. Smith's did not have her newly published novel, *High Meadows*, that 'I am doing a vendetta, not going there ever again if I can help it, I am so angry with them.'[34]

Overall, however, Alison could bask in the glow of considerable success. She was pleased to receive a request for information about herself to be eventually used in a national dictionary of authors and was honoured, in December 1937, to receive Christmas cards from both Mr and Mrs Faber and Mr and Mrs Collins. She was delighted that William Collins asked her to help at the children's book exhibition. Small, but tangible indications of her growing fame gave her inordinate pleasure. Although she had presented the books herself, she was pleased in her dentist's waiting-room to see *The Adventures of No Ordinary Rabbit* and *The Knot Squirrel Tied* lying on the table.[35] She was delighted to receive ten per cent of the proceeds of plaster casts of the leading characters in the Little Grey Rabbit series, and was gratified during the summer of 1938 that the National Society for the Prevention of Cruelty to Children had made lantern slides from three of her Grey Rabbit books.

But the major indication of Alison's success was the publication of six books during these two years. The first to be published, in January 1937, was *Ambush of Young Days*. This was a book of considerable significance to her, chiefly because she saw it as a more truly autobiographical work than *The Country Child*. The arrival of the advance copies (which she held to her heart in rapture) stirred up anxieties as to what she had revealed about herself and four days before publication date she admitted her terror lest prying reporters should come in its wake. Another reason for her feelings of vulnerability over this book may have lain in Alison's realisation that 'it is the first book written since I have been alone, and published, for I did the C Child before 1930'.[36] *Ambush of Young Days* conjures up, with great feeling and fine writing, more scenes from Alison's childhood at Castle Top Farm. Its power is immeasurably enhanced by the beautiful illustrations by Charles Tunnicliffe. Where it differs from its predecessor, *The Country Child*, is in its capacity to reveal rather more of the pain and uncertainty of Alison's childhood; there is a greater candour and a greater freedom in admitting the frailties and misdemeanours of childhood. The opening words of chapter eight, 'Spring Cleaning', might serve as a summary of Alison's whole life: 'I was a restless enquiring child, with strong desires to identify myself with all I saw, to absorb their essence, to take things into my own self, and to get at some inner meaning which I thought they had, as if they lived a life of their own which I wanted to share.'[37]

Ambush of Young Days was by no means a best seller; only 840 copies had been sold by October 1937. It was, however, taken by the Junior Book Club. Although Alison kept an anxious eye on the slowly decreasing pile in her local W.H. Smith's, her chief reaction to the publication of the book was delight at its reception. The *Listener* declared that she had written 'in a prose which is excellently descriptive, and often exquisite. Her book is in a minor key, and it is a work of rare delight and charm.'[38] The *Woman's Magazine* called it 'a gem of a book'[39] and the *Observer* pronounced it one of the best books of 1937, likening it to a ray of sun to the heart.[40] The *Manchester Guardian* thought that its style was 'always simple and unsentimental yet suffused with true poetry . . . it is singularly beautiful and refreshing'.

There was some criticism. The journal *Education* called it 'well written' but 'somewhat dull' and described the character that represents Alison as 'a somewhat proper little girl of Victorian days', noting that the child shrank from using a word like 'stink'.[41] Alison was most hurt, however, by *The Sunday Times* review, headed 'Sensitive Plants', which said, 'The vividness and precision of the writing deserve high praise; but I wish the writer had departed from truth just to the extent of working up some excitement, some "plot" . . . drama does happen to some children, though evidently not to [her].'[42] Alison declared herself 'infuriated . . . it was so unfair. . . . I wrote a scientific study of youth, with no love story or divorce, or eavesdropping conversation.'[43] When, three days later, Lady Crossley sent Alison what happened to be her third copy of the 'hated review', she broke down: 'I felt it was the last straw . . . thoughts of Lady C reading it, and I wept as I, Cinderella, took her cinders from the grates and made the fires. I am not well, I am on edge, frightened, hunted, feeling like a wild little creature with a pack of dogs after me, and the dogs are these Bowdon women with their brown faces and hats and clothes and affected voices and supercilious stares.'[44]

The Knot Squirrel Tied was also published during 1937, adding another charming volume to the Little Grey Rabbit series. Despite the success of these books, Alison declared herself dissatisfied with the royalties she received from Collins in the autumn of 1937: she was sent a cheque for £13. 14s. 4d. against the six months' sales of 1462 copies of *Little Grey Rabbit's Party*, 816 of *Squirrel Goes Skating* and 568 of *Wise Owl's Story*.[45] The six months up to Christmas of 1937 were, however, to see the sale of over 11,000 copies of the Grey Rabbit books. The question of Alison's financial return from these books seems to have come up when she visited William Collins in London on 28 March 1938, since he told her that he gave her 'as much as I dare'.

One considerable, and much delayed, triumph for Alison during 1937 was the publication of *The Adventures of No Ordinary Rabbit* by Faber on

29 November. This much travelled and much despaired of book had been rejected by Nelson early in 1937. Alison, who considered the book 'so original', took some comfort from the thirty pounds that she had already earned from the text from the BBC and *New World* magazine. Refusing to give up, she sent it to Faber. She was relieved at the end of April 1937 when Faber's Charles Stewart wrote back to her suggesting certain alterations to the manuscript. This was encouraging in itself, but as Alison delved further into the parcel which contained the manuscript she found a note from Mr Faber to, she presumed, Mr Stewart. The note read, 'E[nid] E.F[aber] reports favourably on this. She says also, I think rightly, that Alison Uttley seems to have staying power, and is likely to go on and increase her reputation, and is therefore worth sticking to. . . . G.C.F[aber].' Alison reacted rapturously to this news, declaring it 'A feather in my cap, an encouragement for a lovely Mimbles, and it makes me want to write more and more.'[46]

The Adventures of No Ordinary Rabbit was illustrated to Alison's entire satisfaction by Alec Buckels. It ran to 208 pages, and consisted of eighteen homely tales of the boyish adventures of Tim Rabbit. It is characterised by scraps of versified country lore and it shares, in common with the Little Grey Rabbit books, not merely some hissing, threatening weasels in a crooked black house, but also the same schoolmaster, – the rabbit, Old Jonathan. Alison's pleasure at the advance copies of the book led her to observe that although she found Faber 'drier' than Collins, they nonetheless produced her books beautifully.

The book was well-received. *The Times Literary Supplement* remarked that it provided 'The right type of tale for under seven, perhaps under ten will not despise them indeed.'[47] The *Observer* wrote 'With pauses to look at the pictures, the tale goes perfectly.'[48] The book's success was to lead to a series of Tim Rabbit books, which brought Alison further fame and income. More importantly, perhaps, it was her first animal children's book to be published by Faber, who already published her books of country reminiscence and her collections of fairy tales.

In 1938 Faber were to publish two more of Alison's books. The first of these was her novel, *High Meadows*. Early in 1937, Alison was still struggling to put the novel into a form that would be satisfying to her and acceptable to her publishers. One of her chief problems seems to have been that she identified so closely with the Verity family, who represent her own family, the Taylors, and particularly with the heroine Patty, who represents herself, that her emotions sometimes got in the way of her writing. During March 1937 she spent hours typing and retyping the script, trying to disentangle Patty's lovers and once feeling herself lost among the High Leas hayfields.[49] But at the beginning of

April she received invaluable help when her friend LM, to whom the book was eventually dedicated, came on a visit. The two friends read parts of the book: 'It is terribly confused, and not fit for anyone to read, yet I must have advice on it. LM read a great deal, and suggested that Patty ought to marry Jem Crossland. This surprised me, I have half fallen in love with my poacher-gipsy myself, but I never thought of Patty marrying him. Yet that is the solution. I felt so happy that Patty would be happy with him. We worked till nearly midnight.'[50]

Two days later Alison and LM had finished the revision, and she set about retyping one hundred thousand words. At the end of June 1937, while she was working tenaciously on the typescript, she was still agonising over Patty's choice of partner, recording this dialogue in her diary:

'Oh Patty Verity, do you want to marry Martin Dunkerley or not?'
'No, I don't. I want to stay home and hide at the farm.'
'Yes, you'd better. There's a warm fire in the grate, P.V. And happiness, and here it is icy cold and no fire.'[51]

By the middle of July she had rewritten twenty-two chapters in forty-four days. She still had doubts about the book, thinking that perhaps it was too long and too 'placid', although believing that the ending was good. On 27 November she was delighted and astonished when Faber accepted it on the condition that it was cut by sixty pages. On 24 February 1938 Alison received the first six chapters of the book in proof form and was 'Most thrilled to see it in print, and the lovely leafy oblong round each chapter heading. They are the most artistic and excellent publishers, they spare no pains.'[52]

High Meadows was published on 14 April 1938. The book is often mawkish in sentiment, predictable in characterisation, and ridden with clichés. Sometimes the writing is downright banal: '"I'm no milkmaid," pouted Patty, screwing her mouth into a rosebud which Martin thought adorable. . . . "Yes, if you please sir, kind sir," she said. Patty bobbed a curtsey.'[53] There is also something unbecoming in Alison's choice of a surname for the representation of her own family, Verity, which, meaning truth, presents a shining, unduly virtuous image. Here and there throughout the text, however, flickers Alison's genuine and startling ability to recapture so finely life in the countryside.

High Meadows got the reviews it deserved. Among the more favourable notices of the book in the national press was one in the *Daily Telegraph*, which wrote that it 'describes an idyllic country life with all the stock figures . . . everyone who likes good, honest, sweet-smelling books will like it'. *Punch* was able to comment that its 'underlying appeal is so valid . . . so intensely felt'. More typical was the *Manchester*

Guardian which observed, accurately enough, that Alison was not primarily a novelist and that a synopsis of the story would make the book sound a 'terribly old-fashioned tale'. Alison was also hurt by a scathing review in *John O'London's Weekly* and an equally bad one in the *New Statesman*. Despite the mixed notices in the press, two hundred copies of the novel were taken by the Junior Book Club, and seven hundred copies were sold in five weeks.[54]

Both Faber and Alison must have been relieved that the publication of another volume of her fairy tales, *Mustard, Pepper and Salt*, on 6 October 1938 was much more favourably received by the critics. Alison was pleased both by a good review in the *Daily Telegraph* and one in *The Sunday Times*, which remarked 'Alison Uttley's head must be full of stories, and she produces them so easily.' *Books of Today* thought that the stories had 'certain affinities with Oscar Wilde's beautiful tales for children'. The only discordant note was struck by a letter from Eleanor Graham, saying that 'frankly, she doesn't like many of the tales in M. P. and S, they are not worthy of me, and will have to criticise adversely! I told Faber not to put them in, but they would do so. Now my dear book is in the soup, just when I want the money.'[55] This proved to be a pessimistic, though understandable, reaction.

Fuzzypeg Goes to School was also published in 1938. Alison described working on it in the spring of that year: 'Today I have been typing the new Fuzzypeg, looking up flowers and trees, thinking of phrases. I like it very much, and think it will do for Mr Collins, but John must read it first.'[56] Successful as the book was on its publication, its production entailed a bizarre tiff between Alison and Margaret Tempest. During August, Alison expressed delight at the illustrations, 'more adorable things, which pleased me very much. She *is* good. I am sure the book will be lovely.'[57] Despite this favourable reaction, Alison apparently returned the illustrations with a letter containing some criticism, for on 21 September she received a reply from Margaret Tempest 'incensed at my criticisms of the Fuzzypeg book – and rightly so. I was stupid to criticise them when they were done. She said she spent three months over the paintings. So I wrote back, rather apologetic, but I feel rather uncomfortable.'[58] A review in *The Times* confirmed this recantation, praising Margaret Tempest's 'delicate, miniature-like paintings'.

While these six books were being published, Alison was busying herself with various projects. In April 1937 she was writing part of a Little Grey Rabbit play, 'to cheer myself up', and at the end of August 1937 she began writing the story of *The Speckledy Hen*. Of far greater significance for her reputation as a writer, however, was the work she began early in 1937 upon a historical novel for children. She had begun researching for this book partly in response to a letter from William

Collins encouraging her to undertake such a project. She worked on and off at the novel for the next eighteen months. Her idea was to write a book centered on the unsuccessful Babington Plot to rescue Mary Queen of Scots and murder Queen Elizabeth I. The conspiracy had been hatched at the old manor at Dethick, only a few miles from Castle Top Farm. In October 1937 Alison's friend, Winnie Armitage, drove her to Manchester so that she could undertake research into the historical background of the Babington conspiracy at the Rylands University Library. Alison soon became deeply, almost mystically involved in the writing of this story. She chose to tell it through the person of a twentieth-century girl, Penelope, who on visiting an ancient farmhouse, Thackers, was to find herself travelling back in time to watch the unfolding of the drama. She declared herself greatly moved by the tragic tale of Anthony Babington and perhaps fell more than a little in love with his younger brother Francis.[59]

By the end of November 1937 she was typing the final version of the novel, provisionally entitled *Thackers*, finishing it on 11 December 1937. Four days later she posted the typescript, now entitled *The Secret of Thackers*, noting in her diary, 'I always feel romantic when I post a new book.'[60]

The typescript was sent to William Collins who had, after all, suggested that Alison should write a historical novel for him. At the end of March 1938 Alison called on Mr Collins at his London office where he told her 'that Thackers would not do in its present form, too difficult. He was very charming and kind.'[61] Alison later went to lunch with her friend Eleanor Graham, who took the manuscript of the book away with her afterwards. As a result of these consultations, Alison had decided by the end of April 1938 to rewrite the book. The going, though, was difficult and early in May she was complaining that she could not get on with the work of revision and that the characters did not 'live' for her. A few days later, however, she had become so deeply involved with the book that she complained, 'I feel queer, not knowing when and where I live, out of time, partly with doing the sixteenth century tale.'[62] Towards the end of June she had completed her revision, and sent the typescript back to William Collins. In October, Collins finally rejected the book: 'a nice letter from W.A.R. Collins, but he says the characters are not enough distinctive [sic] and not enough action. So that's that! But I didn't repine, for now I've gone back to my first love, the first edition, and I am reading it with pleasure, and shall try Faber.'[63]

Throughout these years the prospect of moving from Bowdon became more and more attractive. Alison refused an offer of one thousand pounds for Downs House in February 1937 and in August that year advertised the property in the *Manchester Guardian*, describing it as a

'Small detached house of character, excellent condition. Two large receptions, five bedrooms, many cupboards, pantry. Power, gas. Quiet road. Garden. Ten minutes to station. One thousand pounds.'[64]

By January 1938, however, Alison was still in Downs House, declaring herself 'very tired of this house, and all the work and turmoil, and I long for a little modern house with a tiny easy kitchen. I feel I am marking time, waiting for spring and a new house.'[65] She concentrated on three areas: Devon, near Torquay, Haslemere in Surrey and Buckinghamshire. At the end of her diary for 1938 she left a list of the houses that she had viewed and her reasons for liking them or disliking them. One problem was cost, since she felt unable to offer more than sixteen hundred pounds for any house; the other was that she did not want to live in anything 'too suburban and squashed'.

Eventually in July she found the house in Beaconsfield in which she was to live until her death in 1976. GL and John approved of the house, and on 20 July 1938 she signed the contract. Early in August she and John decided that the new house should be called 'Thackers' an interesting choice in view of the fact that Alison had not yet persuaded any publisher to take on the typescript bearing that name.

Alison contemplated her move with 'many a qualm. I think we can manage and I think we shall love it, but it is a terrific outlay for a penniless couple like John and myself.'[66] In fact, Alison was far from penniless. Unable to sell Downs House for the price she wanted, she proceeded to let it for an annual rental of sixty pounds. This meant that she was able to buy a new house for £1475 (plus a hundred pound contribution to making up the adjoining road) without realising the capital tied up in her house at Bowdon.

Alison was aware of other ambivalent feelings about the move: 'We had to take the plunge and get away from Bowdon, to more sunshine, and for me to be nearer John, and to have London not far away. To escape from these uncongenial people and dirty old Altrincham. Yet I love Downs House, and I hate to leave W. Armitage . . . and not to have LM so often, or to see darling Prof. A and Mrs Johnson. The die is cast, and I must move forward with no backward glance.'[67]

At 6.30 a.m. on 15 September Alison and John got up to begin the 'great removal'.

CHAPTER FIFTEEN

Beaconsfield In Wartime, 1938–41

> If the Germans come, marching through here, I shall have to fly . . . on my cycle perhaps, and I can't ride more than 2 miles. . . . I wonder if one ought to hide one's silver. . . .
>
> ALISON UTTLEY, diary, 21 May 1940

> . . . I do find life difficult at times, – alone I can do it, but strangers with no 'vision' are as disconcerting as strangers to a child, and I behave childishly too, do foolish things, unworthy. . . . I don't think one can have great imagination and great wisdom. Can one?
>
> ALISON UTTLEY, diary, 17 January 1941

Alison's new house, Thackers, was a fairly solid, two storey building faced with brick up to first floor level, above which were white walls bearing black gables. Inside, the main feature was a long sitting-room which, within a few years, was to become 'crowded with objects she had collected, including, of course, her very remarkable collection of Dutch and Flemish painters, all of them small, incidentally, and things like snuff-boxes, patch-boxes, little ornaments of various kinds . . . she had a passion for these small things'.[1] As Alison got older her house became more and more cluttered, and it was sometimes quite difficult to move about freely, especially with the trailing flexes from several electric fires. Her furnishings were by no means avant-garde. Among other things, the long sitting-room contained a big square armchair in which she often sat, a dresser with rows of plates and items of china, and a grand piano. There was a standard lamp with a pleated fawn shade and similar coloured curtains, giving the overall effect of an oatmeal-coloured room. It is easy to see why she was first attracted to the house by this pleasing and spacious room, where she was to write so many of her books sitting at a desk from which she could see her garden.

Her friend and publisher at Faber, Peter du Sautoy, remembered that:

> Her house was in a perfectly ordinary suburban road . . . but it had a very nice garden, and at the end of the garden, quite a long bit of woodland, which had been kept when the houses were built. This was

very important to her, as her dogs could play in it, and she could watch the trees, very big trees they were, and there were all sorts of wild flowers growing in the wood, which she loved. I always thought that this was something she was very lucky to have, in Beaconsfield, which is after all a suburban town.[2]

Alison was to live at Thackers for the next thirty-eight years, growing in fame as an author and receiving many visitors, including Susan Dickinson who dealt with her Little Grey Rabbit books at Collins:

> She had this house, rather like [Grey Rabbit's] little house at the edge of the wood. It was filled with memories; every single available surface was covered with little figurines and little boxes; and then down at the bottom of the garden were the dogs' graves, where you were taken and shown these little standing stones by the bluebell wood; and of course there was always a Scottie. It was a lovely place to visit, and I always enjoyed going to see her very much. She was such a stimulating person to talk to.[3]

But visiting Alison Uttley was not always easy, as many of her friends and acquaintances found. She could be charming and hospitable, but also abrupt and dominating. She remained a commanding and fascinating person well into old age. She was later to recall that when she moved to Beaconsfield she looked and felt young, apart from the greying of her hair.[4] Her features were strong, handsome and shrewd, she was definite in manner and still spoke with a distinct Derbyshire accent. Although her face and eyes could be kindly, there was a touch of steel in her glance and an authority in her personality. It was difficult to visit Alison except on her terms:

> I always thought one had to get slightly attuned to her atmosphere, her whole way of thinking, her way of life, because she was rather an extraordinary person. You had to get used to the idea that here was somebody who really did believe in fairies . . . and she was also liable to talk at very short notice about things like dreams and ghosts. . . . You had to get used to that, to tune in with her feelings, her interests, and it was sometimes a bit difficult to do that.[5]

Other visitors found her to be a curious mixture: hospitable and intellectually demanding, restless, always turning things over in her mind, enquiring and intuitive. For those lacking the appropriate intellectual muscle, she was an intimidating and disquieting hostess.

The hard edge of her personality was, however, often retracted when children visited her. Charles Stewart, who was her editor at Faber during this time, visited her frequently with his family. His wife and two daughters remember her as 'very lively, with bright, sparkling eyes. She was so sympathetic and prepared nice teas' for them.[6] But the Stewarts were also aware that Alison was living on 'a high wire, and crammed a lot into every day'. They remembered her high-pitched voice when she called to her Scottie dog, as well as the black looks she gave them when the milk was spilled or when she asked them not to blunt her knives by cutting too vigorously on to their plates. Another friend, Sir Oliver Millar, recalls that 'She was always nice to our three little girls' and sums her up as 'a good mixture . . . of a deep imagination and a good shrewd business head.'[7]

Alison seems to have settled quickly into her new environment, in particular valuing her garden which she described on a wet November day two months after the move: 'the beech trees waving gently, irregularly, some lower branches moving violently as the rain catches them, the high boughs swaying softly. Now a roar of wind in the trees. The lawn looks very green, and one dandelion stands upright. The two cypresses guard my doorway, and they don't move at all.'[8]

Although a crop of celebrities lived in or within striking distance of Beaconsfield, including G.K. Chesterton, G.L. Garvin, Editor of the *Observer*, Walter de la Mare, Enid Blyton, Angela Thirkell and the critic S.P.B. Mais, by the end of November 1938 Alison was bemoaning the fact that she was only meeting dull and conventional people, rather like those she had known at Bowdon. Her luck took a turn for the better early in 1939 when Katherine Wigglesworth, who was later to illustrate many of her books, heard from the local librarian that the author she so much admired was now a near neighbour. She called on Alison, but finding her out, left her her card:

> Some days later in the early afternoon I was on my hands and knees blowing at the newly-lit fire in our sitting room, when a voice behind me said 'He huffed and he puffed till he blew the house down!' I jumped up and there, leaning in at the open casement window was Alison Uttley. I let her in the front door, and as I passed through the hall, Nanny came down the stairs with a twin under each arm.[9]

A warm friendship was to develop between the two women, although there were periods of estrangement and disenchantment. Katherine Wigglesworth pleased Alison by calling Thackers 'a fairy house'. Alison called often at the Wigglesworths' house, to talk about the manuscript she was working on and sometimes to ask Katherine to look critically at Margaret Tempest's illustrations for the latest Little Grey Rabbit book. She has left many descriptions of calling on her friends with Hamish, her Scottie: 'A lovely picture. Mrs W, her cheeks like red apples, in her bright red and blue and green overall, holding little Bill in her arms, his head pressed to her cheek, and arms round her neck, and Jane holding on to her skirt.'[10] Alison became particularly attached to the Wigglesworth twins, Bill and Jane, loving to play with them, as once, at night, she lifted Bill high in her arms while he called out 'The moon! The moon!' Sometimes she would invite Katherine Wigglesworth, the twins and their nanny, Eileen, round for supper: 'Such a feast, and the greatest fun. . . . We all washed up. Then we sang! . . . we went on to all the old favourites – and we sang and sang till after midnight, an uproarious trio.'[11]

One problem in Alison's relationship with the Wigglesworths was the difficulty she had in relating to Dr Wigglesworth, a pattern which was to be repeated in her relationships with several of the married couples with whom she became friendly. Dr Wigglesworth, already embarked on what was to become a very distinguished scientific career, was seen by Alison as 'dry, cold, rude. . . . A detestable man.'[12] Once Alison, conscious of her inferior scientific status, complained that he treated her like 'a lab boy'. Perhaps these difficulties were also the result of a competition between Alison and Dr Wigglesworth for Katherine's attention. They were not helped by Dr Wigglesworth teasing Alison that she had simply copied Beatrix Potter. Certainly Alison was to encounter similar problems when she developed a close and affectionate friendship with Lilian King, who lived at nearby Penn. She once asked Mrs King to get rid of two friends who were with her so that she could talk to her properly, and she had great difficulty in relating to Mr King. Once, after Mr King had told her that Lilian was unavailable, Alison left this note on his door:

> My wife is unavailable,
> My kingdom's unassailable,
> I am the King of Penn.[13]

By the end of January 1939 Alison was expressing her exhilaration at meeting so many interesting people at Beaconsfield. During her time there she was to be particularly close to the Gurneys, the Fairbairns, the Kanns, the Athays, Lord and Lady Howe and Margaret Rutherford and her husband Lewis Stringer. Among her more important new friends was Walter de la Mare, whom she visited at the Old Park at Penn for the first time in October 1940. Alison was shown into de la Mare's presence by a butler in a yellow waistcoat, and there met:

> Mr de la Mare, smiling, small, sweet-faced coming to see me across the room. The fire flickering in long flames. . . . We talk of auto-biographies and childhoods, and first memories, and a child's impressions of grown-ups, flowers and smells and colour. . . . We spoke of Prof. A, and of words. . . . I talked to him of his poetry. I asked him to come to tea, and he said he would. Oh joy.[14]

When de la Mare visited Thackers, the conversation ranged as widely as it had at Penn – wider even, this time taking in the nature of dreams as well. Although the friendship was to flourish and grow, nine months later Alison, quick to imagine rebuffs, felt that de la Mare had taken a dislike to her and was treating her with disdain.[15]

The relationship which continued to give Alison the greatest pleasure was, naturally enough, with her son. She remained deeply attached to him, felt really happy only when he was in the house with her and was correspondingly bereft when he left. Although she had expected it, she received a great shock when John was called up three months after the outbreak of war. He was commissioned as a lieutenant in the artillery and Alison was haunted by the prospect of him leaving her so soon for military service. Before he departed on 28 December 1939, she expressed in her diary her great love for him, seeing him as a fine man, an idealist, who had now to get used to the more brutal business of handling guns. On one of their last nights together she 'played Chopin, fumbling, but John loved it. . . . It is marvellous this friendship and love between us.'

Although John was not to go on active service for some time, the prospect of this worried her and she found it 'bliss' when he came home on leave. In the spring of 1941 she was 'washing up after lunch' when 'a camouflaged lorry stopped outside, – and I saw John's scarlet cap. I was thrilled.'[16] John's absence on military service meant his mother felt his worth all the more and she wrote after one weekend leave how much she valued 'the feeling of John in the house, his attitude always intrigues me. I love his acceptance, the careless happiness, yet the careful attention he pays, – never a word against anyone, always jolly and charming.'[17] Although one might wonder what price John paid in terms of repressed anger in order to win such maternal approval, there seems no doubt that the relationship remained very close and loving. It is perhaps a poignant indication of Alison's feeling of loneliness that in January 1941 she asked, albeit jokingly, a man who had just sold her some firewood whether he would sell her his little boy.[18]

Her contact with her relations continued to be distant. She was able to acknowledge occasional 'nice letters' from Emily, but she remained fundamentally disapproving of her Uttley in-laws. She was glad to hear, during the spring of 1940, that Joan Uttley was to marry an airman and that Tony Tolson had been called up, expressing the opinion that it would do them both good. Gertrude she continued to see as a positively malevolent influence, even refusing in May 1940 to give her John's address on the grounds that she was a Fifth Columnist.[19] Although she was delighted in the autumn of 1940 to show her new house to her brother Harry, two months later, at Christmas time, she was expressing frustration that he and his wife had not acknowledged her Christmas presents to them of a new book and ten shillings: 'They have no gratitude. I really will never send them one of my books, or any money, for they don't deserve it. They are the only ungrateful ones I know.'[20] She dismissed Frances's and Harry's present to her, a pair of painted candles, as rubbish and a waste of money. More gratifying for Alison was the appreciation shown by Harry's son, Ronnie Taylor, who, even while serving in the Merchant Navy, showed a ready appreciation of the books which she sent him.

Several of Alison's well-established friends visited her soon after her move. GL came to stay with her several times and in May 1941, amid wartime rationing, touched Alison by sending her a box of eggs through the post, three of which arrived smashed. LM was an equally welcome guest, although Alison tended to notice her primness as well as her 'sweet nature'. Eleanor Graham also came to stay, although in October 1939 Alison found her visit a strain, subsequently rationalising: 'I feel E.G. disapproves of me, – I don't know why. I am myself, and I have my own secret world of magic and beauty. She is matter of fact and practical, and I am not.'[21] The redoubtable Miss Hackforth arrived in August 1939, in a taxi, Alison was rather shocked to notice; perhaps she still nurtured a grievance from earlier in the year when Miss Hackforth had cancelled a visit at the last minute because of it being 'too wet', leaving her with a good deal of superfluous food that she had prepared.

A succession of home helps and gardeners attended Alison's first years at Thackers. She recounted various 'struggles' with her maids, once dismissing as 'absurd' a demand for pay at tenpence an hour and eventually agreeing on eightpence. From April 1940, however, she developed more stable relations with a cheerful and hard-working help, Kathleen.

On balance, the domestic help she received enabled Alison to lead the sort of life she wanted. She was able to visit London as often as she wished, although the outbreak of war was to be an inevitable inhibition. She visited the capital in November 1940, however, 'feeling rather frightened' and taking 'a big hanky for a bandage' in case of an air raid; she noticed 'the great smash at Oxford Street, acres of Lewis's down' and a smashed grand piano among the rubble on the Regent Street pavement.

Back in Buckinghamshire, she greatly appreciated her new surroundings, taking long walks in the woods and cycling further afield to the old part of Beaconsfield to do her shopping. One of her reasons for visiting Beaconsfield so regularly was to have her hair permed or set; she sometimes resented this, considering the two pounds she paid the hairdresser at the start of July 1941 'a wicked waste of good money. I hate it, but it has to be done with my mop.'[22] She joined in local activities, playing cricket for the first time in fifteen years in August 1939 and scoring three runs, and attending – and sometimes being bored by – meetings of the Women's Institute. She took the *Daily Telegraph* on weekdays and at the weekend enjoyed the 'cheap luxury' of *The Sunday Times* as well as the *Observer*.

Despite the many friendships, some of them uncommonly warm, that Alison made in her new surroundings, she continued to set high store by the solitude that enabled her to write. She resented the fact that her next-door neighbours, the Lanigans, were sometimes noisy and she once felt herself to have been particularly self-sacrificing to have invited Eleanor Graham to stay for the weekend. Her diaries contain many descriptions and rationalisations of her often solitary state:

> Sunday, – breakfast in bed, rain pouring, and I read the Observer. Later the rain ceased and I went out with Hamish, over the hill down the field, then through the woods to Knotty Green. I picked bunches of lovely catkins, some of them out, pale green, very soft and delicate. . . . I went in the garden, the first time for days, so many bulbs. . . . I had spoken to nobody except a woman with dogs, but I have not felt lonely, with [the] wireless and Hamish.[23]

She found great satisfaction and inspiration from her solitary walks: 'As I walked this morning I kept singing "Oh the Holly and the Ivy", scraps out of Traveller in Time. I felt happy as I walked along, nobody there, and all the lovely woods and the farm with men throwing turnips in a heap in the big barn, and hens running into it to eat in the straw.'[24]

Alison spent some of her time alone taking stock of herself. On her fifty-fifth birthday she wrote:

> Well, I am now 55, and it doesn't seem long since I was 5, but I am glad I am *not* 5. It wasn't too comfortable for me. I am thankful for all the lovely things of life, for rain and sun and sky, for silence and for sound, for all things I have loved. I believe in immortality and I love God. I pray above all for John's safety and his happiness and his courage, and I am thankful for all my dear ones, those who have died and those living.[25]

She often found the natural world so beautiful that she assumed that it was an indication of what Paradise would be like, 'Heaven is here, if we did but see it.' In January 1941 a complimentary review in the *Irish Times* of her book *Ambush of Young Days* remarked that she had not lost the 'poetic vision of childhood', prompting Alison to write:

> I have not, but I do find life difficult at times, – alone I can do it, but strangers with no 'vision' are as disconcerting as strangers to a child, and I behave childishly too, and do foolish things, unworthy. I want a steadying influence then, a mother to help me, a son to help me, for

John has much more wisdom than I have, bless him. I don't think one can
have great imagination and great wisdom. Can one?[26]

Alison continued to cope with her various ailments and her fits of depression
alone. Her weak knee remained troublesome; on one occasion her feet
swelled up alarmingly; sometimes she slipped and fell, and in the summer of
1941 tumbled painfully off her bike. She coped with her depressions by
enduring the suffering they brought, and finding renewal through rest and
the beauty of the natural world.

Despite her bouts of depression, she was wary of psychiatric remedies,
remarking vehemently, 'I do *not* like psychologists. I feel they make the
theory and put things into it.'[27] Ironically, she continued to set great store by
her dreams, often recording them meticulously in her diary. Much of this
marvellously rich and varied material was later incorporated into her book
The Stuff of Dreams. It is interesting, and an indication of her reluctance to
acknowledge the dark side of her own nature, that she makes hardly any
attempt to analyse her dream life. Why, for example, did she find her dream
of Japanese faces, seen at an exhibition, 'absolute bliss'? What was the
significance of a dream in which Walter de la Mare drove up to Castle Top
Farm in 'a queer antediluvian car', embarrassing Alison by seeing her family
in 'all our workaday affairs'? Why did Alison not think further of the dream
prompted by the news that her niece Katherine was to be married, in which
she retreated from a bull and withdrew into an old house where a man was
writing? She did, however, enter into a correspondence with J.W. Dunne
over the significance of dreams and the nature of time, and felt greatly
gratified when this distinguished authority told her that her dream experiences were 'unique'.[28]

The approach of the Second World War had been an inevitable
preoccupation for Alison in the year following her move to Beaconsfield.
In January 1939 the *Observer's* analysis of Hitler's aggressive intent put
her into a panic, although three months later she felt less frightened at the
prospect of war because she accepted the good reasons for fighting it. Her
anxieties sometimes affected her capacity for work, making her feel
'disinterested'. During August 1939 she laid in stocks of food and
prepared rather anxiously for the arrival of evacuees (she tended to call
them 'slum children'). At the end of August 1939, with the outbreak of
war a few days away, she expressed her amazement that in her new
environment there were no 'backsliders', though she imagined there
were plenty of them up in Bowdon. On 1 September Germany invaded
Poland and two days later Alison wrote: 'War declared today at eleven
o'clock. We heard it at eleven fifteen. It is like a nightmare. But the sky is
blue and cloudy white, [the] flowers lovely. We gathered berries and red
leaves. Four little children, evacuated, came to tea. Now it is a bad time. I
cannot write.'[29]

By the end of October Alison had put many of her doubts behind her and was able to give a clear-eyed assessment of what the war was about:

> We do not fight for Poland. This is no war about a map. This is a war to enable individuals to live in freedom. This tyranny must be abased. Caesar was a conqueror, he extended Roman Law. Alexander spread Gr[eek] civilisation. What does Hitler bring! Torture, concentration camps, secret police, religious persecution. Only [the] defeat of Hitlerism can dispel the dark shadows over the world.[30]

Alison's diaries reveal her detailed reaction to the progress of the war. Her response to the traumas of its first years were in no way remarkable and probably reflected the views of the bulk of her fellow citizens. She expressed her shock at Russia's invasion of Finland in November 1939; she was amazed and outraged at the French collapse during the summer of 1940; and expressed her despair that the United States seemed unwilling to enter the conflict on Britain's side. She maintained a sturdy patriotism, comparing herself favourably with her sister-in-law Gertrude whom she caricatured as a pacifist and pro-Communist, as well as being selfish and a snob. Alison saw Castle Top as a stronghold, ready to fight to the end. After Winston Churchill became Prime Minister in June 1940 she declared him to be a worthy successor to King Alfred, who so many centuries before had led English resistance to invasion. Despite her confidence in Churchill, she recognised the very real perils that Britain faced during 1940 and in the May of that year asked herself what should she do if the Germans arrived: 'If the Germans come, marching through here, I shall have to fly . . . on my cycle perhaps, and I can't ride more than 2 miles, but it would help to have it. I wonder if one ought to hide one's silver, or what one ought to do. Darling John, – I wish I could see you to talk this over, I feel rather lost in this world.'[31]

In common with her fellow countrymen and women, Alison endured various privations and perils during the war. Although she did not always go to the shelter when the air-raid sirens went, at the height of the Battle of Britain she did come downstairs in response to 'guns firing, bombs falling, and planes roaring over'.[32] A few months earlier she had wondered whether the cuckoo still sang when bombs were falling. She did not welcome wartime rationing, forgetting her card once when she went to collect her meat ration and appealing unsuccessfully to Beaconsfield Council to get her small coal ration increased.

At the outbreak of war Alison tended to romanticise the arrival of evacuees from London, noting while taking tea at her friend Mrs Wardle's that 'A jolly little Cockney peeped in at her window.'[33] When Alison's own sense of public duty was put to the test, however, she seems mostly to have failed. In October 1939 she was appalled at the arrival of a Mrs Stafford and her grown-up daughter, whom she had been asked to put up for a while: 'Oh goodness, how disappointed I was to see a frowzy old woman . . . as different as possible from what I expected. I like the daughter, plain but good hearted and kind. . . . The mother bored me nearly to tears . . . such a greedy old thing. . . . Blast her!'[34] Three weeks later Alison was delighted to see them go, comforting herself that she would now be able to get down to her writing. In the spring of 1940 she expressed a willingness to take in some French refugees, but then argued that she was not well enough to undertake the responsibility. A few months later she refused point-blank to accommodate two Czech Jewish refugees: 'the girl with painted lips, the man like an East End Jew, a couple I disliked intensely, the man avoiding military service, the two out for their own fun. Their air was most repulsive, I wondered who would take them in, rich and rotten they looked.'[35] She turned away several other people, including an old woman and a young child in October 1940 and when, early the next year, she was obliged to have a soldier billeted on her, complained bitterly that he was wasting her electricity.[36]

The truth is that the war, despite its high drama, despite her son's involvement in it, was essentially a distraction impeding Alison's insatiable desire to write. From the date of her move to Beaconsfield until the end of 1941 her literary output was staggering. She published nine books and wrote six more. She contributed several tales to *Child Education*, including 'Macaroni Cheese', 'The Little Red Hen' and 'The Firewood Tale'. Early in 1941 she wrote a play for radio about Mary Queen of Scots, becoming so intensely involved in the story that she felt that she knew her intimately and became 'half-frightened' as if the tragic, doomed queen was really alive.[37] The play was broadcast on 17 March 1941. The BBC broadcast a large number of her stories, mostly to do with the characters in the Sam Pig books. But in January 1940 Rhoda Power at the BBC asked her to write something about Hans Christian Andersen. Alison was thrilled with this commission: 'I cannot tell you how proud and happy this made me feel. I thought of the little girl at Castle Top, reading Hans Andersen, and now being asked to write about him.'[38] In 1946 she was to publish *The Washerwoman's Child: A Play on the Life and Stories of Hans Christian Andersen*. Although the BBC rejected four of her country tales in November 1939, there was ample compensation for this disappointment, not only in the success of her broadcasted Sam Pig tales, for which by 1940 she was being paid four guineas each, but also in the knowledge that Uncle Mac of 'Children's Hour' had written to her telling her how often children requested more tales about Sam and his family and friends.

Alison's overwhelming desire, though, was to write stories for publication. She continued to set herself daunting schedules. In January 1940 she noted down her writing programme:

> This year I want to write either a book of fairy tales, or Pig stories continued, or both. Also to clarify the short stories, and make two volumes, one of C. Child tales, the other of stories. There is that novel hanging in the air, and what about a sequel to Traveller in Time? I must work hard now each day and get something done, really finished. So each day to keep myself at the grindstone I will write down what I have done. Really I am lazy. I want to dream, and I must work.[39]

Two months later she had posted off to Collins the typescripts of *Little Grey Rabbit's Washing Day*, and *Water Rat's Picnic*. The former book had been suggested by John as he watched Alison's washing on the line and Alison preferred it to *Water Rat's Picnic*, remembering how much she had chuckled when she wrote it.[40] Margaret Tempest was impressed by the rapid production of these two little books, asking Alison how she managed to write them so quickly and wondering with her whether, with the war in full swing, *Little Grey Rabbit's Washing Day* would ever be published.[41] By the end of the year Alison was writing a story she called 'Grey Rabbit's War', later to be published as *Hare Joins the Home Guard* in 1942, and *Little Grey Rabbit's Birthday* which did not reach the bookshops till 1944. She was by now producing these tales at such a rate that there was a gap of nearly four years between her submission of *Little Grey Rabbit's Birthday* to Collins and its eventual publication.

During the Spring of 1940 she was working hard at her Sam Pig stories, finishing the typescript on 28 March and declaring, perhaps surprisingly for her, 'I am quite sick of the 4 pigs, and don't want to write any more animal tales yet awhile.'[42]

Part of her frustration may have arisen from her difficulty in arriving at a good ending for her new Sam Pig book. But a much more potent factor was her belief that these tales were something of a diversion from 'the real work, the book'. The book Alison referred to was another volume of autobiographical writing, eventually published as *The Farm on the Hill* in April 1941. Alison was working sporadically at this typescript, provisionally entitled 'Susan Garland', from the beginning of 1940. She finished the book on the first day of August 1940, although feeling dissatisfied with the last chapter. At the end of the year she started 'a quite unexpected book "Country Memories".'[43] This was eventually published in 1943 as *Country Hoard*. Alison also sowed the seed for a future book when, while working at some tales of country reminiscence, she dug into her mother's old cookery book for inspiration. Many years later, and at the suggestion of Peter du Sautoy, this book was published as *Recipes from an Old Farmhouse*. One disadvantage of Alison's strict system of schedules was that it made no allowance for human frailty: at the beginning of December 1940 she was racked with guilt that she hadn't managed to write anything for a whole week.

Her professional relationship with Margaret Tempest continued to teeter between fertile co-operation and a jealousy spiced with ill will. Although Alison received a friendly visit from Miss Tempest in July 1939, she had a few months earlier dismissed her as a 'humourless bore'. A little later she apparently triumphed over her in a quarrel over some illustrations, noting in her diary that in the past it had been mostly she, Alison, who had given way in such circumstances. Significantly Alison asked Katherine Wigglesworth to advise her on the draft illustrations for *Moldy Warp, the Mole* in 1940. Margaret Tempest agreed to alter these pictures as Alison wished. In the spring of 1941 Alison was happy to agree to the twenty illustrations Margaret Tempest suggested for *Hare Joins the Home Guard*, and in June of that year admitted that her illustrator had taken her 'awful criticisms' quite well.[44]

The rivalry that existed between Alison and Margaret Tempest found an echo, though at a greater distance, in Alison's positive dislike for Enid Blyton. Too jealous of her reputation to abide comparison with any other author, even the illustrious Beatrix Potter, Alison was also fiercely competitive on the commercial front, finding Enid Blyton's huge sales particularly galling. Her antagonism towards her was compounded by the fact that they both lived in Beaconsfield. The first hint of any rivalry occurred in May 1941, when Katherine Wigglesworth went as Alison's emissary to the local W.H. Smith's 'trying to get him to stock my books': 'he refused. No demand! "Now if it was Miss Enid Blyton's books! They sell marvellously. Do you know her? She is a charming woman. Here is her photograph." Mrs Wig, "She looks rather harassed," – as she looks at the awful picture of a vulgar curled woman.'[45]

Alison only met Enid Blyton once socially. Towards the end of her life, she recalled an interview with a reporter from the *Bucks Advertiser*: 'I could only say that we only met once and when I asked her which books she wrote, she replied "Look in Smith's window", and turned away, and never spoke again.'[46]

Alison was perhaps not the totally innocent party in this encounter. Katherine Wigglesworth has left another account of the meeting:

> Alison was asked to meet her at a lunch party. As they all moved into the dining room for lunch, Alison, doing her best to be pleasant, turned to Enid Blyton and said 'I know the book you wrote about a

horse, but what else have you written?' Enid Blyton drew herself up and replied frostily 'Smith's window is *full* of my books. You can see a few titles if you care to look.' As Alison later said, 'You see, Katherine, I had mixed her up with *Enid Bagnold* and *National Velvet*.'[47]

According to her diaries, Alison was also introduced more spontaneously to Enid Blyton in April 1943 while standing in the queue at the fishmonger's in Beaconsfield: 'At Wilkinsons I was watching a woman ogling [the fishmonger], her false teeth, her red lips, her head on one side as she gazed up close to him – suddenly he turned to me and to my surprise introduced her, Enid Blyton! The Blyton, photographed and boastful!'[48]

Alison's dislike of Enid Blyton personally and her contempt for the quality of her children's books was summed up some years later when she observed that the best place for Blyton's books 'was a sale of work'.[49]

The books which Alison published during these three years ought to have blunted the edge of her rivalry with Enid Blyton. During the month of November 1939 alone, she published *Little Grey Rabbit's Christmas*, *Tales of the Four Pigs and Brock the Badger* and *A Traveller in Time*. *Little Grey Rabbit's Christmas* had sold nearly six thousand copies by March 1940 and the fifty-four pounds in royalties which Alison received seemed to her to lift her money worries for the foreseeable future.

The publication of the *Tales of the Four Pigs and Brock the Badger* led to the writing of twelve more books in the series. Faber had accepted the first book in April 1939, although asking Alison to produce fifteen thousand more words. Just over two weeks later she was able to post off the extended typescript. Although in August 1939 she was worried that various bits of rewriting were not good enough, when the advance copies arrived in November she took them round to her friend Katherine Wigglesworth to share the pleasure of their arrival. The visit to Katherine was particularly appropriate, since she provided Alison with the inspiration for one of the main supporting pillars of the Sam Pig books, Brock the Badger. Alison took a particular delight in the success of the Sam Pig stories, remembering her intimate communication with the pigs in their 'palatial' sty at Castle Top Farm and realising that her child readers 'liked Sam Pig very much. . . . They always ask for another little story of Sam Pig.'[50] Peter du Sautoy remembers that 'Sam Pig was the one the children loved. . . . Sam Pig is like a little boy really, rather mischievous and getting up to all sorts of adventures and so on. I used to think that he was in a way her son . . . John, fictional-ised.'[51]

Within two years of the successful publication of the first Sam Pig book, Alison had published *The Adventures of Sam Pig* in October 1940 and, during 1941, *Sam Pig Goes to Market*, *The Adventures of Sam Pig*, *Six Tales of Brock the Badger* and *Six Tales of the Four Pigs*. Although these books were to become strong sellers and to consolidate Alison's reputation as a highly successful writer of children's books, the contract for the second volume of the series, *The Adventures of Sam Pig*, took some time to negotiate. In June 1940 Alison expressed her displeasure with Faber for offering her no advance, even though the royalty terms for seven per cent against the first two thousand volumes sold and ten per cent on any sales after that were perfectly acceptable. She immediately caught the train to London to see William Collins. Mr Collins was very encouraging to Alison, as well as possibly taking a little pleasure in a rival's discomfort, and said that of course she should get her advance for her next Sam Pig book; interestingly, he also asked her to do a country book for them sometime.[52] The bubble of Alison's indignation was pricked four days later when Charles Stewart of Faber wrote an apologetic letter, saying that he had forgotten to mention that there would be a twenty pound advance for the next Sam Pig book which, curiously, Alison felt to be 'quite good'.[53]

In August 1940 Alison published *Moldy Warp, the Mole*. In March of that year she had objected to Collins's request that she allot each illustration to a particular page: 'I loathe doing this, it isn't fair to do it from the MS. So I just raced over it and got it done ready for posting tomorrow.'[54] With the original manuscript of this book Alison left a note presumably for posterity describing how she had written it: 'This is part of the manuscript of Moldy Warp, the Mole, written on my knee by the fire. Usually I type direct, and rewrite on the typescript.'[55] In 1941 Alison published another book for children, this time with Faber, *Ten Tales of Tim Rabbit*.

This small flood of children's books brought Alison some gratifying reviews. Of *Tales of the Four Pigs and Brock the Badger*, the *Observer* said, 'The animals that figure in these eventful and humorous tales are all the most distinct characters. A delightful book. The illustrations do full justice to the text, which means that they are very good indeed.'[56] *The Sunday Times* said, 'The adventures of four small pigs are full of fun and quite charmingly original. Sister Ann Pig is a joy.'[57] *Books of Today* remarked that the tales in *Sam Pig Goes to Market* 'are all delightful' and the Christmas edition of *The Times Educational Supplement* for 1941 observed, 'It would not be Christmas without some tales by Alison Uttley.'[58] *The Times Literary Supplement*, reviewing a few Sam Pig books and *Ten Tales of Tim Rabbit*, wrote that Alison's prose had 'a simplicity, a lucidity and a realism of detail that can persuade the most fantastic event into a convincing literalness'.

Of all of her books that came out at this time, the one with which Alison felt most passionately involved, and the one which was to prove among her most successful, was *A Traveller in Time*. Published in November 1939, it had caused Alison much anguish during its writing. Very early in 1939 she was willing herself to finish the 'darling of my heart' and a little later cudgelled her wits for a perfect ending and start to the typescript. At the end of January a speech by Hitler, of apparently peaceful intent, inspired her to set about the revisions which the draft typescript still needed. Early in March she completed her third and final revision of the text and sent it off to Faber. Faber accepted the book in May 1939, offering her a thirty-one pound advance and better royalties than hitherto. The publishers still required some revision and, at the end of May, Alison was altering parts of the text while struggling against the distraction of the next-door neighbours' dog, whose barking she found infuriating. She strongly objected to some of the illustrations, particularly one showing a calf feeding from a bottle.[59]

When, in July, Faber asked for autobiographical details and a photograph for their publicity, Alison wrote in her diary, 'I don't have that fear of publicity now, for I feel more secure in my writing and I think it might do me good.'[60] On 9 November, the day on which the book was published, she expressed mixed emotions: 'It is a great thrill that this book which has had so many vicissitudes should be safely launched in a brave blue jacket, and yellow dustcover, with excellent print and paper and all. How nice it looks, bless it!'[61] A letter from the *Derby Evening Telegraph* asking her for autobiographical details threw her into a state of anxiety, however, a condition that was rendered more intolerable by her temporary wartime lodger, Mrs Stafford, driving her 'dotty [with] these continued questions about nothing' as she struggled to write a reply to the newspaper.

Alison's fears for her book's reception were heightened by her friend Eleanor Graham apparently telling her some three weeks before publication that she didn't like parts of it, and that it should be written again. Eleanor proceeded to change her mind, however, subsequently writing Alison a congratulatory letter, and giving her a splendid notice in the *Bookseller*, which Alison thought amounted to perjury.

A Traveller in Time is justifiably regarded as one of Alison's greatest literary achievements. This is partly because the writing is so skilful that the long-ago story of the Babingtons and Mary Queen of Scots is presented to the reader in an entirely real and recognisable form – certainly as genuine as life upon the 'real' Thackers Farm in Derbyshire where the heroine Penelope, her older sister Alison and her brother Ian are sent. But the true power of the story derives from Alison's deep personal involvement in its fabric. She *is* Penelope, coming home to her north Derbyshire roots and at the same time moving in a dreamlike fantasy between the present and the sixteenth century. Alison's deep-seated and childish need to recreate the rural security of Castle Top Farm is thus perfectly in tune with her passionate interest in the world of dreams and time-travelling. The realisation of these needs in the adult writer produced a novel of rare harmony and strength.

Her struggle to write this extraordinarily imaginative book was more than vindicated by its reception. Margery Allingham wrote in *Time and Tide*: 'I found it enchanting. There is no writer who can re-create a summer's day so surely as this author can, and that is no ordinary achievement.' Humbert Wolfe in the *Observer* thought that with this book, Alison 'addresses herself to a wider and wilder world'.[62] Alison responded rapturously to this praise, writing in her diary, 'Oh dear Humbert Wolfe, thank you for that word wilder. True, those are the ones that I write for. It is utterly lovely, this review, and I am grateful to God.'[63] Considerable contemporary literary figures showered Alison with praise. J.B. Priestley wrote her 'a very nice letter', comparing the book to 'a Vermeer picture, rich and vital'.[64] The critic, C.A. Lejeune, told Alison in a letter that she had not enjoyed a book so much since she was sixteen, and S.P.B. Mais also let her know how thrilled he was by the book. She received many other letters from less distinguished members of the public.

There were some unfavourable reactions. A 'rather sniffy' one in the *New Statesman* and a positively hostile one in January 1940 in the *New English Weekly*. Alison was incensed by this notice which called the book 'fake rustic' and wrote angrily to the editor, extracting an apology from him and even eliciting a placatory letter from the reviewer – to which she did not deign to reply.[65] Alison was further disappointed that the book had sold only 999 copies by early January 1940, although there was compensation in the purchase of the United States rights by the publishers, Putnam, in the summer of 1940: 'Oh joy! . . . 250 dollars advance, and ten per cent against five thousand, twelve per cent to ten thousand and fifteen per cent afterwards. Isn't that wonderful news! I am filled with gratitude and thankfulness, not for the money, or the fame, but just to know that people over there will read about Thackers and Penelope, and all my thoughts and love and dreams.'[66]

Alison published one more book during this period, *The Farm on the Hill*, in April 1941. She finished the typescript in August 1940, rather concerned that the last chapter was 'not good enough'. In September 1940 Faber offered her a thirty pound advance for the book, which Alison at various times called *Susan Garland* and *The Farm on the Hillside*. These working titles are enough to indicate how closely Alison identified herself with this book, a direct successor to *The Country Child*, *Ambush of Young Days* and even *High Meadows*. Perhaps this is why she found the arrival of the advance copies in April 1941 so gratifying: 'It is one of the most exciting moments of life, to open a parcel containing a newly published book. What colour will be the cover? The jacket? How will it look? This is a war book, a plain jacket with big lettering, but the book has a cover the colour of the Country Child. . . . It is very nice, I have been dipping into it, welcoming it, with a little ache in my heart for that girl of long ago. Heavens! How clearly it comes back to me! I could write a dozen books of memories! So here I sit by the fire – which I lighted in celebration, – and the book lies on the chair near me, and all the room is looking at it.'[67]

Published at seven shillings and sixpence, the book received mixed reviews. Although *The Times Literary Supplement* was very complimentary, calling it 'a quiet and honest sequel' to *The Country Child*, the *Spectator* wrote: 'Usually Mrs Uttley is an exact and careful observer, but sometimes she lets her pen go off on a whimsicality which is destructive.' The reviewer then quoted the instance where Becky was undecided what to do next and Alison had written 'the harebells shook their blue glass bells with a tinkling assent'.[68] It is perhaps odd that, in her diary for 10 May, Alison called this review 'good'. Despite the variable views expressed about *The Farm on the Hill*, it had sold 1300 copies by the autumn of 1941.

Her prolific output during these years did not stop Alison from expressing her worries about money from time to time. She was relieved in November 1939 to receive a small legacy from James's aunt Alice, since a few months previously she had been very worried about her lack of spending money. In September 1941 she expressed her anxiety that she had only twenty-seven pounds left in the bank. One of the reasons why money seemed short to her was that she was spending at quite a rate. She continued to make various investments, for example putting thirty pounds into a War Loan in December 1940, and four days later feeling overcome with guilt that she had just purchased a chair for fourteen guineas.[69] Her curious double standard is illustrated by an entry in her diary for 24 May 1941 where, having recorded the investment of forty-six pounds in War Savings, she then confessed to buying a box of chocolates for two shillings and sixpence: 'Extravagant, but I have to buy when they are there, or the dream goes.'

In reality, Alison's fortunes flourished during the war. She produced a very large number of books and houses like Faber and Collins found wartime publishing very profitable. Publishers were obliged to use poorer quality, cheaper, paper and the public's demand for reading matter of all sorts became almost insatiable – the *per capita* sales of books increased by fifty per cent between 1938 and 1944. The armed services had a huge demand for books, four hundred libraries were badly damaged or destroyed thus obliging the eventual replacement of over one million volumes, and books remained exempt from purchase tax while other forms of entertainment rocketed in price. Above all, 'The longueurs of war, and the blackout, encouraged the addict.'[70] There was a sharp increase in the demand for more serious books. Alison's sales benefitted from all these factors, and Geoffrey Faber was to remark that she was 'one of the authors who was made a little more comfortable during the war'.[71]

Her royalty payments were substantial and she received such bonuses as income from the publication of Little Grey Rabbit painting books. She also received substantial dividends from Sugdens – ninety-seven pounds in August 1939 and a hundred and twenty pounds, which she described as 'a fortune', in July 1940. She began to acquire some of the trappings of the wealthy, including, by the spring of 1940, several original paintings, a Breughel amongst them.

Despite her burgeoning reputation and what she saw as the 'staggering' sales of the Little Grey Rabbit books in particular, she still retained the capacity to be surprised by her relative fame. In Beaconsfield in December 1940 she overheard a child and her mother in a shop speaking of Grey Rabbit, 'so I told them who I was and they were suitably thrilled. So was I, for it was jolly to find her friends in children with pointed wool caps and little red faces.'[72] But she remained in awe of famous literary figures, noting with a schoolgirlish pleasure in April 1941 that her fifty pound royalty cheque from Faber had actually been signed by T.S. Eliot, one of the firm's directors. For all this, Alison had unquestionably established herself as a major figure in the world of children's books.

CHAPTER SIXTEEN

Much Fame, A Modest Fortune And Great Anxiety, 1942–45

I told John I should be with him day and night.
Oh my darling.

ALISON UTTLEY, on John leaving for active service
18 May 1943

It is incredible . . . I can feel 10 years old easily,
but not 60.

ALISON UTTLEY, on her sixtieth birthday
17 December 1944

The diary entry for 1 January 1942 conveys the densely textured fabric of Alison's days, artfully contrived to hold her loneliness at bay:

Peeping through the curtains at the new year. Misty grey light. I received cheque, letter from LM and reviews, a nice beginning, and I had tea and toast and butter, honey and an apple. I did the fire, swept, dusted, got in coal, and then gardened. I planted 12 raspberry canes, transplanted gooseberries, tried to plant apple trees but I couldn't dig the holes. Then I raked up loads of leaves, cooked till one o'clock. Cooked lunch, sausage rissoles, pot[atoes] and apples, – and then the young man from the wood came with his load. . . . I gave the young man and the boy each a piece of barley sugar. I ironed a big pile of clothes, p. cases, hankies, etc. Then Mrs Dobell and Timothy came to tea. . . . I showed Tim John's early drawings. . . . We talked of books, of the Book of Discovery, and of Odysseus. At the end, I gave him [Hare Joins] the Home Guard which quite took away his breath. I wanted to write, but letters, washing up, supper etc., have taken all evening. It had been a nice friendly day, a happy day, the room lovely with its holly branches and a little tree and my thoughts of dear John.[1]

Housework was a favourite remedy against loneliness and even when her quest for the ideal home help was eventually rewarded by Mrs Allen, who apparently performed 'miracles' and was to remain in her employment for many years, she still continued to do an enormous amount of housework, including the patching of all sheets, the making of marmalade and sometimes spring cleaning, unaided.

But it was John, of course, who remained her surest comfort and nothing could prepare Alison for the shock of his engagement, announced in April 1942 to Dorothy Parker. Her first reaction was 'deep surprise. . . . Well, I am sure he has chosen well, he would for he goes underneath mere skin to character, and I hope Dorothy has strength and character. I only remember a pretty girl. This is a critical moment. I feel intensely for John, his future, his all, bless him.'[2] That night, however, Alison lay awake, 'anxious, troubled, wondering if all would be well. I lost my faith, I got frightened. . . . I wondered if she was good enough, did she love God, could she carry on in adversity? Reading? Music? Interests?'[3] The next day she wrote to John 'asking him if he had truly considered his engagement to a girl he didn't know, a contract for life. Why hadn't we seen more of her before? It was a careful letter, I restrained my anxieties.'[4]

The truth was that Alison, although she struggled to react positively to John's engagement, was overwhelmed by jealousy at the prospect of her passionate and over-close relationship with her son being diluted and disrupted forever. It is no accident that, ten days after receiving the news of John's engagement, she 'staggered' and collapsed – though she revived quite rapidly. When John's banns were called on 24 May she felt 'deep joy mixed up with all kinds of panics'.

John was due to marry Dorothy Parker on 23 June 1942. In the interim Alison alternated between optimism for the marriage and the conviction that it was a wholly unsatisfactory arrangement. The day before the wedding Alison and John travelled by train to Bowdon for the ceremony. Alison had intimations of an impending disaster on the train, noting that John had to stand up and thinking '"ill luck". Then later on in the express [saying] "I feel as if we were off to Edinburgh, and not going to a wedding at Bowdon."'[5]

At the Parkers' house that evening, Alison rememberd 'the sickness that swept over me . . . so that I pushed back my chair, that vulgar young girl. . . . The ugliness.'[6]

What happened next was high drama. At seven o'clock on the morning of his wedding day John came to Alison's room, woke her and told her that he could not go through with the marriage. She recalled 'the tragedy of John's face when he awoke me'.[7] It is not difficult to unravel what led to this abrupt decision. We know that, according to a large number of acquaintances and friends, Alison had 'dominated John all his life'. She had made it clear that she thought Dorothy Parker was not worthy of him, and at the same time had doubtless made him feel agonies of remorse at the pain which his marriage would cause her – lonely as she was. Moreover the intense, often physically expressed, love which existed between mother and son made both of them retreat before the inevitable severance that John's marriage implied. John may also have felt a profound and pervading lack of self-confidence, including an exaggerated anxiety over establishing a sexual relationship with Dorothy – something which he had not so far attempted.[8]

Alison now acted with a speed born of pity and some self-interest. She called off the wedding and even stuck a notice to that effect upon the church door. She and John, accompanied by his close friend David Paine, left for Scotland. When John ought to have been on honeymoon, he was in fact staying with his mother in the hotel in Dumfries to which he intended to take Dorothy.[9] A year later Alison was to remember almost romantically that 'wonderful escape' to Scotland.[10]

Although Dorothy Parker wrote an understanding letter to Alison, returning a brooch she had given her as a present and prompting Alison to remark 'she is a nice girl', other members of the Parker family were not so accommodating. Dorothy's father wrote angrily to Alison, holding her responsible for the catastrophe and referring to the now-revealed secret of James's suicide. Alison was bitterly resentful of Mr Parker 'speaking of John's ancestry as if there were some horrible blot, sneering, asking why, *knowing what I did know*, I didn't stop the engagement, for John after a lifetime of obedience would obey me'.[11]

At any rate, Alison now had John to herself though the experience had unsettled them both. A fortnight after the cancellation of the wedding, Alison found herself guiltily stealing raspberries from the wood of her neighbours, the Lanigans. During September 1942 she endured a 'frightful dream' of lying in a bed in a large room, 'John in bed across the room . . . then I saw 2 enormous birds, cawing fiercely . . . a bird flew in. I was filled with awful fear. It was black, fierce, baleful. It flew over my bed, and I knew it was going to pick out my eyes. I tried in vain to wake the others, and couldn't. I could move no limb, I lay enchained in terror.'[12]

John took six months before he could begin to recuperate. Alison gained some comfort from the knowledge that Dorothy Parker had been engaged before she met John and convinced herself that the Parkers, too, had a skeleton in the cupboard, once referring mysteriously to 'that family and that disease'.[13]

No sooner was the relationship restored on its old footing, however, than John found himself posted overseas. On 18 May 1943, the morning of his departure, Alison wrote, 'I hardly slept last night. I feel stunned. I think of his dear face – as I kissed it as it was half hidden in the bedclothes, and we made our old baby squeak . . . then we had our prayer. I wept. Then we played the old song, – holding arms; I cannot write about it. It is all too sacred.'[14] For the next two months she was haunted by many dreams, most of them illustrating her fears for John's safety. In one particularly graphic dream she was holding a beautiful and precious piece of Dresden china when a brutal Gestapo man came in, questioning her and threatening the safety of the piece of porcelain.[15]

In July 1943 Alison was disturbed to hear that John was among the Allied forces invading Sicily. A month later she was so anxious at not hearing from him that she burnt a candle at the shrine of St Anthony, and was soon rewarded with the arrival of a letter. When Italy was invaded early in September 1943, she felt 'sick' at the news and three weeks later was devastated to be officially informed that John was missing. She promptly dreamt of her son reassuring her that he was not dead, but a prisoner of war; a fact confirmed a month later.

John had been wounded before he was captured and Alison was overcome at the news, often feeling ill and faint, and once lamenting that she had nothing to look forward to until his eventual release at the end of the war.[16] She even protested that she could no longer write her diary, but in fact the entries are as full as ever. Early in November her immediate anxiety was relieved by John's first letter from his prisoner of war camp in Italy, but in the latter part of the war he was moved to a camp in Germany and Alison suffered agonies at the news of Allied bombing raids, often imagining her son's camp being devastated. On 2 May 1945 she received an unexpected telephone call from somebody who had seen John alive and well two weeks previously. On 10 May John spoke to her on the phone, an experience which left her so moved that she could not write down all her reactions in her diary, and by the end of the month he was home in Beaconsfield.

Besides John's vicissitudes other family mishaps paled into insignificance. Alison was genuinely sorry when her sister-in-law, Frances, died of cancer in April 1943, but mainly on account of the grief it caused her brother Harry. When Harry married a thirty-two-year-old woman, Hilda, a year later, she expressed appropriate happiness. The Uttley sister-in-law for whom she had the most time, Emily, died during December 1942 and in July 1944 George Uttley wrote to tell her that Emily's widower, Alfred Byers, was also dead.

Much more vital to Alison's existence were the friendships she developed and maintained during these years. These relationships were not always easy-going. Despite her affection for Katherine Wigglesworth and her twins, the two women became estranged early in 1942. Alison's version of things was that Mrs Wigglesworth was 'neglecting' her, 'telling lies' about her husband's academic achievements and making a bid for the friendship of another of Alison's close friends, Joan Dobell.[17] It is clear that Alison wanted to have Katherine Wigglesworth's friendship largely to herself. She also continued to feel that Dr Wigglesworth disliked her and was rude to her. This tangle of rivalries and mutual disappointments led to a two-year interruption in relations between the two women. Alison's rejection of Katherine was such that she refused to believe that the latter had 'done many accurate drawings for the British Museum. . . . I don't believe it . . . mediocre talent.'[18]

A partial reconciliation was effected in September 1944, when Katherine and her twins came to tea at Alison's for the first time for two and a half years. The visit prompted her to remark that she felt glad, but would go slowly in re-establishing the relationship. On 14 February 1945 she was touched when the Wigglesworth twins bought her a Valentine card and two weeks later she was invited to tea at their house for the first time for three years. Although the friendship had now been re-established, there were further fluctuations to come.

Her friendship with Walter de la Mare went from strength to strength. They visited each other regularly and exchanged letters full of mutual respect and affection, de la Mare taking a keen interest in John's fate after he became a prisoner of war. Alison found particular pleasure in the high regard the poet showed for her writing. She presented him with copies of her books, particularly her collections of essays. Typical of de la Mare's response to such gifts was a letter he wrote to her in September 1943, having received a copy of *Cuckoo Cherry-Tree*:

> I devoured a handsome slice of it in bed last night. What natural all-round children they are, and what a joy your stars and weather and flowers and birds etc are; the most unfailing of all company. You know them 'by heart' – the only way to *know* anything. . . . The English too is so true and full and fluid in rhythm. . . . I love too the occasional lost or half-lost country word.[19]

As well as her perennial friends, LM and GL, to whom Alison, as she became wealthier, gave presents – such as the brooch she sent them each in May 1943 – Alison continued to see quite a lot of Eleanor Graham. Although she felt from time to time that Eleanor disapproved of her, she reaped some practical benefits from the relationship when her friend moved into an editorial position at Puffin Books in May 1944.

One particularly close and valuable friendship was made in July 1943, when Alison met the actress Margaret Rutherford for the first time at a dinner given by Miss Collins, G.K. Chesterton's secretary. Alison thought that Margaret Rutherford 'looks about 60, but I don't suppose she is that, a nice face, keen clever mind, fair hair faded and light, and fluffy'.[20] A warm and mercurial friendship sprang up immediately between the two women, perhaps strengthened by their mutual capacity to play the prima donna. Soon they were taking tea and dinner with each other; Alison went to London to see Margaret in her plays and the latter suggested that the two of them should work together on a film. Alison considered Margaret Rutherford a 'wonderful woman' and confessed how much she liked talking to her. In the spring of 1945 she was delighted to learn that Margaret was to marry Lieutenant Lewis Stringer, although she looked older than him, and sent her a tea caddy for a wedding present.

Joan Dobell, whose apparent closeness with Katherine Wigglesworth had caused such anguish, was another valued friend of the period – although Alison was once so upset by the behaviour of her children that she vowed 'never to go when the children are about'. Other Beaconsfield contacts were Mrs Hamp and the vicar's wife, Mrs Routh. Although she was once invited to tea to meet the poet and novelist Hilaire Belloc, the meeting never took place. Barbara Healey, the wife of John's friend from Cambridge days, was someone she saw from time to time, as well as Marie Marques. Of her publishers, she had most social contact with Charles Stewart of Faber and his family, sometimes staying with them when she went to London. She was deeply upset when Charles Stewart was killed in an accident on the London Underground in May 1945.

Her relationship with Margaret Tempest was somewhat warmer during these years. Alison approved of her 'charming' pictures for *Water Rat's Picnic* in August 1942, although offering some criticisms which her illustrator took 'very well' (Alison protested in her diary that she hated to find fault with her!) When Alison went for a holiday in the Lake District in August 1942, she stayed overnight with Margaret Tempest and in the summer of 1944 was glad to receive parcels of *Country Life* from her. A few months later, however, the old rivalry flared up when she noticed that a front page advertisement for the Grey Rabbit books in the *Bookseller* had Margaret Tempest's name before hers, causing her to vow that she must do 'something' to restore her prestige.[21]

Inevitably the progress of the Second World War continued to preoccupy her. She remained a passionate supporter of Winston Churchill and became furious at what she considered to be defeatist talk. The fall of Singapore early in 1942 had depressed her considerably, although her spirits rose when she noticed a robin in her garden. In these dark days, she wished that Drake was still alive and ready to inspire the British war effort. She followed the heroic Russian defence of Stalingrad closely and even felt that the rich in Britain were not working hard enough for victory, a poor contrast with the total commitment of the Soviet nation. Although on her visits to London she was horrified at the devastation caused by bombing and was once shocked to see the wreckage of a Halifax bomber hanging on Nelson's Column, she was unexpectedly saddened by the implications of the first thousand-bomber raid on a German city, Cologne, in June 1942.

The Allied landings in North Africa in November 1942 cheered her, but John's involvement in active warfare from the summer of 1942 onwards made her more keenly aware than ever before of the price to be paid for victory. Once while eating in a restaurant in London, she rebuked a woman sitting at a table nearby for complaining about her food, telling her that the people of occupied Europe would be glad to eat it. The D-day Landings both exhilarated and worried her, chiefly because the fierce fighting would move closer and closer to John's prisoner of war camp. She was also upset when the offices of Collins were bombed in the middle of the war and found it even more 'horrid' that Faber also suffered damage in June 1944.

She greeted V-E Day with predictable relief and enthusiasm, knowing that it would soon mean John's return to her. It is interesting that her diaries contain no mention at all of the victory over Japan, something in which she had by now no personal interest. One further development during the war caused her to react sharply. That was the landslide Labour victory in the summer of 1945, between V-E Day and V-J Day. Alison, the one-time close friend of Ramsay MacDonald and his family, wrote, 'Socialist Govt. in. I can't write about it, the ingratitude of people when Churchill has saved us from death and dishonour.' A few days later she wrote: 'I feel we have betrayed the lion-hearted Churchill. It is awful to think Attlee and Bevin are at Potsdam instead of Churchill and Eden. Railway workers striking in order to compel the govt. to nationalise the railways. And then, where will they be? Still striking?'[22]

These somewhat sanctimonious pronouncements are consistent with change in her personal fortunes, for the sums she received from royalties had increased steeply. She was 'staggered' in March 1942 to have received £297 in royalties from Faber, writing that she had never known such sales. A day later William Collins told her that he could sell 100,000 of her books if he could get them printed. In January 1943 she declared herself 'amazed' at receiving £200 from Heinemann after 'colossal sales' for the first four Little Grey Rabbit books.

In March 1943 she received a Faber royalty cheque for £1090: 'I . . . could hardly believe my eyes. £200 was the utmost, my wildest hopes. It is quite amazing and very wonderful, – I think of my small beginnings, my timid efforts all alone with no-one to give advice. I feel very grateful and humble. . . . Did my work, feeling queer. I'm not used to having any money.'[23] Faber had sold more than 82,000 copies of her books in the six months that had produced this large cheque. In September 1943 an even bigger royalty cheque arrived from Faber –

£1268, a good deal of it due to the success of *Country Hoard*. The discrepancy in the royalties Alison received from her three publishing houses partly reflected the fact that her income from the Little Grey Rabbit books was split on a fifty-fifty basis with Margaret Tempest. But there was another factor, too. Faber was sole publisher of her books of country reminiscence, whose nostalgic appeal to a beleaguered and often deprived wartime readership was clearly very powerful. Her Sam Pig and Tim Rabbit books were also selling well. Alison's income continued to run roughly at this level for the rest of the war.

Her reactions to the arrival of big royalty cheques are interesting. After receiving her largest half-yearly cheque of 1943, she rushed out into the garden and beat a rug to 'let off steam'. More typically and predictably, she felt rich enough to go shopping in Beaconsfield and London, buying things which hitherto she had felt herself deprived of. In April 1943 she bought a squirrel fur cape for £46. 10*s*., and she continued to build up her collection of antiques, shopping often at Brown's in Beaconsfield and buying there, for example, some Queen Anne spice cupboards in February 1943. She also continued to put large sums of money away on her and John's behalf in National Savings and various investments. By September 1944 she had made up the amount held in John's name in War Bonds to £900. One of the prices she paid, of course, for this success, was to receive large income tax bills. In December 1942 she found a tax bill of £79 'terrific', but by July 1944 the Inland Revenue was demanding a 'prodigious' £2500 from her.[24] Two months later she declared herself amazed, but secretly a little pleased, that she was liable for Super Tax.

She received many other examples of her success. In London, in the spring of 1943, she noticed that the Sam Pig books were in all the shop windows and waved to him. Five months earlier Omnia Films had bought a one year option on her book, *A Traveller in Time*. In November 1944 she was invited by The Book Circle to their show for authors in London. More touchingly, a marine wrote to her in March 1944 telling her that, while serving in the Pacific, the two authors that he cherished most were herself and Jane Austen.

Yet Alison did not always feel accepted. She refused to join the local Penn Club in February 1943, on the grounds that 'I know nobody, none of the famous ones, and I won't join it.'[25] She quite frequently felt old and depressed and 'stupid'. In December 1943 she awoke one morning hardly able to lift her arm in bed. Her neck was X-rayed in the summer of 1944 and she was diagnosed as suffering from arthritis. She sometimes underwent the agony of 'black dreams', screaming for her mother in her distress. On her sixtieth birthday, however, she could write, 'It is incredible . . . I can feel 10 years old easily, but not 60. It has been so grand and exciting, all these years. I hope I shall have lots more left, to write books, to play with grandchildren, and to enjoy the sun and moon and earth.'

Through all this, her output was even more spectacular than hitherto. Between 1942 and 1945 she published fifteen books and a play, produced various articles and had a considerable number of her tales broadcast. She continued to work exceptionally hard, in May 1942 writing twelve tales in six days, considering it 'a record' even for her, and continued to find inspiration and ideas on all sides. From April 1942 she became very interested in Mr Norris, a local countryman who regaled her with a variety of rustic tales and experiences. Merely to take a walk was an inspiration: 'Then off I went with Hamish, for the sun shone in a lovely day. We went through the wood, and I thought of tales I might write. Every tree, every jolly thing reminded me, so that my mind . . . brimmed with stories.'[26]

During the latter part of 1942 she posted a draft sequel to *A Traveller in Time* to Faber. Charles Stewart replied that he quite liked the typescript, but nothing much seems to have come of it. In April 1943 she began typing a new novel, which eventually saw the light of day as *When All Is Done* in 1945. She thought of writing a story of Sam Pig at the ballet. Early in 1944 she produced the manuscript of *Little Grey Rabbit and the Weasels* in 'record quick time', explaining that she 'got so intrigued' by the idea 'I just went on'.[27]

Eleanor Graham's move to Puffin Books produced the offer of a paperback edition of some of the Sam Pig stories in the summer of 1944, but Alison later declared herself glad when Faber refused to co-operate on the grounds that it would spoil their sales of the books. In February 1945 she dedicated her play about the life of Hans Christian Andersen, *The Washerwoman's Child*, to her friend Margaret Rutherford. In July 1944 she was flattered and surprised to receive a letter inviting her to write the history of the county of Buckinghamshire for the publishers Robert Hale. After some negotiations over terms, she went ahead with this book, publishing it in 1950.

One indication of her enormous productivity, and also of her new sense of financial security, was her employment of a typist, Mrs Sibbring, in the autumn of 1944. Alison declared herself well-pleased with her new assistant, agreeing to pay her three shillings an hour. She continued to employ a typist on a part-time basis for the rest of her life.

Among the stories she produced during these years were several for the prestigious publication *Junior Bookshelf*; 'Grey Rabbit and the Bit Bat' and a 'Cock and Bull' tale for *Child Education*; 'Tom Tit' for *Farmer's Weekly*, and several articles for *Housewife* and *Good Housekeeping*. She also sent, in September 1945, the proofs of an operetta to

Good Housekeeping. Her one rebuff occurred when she sent an article to the magazine *Field*, which sent it back, prompting Alison to observe that, of course, it was 'a mistake'.

The BBC continued to be a consistent and fairly profitable patron, with Sam Pig and Tim Rabbit providing most of the material for her broadcasts during these years. Although in March 1942 Alison declared herself bored with copying out tales for the BBC, she admitted that she loved to hear them on the air and that she also needed the money.[28] In 1945 she even wrote some incidental music for one of her programmes. Not that her relationship with the BBC was always smooth: in February 1944, on being interviewed by Janet Quigley, she dropped a 'clanger' by saying that she didn't like 'Woman's Page' – apparently one of her interviewer's favourites. In June 1944 she entered into a bizarre controversy with the BBC, rehearsing her arguments in her diary and accusing them of trying 'to influence children so that they think no generation was any good till they adorned the world with their presence. . . . Is it true that this year of grace, 1944, is the height of civilisation? Tractors on the ploughland & tanks on the battlefield? It is a Nazi theory that only this generation is any good and all else must be scrapped. . . . Look at us, gods with electric light and neon light, and water laid on, all invented by those people who lived in candlelit days.'[29]

Free of such controversies, Alison derived a greater pleasure from the publication of her books. During 1942 she published four, beginning with *Hare Joins the Home Guard*. This is one of her few books for children to reflect the contemporary scene, with Hare, Grey Rabbit, Squirrel, Moldy Warp, old Hedgehog and the rest pitting themselves in a successful struggle against an invading army of weasels. The book must have reassured thousands of young readers aware that Britain faced imminent invasion and defeat, and in March 1942 William Collins showed Alison a letter from a child saying, 'Goebbels won't let the Nazis come now because Hare will stop them.'[30] This undoubted success was followed later in the year by *Little Grey Rabbit's Washing Day*. In the autumn of 1942 Alison published *Nine Starlight Tales*, which Faber had accepted with a thirty-pound advance in March of that year. This collection of fairy tales received generally good reviews and by February 1943 seventeen thousand copies had been sold. Another Sam Pig book appeared in 1942, *Sam Pig and Sally*. *The Times Literary Supplement* remarked during September 1942 that 'Christmas without [a Sam Pig book] would certainly lack something for the many children who have listened to his broadcast adventures, and for them . . . an ideal present would be *Sam Pig and Sally*.'

During 1943 Alison published a further Sam Pig book, *Sam Pig and the Circus*, for which she received in March 1943 her first hundred-pound advance. As usual she had taken care to research the book, checking with her Irish friend Mrs Corsellis the authenticity of the words put into the mouth of the Irish cook at the big house. Alison approved wholeheartedly of the fine black and white illustrations by A.E. Kennedy and was gratified to learn, in December 1943, that the first print run of ten thousand books was oversubscribed. The only Little Grey Rabbit book to be published during this year was *Water Rat's Picnic*. Another collection of fairy tales, *Cuckoo Cherry-Tree*, was published on 17 September 1943. Alison had been working hard at these stories since Christmas 1941, finishing them at the end of May 1942. Faber accepted the typescript promptly, offering her a thirty-pound advance. The book contains some of her best fairy stories, like 'Rag and Bone', a very haunting and powerful tale. Dedicated to Alison's nephew Ronnie Taylor who was serving in the Merchant Navy, by early December 1943 it had sold out of its first edition.

The book which probably gave Alison the greatest pleasure to publish during 1943 was *Country Hoard*. She had originally 'loathed' the illustrations and had even sought Walter de la Mare's advice over them. In the summer of 1942 Faber decided to ask Charles Tunnicliffe to illustrate the book. Alison was delighted with this move, chiefly because she appreciated the consummate skill of Tunnicliffe. She had a professional relationship of great mutual satisfaction with him and was glad to receive his grave and intelligent letters written in his beautiful script. This accord did not always extend to personal matters and once when Tunnicliffe called unexpectedly at her house in Beaconsfield, she hid from him in an upstairs room, refusing to answer the door. Despite this contretemps, Alison considered Tunnicliffe to be her best illustrator and once was shocked to learn that Margaret Tempest did not like his drawings, remarking, 'It shows how inartistic she is. He is a real artist, she is very poor.'[31] *Country Hoard* was a book very dear to Alison's heart. She felt that her mother would have loved it and was greatly relieved to receive very complimentary reviews. The *Manchester Guardian* wrote 'It's "still dews of quietness" are dropped unconsciously by one who, a perfect artist in miniature, is completely absorbed in her own re-living of that "hour of splendour in the grass, of glory in the flower".'[32] The *Listener* commented that 'Country pleasures, like country food, were home-grown, and those Miss Uttley has hoarded and described for us are as sweet and wholesome as red-cheeked apples in a loft.'[33] In *Home Chat* Alison's acquaintance, S.P.B. Mais, remarked, 'she is a born writer with a peculiar gift for conjuring up a scene in a phrase. A very happy book this, to hoard as a squirrel hoards nuts.'[34] A.A. Milne wrote in *The Sunday Times*, 'Mrs Uttley's charming memories of childhood have been ringing the bell with every chapter.'

Six thousand copies of the book had been sold by the beginning of June 1943 and *Country Hoard* went into its fourth impression in November 1944.

1944 saw the publication of *Little Grey Rabbit's Birthday*, and another book of fairy tales, *The Spice Woman's Basket*. Less happy was Alison's half-share in a book, *Mrs Nimble and Mr Bumble* and *This Duck and That Duck*, published by Francis James. Alison wrote the part called *Mrs Nimble and Mr Bumble* and Herbert McKay the second part. Quite apart from Alison's contribution being unremarkable, she was outraged to discover in December 1944 that the book had been pirated by another publisher. The ensuing lawsuit was settled by a sixty-pound outright payment to her early in 1945. During the last year of the war, Alison published *The Adventures of Tim Rabbit* in March. This was another children's book for which she was offered a hundred-pound advance by Faber. In accepting the typescript, Charles Stewart had teased her by remarking that he was glad that her fairies were 'dangerous'. This was followed by another collection of tales, *The Weather Cock and Other Stories*. Alison created a fuss over the publication of this latter book, declaring that she detested Nancy Innes's pictures and forcing through some alterations. She completed her publication of books for that year in October with *When All Is done*, another relatively undistinguished rustic novel, out of the same stable as *High Meadows*. She found the early reviews 'disgusting', but was later cheered by Nan Duncan's opinion that it was the best of her books.[35] Better reviews followed and Alison's self-esteem was restored by Eleanor Graham's judgement that 'You have a lovely gift of words and such a wonderful power of observation and memory.'[36]

The publication of a play, *Little Grey Rabbit to the Rescue*, rounded off a triumphant year for Alison. She had first shown the typescript of the play to the Windsor Theatre in August 1944, but they had rejected it. She had then sought Charles Stewart's advice and he had responded by sending her the address of a children's theatre that she might approach. In November 1944 Faber told her that they would publish the play if she would wait until 1945 and offered her a forty-pound advance. In December 1944, when Faber's offices were bombed, the typescript was destroyed. Four days later Alison was working solidly every day, restructuring and rewriting the play. Eventually, however, and perfectly logically, it was Collins who published *Little Grey Rabbit to the Rescue*, a clear indication of Alison's capacity to switch with confidence from one publisher to another. It was a confidence that was born of her now striking and unassailable success.

CHAPTER SEVENTEEN

Bereft Mother and Prolific Author, 1945–50

Sometimes I feel my heart is broken but it must
not be. There are so many things, and human love
is not all. There is the companionship of trees and
grass and the feeling of the earth.

ALISON UTTLEY
on John's engagement to Helen Paine,
14 December 1946

With her son's return to her at the end of the war, Alison's life seemed at
first to resume a familiar pattern. The financial rewards of her writing
enabled her to live very comfortably, somewhat at odds with the
privations felt by much of the nation during the austerity years of post-
war recovery. In September 1945 she bought a car, spending two
hundred and fifty pounds on a Morris 12. For two years she relied upon
John to drive her wherever she wanted to go, and was particularly
grateful when he acted as chauffeur in her researches for her book on the
county of Buckinghamshire. In May 1947 she was expressing her joy at
having driving lessons, eventually passing her test in October 1948.

Although she was an erratic driver and had a number of scrapes and
bumps, she managed remarkably well for someone who had only begun
driving in her early sixties. Above all, she felt a sense of liberation: 'With
joy driving all alone for the first time, to B. and then on to Penn to see
Mrs King, singing as I drove, under the golden trees, happy and
excited.'[1] Two months after passing her test, Alison had acquired the
services of a part-time chauffeur, whom she always called Olley, sharing
him with Mrs Garvin, the wife of the editor of the *Observer*. As so often
with those who worked for her, Alison found the services of Olley both
a blessing and a trial. He cleaned her car and generally helped to
maintain it in good working order; he even drove her to Tintagel where
she took her holiday in September 1949. She was, however, sometimes
resentful if he was unable to take her where she wanted to go, and was
once so cross he was unable to polish her car that she straightaway went
out and did it herself.

She went regularly to London – often, during these years, to visit her dentist. When in London, she frequently lunched at Fortnum and Mason and bought increasingly expensive items in the shops. She became a regular visitor to Slatter's Gallery, feasting her eyes on the 'glorious' Flemish and Dutch paintings that she found there. After a visit to this gallery in May 1948 she suddenly realised how valuable her own Breughel painting was, although the rest of the pictures that she accumulated over the years were, according to a highly reputable authority, 'not a very distinguished lot'.[2] In 1947 she went to the Chelsea Flower Show for the first time and remained a dedicated visitor thereafter. She maintained her intense interest in an enormously wide range of topics, becoming more intrigued by the esoteric and downright quirky. Her interest in spiritualism grew, she began taking note of the reported landings of flying saucers, and in February 1949 recorded a telephone conversation with a Miss Wood who had, it seems, recently seen fairies in her garden: 'She saw them at 8 pm on a summer night when she opened the door to shake the supper cloth. . . . She stood watching them. Holding hands as they danced. Their faces indefinite, not strongly featured, but pointed faces, and radiantly happy. . . . About two feet high. Suddenly they disappeared. . . . Not a sound.'[3]

Perhaps Alison's increasing sense of loneliness led her into these odd imaginative byways. Although still incredibly vital and active, she was at times forced to acknowledge the fact that she was aging. Her diary entry for 6 January 1946 paints a rather pathetic self-portrait: 'In bed, in blue dressing gown, hole in the elbow, with white scarf-shawl over my shoulders, my grey hair tumbled, as I sit here, a sore throat, but not so bad.'[4] She applied various remedies for her loneliness. One of the most successful was always to have a dog in the house. The beloved Hamish had died in April 1944, a bitter blow. A year later she recorded the anniversary of his death in her diary, shedding tears that made the ink on the page run. In the summer of 1946 she acquired a new Scottie, at first calling him Angus but later naming him Macduff, the subject of a book published in 1950. Although her succession of Scotties were a great solace to Alison, they were not always easy pets. She found Macduff particularly difficult to house-train and only gave him his first bath a year after she acquired him. Local friends were to remember her dogs as 'smelly' and 'mangy'.[5] Once when a visiting child was nipped by Macduff, Alison's response was to tell the victim what a privilege it was to be bitten by her dog.

In 1947 Alison experimented with the idea of a female 'companion'. A Mrs Drysdale arrived in the middle of November. The next day Alison felt ill, 'very ill'. Two weeks later the two women had a lengthy conversation, with Mrs Drysdale saying that she must 'have Freedom, to think, to act, to do. So I agreed. She spoke interestingly. I was touched by her manner and what she said, but after a time I found myself thinking "Here is a crank, so set on self development and freedom that we shall never get on.""[6] For the next week Alison struggled with her ambivalent feelings towards her companion, sometimes liking her a good deal, at other times being exasperated by how little work she did in the house. On 5 December she was thankful when Mrs Drysdale gave notice: 'It couldn't go on. No companionship or help. She knows no poet or writer, no music or art. All her thoughts on (1)Make-up, (2)Divinity!!!'[7] On 8 December a delighted Alison paid Mrs Drysdale nine pounds and she left.

Alison suffered more than her fair share of depression and illness during these post-war years. She often described herself weeping in bed, or being so tired that she wanted to stay in bed all day. In July 1946, perhaps sensing that John was about to get engaged for the second time, she wept bitterly, wondering what was going on and anxious lest what she called 'Old Fear' had got her. She consulted her GP, Dr Milner, on several occasions. Dr Milner, although recognising what an awkward customer she could be, was generally very supportive, getting her out of jury service in the autumn of 1949 on the grounds of 'nervous exhaustion' and telling her in the spring of 1950 that she must slow down. Sometimes Alison's anxieties manifested themselves dramatically. In October 1945 she suffered a claustrophobic panic while staying in a hotel and became convinced that fire was about to engulf her.[8] A few days later she visited Margate to give a lecture to an audience of schoolchildren on 'Country Life', which she felt to be so unequivocal a disaster that she vowed never to give such public talks again – a vow she did not keep.

Often she believed herself unappreciated and unacknowledged. It was nothing new to feel that her Uttley in-laws and her brother Harry thought little enough of her, but early in 1946 she was overcome with doubt as to her skills as a writer, flinching from what she imagined to be the 'sneers of Bloomsbury'. In July 1946 she wrote poignantly in her diary: 'I long for a friend, like GL or LM or W. Armitage, or Mrs Edward. I seem to write for nothing, and nobody now [Charles] Stewart is dead.'[9] It is odd that John should have been left so completely out of her reckoning and it suggests he may have been the root cause of her trouble in the first place – a depression born of the complexities and disappointments of her relationship with her son.

For two years after the end of the war, Alison was preoccupied with John's failure to cope with the new teaching post he took up on his return to civilian life, that of form master at Eton College. Within a few days of his instalment in September 1945, he was complaining that his memory was gone, that he had no confidence in front of his classes and that he dreaded each day's work. In November 1945 he began seeing a psychiatrist. Alison became very agitated by this and quoted with approval the views of a local acquaintance, a priest, who did not like 'these psychologists' and who doubted whether John's was a Christian. Alison's anxieties over John's psychological problems were inevitably heightened by her memories of the depressions which had led to her husband's suicide. Nor can it have helped much to have been told by her brother Harry that 'If he [John] wants to do a James, you can't stop him.'

Alison encouraged John in a form of therapy which she had always found useful herself – she encouraged him to write a book. Early in 1946 the manuscript was sent to Faber, who returned it with the comment that it was not original enough. The book went off to Dent, but it proved unworthy of publication. Throughout the summer of 1946 John continued to feel his inferiority and inadequacy as an Eton teacher. In June he applied for a post at Leeds Grammar School, amazing Alison that he was prepared to make such an exchange. In July he applied successfully for a post at Stowe public school, although he was so nervous before the interview that he spilled his drink. John's career at Stowe, however, was eventually to be beset by some of the same difficulties that had dogged him at Eton.

At the end of August 1946 Alison's relationship with John took a new and dramatic turn when he wrote to her announcing his engagement to Helen Paine. Alison's response was almost identical to that when John had earlier become engaged to Dorothy Parker:

> Well, I didn't like her when I met her, too painted, and 'rather fast' I thought, – she took John dancing when there were all the wonderful fireworks to see in London. I think she is a town type. But I foresaw this would happen before John went, yet I couldn't mention it. Sweet darling, I do hope he will be happy with her. I adore him, and I know his goodness. I've not felt upset, only resigned. At any rate a nice family.[10]

Three days later Alison's attempt to be cheerful gave way to grief: 'I wept in bed last night, sorrow and loneliness and distress. Poor John. I fear he is throwing away all his chances, and the fun and joy of life.'[11] This fundamentally selfish and mistaken reaction on Alison's part was put into its proper perspective the next day, when John came to see her 'smiling, very brown and happy'. Alison, for her part, felt 'queer and glum and very sick, that queer sickness that comes over me. We talked a little, and he said it was only an "informal engagement," – both of them not decided. However, I fear *she* is. I am sure John is not in love, but he has been deluded.'[12] Among her haunting dreams at this time was one of mislaying a baby.

In the eight months between the anouncement of John's engagement and his marriage to Helen on 12 April 1947, Alison's emotions swung between morbid self-pity and an attempt to think positively about her son's future. She contrived to find fault with Helen on almost every occasion. When John and his fiancée began visiting her fairly regularly from October onwards, Alison's diaries contain a good many unfavourable impressions of her future daughter-in-law. These included the fact that Helen had 'scarlet nails' and was 'continually' filing them; that at Thackers she wandered around the kitchen opening Alison's cupboards and looking inside them; that she bought four tickets to the ballet in Alison's name and with Alison's money; that she was 'not interested in poetry, books, or anything. What is the Eucharist? she asked'; that Helen had a 'colossal self-importance' and that she hated receiving a letter from her; and, perhaps most damning of all, that she had been married once before and was thus denying John the rapture of a young, green love.

Although there was some substance in Alison's criticisms, her view of Helen was greatly distorted by feelings of jealousy and rivalry. As even she had been forced to recognise, Helen's origins were perfectly respectable and solid, since her father was a Methodist minister. Nor was Helen the scheming 'older woman' that Alison represented her, being in fact three years younger than John. Moreover, theirs was no fly-by-night affair but, on John's part, a steady attachment that had lasted since Cambridge days. Helen's sister recalls that:

> Several times John came to Guernsey for his summer holiday and stayed with us in my grandmother's house, where he grew to love Helen, but she didn't return his love at that time. She met and married someone else in 1940, who unfortunately was killed in 1941. John was a P.O.W. When he came home, he heard about Helen, got in touch with her, and they married in 1947.[13]

Helen Uttley has her own version of her early relationship with Alison. She recalls the first time John took her 'to lunch in Thackers in 1946, a disastrous occasion because of her behaviour – and even worse on the night we entertained her on our official engagement. . . . She didn't address a word to me for a very long time; it was always "John, do you remember. . . ."'[14]

If Alison found it almost impossible to think well of Helen, the latter had a generally low opinion of her mother-in-law. She believed that she was a great 'story-teller', in personal as well as in professional matters, and summed her up, revealingly, thus: 'She *was* a very odd person, and very rude, so presumably had always been so – She told me I was a designing widow! and never once asked me about my training, for instance; if you hadn't been to university she had no further use for you. I have been very unfortunate with my Ma-in-laws. The first one was a snob . . . the second was an intellectual snob.'[15]

Quite apart from their different personal styles and cultural tastes, although Alison seems to have misrepresented the latter difficulty, the relationship between the two women was doomed to failure on one simple issue: they were rivals for John's affection and, despite Alison's attempts at obstruction, Helen won the battle. Certainly Helen recognised the need to establish an early hold over John and once told a close mutual friend of both of theirs that '"Ma Tut" as she called [Alison], would have kiboshed their marriage if she had not hooked John first.'[16] Getting John 'hooked' implied establishing a sexual relationship with him, almost certainly the first that he had enjoyed. Helen's sister, on the other hand, believes that 'it was John who did all the "running"!' Helen also held strong views on many subjects and her liberalism was in strong contrast to Alison's deepening conservatism. She was also able to talk more freely than Alison about her private emotions. Most significant of all, Helen had as tough a personality as Alison and thus tended to stand up to her and be disliked for it.[17]

John was caught in a tug of war between two strong and demanding personalities. Although Helen was conscious of Alison's wish to control John, she in turn 'said she *had* to be tough with John, as he would never make decisions and it was always left to her to decide; though I can tell you she has always been a "bossy type"!!!'[18] Many years later Helen was to complain of John's 'lack of standing muscle', an indication, perhaps, that his failure to exert himself with her sometimes included a sexual incapacity.

Alison recognised her defeat at Helen's hands at the end of November 1946, when she broke down and wept at the theatre where she had gone with Helen and John: 'A devastating day. Theatre, lovely ballets, but I suddenly collapsed with nervous tension, the snubs of John, the slights . . . I sat weeping in the theatre!'[19] She continued for a few months to feel that John was inclined to discount her, to 'snap' at her. She was once enraged when he wrote a letter 'Reprimanding *me*! Saying I must rely more on myself. It makes me laugh. Fancy John telling me to rely on myself. My God. But I am laughing – & I won't care. For I know now how weak he is and always has been.'[20] Two days later Alison had convinced herself that 'He has never been a jolly companion, shopping with me, sharing things. Always reticent and cold, telling me nothing. Showing me no letters. . . . So this final blow is only part of it. I shan't lose much. Sometimes I feel my heart is broken but it must not be. There are so many things, and human love is not all. There is the companionship of trees and grass and the feeling of the earth.'[21] In the months before John's marriage, however, she continued to torture herself with thoughts of him sleeping in 'that woman's flat' whenever he was in London, of Helen's drinking habits and their pernicious influence, and of John's new reserve – he never called her 'darling' any more.

After John and Helen were married in Guernsey, Alison pronounced herself relieved, even happy that she was now more free. In May 1947 she declared that she had that month recovered her strength and vitality. She remained, however, locked in a close and untidy triangular relationship with her son and daughter-in-law. Nine days after the wedding, the three of them holidayed in Cornwall together where Alison noted tartly that Helen looked about forty. When she motored to see John in his new job at Stowe, she noticed that although he looked proud, happy and older in his new life, his cottage was littered with empty bottles.[22] The three spent the Christmas of 1947 together, when John's status was perhaps symbolised by his bringing both mother and wife breakfast in bed. Alison was shocked to notice that Helen wore John's pyjamas. She later broke down and cried bitterly, but was gratified when both son and daughter-in-law did their best to cheer her up. On the last day of the year she confessed that she was sorry to see them go, but felt at the same time glad: 'it has been a great strain. Helen isn't like ordinary nice girls – she is different, older, and she offends my eye by her ugly face and queer eyes. However when she smiles, which is seldom, she looks different.'[23]

A year after the wedding Alison was still drawing unfavourable comparisons between the two: 'Helen's private conversation. Oh dear. John looks so handsome, nay, beautiful and young & Helen so old – pouched under [the] eyes. I think of the unborn children who might have been born.'[24] As Alison had somehow divined, the marriage was to produce no children. Helen was particularly concerned at her failure to conceive and suffered a cruel blow some years later when her one pregnancy ended in a miscarriage.

Alison never managed to reconcile herself fully to her son's marriage. One of the ways in which she showed her irritation was by transferring shares she had originally allotted to John back to herself in July 1947, arguing that she was worried about her financial security. Unable to destroy Helen's hold over her son, she plotted a posthumous revenge. In June 1949 she travelled back to Bowdon to her solicitor to make her will. John accompanied her and asked about Helen's position in the event of him predeceasing her, to which Alison's conclusion was, 'I cannot leave all to her.'[25]

As John and Helen sank in Alison's estimation, one member of the Uttley family rose in it. Martin Byers, Emily's son, had sent Alison food parcels from Kenya at the end of the war and had gratified her by telling her that the bookshops of Mombasa were full of Grey Rabbit books. Although Alison found Martin and his bride Rosemary 'a darling pair' when they called on her in November 1946, it is strange that she only managed to buy them a wedding present six years after the event. Of her other Uttley relations there is hardly any mention in the diaries during these years.

With John gone, or so she believed, Alison's friendships were more important than ever to her. She was upset when the Wigglesworths moved to Cambridge at the end of 1945, but visited them on several occasions during the next few years. Significantly, when Alison sold her idea of a series of Little Brown Mouse books to Heinemann at the end of 1949, she chose Katherine Wigglesworth as her illustrator. She kept up with Margaret Rutherford, and in 1948 Walter de la Mare particularly moved her with his Christmas present of a poem written specially for her, 'with love and all good wishes':

> Solitude
> Space beyond space; stars needling into Night;
> In wonder and love I gaze from Earth below.
> Spinning in unintelligible quiet beneath
> A moonlight drift of cloudlets, still as snow.[26]

Among the new friends that Alison made during these years, by far the most important was Peter du Sautoy who had taken over from Charles Stewart at Faber. Alison soon established cordial relations with du Sautoy, his wife Mollie and their two sons. Eighteen months after first meeting her new editor, she recorded a 'delightful' visit to them at Windsor. By which time she had already entertained them at Thackers – also enjoyable, though the preparations for their coming apparently left her feeling 'worn out'. Another fresh acquaintance was Mary Treadgold, whom she liked so much that she hoped 'to share some of my life with her'. Although she occasionally saw Eleanor Graham, she felt relief that she was 'no longer under her spell'. She made her first visit to Leonard and Joyce Kann in Beaconsfield in January 1950, and among the aristocratic acquaintances that she was then cultivating, she especially valued Lady Tweedsmuir, the widow of John Buchan. In August 1949 she met Lord Curzon, later Earl Howe, whom she found 'a delightful man, a joy to talk to, and how we talked'.[27] She was particularly intrigued by his distinguished naval ancestor.

Her recorded reactions to public events during these post-war years are sparser and more muted than hitherto. She reacted hardly at all to external affairs, although the crisis of the Berlin airlift caused her to describe Russia as 'a great bully' and to fear that war with the Soviet Union was near. At home she became a stern opponent of the Labour government, complaining about food rationing and claiming that everybody was depressed by the administration's 'stranglehold on industry'. In the midst of the great coal shortage of 1946 she accused the government of mismanaging the economy, considering it obsessed with nationalisation and restrictions. Who, she asked plaintively in February 1946, was going to pay for all this social welfare? She voted Conservative in the county council elections of April 1946 and was driven to the polling station by a Mrs Hall, talking of 'socialism and bathrooms'. A month later she joined the local Conservative Association but was level-headed enough to tell one of the local officials, who had been congratulating himself that most of the families in a wealthy road had joined the association, that it would be far better if a poor road had joined.

Alison's political responses were perhaps so orthodox and self-interested as a result of her high wartime earnings. Perhaps her creative activities left her with little time for political soul searching. Certainly, her output remained prodigious. Between 1946 and 1950 she published, in addition to a good many articles and reviews, thirteen new books as well as a play. She edited an anthology of country life, had a considerable number of stories broadcast on the radio and broke into television as well.

Her royalty payments stayed at a high level during these years, several times exceeding a thousand pounds. She received £1153 from Faber, mainly for her book *When All Is Done*, in March 1946, £1370 from Collins in April 1948, a sum which made her feel 'dizzy' with surprise and pleasure, and a further £1236 from Collins in March 1950. In between these financial high points, she received sums which often exceeded five hundred pounds, and which, on two occasions, were well over eight hundred pounds. Sugdens also paid dividends of a little over £180 per annum. The first four Little Grey Rabbit books published by Heinemann made a respectable contribution, and in September 1946 Margaret Tempest wrote joyfully to inform her that the publishers were prepared to give them a five per cent royalty on these first books in the series. In general the Little Grey Rabbit books continued to sell extremely well, and in March 1947 William Collins told Alison that the series had sold over one hundred thousand copies in the previous year and that his target for the current year was one hundred and fifty thousand.[28]

Her relationships with her publishers were generally smooth. One of her editors at Collins remembers:

> She was a very professional author. The manuscript arrived very clearly typed, and it was quite obvious that she knew exactly how she wanted it presented, and we would read it and go back to her with any small suggestions that we might have, and she either agreed with them or not. And then we sent it to Margaret Tempest, who told us what she would

like to illustrate, and it then went back to Alison Uttley. Yes, she was quite an easy author to deal with, but if she made up her mind about something, and we didn't agree with her, then she would dig her toes in quite firmly.[29]

The going was not always so smooth. In July 1949 there was some haggling with Heinemann about the proposed payments for a new edition of the first four Grey Rabbit books. Early in 1950 there was a struggle over terms for future Grey Rabbit books with Collins, and in April of that year Alison vowed that she would not let them have her next two tales in the series. It is interesting that at the height of this conflict she dreamed of being 'unhappy and lost. I got out of a train at Cromford . . . I didn't know where to go. I had no hat, no coat, a thin dress, no shoes or stockings. I knew I couldn't go home, or who would shelter me.'[30] Although this conflict was resolved, Alison was perhaps guilty of a little sharp practice when in September 1949 she sold the idea of a series of Little Brown Mouse books to Heinemann. When the advance publicity for this series reached her in March 1950, she confessed to feeling excited and frightened. 'Collins will be so cross, and so will M.T.'[31]

Among her triumphs at this time was a 'charming' reply from Princess Elizabeth to Alison's gift of the Little Grey Rabbit books for her wedding in 1947. Alison was probably equally gratified to learn from an American fan of hers that Beatrix Potter had actually sent her a copy of an Uttley children's book. *A Traveller in Time* was offered to Twentieth Century Fox as a possible film, but was later rejected. In April 1949 Alison was invited to be the distinguished guest on 'Woman's Hour'. In January 1950 Harrods telephoned asking her to attend a book-signing session for them, prompting her smile at the incongruity of their timing as the telephone call found her 'struggling with fire and rugs, and kitchen floor, all dusty'.

Not that Alison's fame was universal. She was irritated in September 1945 to hear someone asking, when she and John went to a children's home to present Little Grey Rabbit books, 'Who is Alison Uttley?' Nor were all the letters she received from her readers gratifying. She was not particularly helpful to a woman who sent her a TV script to read through, and she was once infuriated to be asked whether the characters in her novel *High Meadows* were essentially drawn from the world of Thomas Hardy.

Among her other trials was her relationship with Margaret Tempest, which remained uniquely troublesome. She never encountered such problems with her other illustrators. She continued to be enchanted by Tunnicliffe's illustrations and was very pleased with Irene Hawkins's illustrations for *The Cobbler's Shop and Other Tales*, but with the illustrations most often associated with her it was a different story. At the heart of the conflict, as we have seen, lay the dispute as to who was the main begetter of the Grey Rabbit characters. This controversy surfaced again early in 1950, when Margaret Tempest refused to back the demands Alison made of Collins over future books in the series. Although it is reasonable to suppose that Alison gave as good as she got, she declared herself on several occasions horrified at the contents of letters from Margaret Tempest which were, apparently, full of 'jealousy and spite'. By April 1950 things had reached such a pitch that Alison declared she would do no more books with Miss Tempest: 'I hate her to touch my little sweet people.'[32]

Nothing, however, could take away from the scale of Alison's achievements during these years. She continued to receive many requests for articles. Among the journals she wrote for were *Good Housekeeping*, *Child Education*, *Farmer's Weekly* and *Housewife*. A typical fee for these stories was twenty pounds. Above all, she declared herself honoured to be asked to write for the *Saturday Book*. Another indication of her standing in the world of letters was *The Sunday Times*'s invitation to review a book on windmills in September 1948. Other requests for reviews followed.

The BBC was still an enthusiastic patron. Among her more successful radio broadcasts were more tales of Tim Rabbit. Uncle Mac of 'Children's Hour' remained a great admirer of hers and even read the Tim Rabbit stories, which Alison considered to be an honour though finding his style a little dull. In November 1947 she read her script of 'King Arthur's Country' herself and believed that she had done it well. The first part of her play *The Washerwoman's Child* was broadcast in March 1947 and in November 1948 she was flattered that the Third Programme wanted to broadcast an adaptation of *The Country Child*. Perhaps her most important breakthrough came when the puppeteer Anne Hogarth proposed an adaptation of the Grey Rabbit stories early in 1950, but when adaptations of the first four books were eventually shown on television, Alison had to go to friends at Penn in order to see the programmes, having no TV set herself.

An illustrated edition of *The Country Child* was published in 1945, an occasion somewhat marred for Alison by a review in *Punch* which gave more space to Tunnicliffe than to herself. She was pleased by a reprinting of *Ambush of Young Days* early in 1950 and a Belgian edition of *Six Tales of the Four Pigs*. Sam Pig was also translated into German for the Austrian and German markets. The Grey Rabbit books were translated into Dutch, and in January 1950 Alison was delighted to learn that *The Country Child* was being issued in Germany.

During this period Alison published four Grey Rabbit books, *The*

Speckledy Hen in 1946, *Little Grey Rabbit and the Weasels* in 1947, *Grey Rabbit and the Wandering Hedgehog* in 1948 and *Little Grey Rabbit Makes Lace* in 1950. *Sam Pig in Trouble* appeared in November 1948 and a book about one of her Scotties, *Macduff*, in 1950. Her play, *The Washerwoman's Child*, came out in December 1946, although she was irritated to find it dedicated wrongly to Mark, rather than Margaret, Rutherford and blamed Richard de la Mare for the mistake. Two books of fairy tale and magic appeared, *John Barleycorn* in May 1948 and *The Cobbler's Shop and Other Tales* in 1950. Her book *Buckinghamshire* in the County Series was over five years in gestation, eventually appearing in 1950. This book was not easy to write, though Alison did a good deal of research for it. She felt herself to be the 'most humble' of the various authors in the series and had some disagreements with the editor over different revisions. In April 1948 she was devastated when the proofs were destroyed in a fire at the printer's, declaring that she had a sinister feeling over the book and that the publishers, Hale, were 'a sickening lot'.

More satisfying for her were her two books of country reminiscence, *Country Things* published in June 1946 and *Carts and Candlesticks* published in 1948. *Country Things* received an excellent review from Cyril Ray in *The Sunday Times*, but a supercilious notice in *Punch* and the view, expressed in *Time and Tide*, that she could not write. *Carts and Candlesticks* received more even treatment. Cyril Ray wrote: 'Alison Uttley . . . is as true and tender as a north-country woman should be. . . . For in spite of everything, an older tongue is spoken among the northern fells than in the softer downs and woodlands of the south, and they are haunted still by an older magic. In book after book – this latest one is no exception – Mrs Uttley recaptures it as no-one else can.'[33]

But Alison was not merely successfully replaying and adapting her well-tried themes and harmonies. The publication of the first Little Brown Mouse book in 1950 heralded a new series which, by 1957, included twelve volumes. The Little Brown Mice, Snug and Serena, are pleasant enough characters, though lacking the true originality and fascination of Alison's earlier animal creations. The whole series was illustrated by Katherine Wigglesworth, but Alison declared herself disappointed with the first pictures she received in March 1950, considering them to be 'too loud and crude'.[34] She telephoned her editor at Heinemann, Dwye Evans, and got them altered. In April 1950 she was writing the third Little Brown Mouse tale with undiminished energy.

CHAPTER EIGHTEEN

Seventy Years Old,
But Still Going Strong,
1951–55

I felt a little sad, nothing from G.L. or John or
Harry or Ronnie on my 70th birthday. However,
freesias came from K. Wig., lovely, & a telegram
from Margaret [Rutherford] and Stringer . . . I
was touched nearly to tears by this.

ALISON UTTLEY, diary, 17 December 1954

Alison celebrated her seventieth birthday in December 1954. She wrote,
'I feel as I did at 20, only more carefree, but more tired! A lovely lovely
day of sun and shadows and bliss.'[1] Despite these positive feelings on
becoming seventy, Alison had previously shown some resentment at
attaining this significant age. Early in 1953 she had bemoaned the fact
that because she had begun driving a car so late, she was now difficult to
insure and in November of that year had reacted furiously to her
accountant suggesting that, because she was nearing seventy, she
doubtless took no pleasure in travelling.

During 1951 and 1952 she seems to have been rather depressed and,
for her, uncommunicative. Her diary entries for these two years are
remarkably thin, even scrappy. Perhaps one explanation is her ill health.
In July 1951 she fell awkwardly down her stairs and lay in agony by
herself for some time. She had broken a rib and badly torn some muscles
and although friends like Katherine Wigglesworth came to look after her,
she resented her incapacity.

It is perhaps indicative of deep-seated anxieties that she developed at
the same time an extremely unpleasant form of dermatitis. Some of her
friends privately believed that her Scottie, Macduff, who was later discovered to be suffering from chronic eczema, had infected Alison. Whatever the cause, her dermatitis was a very inconvenient and unbecoming
affliction. Alison's diaries for these years show how much she suffered:
her legs, and eventually other parts of her body, were covered with
running sores; sometimes she thought that the itching would drive her
'crazy'; once she felt that she ought to be excited at a publishing triumph,

but instead could only stay at home and 'anoint her hundred wounds'; on another occasion she dreamed of a dark-haired woman whose body was scarred the same way as hers; early in 1953 she suffered such a bad attack that, as she wrote pitifully in her diary, although Macduff did his best to comfort her, only her mother could really have helped.[2] Her dermatitis had significantly improved by the autumn of 1953, although it returned to plague her early in 1955.

She continued to be visited by depression, feeling particularly distraught on the anniversary of James's suicide in 1951. She sometimes showed excessive grief over everyday accidents, bitterly lamenting in the spring of 1954 that some workmen had broken a passion flower tree in her garden. A year later she lay awake until four o'clock in the morning, worrying over what she admitted were trifles. In May 1955 she haemorrhaged and had to go into the Princess Christian's Nursing Home at Windsor for several days for some gynaecological investigations which included the scraping of her womb. She wrote to Charles Stewart's widow, Agnes: 'It is a great shock. I felt so well . . . I have never been to hospital or nursing home – I thought I should be free, having a country constitution.'

Despite these various problems, Alison seems to have recovered a good deal of her spirits from 1953 onwards. Her diary for that year is far fuller than for the two previous years, blooming like a flower reviving after a drought. She also felt contented enough to allow some not always flattering introspection. In March 1953 she wrote, 'I am not a lovely person, I fear', and a little later admitted that she was 'a poor judge of character, – except that my first impressions are usually right'. Although she occasionally toyed with the idea of a resident companion, she was realistic enough to recognise that she could only continue to write so productively by managing alone, 'thinking, dreaming and writing'. Sometimes she positively revelled in her solitary life, and on Twelfth Night in 1951 'took down the holly and ivy, which no-one has seen but *I* have seen it and all the invisible ones have had its joy'.[3] Two and a half years later she described the essence of herself as floating in the air, a little above her corporeal presence.

She expressed a variety of old-fashioned views. She seems to have resented the fact that contemporary opinion tended to blame mothers for the problems of their children, rather than the Devil, as in her childhood. She was deeply embarrassed when she called on a female neighbour and found her walking about in red shorts, 'a hanky round her breasts'. She once wrote a passionate denunciation of the intellectual arrogance typified in her mind by Dame Edith Sitwell, an attitude which she considered to be essentially crooked and evil.

Alison was as avid for life as ever, experiencing it as fully as she could.

She eagerly talked to some gipsy boys that she met, went regularly to London – going to her first cricket match for some time in July 1953 – took regular holidays and in the spring of 1953 went 'naughtily' into her garden at the dead of night in her nightdress, there to be thrilled by finding an owl perched in the apple tree. She continued to absorb and ponder over many theories. She remained intrigued by the concepts of space and time, accepting that they implied each other mutually. She also became increasingly obsessed with the contemporary interest in Unidentified Flying Objects. In November 1953 she read the best-selling book *Flying Saucers Have Landed*, declaring that she absolutely believed it and that it fulfilled all her ideas and the needs of her imagination.[4]

Music was a source of delight and once she felt that Paganini's Caprices were 'so marvellous I am even more convinced . . . that he got supernatural help'. Bach's cantatas she found 'ravishing', and she was often deeply moved by the music of Brahms who remained a favourite. She continued to read ravenously. In January 1953 she was reading Carlyle's *Letters* and Tunnicliffe's *Shorelands*. In February 1955 she turned again to Keats 'that glorious, astonishing poet'. She began to attend church more regularly, but found the order of the service so changed she knelt at the wrong times. At the end of 1953, however, she declared herself stupefied by the clichés that bedevilled the sermon being preached, and decided it was best not to listen. Although later she took out a modest covenant for Penn church, she resented requests to increase it. She became interested in Jordans, a nearby Quaker settlement with a hostel and a meeting house, but subsequently denounced it as 'unnatural, like a Communist state. It is rich, pretending to be poor.' She visited a local school, High March, several times.

Her behaviour was sometimes eccentric. In March 1954 she lit the fire with the contract for her next Grey Rabbit book and had to ask for a replacement, and once overreacted and stormed away when a woman standing in a queue for fish asked her to take her turn like everyone else. Her dream life was extraordinarily full and complex, offering sidelights on the otherwise repressed yet extravagantly emotional side to her nature. There was the time when she dreamed of an Italian showing her the most gloriously coloured clothes: 'I bought a pair of knickers, partly deep heavenly blue, partly a kind of red like a fuchsia, slit and lined with the different colours, and I looked at the marvels of silk, texture and shade, petticoats very low and frilled, shot silk, and a dressing gown of silk, and vests etc. I wanted a vest like the knickers. Medici colours.'[5]

Immediately after this entry in her diary she has written, 'I have got the sun in the morning and the moon at night.'

Her relationship with her son and his wife seems to have been a little more satisfactory. The marriage was clearly successful enough, despite, or perhaps because of, Helen's tendency to dominate John. In general, John took Helen's side in any conflict with Alison and the love he felt for his wife is perhaps best summed up by a poem he wrote to her on the twentieth anniversary of their wedding:

> We have been happy for twenty years, eh what!
> We have been happy for twenty years, eh what!
> I know there have been ripples in the stream
> I know it may not have been an idyllic dream.
> But it has been life, and we have marched on,
> With love and forebearance in unison.
> And I for my part look forward to
> Another twenty years or more with you.
> Eh What![6]

Alison enjoyed several visits from John and Helen which she later described in her diary as 'lovely' or 'happy'. Perhaps she was relieved to see that John was evidently content in his marriage, and was reassured by both his visits and his letters – such as the one she received in August 1953, telling her how happy he was on holiday in Guernsey, sketching, bathing and reading. That Alison felt more positive towards her son and his wife is indicated by her decision in December 1953 to transfer the ownership of Downs House to John. The competitiveness between mother-in-law and daughter-in-law abated sufficiently to allow John sometimes to go off with Alison for short holidays to the Cotswolds. His comparatively comfortable position between the two women in his life is perhaps symbolised by the message on the valentine he sent Alison in February 1953: 'I am neither oak, nor weeping willow.' But not all was sweetness and light. In September 1954 Alison made a bonfire of John's childhood golliwog and scout uniform, as well as burning hundreds of letters from James to her. She expressed disappointment that John, although clearly far happier in his job at Stowe than he had been at Eton, was not promoted to housemaster in December 1954. After spending Christmas of that year with John and Helen, she recognised that the experience had been a pleasant one, but felt she could no longer fit into their lives. She still found it easy to criticise Helen, once regretting that her whispering during a midnight mass had 'quite spoilt' the service for her and on several occasions expressing alarm at her daughter-in-law's temper.

Her relationship with her brother Harry continued to be fundamentally unsatisfactory. She expressed her disappointment that he had not written to her during her illness of May 1953, and during November 1954 responded negatively to his suggestion that she should go and live with him as they were both getting old: 'But I cannot as we

should neither of us enjoy it, too different. I would have him here –
much easier. No use to ask for disaster.'[7] Alison sent regular payments
to her cousin Sissy, and was once so enraged when the bank failed to
make the payment that she stormed into the manager's office and later
described him as 'a little wretch'. Three years later, however, Alison
was shocked to learn from Sissy that she had been left several cottages in
a will which she proposed to sell: 'She is quite wealthy. I had no idea!
She must have had 9 or 10 houses, and I gave her twenty shillings a
week!'[8] There seems to have been little more contact with the Uttleys
during these years, though George and Doris Uttley paid her a visit
during 1951 and for Christmas that year she sent a tiny bottle of scent to
Gertrude. Sugdens went through one of their not infrequent financial
crises early in 1953, with the younger generation finding fault with
George Uttley's management – a conflict which moved Alison to wish
'a plague on both your houses!'

Both of Alison's oldest friends became something of a trial during
these years. During her various visits to Beaconsfield she was irritated
by LM's deterioration into a slow, old woman, who usually aroused her
impatience. But she was also mostly sorry when she left Thackers,
recognising her as 'a brick', although confessing that she was weary of
hearing endless stories of LM's dog and of her neighbour's television.
GL continued to send her boxes of eggs, most of which, in now
traditional fashion, arrived smashed. GL's sister died early in 1951 and
in June 1954 Alison, though not really meaning it, offered her a home at
Thackers. In fact, she was convinced that they would never get on, since
she was too active and GL too passive. A little later Alison was annoyed
that her friend asked her to buy her house for £2950. From the summer
of 1954 Alison's comments on GL are mostly derogatory, insisting that
she was stooping and old, that she was half-crazy and made noises like a
horse, that she was unduly obstinate, that her mannerisms had become
exaggerated through living alone and that she could only write
platitudes in her letters. Alison was forced to revise this low opinion
when she and John called on GL in the spring of 1955 and were amazed
and impressed by the portraits of her dead brother, Gilbert, that she had
painted.

Katherine Wigglesworth continued in Alison's good books. She records 'jolly' meals with her and was glad when Katherine responded
positively to some of Alison's criticisms of her illustrations. Mostly, the
two women seem to have been on very close terms. Once after
Katherine had gone down on her hands and knees to help clean up after
the sweep had been to Thackers, Alison lent her a blue rest gown and
then insisted that she looked like Catherine Parr, Henry VIII's last wife,
a conceit which made them both laugh till they cried. It is clear that

Katherine sometimes longed to share other flights of Alison's imagination, once writing from Cambridge of the city's depressing effect and her longing to chat about mermaids and unicorns.

Mermaids provided one of the subjects which Alison enjoyed discussing with Walter de la Mare. She wrote an essay on him in the spring of 1951, which he told her he loved more than any other appreciation he had yet received. When she visited his sickbed in May 1952 she was relieved to perceive his warmth and vibrancy. But in July 1954 Alison was shocked to see how much he had aged and how easily he talked of death. De la Mare did not die, however, and for her birthday in 1955 Alison received a letter from him which delighted her by declaring she was composed of the very essence of England.[9]

The acquaintance with Margaret Rutherford had ripened into one of the most successful of Alison's relationships. They visited, wrote to, and telephoned each other regularly. In January 1953 Alison was flattered when Margaret told her that she thought of her every day. Other encounters proved less satisfactory, though. She found the visit of Joan Dobell a strain in May 1951, particularly because she was obliged to listen to her many complaints about her marriage; Alison put her own particular gloss on it when Joan told her that she had a walnut tree, saying, 'I wouldn't mind what kind of husband if I had a walnut tree.'[10] She was disappointed in August 1953 on meeting her old tutor from Manchester days, Sir George Simpson, to find him far duller than she remembered and speculated that perhaps academic life at a small university narrowed the mind. Eleanor Graham visited her once, when Alison was reminded how ill their personalities fitted together.

Somewhat surprisingly, perhaps, Alison did not simply fall back on old friends now that she was entering her seventies, but continued to forge new contacts. Among others in the locality, there were the Wailes and the Wilmots and, particularly important, a young woman called Georgina Jenkinson who had often written to Alison before she visited her in March 1953. Alison immediately warmed to her, kissed her when she left and was to retain a great affection for her. She was more excited at meeting the author Eleanor Farjeon in June 1954, and wished afterwards that she had known her years ago. A few months later she received a heart-warming letter from Eleanor, beginning, 'Lovely, dear, brave, gay Alison', and promising that, 'she will join me in my hollow tree, and squat beside me . . . "a clay pipe in my teeth".'[11]

Away from the circle of her friends and acquaintances, Alison kept a fitful eye on public events. She was delighted with the Conservative victory in the general election of 1951 and declared herself thrilled that 'Winston was supreme again.' In November 1954 she once more expressed her deep admiration for Churchill and her equal hatred for the

Graham Sutherland portrait that was presented to him at that time. Otherwise, her main preoccupation was with the Royal Family. She felt the death of George VI 'like a sword' through her heart and, a year later, Queen Mary's funeral service reminded her of that upright woman's 'unquenchable zest for life'. She identified strongly with Queen Elizabeth II, declaring herself glad to be English on Coronation Day in June 1953, and a year later calling the Queen 'a wonder girl'. The controversy over Princess Margaret's love affair with Peter Townsend shocked her during the autumn of 1955, and she denounced her for being a 'selfish girl'. When Princess Margaret eventually announced that she was not, after all, going to marry Townsend, Alison pronounced it 'a great relief, and [a] weight off our minds. Thankful she has made this fine decision. . . . Feeling happy about the Queen now, who has her sister.'[12]

Alison seems also to have felt reasonably happy about her writing career. Having safely weathered the late 1940s and the crisis of confidence they brought, she began the new decade with her powers undiminished. Her fertile imagination continued to toy with many projects. One of her few failures to comply with the suggestions and requests of her publishers was her inability to oblige Faber with another *A Traveller in Time*. Otherwise, she was able to snap up the merest trifle, writing her book *Hare and Guy Fawkes* after some little boys had suggested to her in January 1953 that she should write a story about Grey Rabbit and Guy Fawkes. In December 1954 she woke up after dreaming of an atomic power station with a perfect short story already formed in her head. Not all of these ideas saw their way into print, but Alison's productivity continued unabated – so much so that in January 1955 she berated herself for breaking her rule of writing at least a thousand words a day.

Quite apart from the continuing heavy sales of many of her books – *Buckinghamshire* was amongst the few exceptions to the rule, with only three thousand copies sold six months after publication – her stories were beginning to find their way into profitable anthologies. By the end of 1954 Eleanor Graham was choosing tales for a Puffin edition of her work, surprising Alison by insisting that there could be no Tim Rabbit stories included because of the public's current revulsion at myxomatosis. A year later Alison met Kathleen Lines at *The Sunday Times* Book Exhibition and was told that the latter wanted to publish a book of her fairy tales.

Her finances for the period made the usual impressive showing when, apart from her high royalties, her various investments yielded handsome returns. The size of her income now necessitated the services of an accountant – an 'awful' man, according to Alison, who longed to be free of his questions. She was discomforted by her heavy tax demands, nearly £1000 for the financial year ending in April 1953, complaining 'I never save a penny.' But in March 1951 she bought £1500 worth of Defence Bonds, and also invested heavily in works of art and in antiques. In the spring of 1951 she bought an Ambrose Breughel painting for 400 guineas and further purchases of Breughel paintings followed, including a painting of a windmill priced at £200 by Jan Breughel in August 1953. Eight months later she spent £450 on another Breughel. She became a regular visitor to antique dealers' fairs, purchasing a diamond brooch for £175 and a Queen-Anne chair for £135 in the summer of 1951. She also bought two paintings by David Cox in December 1951, eventually leaving these to Charles Tunnicliffe in her will. Apart from her son, and a few chosen relations like her brother Harry and her cousin Sissy, Alison was not free with her money and in April 1953 declared herself 'staggered' by her friend Del Anderson's request that she should lend her some money in order to buy a house.

Hand in hand with this financial success went Alison's widespread fame. She took variable pleasure in the large number of fan letters she received, although feeling touched by one addressed to 'A Uttey and M Tempy'. She was flattered to hear in the spring of 1951 that the Queen wanted to borrow her book on Buckinghamshire. She also gave quite a large number of lectures during these years, to book leagues and clubs, mostly on the subject of 'Writing for Children'. She opened a variety of fêtes and bazaars and was generally in considerable demand. Occasionally, however, in well-heeled gatherings, she asked herself what she was doing there in the midst of 'a rich, important, chattering crowd, knowing nothing of the country or flowers'. She sometimes still felt amazed that the outside world was interested in her at all, secretly wondering in October 1953 why anyone honoured her, or read her.

She remained, however, fiercely proprietorial over her literary creations, especially the Little Grey Rabbit characters. In the autumn of 1951 she began a fierce and rancorous dispute with Margaret Tempest over the adaptation of some of the Grey Rabbit stories for television. At the heart of the quarrel was Margaret Tempest's annoyance that Alison had not properly asked her permission to offer the stories to television at the outset. But money also came into it. Alison felt that she was being morally blackmailed by her illustrator and even thought of seeking legal advice. Eventually a common-sense peace was patched up whereby both women agreed to share the proceeds from television equally. Not that Alison seems to have forgiven her rival easily, and in October 1953 she responded to Margaret Tempest's confession that she was bad at drawing horses by observing that she was 'bad at all drawing'. Perhaps one of the problems in their relationship was Alison's continuing unease at Margaret Tempest's superior social origins and position, an unease she once pinpointed after a visit to one of her illustrator's friends, as having to do with 'stalwart women of ladylike mien' in cottages too small for them, 'They are so out of place, so big.'[13]

Despite the differences with Margaret Tempest, Little Grey Rabbit proved to be a great success on television, skilfully brought to life by the puppeteers Jan Bussell and Anne Hogarth. *The Washerwoman's Child* was also accepted for television presentation in April 1951, and in February 1955 Alison received a proposal from Independent Television that they should adapt some of the Tim Rabbit tales. Radio broadcasts of Little Grey Rabbit stories and one Little Brown Mouse story were also transmitted, as were some individual fairy tales. In January 1952 Alison was interviewed for BBC television by Mrs Kennish.

The spin-offs from her books at this time included, apart from the various Little Grey Rabbit toys and games, a Tim Rabbit song book with music specially composed by David Davis and, more indirectly, the offer of a regular gardening column – like that of Vita Sackville-West – in *The Sunday Times*. Surprisingly perhaps, Alison declined: 'I felt flattered and honoured, but refused, – no Botany and Latin.'

Above all, though, Alison valued the publication of her books. Among the newcomers to her creations during these years was the Little Brown Mouse series. So well did Alison feel she was getting on with Heinemann over these books in the spring of 1951, that she toyed with the idea of writing some more Little Grey Rabbit tales for them. This optimistic impulse was replaced a month later by fury when Heinemann's Dwye Evans complained that the latest Brown Mouse books had insufficient plot, prompting Alison to exclaim that she could not write for him any more. Little Brown Mouse books continued, however, to appear at regular intervals – twelve in all by 1957. The success of this series prompted Alison to offer another manuscript, the *Little Red Fox and the Wicked Uncle*, to Heinemann early in 1953. The book was published on 26 October 1954 and received some complimentary reviews. This was to lead to further Little Red Fox books.

This series, like the Brown Mouse books, was illustrated by Katherine Wigglesworth. The illustrations, both in colour and in black and white, are attractive, neat and appealing. It ill-became Alison, when Katherine complained in April 1955 that the sale of the first Little Red Fox book was poor, to write, 'I really feel very sick with her. Her work isn't wonderful, the sales are good, she has half the income. I feel that I shall refuse to write these books. I am infuriated, for she grumbles so much, not only in letters.'[14] Alison was more at ease with the publication of two more Grey Rabbit books, *Hare and the Easter Eggs* in April 1952 and *Little Grey Rabbit Goes to Sea* in 1954. She had been working on the latter book since January 1953, reminding herself that she must always have one in reserve in order to maintain her momentum. The book sold over twenty thousand copies during its first six months. Two more of the popular Sam Pig books were published: *Yours Ever, Sam Pig*, described on 'Children's Hour' as a welcome addition to 'the enchanting . . . series', during 1951; and *Sam Pig and the Singing Gate* in 1955, of which the *Birmingham Post* remarked, 'The stories are a little shorter, and perhaps on the whole slighter than usual but the little pigs have lost none of their charm and the writing is as good as ever.'

A further book of country essays and reminiscence, *Plowmen's Clocks*, was published in 1952. Alison was not overpleased with the book's reception, complaining of a 'sneering' *Sunday Times* review in January 1953. More rewarding was the view of the *Irish Independent* that 'This little book is delightful in its urbanity, its craftsmanship, its simplicity of style and its power to stimulate the imagination.'[15] *The Times Literary Supplement* also thought that 'Readers . . . will return with pleasure to the North Country farm life which she knows so well and describes with feminine awareness of detail and poet's clarity of vision.' Alison was particularly upset by one review which disliked her nostalgic memoirs, writing trenchantly and a little dishonestly, 'I much prefer the present.'[16]

Perhaps the most significant book which she published during these years was *The Stuff of Dreams*, on 22 October 1953. Alison sent the manuscript to Faber early in January 1953 – interestingly, at the same time that she believed she had seen 'phantoms' after giving a party which was crowded with too many people.[17] While waiting for her publisher's reaction to the manuscript, she wrote in her diary that she was able to see into time, very dimly, during dreams.[18] She was delighted by Peter du Sautoy's acceptance of the book in the middle of February 1953. A little over a month before publication, however, she declared herself frightened at seeing it on Faber's summer list. This anxiety doubtless sprang from her deeply entrenched dislike of exposing the intimate details of her private life. It was understandable that she should feel so threatened by the publication of the book, for although she herself makes almost no attempt to interpret her dreams, simply by recounting parts of her dream life she was exposing herself to potentially unfriendly scrutiny and analysis. As it happens, her dreams reveal an internal world no more disordered and unacceptable than that of the average person. They also show the rich, imaginative texture of her thoughts. Yet she clearly felt that many of her recorded dreams exposed the unacceptable face of her personality and the dark workings of her unconscious mind. She tried to put dreams into her own perspective in the foreword, writing:

Dreams are an entertainment of stories never written, of music unknown, of a hidden way of life with beauty transcendent, but we may
ask if the mind of Nature itself is revealed, with enchantment and
something else, dangerous and unknown. Can it be that the natural
world is imbued with life into which we are allowed to glimpse? Or is
it only a heightened illusion, such as one sees on a winter's day, when
through the closed window there is a vision of a company of little
golden flames dancing on the snow, leaping high and flicking their red
tongues on the whiteness? We move aside, the reflection vanishes, a
fire is on the hearth, snow on the lawn, all is explained, the miracle of
fire and snow remains in the memory.[19]

The critical reception for the book was generally favourable. It took a
month, however, for the first complimentary review to be published in
John O'London's Weekly, Joanna Richardson observing, 'Mrs Alison
Uttley . . . has long given us pleasure with her country books in which
everyday life is drawn so perceptively that it almost turns into a fairy-
tale . . . but only now, in *The Stuff of Dreams* . . . does she show that
she is a qualified scientist; she retains her happy qualities and records her
fantasies with scientific precision. She has written, I think, an exciting
book.' *The Sunday Times* called it 'a fascinating record, rich in wonder
and mystery and stamped all over with the mark of a highly lovable
personality'.[20] *The Times* considered it to be 'a great tribute to the
charm and spontaneity of Mrs Uttley's writing. The dreams she has
collected here . . . continually sustain her readers' interest.'[21] Alison
was horrified at a review she received in the journal *Psychic*, which took
her to be some sort of spiritualist. This speculation offended the scientist
in her. She received a good many letters about the book, but treated
them with circumspection, feeling 'I must be careful about these Dream
fans, they go hay-wire.'[22] Such admirers were, however, but a small
part of her by now extensive public.

CHAPTER 19

Dropping Into Old Age?
1956–60

An hour or two with one of Mrs Uttley's books is
as refreshing as the smell of a wood after rain, as
homely as muffins by a Sussex fire.

Time and Tide ,1956

On New Year's Day 1956 Alison settled down by a fire after lunch and
heard the radio playing 'Alone':

> which makes me think of a young workman on the roof of a Bowdon
> house, tapping and hammering the gables, singing 'Alone' very loudly,
> and my secret joy and laughter as I heard him perched so high. A wet
> day with brilliant sun between, – and I am the same, depressed still by
> the tension of Christmas, and yet full of joy in life and beauty, and
> 'Here's a new Day'. The trees, especially my beech, so glorious, so
> immortal in spite of mortality.[1]

As Alison approached her seventy-fifth birthday, she carried out more
than her usual quota of stocktaking. Her new year resolutions for 1957
were 'to be patient and kind, – to keep my own council [sic] and to be
careful what I say, especially to John and Helen, lest they think I boast.
To look for the hidden marvels, the beauty in the world, the secret
Heaven. To laugh, to dream and not care too much.'[2] In June of that
year, having agonised over whether to ask her friend Richard Fairbairn
to draw up her will, she went to a London solicitor to arrange her affairs:
'It was quite fun, no depression, in fact I enjoyed doling out my jewellery
to dear friends.'[3]

When she attained the age of seventy-five she wrote in her diary, 'it
seems absurd, – I cannot believe it, for I feel just the same as ever, full of
joy and life, only a bit tireder, so that I have to rest after lunch.'[4] On New
Year's Eve she wrote, perhaps more realistically, 'Now I feel I have really
dropped into Old Age. But I can think quickly and manage to do things;
and I have written 4 books for next year.'[5]

Various scientific phenomena excited her more than for many years,
and also gave her cause for further introspection. In April 1957 she was
so thrilled by seeing a comet that she drew a map of the night sky and

counted the experience among a long list of her blessings. She was even more stimulated by the news of the launching of the Russian satellite, the Sputnik, six months later. These two events seem to have put her more in touch with her early scientific training, and she recalled shortly afterwards lying awake till three o'clock in the morning, 'thinking of Scientific work, the urge and thrill of it. The bliss when we calculated the number of atoms in a space. . . . So I lay awake, thinking of what I might have done, yet I might have found it sterile, and my life is human now.'[6] A few months later she listened to a panel of scientists on a radio programme answering questions from the public, and found that 'I knew all the answers since schooldays. . . . So [the] sceintific work did me much good, mentally, as I knew and remembered all the answers.'[7] Then came her first sighting of the Sputnik, which thoroughly amazed her. Perhaps she was attracted once more by the concrete realities of scientific achievement because, as she grew older, 'Sometimes I think I withdraw from this Life, seeking something in the Future Life, seeing it here around me, half visible.'[8]

For the most part, however, Alison's feet were firmly on the ground. The end of May 1956 saw her home help, Mrs Allen, spring-cleaning the top landing while Alison coped with the rest of the house. Mrs Allen seems to have grown in her estimation during these years, perhaps partly because she found her other help, Kathleen, increasingly unsatisfactory. Although Kathleen eventually left her employment, Mrs Allen, with 'her country face and good manners' remained to give invaluable service. When her husband died in February 1957, Alison wept for the death of this 'nice' man. In the middle of 1958 she gave Mrs Allen an unsolicited rise in wages, now paying her 6s. 6d. an hour. This was an unusual gesture, and she continued to scrutinise the payments she made to others. She objected to being overcharged by a firm that mended her garden fencing and was delighted when they reduced the bill by three pounds, as well as admitting their error in a letter written in Little Grey Rabbit language; later on she accused her milkman of cheating her and was alarmed when he responded by threatening her with a libel action.

Sometimes Alison's determination to do things for herself proved hazardous. A keen motorist still – she bought a new Morris Minor in the autumn of 1956 – she was by no means the safest of drivers, and once called out to a fellow motorist with whom she had become entangled: 'I'm not a good driver.' Things sometimes went wrong in the kitchen, too: 'My egg fell off my breakfast tray, and rolled under the bed. I chased it with a *sword*, couldn't reach it, and Mac[duff] thought I was playing ball. Hilarious as he dashed about, and the egg rolled sideways.'[9] There were other accidents, as when she set a mousetrap in her bedroom and then was horrified when a robin that used to fly in through the window was inadvertantly killed in it. Two of her Scotties died during these years, Macduff early in 1958 and, inexplicably, MacTavish eighteen months later. By the end of 1959 a new dog had been installed, Dirk, although Alison declared herself 'staggered' that he had cost her eighteen guineas. She now took *The Times* for a daily newspaper, finding it far more satisfying than *The Daily Telegraph*, and went a good deal to the cinema. Among the films she saw during these years were *Richard III*, in which she considered Claire Bloom 'perfect' though she thought that the film as a whole did not contain 'enough Shakespeare', and *Great Expectations*, which she found 'frightening, I think all my childhood fears came from Dickens'. She detested Ingmar Bergman's *Wild Strawberries*, shutting her eyes through most of it, perhaps because she found it too painful. She also kept up with contemporary literature, another indication of the breadth and vigour of her interests. She approved of Iris Murdoch's *The Bell*, observing 'How brilliant it is, the characterisation, presentation, perfection. But too much homosexuality, – obsessed by it.' *Lord of the Flies* she judged to be brilliant, but frightening. *Lady Chatterley's Lover* she thought would harm the young and declared herself glad that she had not read it when she was eighteen years old.

She seems to have coped better with her various ailments and fits of depression. When Mrs Allen broke a candlestick early in 1956, she was able to take it quite philosophically, as she did her spell in a nursing home where she was admitted with a high temperature in February 1956. Her dermatitis returned to plague her, causing her legs in particular to swell up and bleed. She damaged the joint of her knee in the spring of 1958 and required medical attention, including the visit of a London specialist to whom she lied about her age, telling him she was seventy years old when in fact she was seventy-four. It is significant, though, that her GP Dr Milner, did not need to call on her for a period of eighteen months during these years.

She inevitably remained preoccupied with the lives of John and Helen. In September 1956 she was delighted to be told that Helen was pregnant and that a baby was due at Easter. But two months later when she visited them at their cottage at Padbury she was seized by a terrible presentiment of disaster while Helen chatted about the pregnancy, putting her sudden depression down to the fact that she was 'too psychic'. Her intimations of misfortune were unhappily fulfilled when Helen later miscarried. It is significant, though, that Alison's diaries contain no reference at all to this tragedy. Helen's father died during 1957, a loss that found Alison prepared to realise how much John had come to love his father-in-law. It was a small enough concession, but one which won a response from Helen in the form of a warm and constructive letter, which went on to tell her what she already believed herself – that John should face up to the psychological difficulties which were now besetting him.

This unhappy theme remains constant throughout these years. Although John was made Housemaster of Walpole House for the autumn term of 1956, within a few months of taking up his new position he was beginning to tell Alison of his anxieties and depressions. His complaints included 'feeling constricted', the conviction that he was not able to keep proper order among the boys in his house, that he had lost his courage, and that he found it difficult to remember things. The death of Helen's father seems to have coincided with the onset of a particularly deep depression, perhaps because it was a reminder of the crippling blow James's suicide had dealt him. Nor were his anxieties helped by the appointment of a new headmaster at Stowe, and by September 1958 he was complaining that the new head was to severe. A few weeks later Alison wrote despairingly in her diary, 'I cannot help him. It is most strange this heavy cloud. It reminds me so much of James, alas.'[10]

During November, John suffered a complete psychological collapse and was admitted to the Warneford Hospital in Oxford, where he received electro-convulsive therapy. Although there was some temporary improvement and he was back at his job in January 1959, his anxieties soon began to manifest themselves once more. Later when he visited an osteopath who, no doubt to Alison's approval, put his problems down to a blow he had once received on his head, the relief afforded was only temporary. By Christmas 1959 Alison was alarmed to hear that whenever her son received a letter from the headmaster he thought it was a notice of dismissal. In the spring of 1960 John was, in fact, dismissed as housemaster, the head arguing that a tougher man was needed for the job. Although John toyed with the idea of taking a year's leave, he decided to leave Stowe at the end of the summer term of 1960. For a while it is clear that Alison felt she had regained some of her lost intimacy with her son, recording in October 1960 that although he had confessed to her a phase of near apostasy, they had said their old prayer together and that his religious faith was now restored. She reacted with dismay, however, when John told her at the end of the year that he had decided to give up teaching altogether and instead to live in Guernsey and seek to develop property there. She put on a brave face in public, however, telling Peter du Sautoy that, 'the strain of teaching might bring back a recurrence of the illness' and agreeing that John was right to live in a quiet island like Guernsey.[11]

In truth, John's removal to Guernsey was a bitter disappointment to Alison. It was now more difficult to see him on a regular basis and the sense of loss produced by his marriage was accentuated. Alison had given John some financial help while he was at Stowe and was generally sensitive to the fact that he earned relatively little money. But she could not, despite her generally improved relationship with Helen, rid herself of the idea that her daughter-in-law was extravagant and would, if given the chance, 'dissipate a fortune'.

The subject of money cast its shadow over her relationship with other members of the family. She consistently felt that her brother Harry was ungrateful for the presents she sent him and once wrote him a frank letter telling him that he should acknowledge with better grace her present of a ten pound premium bond. Harry continued to disappoint her in other ways, once prompting her to observe after he had tactlessly said that she looked a good deal older, 'He has *no* feelings, he is blank as a wall.'[12] Even when Harry and his family visited her in the summer of 1957 and gratified her with their news of how Mrs Clay, the new owner of Castle Top Farm, was managing the property, Alison was hurt that they offered her no praise for her own house or garden.

Although she had for so many years treated Gertrude with an icy disdain, she was touched when her sister-in-law's daughter, Katherine, invited her to come and see her children in their house at Kew in the spring of 1957. In the summer of 1959 Alison recorded a happy visit from Katherine and her two little boys, whom she found very likable. A crisis in the fortunes of Sugden's led to a renewal of contact with other members of the Uttley family from November 1957. Harold Armfield, Gertrude's husband, wrote to her at the end of the month about Sugden's crisis, the first letter Alison remembered receiving from him for twenty-seven years. In May 1958 Alison wrote a letter to Gertrude and was gratified to receive a friendly reply. Sugden's was in its death throes by 1957. Although the firm had prospered during the Second World War, largely because of the imposition of cotton quotas and the sharp fall in competition from imported cotton goods, there had been a steady decline thereafter. Hardly any of the profits were reinvested in the firm and the designs used were becoming increasingly out of date.[13] Eventually the decision was made to wind up the firm and to provide George Uttley, who had for so long been in charge of it, with a pension. Tony Tolson, Alice Uttley's son, who was employed by Sugdens at this time, played a leading part in the negotiations.

Alison resisted the move to provide George Uttley with a pension, harbouring resentment over what she remembered as his ungenerous attitude towards her at the time of James's death. She also bitterly resented a request made by George Uttley that she should lend ten thousand pounds to Sugdens to guarantee their future borrowing for trading purposes: 'Colossal cheek, – nay, it is incredible. I haven't the money, and I would never lend it to that crazy firm which has squandered a fortune already and gave me no help in my direst need, when I was penniless.'[14] Eventually, calmer counsels prevailed, including that of John who decided to put something towards George's pension. Alison received just over £403 from her shares in Sugden's in the middle of December 1957, out of which she grudgingly agreed to contribute to a covenant for her brother-in-law, writing in her diary 'A queer business. . . . Would they do it if anybody else was affected, – if Tony went bankrupt for example?'[15]

Death wrought havoc among Alison's private relationships during these years. Walter de la Mare died in June 1956, GL in March 1959 and LM in February 1960. Alison continued in close contact with Walter de la Mare right up to his death. In April 1956 she was touched when he told her that if he were a king, he would make her a dame. But when he celebrated his eighty-fourth birthday a day later, she only sent him a face cloth for a present, noting in her diary, perhaps rather guiltily, 'But so pretty, green edge and roses on it, – and a card and letter.' This apparently miserly gift was certainly no true indicator of the strength of her feelings for de la Mare. His death in June moved her deeply: 'The saddest news. W.J. died early this morning. I can't believe I shall never see him again. I loved him. I adored him. . . . I went in the garden to think and to pray. The cuckoo was calling in my wood, over and over. It seemed to be immortal, and it brought W.J. to me.'[16] For three days Alison wrote nothing in her diary. She continued to feel close to her old friend, valuing contact with his daughter Florence Thompson and once sensing, when she listened to a radio discussion on his work, that he was not far away.

During GL's last years, Alison was a generous friend. She sent her a hamper of food for Christmas 1957 and received this reply:

> My Dear Alice,
>   It has come! by a special messenger. . . . It is wonderful: a great chest of treasure, all spread out in my little room & every single thing most welcome & delightful. The pudding of course, and the various pickley things . . . the soup and fruit salad. . . . Nothing – books, pictures, jewelry, could have brought more joy & happiness to the heart of this greedy woman.[17]

The approach of GL's death aroused mixed emotions in Alison. She felt both distraught and exasperated to have news of her oldest friend's increasingly eccentric behaviour during the summer of 1958. Neighbours were obliged to put GL into a nursing home early in June, and Alison telephoned her friend's bank manager to assure him that there were sufficient resources to meet the expense. Ten days later GL insisted on coming home. In March 1959 Alison learned that GL was dying: 'Poor GL. She is unconscious. . . . Yet what can we do? . . . Poor GL. I think of her long ago, when she was young and happy. Now she is old and miserable, and no desires or hopes. Life is sad, it has been sad for her, and yet much happiness for her, the school, and the adulation of girls and parents.'[18] GL died a few days later. John and Helen accompanied Alison to her funeral at Chedworth. As she sat in the church with GL's coffin before her, laden with wreaths, Alison 'kept saying "Gwladys! GL. Gwladys. Here we are."' Although GL bequeathed two thousand pounds to John, Alison inherited the bulk of her friend's estate, receiving £5685 in July 1959, and deciding to use the interest for daily living and to leave her son the capital.

Eleven months later LM died at Preston on 7 February. On hearing the news, Alison wrote in her diary:

> I am so grieved. I loved Lily and admired her for courage and bravery in [the] face of many difficulties. . . . She encouraged me with my writing, she brought sweets and good things and flowers in our poverty when J died. I was always excited to open the door at Bowdon and see her, pretty blue hat and pretty dress, gloves, carrying a pile of parcels and her suitcase. And the cricket matches we saw together. Poor dear Lily with her er . . . er . . . er that annoyed me a little . . . dear Lily. I shall think of you always.[19]

Two other close female friends of Alison's survived, however, full of vigour. Katherine Wigglesworth and she continued to cooperate on their books, to visit each other and in the summer of 1956 spent a week together at Rye in Sussex. Alison expressed relatively few resentments at her friend's behaviour during these years, although she quite wrongly doubted the news that Katherine's son Bill had been awarded a scholarship at Magdalen College, Oxford, in January 1956. Margaret Rutherford caused Alison some concern during 1956 by confiding in her that she had fallen in love with another man, who appears in the diaries as Malcolm T. In order to help her through her crisis, Margaret went to a psychiatrist and also to a medium. By the autumn of that year the crisis had been surmounted and Alison was glad, on meeting her friend in London, to see that she was looking much more relaxed. Two years later Alison spontaneously decided to join Margaret and Stringer on a holiday at Brighton. On another occasion she enjoyed accompanying 'MR' to the home of the actor Robert Morley where she met his three children, including Sheridan, 'fat, delightful, most attentive, good manners and amiable'.

In the world of books, Peter du Sautoy, who became vice-chairman of Faber in August 1960, was Alison's most trusted and admired friend – surpassing even William Collins in her estimation. She relished going to the annual National Book League cricket matches with him and being invited into the family circle. She fostered her friendship with Eleanor Farjeon and cultivated her latest literary acquisition, the poetess Ruth Pitter, whom she met in the spring of 1956. Warm letters passed between the two women and Alison visited Ruth, whom she had earlier described as 'very correct and strong-looking, not like a poet', at her country home at the end of June 1956, finding her in 'open blouse and trousers, working in [the] garden.' Katherine Wigglesworth accompanied Alison on her visit, thus providing her with support in the face of the hostility of Ruth Pitter's female companion, Miss O'Hara, 'very peevish, hardly let me in but I thrust flowers at her'.[20]

At Beaconsfield, Alison continued to feel very close to Lilian King, declaring that she adored her and that she was 'a saint'. Donald de Hirsch grew so rapidly in her estimation that she felt she had met nobody like him except Walter de la Mare. Alison had some contact during these years with Ruth Plant, who was interested in spiritualism, but whom she found too overwhelming, and sometimes 'too hysterical'. In addition to her well-established friends, she also liked Del Anderson, although privately expressing her disapproval of her daughter Rosemary's make-up. Early in 1960 Alison very much enjoyed the visit to Thackers of Susan Dickinson, who was to become responsible for her books at Collins and whom she was delighted to discover was the grand-daughter of the writer H.M. Tomlinson, whose books she had admired for many years. More surprising, perhaps, was the warm friendship she struck up with a young Russian journalist, Tatiana Tess, who interviewed her in London in July 1959. An affectionate relationship sprang up between the younger and the older woman. Tatiana gratified Alison by telling her how much she admired her writing, and it is a tribute to Alison's feelings for her new friend that she struggled over the next twelve months to learn Russian.

Alison's lapsed liberalism seems to have enjoyed a modest revival during 1956. In May of that year she expressed her anxiety that the British authorities in Cyprus had condemned to death a man who 'did no murder' for alleged terrorist activities. By far her greatest preoccupation, however, was with the Suez crisis. Although in July she noted censoriously in her diary that the Suez Canal had been 'stolen by Egypt', the transparently contrived British intervention in the Egyptian-Israeli war at the end of October dismayed her. For all her Conservative sympathies, Alison saw the British invasion of Egypt for what it was – a device to regain control of the Suez Canal. She became rapidly disenchanted with the Prime Minister, Anthony Eden: 'Britain has bombed Cairo. Well, I hope Eden will be turned out. He is crazy.'[21] Eden's broadcast to the nation on 3 November, justifying his gov-

ernment's action, provoked Alison's scorn: 'We did *not* go in because of
the little raids between Egypt and Israel [in] the last ten years. Lots of
places have raids. We went in to seize the Canal and to fight Egypt, and
we are the aggressors, attacking a country that can't fight back. Horrible!'[22]

The next day Alison thought that the answering broadcast of Hugh
Gaitskell, the Leader of the Opposition, was 'absolutely true. He did not
rant or exaggerate. I thought he might have been more firm, but every
word told.'[23]

She expressed no regrets at the news of Eden's eventual resignation in
January 1957 and it is interesting that a year and a half later she wished
that she had refused to give copies of her books to a local Conservative
bazaar. Nonetheless, during the General Election of 1959 she voted
Conservative with some conviction, later declaring herself relieved that
Labour was not in 'to harry everyone'. Although she received several
letters from pacifist organisations during these years, she automatically
threw them into the wastepaper basket. She reacted with an almost
fulsome patriotic delight at the birth of Prince Andrew in February 1960
and sent him *Grey Rabbit Finds a Shoe* as a present. She subsequently
received a letter from a lady-in-waiting, 'saying how much the Queen
likes the GR books which she accepts, and will read to the baby Prince.
A charming letter which gave me joy.'[24] While the monarchy remained
a reassuring symbol of social stability, Alison was increasingly aware of
a new element in British society, the black immigrant. Her reaction
generally seems to have been sympathetic, though a little patronising, as
when she commented after visiting a children's home, 'many of them
Negro children – but jolly little people'.[25]

Compared with her very high earnings of the previous fifteen years,
Alison's income dropped quite significantly during the late 1950s. In
March 1957 she was disappointed to receive only £153 from Collins for
the preceding half-year's royalties, although she seems to have been
unnecessarily disappointed by Faber royalties of £740 three weeks later.
The modest success Heinemann were having with her Brown Mouse
and Red Fox books did little to comfort her, and out of an exaggerated
concern at her reduced earnings overall, she refused to take out a bigger
covenant for Penn church – persuading herself that she had no private
means and could not even afford to buy a television set. Six months
later, however, she had bought an option on some shares in De-
benhams; early in 1958 she applied for £500 worth of LCC stock and was
disappointed to be allotted only £100 worth. Nonetheless, she does seem
to have bought far fewer works of art or antiques during these years.

Her declining income does not seem to have been a reflection of a
decline in popularity. Alison was gratified to learn that Dr Irvin Kerlan, a

generous American bachelor whose passionate interest in children's literature led to the foundation of the famous Kerlan Collection at the University of Minnesota, was interested in her writings. Dr Kerlan began to buy manuscripts and first editions of Alison's work from the summer of 1959. She was honoured by his interest and glad to receive the money, noting in her diary that no one in the United Kingdom would pay her the equivalent attention. A substantial number of manuscripts had made their way to the University of Minnesota by the time of Dr Kerlan's death in a car accident in December 1963.[26]

Alison remained much in demand to give lectures, present prizes and open fêtes. Although she felt that some school prizegivings were so dull that she needed a rest the next day, she was flattered to be invited to open the Thame Library in June 1964. Sometimes she thought it absurd to give a talk on 'rabbits and magic' to audiences she saw composed of businessmen and 'sophisticated women', and was often rather surprised to find how much they had enjoyed it. Newspapers wanted to interview her, always something of a mixed pleasure for Alison who still liked to retain control over any publicity concerning her private life. She was, however, honoured to be asked by *The Times* for an interview for their women's page. The interview was published at the end of 1959 and entitled 'Poetic Scientist'. It contained a very perceptive description of Alison:

> What does she look like, this Country Child so many years farther along her indomitable way? Of medium height, sturdily built: her almost white hair is cut short, parted in the middle, and kept in place by a simple bandeau such as a child might wear. Indeed, despite the evident sign of the years, were it not for the eyebrows and eyes one might be tempted to guess that the child had changed but little; the features have retained a child's candour coupled with a child's instinctive secretiveness – an ability to withdraw at will into a delicious storehouse of sensations and impressions which can only be savoured by the tastebuds of the soul, as it were, like bulls-eyes or aniseed balls on the tongue.
>
> But the eyebrows are thick and black, and the eyes dark and bright and knowledgeable – youthful and direct, but not a child's eyes. They do not belie the serenity of the rest of the face, but rather give it depth and meaning, an intellectual sanction to an intuitive simplicity.[27]

Alison was often critical of articles about her in the press, but she approved wholeheartedly of *The Times* interview. Margaret Tempest wrote her a warm letter on reading it and her friends hastened to pay tribute. Her recently acquired friend Georgie Jenkinson told her that the article did not capture her 'wonderful aliveness and joy of living' and Katherine Wigglesworth thought that justice had not been done to

Alison's 'poetic side'. A year later Alison was gratified at what she described as 'a nice article on me (not all true!)' in the *TV Times*, which was linked with what she saw as a 'well-contrived' adaptation of *A Traveller in Time* on Independent Television. Shortly after, and untypically for her, she told Peter du Sautoy that she would be delighted for him to write a monograph of some ten to fifteen thousand words on her for The Bodley Head: 'I am sure you'll do it very happily, and it will give me great pleasure.'[28] That Alison consented to the project was a supreme mark of her confidence in du Sautoy's discretion. He was later to deal tactfully with some autobiographical notes of hers that covered the year of James's suicide, prompting her to write, 'It is much safer, and very good – you got over the difficulty very smoothly.'[29] In the end, however, du Sautoy's increasing responsibilities at Faber, where he was eventually to become chairman in 1971, as well as his deepening involvement in the work of the Publishers Association, proved a serious obstacle to the writing of the biography and it never saw the light of day.

Alison's phenomenal literary productivity was beginning at last to show signs of slackening off. Sometimes unable to meet her daily target of a thousand words, she described a period of relative inactivity in the summer of 1957 and then how 'I suddenly got my wits, and finished a Tim Rabbit tale, writing swiftly and enjoying it.' Alison also left an account of the writing of *Little Grey Rabbit's Paint Box*:

> A lovely day. I made the most of it. I determined to get on with the GR book about the May Day festivities, & I paced about and wrote & waited and wrote & gardened and wrote. Suddenly [I] got it & rushed along hard till I was dead tired but happy, & I finished it. (Rough of course, & a bit long). . . . I was tired & hungry with writing, & I made a supper, a delicious meal. I grilled, no fried, chicken leg, with bacon, got it just right.[30]

But while the chronicling of Little Grey Rabbit's small but well-ordered world remained, for the most part, a pleasure, the Brown Mouse stories were becoming something of a burden on her: 'Writing a Mouse story, botheration. I am sick and tired of them, and yet I have to go on. GR goes on easily, and so does the Fox, but these bore me.'[31]

The Little Grey Rabbit series provided most of the commercially viable spin-offs from Alison's books. She received a modest income from gramophone records during these years and Grey Rabbit 'scenes' were merchandised. Most important of all was the production of a variety of models by Peggy Foye. Alison kept a watchful eye on Miss Foye's work, recording a conversation with her and her assistant in August 1957: 'A great discussion on characters. I told them about S. Pig whom they did not know. I said I did not want a *cat* in GR, nor three old mice in Snug and Serena.' A few months later Peggy Foye was expressing indignation that Alison had criticised some of her Little Grey Rabbit models as being badly coloured. Radio and television adaptations were still a profitable source of income. The Grey Rabbit books held their own as the most popular inspirations for broadcasts, but Sam Pig, and Snug and Serena were also in demand. Among the countries which broadcast her stories were Australia, Norway, South Africa and Malta.

Alison seems to have been less in demand as a reviewer and a writer of articles. It was perhaps her failure to receive many commissions for *The Saturday Book* that led her to believe that 'It has got so vulgar, so mock-Victorian, and quite a bore.' She was asked to review *The Children's Guide to Knowledge* in early 1958. But, although she pronounced some of it excellent, she considered that 'a lot is crude propaganda for the Socialist State. It made me angry.'[32]

Three Grey Rabbit books were published during this period. *Hare and Guy Fawkes* appeared in 1956, *Little Grey Rabbit's Paint Box* in August 1958, and *Grey Rabbit Finds a Shoe* during 1960. Alison expressed most satisfaction with *Little Grey Rabbit's Paint Box*, agreeing with the Collins editor, Robin Denniston, in March 1956 that it was as good as anything she had written. She was perhaps unnecessarily irritated, however, by a review which remarked that while at Manchester University 'little did I think I should get fame by writing about rabbits, three million or so. Such cheek! Cheek!'[33]

Margaret Tempest's intimate involvement with the success of the Grey Rabbit books continued to arouse widely differing reactions on Alison's part – mostly negative ones, even though she admitted in August 1958 how much she liked Margaret Tempest's 'clear pure colours' and was pleased six months later when her illustrator proposed that the Grey Rabbit characters should become the subject for some Sanderson's wallpaper. She was irritated to receive a letter from a boy pointing out that weasels had no black tips to their tails and remarked that she left that sort of thing to Margaret Tempest; she was even more irritated that, as she saw it, her illustrator was still claiming it was she who had truly invented the famous characters; she begrudged sharing half of an Australian Broadcasting Company fee with her and described her vehemently, in October 1957, as 'such a grabber'. Alison was perhaps guilty of some self-delusion when she wrote on receiving the illustrations for *Little Grey Rabbit's Paint Box*, 'not a word of praise or thanks for the book, she says nothing, – I always try to praise her pictures, to cheer her, but she does not need to be cheered'.[34] She then added 'Too much alike', a clear reference to herself and Margaret Tempest.

Two Little Red Fox books were published. The first of these, *Little Red*

Fox and Cinderella, seems to have aroused very little critical interest, but the second, *Little Red Fox and the Magic Moon*, had a far more enthusiastic reception. The *Observer* wrote 'Miss Uttley has discovered for herself a magic recipe – homely detail and unearthly fantasy, pathos and humour, with a dash of folk tale. There is no archness here, only the lightness that comes from an expert touch . . . charmingly illustrated by Katherine Wigglesworth.'[35] *The Times Literary Supplement* thought that 'although it lacks the special charm of her miniature books it has its own individual appeal. The larger format makes for easier reading, and allows more scope for Katherine Wigglesworth's delicately coloured illustrations . . . compounded of a curious blend of fact and fantasy which this author writes so well.'[36] Two more Little Brown Mouse books were also published during 1957, *Snug and the Silver Spoon* and *Mr Stoat Walks In*. The *Daily Worker* welcomed these 'two very attractive little books by Alison Uttley, with lovely pictures by Katherine Wigglesworth'.[37] *Snug and Serena Count Twelve* was published in October 1959, provoking what Alison thought to be a cynical review by the *Manchester Guardian*, as well as this comment in the *New Statesman*, 'Alison Uttley's little animals derive directly from Beatrix Potter.' The Red Fox and Brown Mouse books achieved sufficient success for the American publisher Bobbs Merrill of Indianapolis to bring out three volumes in 1962.

A Tim Rabbit book was published in March 1959, *Tim Rabbit and Company* in which the *Daily Telegraph* noted, 'Alison Uttley exercises her own special, story-weaving charm.' In December 1959 Alison was writing another Sam Pig story, completing it in the middle of February 1960 and sending it off to Peter du Sautoy feeling that 'I have tremendously enjoyed doing this book, the tales have flowed with no effort.'[38] *Sam Pig Goes to the Seaside* was published in November 1960 and the *Scotsman* described it as 'a joyous young book, full of fun as well as of magic touched with poetry'.[39] It is interesting that Alison should have regretted Faber did not publish this book earlier in the autumn. For their part, Faber felt that she tended to hand in her typescripts too late in the year to achieve earlier publication.

Another collection of tales, *Magic in My Pocket*, was published in December 1957 with a preface by Eleanor Graham. Alison had originally found the preface 'offensive' in proof form, because her friend referred to *The Country Child* as having been written a long time ago. She protested at this reference, but, on receiving advance copies in August 1957, was angry to see that Eleanor had not altered the preface as she had wished. Not only did the book sell very well, however, but it was also a great critical success. Published by Penguin Books in association with Faber, *The Times Literary Supplement* called it 'A welcome reprint of some of Alison Uttley's best-loved stories in pocketable form.' The reviewer went on to wonder how the latest generation of seven-year-olds would enjoy these 'gracefully written fantasies of animal life', noting that children's stories nowadays tended to be tougher and to rely less on sentiment. The *TLS* concluded that 'these tales wear well. Whatever one's views on animals who behave like humans, and even mix with them on equal terms, Tim Rabbit, Sam Pig and the rest are entirely engaging creations, and their adventures are recounted with imagination, humour, and what can only be called affection.'[40] Alison was pleased with the excellent reviews in the *Manchester Guardian* and the *Evening Standard*, and was delighted when the *Observer* chose it as one of the best children's books of the year.

Some of Alison's fairy stories were included in an anthology edited by Kathleen Lines in 1958, *A Ring of Tales*. The *Times Literary Supplement* commented that the collection 'included some efficient present-day tale-tellers in Alison Uttley. . . .' Kathleen Lines was to remain a great admirer of Alison's fairy stories and summed up her respect in the foreword to *Fairy Tales*, an anthology she published with Puffin Books in 1979:

> Although many of the stories have their roots in folk tales, and a few seem 'translations' of well-known stories, all of them show the unmistakable characteristics of Alison Uttley's treatment and style. They also give proof of an amazingly long span of imaginative writing.
>
> Mrs Uttley said of her fairy tales: 'So each and every tale holds everyday magic, and each is connected with awareness of everyday life, when reality is made visible, and one sees what goes on with the eyes.'[41]

Four books of country reminiscence and lore completed Alison's publications during these years. *Here's A New Day* was published in October 1956, a book of twelve essays that moved the *Daily Telegraph* to declare 'whether she describes a country auction or the petals of a flower, Mrs Uttley is precise, graceful, and fluent. Her book distils her delight.' *Time and Tide* thought that 'An hour or two with one of Mrs Uttley's books is as refreshing as the smell of a wood after rain, as homely as muffins by a Sussex fire.'

A Year in the Country was published a little over a year later. It was written in under a month, with Alison working hard into the small hours, and she was thrilled when Peter du Sautoy told her he liked the book in principle. Du Sautoy visited her at Thackers on 17 February 1957 to discuss potential revisions to the text. It seems to have been a very enjoyable meeting. Alison cooked a huge boiling fowl for the occasion and the discussion ranged over books like Faber's newly published *Justine*, which du Sautoy thought, to Alison's amusement, she would not like. A week later she had finished her revisions and was promptly offered a contract. The proofs were returned in one day, and a party thrown on the day of publication. But, despite these good auguries, the book had sold only a modest fifteen hundred copies by the end of 1957 and received a mixed reception at the hands of the critics. Alison was particularly hurt by a sneering review written, she imagined, by an 'angry young woman' in *The Times Literary Supplement*, but other critics were more friendly. The *Scotsman* thought that 'Her book is best enjoyed in small doses, and provides a pleasant companion for the country-lover,'[42] the *Birmingham Post* claimed 'One can always rely on Alison Uttley to write with grace and sensibility.'

The Swans Fly Over had been offered to Faber many years before when it had been rejected by Richard de la Mare. Alison now calculated that her current fame would materially improve its chances and, after some re-working, Peter du Sautoy accepted it for publication in 1959. It did encounter one final hitch, though, in Charles Tunnicliffe's refusal to accept what he called a 'pre-war offer' from Faber for the illustrations. Alison, declaring that Tunnicliffe's work was worth any amount, put pressure on Faber who eventually paid the illustrator an improved fee. The book evoked a warm reception. *Books and Bookmen* thought that 'Alison Uttley is a delightfully subtle writer' and *Country Life* wrote, 'she is still the child crossing the dark landing with a lighted candle, to enter a room full of "shadows grim and menacing", but she is also a woman; and the combination makes her an artist. May her books live forever on the bedside table!'[43] *The Sunday Times* complimented her on her 'elegant style' and *The Times Literary Supplement* observed 'These essays are of small matters, but not unimportant, since Mrs Uttley restores to them the newness they have to the child's eyes.'[44] The volume was eventually taken by what Alison considered to be 'a miserably paid' book club.

Something for Nothing was published in November 1960. The manuscript had prompted Peter du Sautoy to say that it was as good as anything that Alison had ever written. He also found the essay on Professor Alexander very moving.[45] *The Times Literary Supplement* sounded a cautionary note, by arguing that 'if the essay is to regain the appeal it had in the days of Robert Lynd and Chesterton, readers will want something more robust than these pieces by Mrs Uttley. This is not to say that she does not express herself with insight and charm, but fine writing by itself is, alas, insufficient.'[46] Ronald Blythe, writing in the *Countryman*, was far more complimentary: 'Each year this delicate and gifted writer offers her thoughts about living in the country in delightful books which contain all the felicity of a correct observation.'[47]

The last book that Alison published during this period was *John at the*

Old Farm. Here was another old manuscript dug out and refashioned for publication. First she sent it to the BBC, who refused it. In April 1959 it was in Faber's hands, where it received a damning reader's report:

> I am afraid I find this very tedious. Mrs Uttley doesn't seem to have *used* her memories, she doesn't build anything out of them, but just recounts. There is an indirectness about it: one observes the boy John, and observes him observing, but never *is* John. There is no continuous narrative, and very little action. . . . It all seems very remote, not so much because of its period, as because of the nostalgia, the 'aged man', the 'ancient' byre. It is charted for adults, not really a story for children.[48]

Alison reacted defiantly to this rejection: 'I am sorry, but I don't care. I still feel in this nether world, not caring about things, material things.'[49] She promptly offered the manuscript to Heinemann, who decided to go ahead with publication. Although it had sold 2200 copies prior to publication, the book was not particularly well-received by the critics, confirming the accuracy of Faber's misgivings. The most favourable comment upon it seems to have been made by *John O'London's Weekly*, which observed that 'Mrs Uttley knows everything there is to know about the countryside from a young person's point of view.'[50] With her reputation so firmly established, however, Alison could afford a few stumbles.

CHAPTER TWENTY

Joyous, Despite The Mounting Years, 1961–65

No-one writes quite so well in the field of rural
belles-lettres as Alison Uttley. . . . On the face of it
her art is slight – and deeply feminine – but there
is nothing else quite like it.

RONALD BLYTHE, *Countryman*, 1963

Towards the end of 1962 Alison listed her likes and dislikes. Among her likes were music, beauty, silence, birdsong, some modern art and seventeenth-century Dutch paintings. She professed a dislike for noise, crowds, loud talk and bluster, and modern sculpture, though she excluded Epstein from this category.[1] This bald and incomplete list does insufficient justice to the range of her interests, and her still enquiring and vivacious mind was best summed up at this time by Peter du Sautoy: 'in short, she is endowed with that divine spirit of curiosity that has been the mark of an intelligent mind from the days of the ancient Greeks'.

The intensity of her reactions tell their own story. On New Year's Day 1961 she looked at her Christmas decorations and felt 'A queer content, like a silence in earthquake country. One almost feels guilty of happiness.'[2] She felt 'joyous' on her seventy-eighth birthday, though she confessed that she did not like 'the mounting numbers' and, despite advancing age, remained astonishingly responsive to the infectious atmosphere of a sporting event. She herself wondered why she felt so moved by cricket and rugby matches, and nearly wept with excitement during the Grand National of 1962. Reminders of her childhood were particularly powerful. In the summer of 1962 she received a box of wild lilies from Cromford which 'touched my heart, they are like a little child, which once I was, shy, timid, intensely alive. They seem to speak.'[3] After receiving the lilies, she went and sat in the garden as dusk fell, feeling 'drunken' with the beauty that surrounded her.

When she felt threatened and persecuted by the outside world, her negative and fearful reactions could be equally intense. In January 1965, conscious that one of her heroes, Winston Churchill, was dying, she wrote of a great storm that howled round the house: 'the rain makes a very peculiar noise, – hissing and beating with a million fingers, sinister, as if it is trying to get in [and] destroy, kill, with hatred of humankind. It is not English rain, it belongs to a foreign country, I feel. I lie in bed, holding tight to [the] bedclothes thinking I am being swept away forever, lost in the universe. I know again all the fears of childhood, and they are many. I do *not* know how I endured some things.'[4]

Her other trials ranged from the petty to the significant. She sometimes felt frustrated by housewifely problems, such as her vacuum cleaner's insistence on shooting out the dirt rather than sucking it up. Two door-to-door salesmen alarmed her by wishing her bad luck when she refused to purchase any of their wares, though she quickly responded by saying, 'bad luck yourselves'. She tended to be more forgetful and clumsy than hitherto. Once she got her petticoat so badly stuck in the zip fastener that she had to cut it away and then sew on a patch. She lost half the proofs of her book *Wild Honey* in August 1962, and a month later was distraught at the disappearance of two valuable diamond rings which she assumed had been stolen. She went to the expense of buying a replacement ring, only to have the two missing objects returned to her by her gardener who found them a year after they had vanished. In the autumn of 1963 she crashed her car, willingly admitting her responsibility. Once, walking in Beaconsfield, she felt the town to be full of ugly women eating huge yellow lollipops and asked herself why she continued to live there.

She sometimes felt sorry for herself: 'Sundays are too long when I am alone, and when I don't go to church or go out. I can see how old people feel, – lost and forgotten on Sundays! I am always glad to welcome Mondays . . . and warm washdays! Homely things.'[5] Normally, her current Scottie provided comfort. Dirk, however, went through a phase of escaping from the garden, even smashing the fences in his desire to explore the outside world. After one such episode, Alison was deeply offended when a neighbour told her that 'a lady of advanced years like you should not keep a young dog'. One way of filling her periods of loneliness was to acquire a tele-vision set. But, incurably careful with her money, she refused to buy one herself, eventually accepting her son's old set as a present in the spring of 1961.

Ironically, in view of this gift, it was John who needed financial help from her early in 1961, when he wanted to buy an apartment house in Guernsey as an investment. Alison lent him two thousand pounds towards the purchase price, even though her accountant later chided her for offering such a low rate of interest. When she subsequently received John's repayments of interest, Alison felt ambivalent. Once she almost decided on sending the interest back, but then comforted

herself with the thought that, if she did so, Helen would think she was
far richer than was the case.

John's psychological problems did not vanish during these years,
though the move to Guernsey seems in general to have been a great
success. He was still receiving injections of drugs early in 1961 and the
continuing friction between his mother and his wife must have taken a
certain toll. Alison's annual holidays in Guernsey, much though she
seems to have enjoyed them, frequently provoked a clash – usually over
what Alison saw as Helen's meanness. On one visit, she found it
difficult to get an extra blanket for her bed out of her daughter-in-law
and was upset by the latter's observation that she must have very thin
blood. On another, she deliberately dirtied the bathmat in order to get a
clean replacement. She was once resentful that Helen, treating her like a
potentially difficult child, did not give her a big breakfast on the
grounds that she would then not eat her lunch. One extraordinary
confrontation took place when Alison begged a little box from Mrs
Paine, Helen's mother, in order to send some roses through the post.
According to Alison, Helen subsequently accused her of meanness in
taking the box: 'I was amazed at her bitterness. I've never been called
mean before. I explained [Mrs Paine] had agreed but she turned away
furiously.'[6] There was more conflict when Helen, with her strong
Methodist background, dared to criticise the Anglican clergy, and
again when Alison objected to a television programme which seemed to
her to be to soft on delinquents. Alison was also particularly outraged to
be sent what she considered to be a big, ugly bonnet by John and Helen
for her 1964 Christmas present.

Despite these skirmishes, Alison was generally able to admit how
happy her son and his wife seemed to be and, as well as recording her
criticisms of Helen, she wrote several favourable comments in her
diaries. But sometimes she still failed to thank her daughter-in-law
adequately when she wrote 'thank-you' letters to Guernsey. In the
summer of 1964 John took her to task over this and she wrote in return a
model letter, which included such placatory phrases as 'Thank you
Helen, for your nice meals, – lobster and crab and many delicious
strawberries and peaches.' She signed herself 'love Mimbles'.[7]

One way in which Alison was particularly helpful towards John
during these years was in encouraging him to persevere with his plan to
write a history of the Channel Islands. She discussed the project with
Peter du Sautoy early in 1963, and contributed herself by retyping parts
of the manuscript and declaring herself 'fascinated' by it. Not that
Alison was without criticisms of her son's text, submitted in an almost
indecipherable italic typeface, finding it 'most difficult, so cramped with
that type, so economical with his paper, I felt despairing, but I

persevered. . . . Sentences too long and too involved. I got lost in the maze.'[8] One of Alison's motives for encouraging John, despite some of the feelings of rivalry that his potential authorship provoked, was to help him build up his self-confidence. After revisions suggested by Faber, his book was eventually published in September 1966 as part of a series on different units in the Commonwealth.

Perhaps John's comparative happiness helped Alison to enjoy better health herself during the early 1960s. Although she was sometimes plagued by bronchitis and her weak knee, as well as the odd bout of flu, she seems to have been as physically robust as a woman of far fewer years. Her dreams were, however, sometimes particularly disturbing. She occasionally felt reassured by the warmth of her father's presence during nightmares, and once when she dreamed that rats and ghosts were scrambling over her body, she called repeatedly for her mother.

It was at this time that her dead friend GL appeared to her in a dream, and Alison asked what the afterlife was like. GL replied, 'Not so bad', prompting Alison to speculate that maybe she had ended up in Hell. One of her most valued local friends, Leonard Kann, died during these years and Alison mourned him as a 'gay pagan'. The death of Dr Kerlan late in 1963 also distressed her, though she went on sending manuscripts to the collection that he had founded. She continued to see something of Mary Treadgold and went on several drives to places of interest with Miss MacFarlane. She exchanged many letters with Tatiana Tess and was glad to receive copies of *Soviet Woman* from her. Her warmth of feeling for Tatiana is indicated by her response to her friend's news that she was visiting the United States of America to work for a women's peace organisation; Alison, by no means a nuclear disarmer, wrote in her diary 'Bless her heart.'

Alison also felt great affection for Angela Reed, who had interviewed her on behalf of the *Daily Telegraph*. Angela was able to tell Alison quite intimate details of her personal life and the relationship that developed between them had some of the characteristics of that between an aunt and a favourite niece. Alison welcomed Angela's marriage to David Caccia and was delighted when they visited her with their 'exquisite wee baby' in December 1963. An affectionate relationship between her and the Caccias was to endure for the rest of her life. Her romantic imagination was fired by the knowledge that David Caccia's ancestors had been supporters of Garibaldi, and had been driven out of Italy as a result.

Increasingly during these years, Alison turned to Peter du Sautoy for professional advice as well as friendship and support, consulting him over contracts offered by other publishers and remaining very attached to his family. Her friendship with Katherine Wigglesworth, however, was going through one of its more problematic phases. Old resentments resurfaced, with Alison considering Katherine guilty both of neglect and of barefaced fabrication. So convinced was she that her friend often exaggerated her family's success that Alison actually wrote a page-long denunciation in her diary, headed 'The Private Life of "Walter Mitty" (alias Mrs X)'.[9] Unfortunately, it was Katherine's daughter Jane who was caught in the crossfire when Alison gave only grudging support to her attempt to find a place at the BBC. Jane also lost out on what should have been a handsome wedding present when, having bought her some dishes, Alison subsequently unpacked them, sending her the book *Cranford* instead: 'Jane doesn't deserve the dishes. I never see her or hear from her. . . . Mrs Wig never writes. So I unpacked the dishes which will be lovely for Xmas presents.'[10]

Alison's brother Harry died in April 1964. Despite her ambivalent, sometimes angry, feelings towards him, Alison reacted with concern and generosity to the news that he was stricken with terminal cancer. She contributed substantially to the cost of his nursing home and was genuinely grief-stricken when he died on 5 April. Although oddly, she did not attend his funeral, she 'thought of this all day, never to see the sun or the brightness, and yet I think he will see a greater brightness with God'. Her cousin Sissy also died at this time, bequeathing her five hundred pounds.

Alison's imagination was caught in the spring of 1961 by the Russian achievement of putting the first man into space. She wrote, 'Major Gagarin. 25,000 mph flight. Thrilling, and very brave to endure the agonies he must have felt. The speed, the loss of gravity, – or was he still under gravity?'[11] This startling achievement by the Soviet Union led Alison to complain that in contrast the British did not seem to care enough about science. She seems generally to have been more sympathetic towards Russia during these years, perhaps because of her friendship with Tatiana. She felt that Khrushchev was acting in an amenable fashion during the Cuban missile crisis of 1962 and was sorry to hear of his overthrow in the autumn of 1964. At one point she wondered whether Russian people were kinder than the English and felt that Soviet cosmonauts were 'Brave people. I think they will be the world leaders in the future.'[12] Man's first contact with the moon, however, aroused more doubt: 'The moon has been hit with a rocket, – poor Moon. That is the start of the Moon Invasion. Yet it is thrilling.'[13]

Closer to home, she was deeply affected by Winston Churchill's death and was moved to tears by the news of President Kennedy's assassination. The Profumo affair of 1963 caused her to sympathise with Harold Macmillan as he faced the attacks of his political enemies. She supported Rhodesia's unilateral declaration of independence in the autumn of 1965, arguing that the British were 'too black-prejudiced'. She also disapproved of mixed race marriages, on the grounds that 'they are against our innermost nature'. She reacted to the Labour victory in the general election of October 1964 with considerable forebearance: 'I think it is better than the Conservatives getting only a tiny majority. Now the Conservatives will I hope help, and not heckle too much as Labour tries to clear up the mess.'[14] A few days later she expressed her strong approval of the way Harold Wilson was tackling the nation's affairs, declaring that she felt far more faith in him than in the outgoing Prime Minister, Sir Alec Douglas-Home.

Her fame continued to be both a source of gratification and of irritation. She sometimes reacted wearily to requests for interviews. When the magazine *Tatler* contacted her, she felt honoured but not particularly pleased. Strangely, perhaps, she developed a close relationship with a *Daily Worker* journalist, Robert Leeson, who was himself later to become a best-selling children's author. Towards the end of 1965 she was particularly hurt by what she considered to be a 'sneering' article about her in *The Sunday Times*. She had been interviewed by Alix Coleman and was perhaps irritated that the resulting article had compared her to another brilliantly successful children's writer, Dr Seuss. Although the article was overall a very complimentary one, she was particularly upset by the assertion that she found adult fans wearisome: 'They will write to me and send me pictures of their grown-up families. I don't give a *button*, and they're terribly dull.' She could not have been overjoyed either by this observation: 'For a good many years now she has been our most profligate provider of crocheting bunnies and clock-winding badgers since Beatrix Potter (her books sell at around 10,000 a month). The comparison is inevitable but Mrs Uttley doesn't relish it much.'[15]

Although Alison must have been secretly gratified by the accidental slip of Alix Coleman's pen that awarded her a 'first-class honours degree', she found the article 'most insolent and vindictive. . . . I won't mention what she says because I must forget, and not have [my] life spoiled by this woman.'[16] She was so enraged that she cancelled her order for *The Sunday Times* and started once more to take the *Observer*, finding it 'much nicer'. She was pleased with the article on her published in the *Observer's* colour magazine early in December 1965.

She was gratified to learn that Prince Andrew's favourite books were those in the Grey Rabbit series, but reacted sceptically to a card from a child admirer, 'saying that "Millions of children adore you" – I wonder!!' She positively resented some enquiries into her writing and refused to help a student from a teacher training college, who asked whether her stories had grown in part out of her childhood experiences.

She resented a bank clerk observing to her that writing was women's work and replied that it certainly was not, adding 'I often wish I were a man. One can speak to strangers more easily, and get information about what one writes about. And travel more in difficult places.'[17] She was even more annoyed when a reader criticised her for using the phrase 'black niggers' in her book *John at the Old Farm*, even though she later agreed with Faber's suggestion to delete the offending words.

She was still much in demand as a lecturer and speaker. She also found particular enjoyment in attending as a guest of honour public events like Children's Book Week, and the Women of the Year lunches held at the Savoy. Not that such events were always totally satisfactory. At the Women of the Year lunch of October 1963, Alison was announced as 'Mrs A. Buttley' and, despite finding herself 'refreshed mentally with these people', considered that 'the speeches were awful, – especially one by Mary Quant, who looked Beatnik, and stammered and spoke bad English. . . . Such a jumble, the worst speech I have ever heard in all my life.'[18]

Although Alison once declared that the luxury of *Vogue* magazine made her sick, reminding her how materialistic the world was, her own private fortunes continued to flourish. Nonetheless she remained apt to complain that she found it difficult to meet the burden of her taxes, the repairs to her house and other expenses, and every year's income tax demand seemed to cause her a surprising degree of discomfort. In the spring of 1963 she scandalised herself by spending ten guineas on a pair of shoes from an Oxford Street store, the most she had ever spent on footwear. On one occasion she even asked her son to lend her a hundred pounds, pleading that she had very little money that was not tied up in investments. It is symptomatic of her mean streak that, although she received £435 from Faber in royalties a few days after this request, she made no immediate attempt to repay the loan. It was left to John to approach her directly with the plea that he could not pay his television bill unless she repaid him. She also altered her will towards the end of 1961, withdrawing her bequest of diamond rings to Margaret Rutherford and Joan Dobell, arguing that it was better that these items should eventually go to John. She did, however, make donations ranging from five shillings to a pound to a large number of charities, thirty-six in all during 1961, for example.

Her payments from her three main publishers were boosted by the sale of a number of subsidiary rights. The Delysé record company concluded a deal with Heinemann during 1963 and various other agreements followed. In August 1964 Heinemann informed her that twenty thousand records had been sold by Delysé, and a year later Alison learned that four thousand records of *Sam Pig in Trouble* had been bought, of which she received five per cent of the purchase price of six shillings. The BBC and the Australian and New Zealand broadcasting services also used some of her stories. She wrote several articles, including one for *Soviet Woman* and other pieces for *Ideal Home*, the *Teacher* and *Homes and Gardens*. In 1964 she reprocessed the story 'The Farm Kitchen', which had earlier been rejected by the publishers Nelson, for *Homes and Gardens*, receiving a fee of twenty-five pounds. The *Teacher* magazine also asked her to review five books in October 1964, which she did, though consciously softening her criticism of the two she disliked most.

The slight slackening in the rate of Alison's productivity first evident in the late 1950s was chiefly the result of her advanced age and the extra effort which writing now demanded; but her inspiration also began to falter during the early 1960s. When she did find inspiration, it was in sometimes eccentric, even fey fashion. For instance, when she was on holiday in Guernsey in July 1961, she recounted:

> Wind in the night. I suddenly heard marvellous music, harps and strings, glissando, chromatic, with the smallest intervals, & voices singing 'Alleluia'. It went on for quite ten minutes, ravishing. I was wide awake. I got up once . . . it must have been an Aeolian harp effect, but the words of the singing were human (or divine), as if all the spirits of the air were chanting the words . . . a magical experience that made me very happy.[19]

Significantly, a comparatively large number of projects aborted or were judged unsatisfactory during this period. Alison completed the manuscript of *Grey Rabbit and the Dumplings* early in 1962, but the book was never published. A year later she heard from Heinemann that they were ending the Red Fox series on the grounds that it had become too expensive. She immediately began thinking of another series, toying with the idea of writing about a bear or a hedgehog as the central character, but the sole product of this initiative was *The Mouse, the Rabbit, and the Little White Hen*, published in 1966.

Alison now also received a surprising number of rejections. Although it was only at William Collins's request that she undertook to adapt for publication some of the stories sent to her by children, a month later – in November 1964 – Susan Dickinson had to tell her that the typescript was not acceptable. Alison wrote resignedly in her diary, 'I agree. Very tired.'[20] She wrote part of an account of 'The Renaissance', but did not get anywhere with it. Even Faber rejected a short book she sent them on the childhood of Shakespeare in the summer of 1964. Alison accompanied the typescript with a rather defensive note, telling Peter du Sautoy, 'I have done quite a lot of research. Not sure if bacon and eggs for breakfast, but it is again probable. He could have pickled herrings, but not so nice.'[21] At Faber, Phyllis Hunt gave it a poor report: 'I am afraid I found this story rather absurd. In the descriptions of the Stratford countryside there are touches of the innocent charm of Alison Uttley's stories for small children, but the total effect is to make Will Shakespeare sound rather like Tim Rabbit. . . . I suppose it might sell on the strength of Alison Uttley's name. But I think we should be inviting criticism if we published it.'[22]

Although Alison was shielded by Peter du Sautoy from the full hurt of Faber's rejection of her Shakespeare story, she was not so fortunate in her negotiations with Nelson, which were taking place at the same time. Nelson had approached her in June 1964, offering her a seventy-five pound advance for the story of her choice. Draft manuscripts began to pass between Alison and the Nelson editor, Lelia Berg – now a children's writer in her own right. At first Alison was comparatively philosophical: 'MSS returned by Nelson's, as I expected. Too autobiog[raphical], and they want a real story for city children . . . which has no fantasy or fairy or animals! Can I do it? – feel flummoxed because I can't keep out the supernatural which is always present for me and always has been, even in atomic structure days. I feel depressed, but I have been keeping up my head, – housework, and to B for shopping.'[23] Two weeks later she was enraged at the rejection of her story 'The Explorers' and by Leila Berg sending 'pages of written stuff, with alterations, most disconcerting and rude. So I have written to say I won't write any more. . . . I was weary and discouraged, not *free* to write as I wish. P. du S. will agree.'[24] Alison almost certainly overreacted to the criticism from Nelson, but this rejection is another indication that her previously sure touch was faltering.

Far greater success attended previously published works. She was overjoyed by the Peacock, later Puffin, edition of *The Country Child* and at a subsequent paperback of the Sam Pig stories. Puffin bought her book *Little Red Fox and the Wicked Uncle* in December 1964 and six months later she was pleased to receive royalties of sixty-seven pounds from Penguin for the paperback of *Magic in My Pocket*.

American publishers showed a greater interest in her than at any time hitherto. Bobbs Merrill of Indianapolis paid a three hundred dollar advance for both *Little Red Fox and the Wicked Uncle* and *Snug and Serena Count Twelve*. Alison approved of the American editions of these books, although thinking that the colour in the latter was rather strident. More significant was the sale of *A Traveller in Time* to Viking Press during 1964. Some confusion surrounded the negotiations, chiefly because it appeared that the book had already been published in the United States by Putnam in 1940, and in Canada by Ryerson during the same year.

Negotiations to sell the book to an American publisher had begun late in 1962. It was first offered to Harcourt Brace, for whom Margaret McElderry felt:

> it was a very difficult book to decide upon, for there is great quality there . . . and a haunting mood and feeling of place recreated. However, I could not get over the feeling that in the last part it bogged down greatly, and grew very slow, picking up again . . . at the end. . . . I may live to regret my decision and to see it going great guns on someone else's list.[25]

Two months later Van Nostrand made an offer for the book, then backed down, puzzled by the confusion over its earlier publication in the United States. It took a year for Putnam to unravel the mystery. Although they could not find a contract, they did 'know that the book was actually set up in this country, for we have a record of producing plates in October of 1940. The book was declared out of print in June 1945, but the plates had been melted already in June of 1942 . . . we have no interest in the book, and you are perfectly free to sell it.'[26] It is clear that Alison's books did not have an enormous appeal in the United States of America, a factor neatly summed up by Peter du Sautoy: 'She is just the sort of author who is obviously very difficult to place with an American publisher, but is yet likely to appeal to a small circle of lovers of the English countryside and country life, perhaps very often immigrants from England. A rather small core of enthusiasts will definitely want her books, both in Canada and the United States, if they can be found.'[27] No such problems had attended the publication of *A Traveller in Time* in the United Kingdom, and at the time of the negotiations with the various American publishers, the book had already sold twenty thousand copies in hardback.

During these years Heinemann was toying with ideas of how best to exploit the Grey Rabbit series. Dwye Evans suggested to Alison that they reissue the first four books again, with new pictures. At about the same time Faber were thinking of obtaining permission from Collins and Heinemann to use various of her stories in a new collection, but without the original illustrations. Both publishers recognised that the proposals might cause difficulties with Margaret Tempest, although Dwye Evans was confident they could be surmounted.

Margaret Tempest, although suspecting in early 1962 that her eyesight was beginning to fade, produced illustrations for *Hare Goes Shopping* two years later that delighted Alison: 'Very successful pictures – MT is good at creating animals and people.' But there was still friction. Both women blamed the other when they felt that the illustrations for *Grey Rabbit's May Day* were not as satisfactory as they should have been. As a result, Collins put off publishing the book for a year. There was yet more squabbling, entirely predictable and very tedious, in December 1964 when Alison once more felt that her illustrator was claiming most of the credit for creating the Grey Rabbit characters.

Alison's relationship with Charles Tunnicliffe remained as harmonious as that with Margaret Tempest was stormy. Alison felt flattered, even amazed, 'at his imaginative way of entering my stories as if he really enjoyed them'.[28] Early in 1964 she was upset at false rumours that Tunnicliffe was dead. One of the other illustrators who gave her great pleasure, A.E. Kennedy, did die in January 1963. A few weeks earlier he had writtten to Alison thanking her for her Christmas card, and hoping that she would be soon writing 'another collection of the delightful Sam Pig stories' and that he might have the pleasure of illustrating them.[29] On hearing of his death, Alison wrote, 'I am very sorry, I always liked him so much.'[30]

Eleven of Alison's books were published during these years. When Heinemann brought out the three Little Grey Rabbit plays at the end of 1961, *Teacher's World* thought 'young children will love to act these three little plays with this delightful little creature as the central character'.[31] *Little Grey Rabbit and the Circus* and *Snug and Serena Go to Town* were also published in 1961.

Little Red Fox and the Unicorn appeared during 1962, together with two books that greatly enhanced Alison's reputation. The first of these consisted of twelve tales of magic entitled *The Little Knife Who Did All the Work*, published on 26 October. Alison had had a struggle early in 1961 to get these tales 'untangled', although she had been fascinated by the process of writing them. She posted off the typescript in the spring of 1961 to an initial Faber reaction that was quite critical. Phyllis Hunt thought that the stories took a long time to get under way and that they contained rather too much poetical writing and old-fashioned sentiment: 'If these stories were not by Alison Uttley I do not think we should publish them.'[32] Six weeks later Peter du Sautoy accepted the typescript, requesting only that the last story should be omitted; he also decided to keep the title despite Alison's fears that it was too long. The book sold over three thousand copies during its first six months and was generally highly praised. The *Guardian* welcomed the stories 'by the queen of enchantment. Mrs Uttley's book is really in a class of its own, and should be marked "For Changelings Only".'[33] The *Times Literary Supplement* thought that each tale was 'written with the heightened sensitivity, the sure touch and attention to the smallest detail which makes fantasy believable'.[34]

Wild Honey was published on the same day and its twelve essays earned a variety of complimentary responses. In the *Guardian*, Robert Nye found them 'fresh, neat and wholesome as a basketful of blackberries: Mrs Uttley's essays are always a delight.'[35] In the *Countryman* Ronald Blythe, who had become – like Robert Nye – a devotee of Alison's writing, wrote thoughtfully:

> No-one writes quite so well in the field of rural *belles-lettres* as Alison Uttley. Her new essays . . . show her sensible imagination at its best. She is never afraid of being intellectual when it is necessary, and she never bullies us into sharing her tastes. She thinks freely in a moral climate untouched by the stale air of the ready-made rule. On the face of it her art is slight – and deeply feminine – but there is nothing else quite like it.[36]

Only one book appeared during 1963, *Grey Rabbit's May Day*. *Tim Rabbit's Dozen* was written during January 1963 and published a year later. One reviewer found these stories by 'the rightly famous Alison Uttley . . . sometimes stranger than fantasy, but lyrical and lovely, too'.[37] The typescript of *Cuckoo in June* had been completed in October 1963, and the book was published during 1964. *Country Life* thought 'It has a promissory touch of solid joys to come. Alison Uttley's approach to the countryside is like that of the Northamptonshire poet John Clare, detailed and almost matter-of-fact; she, too, impregnates that detail with a quiet thankfulness, a sort of worship.'[38] The *Tablet*, although remarking that Alison, unlike the cuckoo, had not changed her tune in June, went on to say:

> Her style is pellucid as the water of her beloved fern-fringed stone troughs, and springs from as rich a depth. That such writing is worthily illustrated is no ordinary achievement. . . . What Sullivan was to Gilbert and Phiz to Boz, C.F. Tunnicliffe is to Alison Uttley, and, for lovers of the old rural life and crafts, their perfect partnership is as much a part of the English tradition.[39]

The *Countryman* thought that the book lay somewhere between essays and poetry in 'an area of pure and sensible language'.[40]

Two old favourites completed Alison's list of publications during these years. *Hare Goes Shopping* in 1965 and the very popular *Sam Pig Storybook* during the same year. Although Sam Pig never achieved the enormous sales of the Grey Rabbit books, his original and wry good humour seems to have pleased the critics more. The *Queen* thought that 'few authors can make animals so endearing or capture so well the scents and sounds and busy rustlings of the countryside'.[41] *Punch* welcomed the 'chance to renew the acquaintance of enchanting, lazy Sam in the idyllic, pastoral world in a just-motorised England'.[42] *Children's Book News* wrote, 'The humour and affection in the stories, the graceful and precise image of the countryside, have endeared them to more than one generation of children.'[43] Perhaps, though, Alison was best pleased by the *Daily Worker's* judgement that the book was 'by one of the most popular children's authors'.[44]

CHAPTER TWENTY ONE

Full of Honours, 1966–70

Each year may be the last so I must enjoy it and work hard.

ALISON UTTLEY, 1970

On the first day of 1967 Alison wrote, 'I want to see some small beauty and record it each day.' Her diaries bear witness as to how faithfully she fulfilled that ambition. They are full of astute, sensitive and beautifully written observations of what she saw. The song of a robin at night was 'so piercingly sweet' that it touched her heart. She took to tempting butterflies into her house by putting out some sugar for them. She found the beauty that she beheld in nature, or in music, books and art often unbearably moving. A radio broadcast of *The Country Child* recaptured her childhood so vividly that she 'felt unhappy. Yet it was marvellous. I feel like a ghost – a queer feeling.'[1]

She became increasingly aware that she could die at any moment and in October 1970 reserved a space for her grave in Penn churchyard for the sum of a hundred pounds. Yet on her eighty-fourth birthday she was no closer to recognising her advanced age than on her seventy-fifth: 'I don't feel old, only tired when I do a lot – and I enjoy doing nothing, just sitting, and looking about me.'[2] She was touched when Tatiana Tess wrote to her, 'You love works of art as if they are human beings.' Tatiana might have been nearer the truth if she had remarked that Alison tended to love works of art rather more than the average human being. Later Alison mused upon the subject herself:

> I realise that I still like men and women alike, for their aura or what I feel. Never sexually, always as I like a sunset, or clouds, or Brahms's 2nd Symphony or . . . the moon, or art. I fall in love with a painting, Van Gogh, or Cezanne or Breughel, and it is the same as my love for the artist. His work is himself. It is the atomic structure I love in men and women, and poets' words get [to] my heart. But women do not understand. They are catching and holding for the sake of sex. I love the invisible, the secret soul of man.[3]

While she was increasingly prone to believe in flying saucers, fairies, magic and 'a great creature in Loch Ness', in other ways her mind became more closed. Early in 1967 she announced that she did not like any novels and would only read books of travel, philosophy and essays.

She was once shocked to find photographs of nude women in *The Sunday Times* colour magazine and promptly 'burnt it up. . . . Sick of all this stuff. Why, O why?' She enjoyed becoming reacquainted with books she had read earlier, declaring that her admiration for J.B. Priestley's *Good Companions* was higher than ever.

She seems to have been less depressed than at some other periods of her life, although, untypically, she declared herself distressed at the prospect of going to London in October 1966. It was perhaps a premonition of death, or at least an anxiety over the confinements of serious illness, which made her reject the idea of double glazing because she did not want to feel shut up in her bedroom. In December 1967 she did become quite badly ill with an attack of bronchitis that nearly developed into pneumonia. She was taken into the Nuffield Nursing Home at Slough, which she paid for out of her private health insurance. Although she was well enough to come home after only ten days, she later confessed that the nurse's request for the names of her next of kin – she gave the names of John and Peter du Sautoy – had really frightened her. Two years later she suffered another serious attack of bronchitis. Once her sensitive skin erupted after using face cream: 'I saw a frightful face in the mirror, scarlet, covered in blood, with huge puffs by the eyes, and a corrugated forehead, as if something had been drained from me.'[4]

John continued to send her valentine cards and to visit her regularly. Early in 1966 Alison was feeling sufficiently optimistic about her relationship with him to make an outright gift of the two thousand pounds she had earlier lent him, thus ending his obligation to pay her further interest. She once considered giving him a private income of one hundred pounds, but then convinced herself that she could not afford it. By the spring of 1967 she had given up all hope of ever having grandchildren, throwing out a pile of baby clothes she had kept against such a day.

John and Helen spent the Christmas of 1968 with her at Thackers – a happy time, according to Alison. Less happy were her annual holidays in Guernsey, although she found much contentment in 'a place of complete tranquillity and timelessness . . . you walk a short distance across short turf with no real paths, to the rocks where you can lie back and breathe the air while the sea is very near. I don't bathe, I'm not a good swimmer, but I rest by the sea, and above it, when I am there.'[5] But her visits to Guernsey were still marked by conflict, mostly between herself and Helen. Although Alison once described Helen's mother, Mrs Paine, as obstinate and a narrow Cromwellian, the two old ladies sometimes formed an alliance. In the summer of 1970 Alison felt that Helen had scolded her mother too harshly, reducing her to tears. She tried to comfort Mrs Paine by singing:

> O dry those Tears
> O calm those Fears
> Life was not made for sorrow.
> Twill come, alas!
> But soon will pass.
> Life will be happy tomorrow.[6]

Apparently Mrs Paine 'joined in, and our squeaky old voices sang, a pathetic, comical duet. But it did us good.'

One perennial cause of friction was what John and Helen saw as Alison's ungrateful behaviour. Several times after her holidays, John found it necessary to write letters pointing this out: 'Of all our many guests, you do the least to help us.' After one such reprimand, Alison replied with a poem entitled 'Lament for a mother-in-law':

> She never did the dusting.
> She never swept the floor.
> She never washed the linen,
> She thought it was a bore.
> She sat out in the garden.
> She read a fairy book.
> She ate the wholesome fishcakes
> Which she had not helped to cook.

The fifth and final verse of the poem contained a rather poignant reminder of Alison's advanced years:

> She wrote a little letter
> And sent it to her son.
> 'I'll soon be off to Paradise
> To sweep in Kingdom Come.'[7]

In June 1970 Alison prepared for her annual trip to Guernsey apprehensively, confessing that she would rather stay at home with her roses, books, television set and her writing tasks. On the last day of her stay she recorded her version of a most unpleasant confrontation with Helen: 'She said "So you've come back. Look at the way you've left your room! Flower petals all over. Sheet stained. What are these stains?' She dragged [the] sheets to my face, I could see nothing . . . she was furious, demented, [almost] out of her mind with anger. I was bewildered.'[8]

Whatever the truth of this encounter, and John was later to tell Alison that he had seen the stained sheet as well, it symbolised the extreme fragility and potential explosiveness of the relationship between mother-in-law and daughter-in-law. The two women were certainly to become no closer to each other during Alison's last years.

Alison had little to do with her other relations at this time. One exception was an unexpected letter she received from Gertrude just before Christmas 1968, saying, 'I have such admiration for all you have succeeded in doing; giving pleasure to thousands. You are wonderful.' A year and a half later Gertrude made another overture, suggesting that she should come and see her. Alison's deep-seated resentment prevented this and she declared that she did not want to get involved in Gertrude's life. One unexpected bonus came with a visit from Hilda, her brother Harry's widow. So well did the two women get on that after Hilda had told Alison that Harry died leaving only seventy pounds in the bank, she wrote, 'I wish I had known she was so nice, I would have helped her more even than I have done, poor girl.'[9]

Apart from her local friends, Alison particularly enjoyed contact with the exotic Tatiana Tess. She visited her in her hotel in London in July 1966 and was struck by her lovely eyes and hair. Two years later Alison was delighted when Tatiana observed that British birds sang in the rain but that Russian birds did not. Angela Caccia visited her several times, sometimes confiding intimate details of her marriage to her. David Caccia was a less frequent visitor. Once when he telephoned Alison to tell her he was arriving the next day and she asked him what he was like now so that the taxi driver would know him, she muddled up the description by repeating, to their mutual amusement, 'blue hair, and fair eyes, and corduroy suit'. Margaret Rutherford saw a little more of her than in the preceding few years, although in November 1969 Alison was shocked to find her friend so old and bent. Peter du Sautoy continued to be her greatest prop and friend in the world of publishing and she wrote in her diary, having read in *The Times* that he had been elected President of the Publishers Association, 'he deserves every nice thing'.

During the summer of 1969 Alison was delighted to have renewed old ties with the University of Manchester. The initiative for this came from Dr Frederick Ratcliffe, the university librarian, who visited her chiefly to discover whether she would like her old alma mater to become a repository for her manuscripts and letters. Dr Ratcliffe, a man of undeniable charm, made a profound impression when he visited Alison at Thackers in the summer of 1969: 'Dr Ratcliffe came at 10.00 am, – and I liked him at once, great fun, and a happy man. He enjoyed every minute and so did I, for [it] felt like meeting a long lost brother, so in tune with my likes and loves and desires, so happy in the sun, and thrilled with the house.'[10]

Dr Ratcliffe bought seven of Alison's books for a total of sixty pounds. When he left, after spending eleven hours with her, Alison wrote rather regretfully: 'A darling man, whom I wish I had met long ago. Shades of Professor Alexander.' After another 'dreamlike visit' by Dr Ratcliffe, Alison agreed, having consulted Peter du Sautoy, that she should bequeath her library and various manuscripts and typescripts to Manchester University.

It is perhaps no coincidence that six months later Manchester decided to award Alison the honorary degree of Doctor of Letters. Alison, who had known for some time that the proposal would be put to the University Senate, wrote, 'I am thrilled it has gone through and I am rewarded for a lifetime of work.'[11] The honorary degree was to be awarded in May 1970 and Alison prepared for what she saw as the crowning glory of her career with considerable pleasure and a little anxiety. She invited three people to accompany her, her son, Peter du Sautoy and Joyce Kann. She justified the inclusion of Mrs Kann by describing her as 'a companion-private secretary. A very nice woman, and my great friend.'[12] After a little further thought, Alison invited Angela Caccia to accompany her as well, even though it meant her flying back from Italy. Although Faber were prepared to pay for Alison's and John's journey to and from Manchester and for their accommodation in the Midland Hotel, the cost of including Joyce Kann and Angela Caccia in the party was set down against Alison's royalty account.[13] A month before the degree ceremony Mrs Barbara Lees, Warden of Ashburne Hall, came to visit Alison at Thackers. Alison immediately liked her 'very much. Warm hearted and friendly and capable. A good person for a Warden.'[14] The two women reminisced about Ashburne Hall and its past wardens and members.

Alison was to remember her two-day visit to Manchester as a 'marvellous time, the best of my life'. She revelled in the excellence of her hotel bedroom, in the luxury of chauffeur-driven cars in Manchester and above all in the companionship of the small group of people whom, in various degrees, she loved. The account she has left in her diary is touching and endearing, and paints a picture of an old yet vivacious lady delighted by the private attention and public honours that were being bestowed upon her. There was much laughter, as on the first evening, 12 May, when her party went to a French restaurant and had 'a crazy dinner, all laughing'. On the second day their hired car was driven with some incompetence by a man who 'kept asking where he was, as he got stuck in traffic, and [the] downpour of rain. We laughed till we cried! We all felt so giddy as if at a wedding as we drove packed 6 in [the] car with driver [and] 2 hat-boxes on our knees.'[15]

Yet despite the jollity there was also considerable tension. The strain of the journey and the almost continuous excitement took their toll of Alison, who complained several times of being very tired, and was too

exhausted even to visit Dr Ratcliffe's library. In the hotel on the night
before the degree ceremony she became hysterical and needed Joyce
Kann to calm her down.

The ceremony itself was compensation for all this. Alison enjoyed
dressing in her ceremonial robes, 'a lovely robe of scarlet with pale gold
linings and gold in the collar. . . . Big black Tudor hat that suited
me.'[16] During the procession for the presentation Alison felt 'I could
have wept, I felt so moved by the beauty'. She was particularly gratified
by the speech made by Professor W.I.C. Morris when he presented her
to the chancellor of the university:

> I present to you Mrs Alison Uttley, already a graduate of this Univer-
> sity, the holder of an honours degree in Physics. No doubt, if she had
> pursued her studies in the entirely physical sciences, she might have
> shaken the earth or cleft the skies. The distinction which we now
> desire to honour has been obtained in other fields, in pastures not new
> but ancient, in sheltered gardens, in vacant wine-red moors and in
> bosky country lanes.
>
> All her life Mrs Uttley has been a teller of tales, at first of entirely
> spontaneous stories which sprang fully fledged from her rich inner life
> as a vivid dreamer . . . [of] not only Little Grey Rabbit, but Sammy
> [sic] Pig, Brock the Badger, and a host of other vividly drawn and
> entirely credible characters.
>
> While Mrs Uttley is most famous for her wonderful children's
> books, in the field of *belles lettres* her essays are admired by adult
> critics. *The Country Child*, first published in 1931, has never been out
> of print, and her other works intended for her more mature public
> share with *The Country Child* an evocative and nostalgic charm which
> has made her one of the significant English writers of the present
> century.[17]

Even if Alison's achievements had not been confirmed by the award of
an honorary degree, she could have been in no doubt as to her fame –
so many were the marks of esteem she received during these years. She
was much in demand as a lecturer and was the subject of a good deal of
journalistic interest. Alison did not always find such attention
gratifying, particularly as she remained fiercely defensive over certain
details of her past life. She expressed her alarm at seeing Peter du
Sautoy's putative biography of her listed by Blackwell early in 1966,
and considered it 'a cheek' when she was asked questions about her
earnings or whether her son had children. Perhaps because she felt that
she was approaching death, she reacted oversensitively to reminders of
how old she was. Once, after giving a lecture at Beaconsfield, she
answered a question as to her age when her first book was published
'untruthfully', saying she was thirty years old when in fact she was
forty-four. She was shocked at a 'horrid interview with the Daily Mail,

who called me a "white-haired" widow who wrote children's stories and by a coincidence lived like Enid Blyton in Beaconsfield'.[18] When the *Evening Standard* published photographs of her in the spring of 1970, she felt they showed her as 'all wrinkles and shut eyes and loose drooping mouth, as I held two snowdrops. The worst I have ever had, a caricature. It might be spite!!'[19]

Alison was far more gratified by an article in the *Guernsey Star* in the summer of 1970, which described her as '"tall, graceful and white-haired". It is one of the nicest interviews I have had, as good as that of Angela years ago.'[20] She was also pleased by an interview published in the *Sunday Telegraph* in the spring of 1969. Most flattering of all was a BBC television programme made for the series 'Line-Up' and broadcast in May 1970. Its opening shot showed Alison, waddling slightly, walking with Dirk on a lead and turning into Thackers. She looked very fit and far younger than her years. She wore a light dress with a belt and a twin string of pearls. Her white hair, which reached to the nape of her neck, blew in the wind. When she was interviewed she spoke at first with a rather refined accent, which got broader and more 'Derbyshire' as she talked about her childhood at Castle Top Farm. The programme presented a woman with a strong, handsome face and shrewd but kindly eyes, talking in a very definite and precise manner. She read well and clearly from her books, not needing to wear glasses. One shot showed her typing at her desk by the window in her long living-room, using the index finger of her right hand and two fingers of her left hand.

She explained on the programme that when she wrote she always told children 'about what I like very much, hoping they will like the same things'.[21] She also wished that adults would realise children were more interested in animals than people when it came to stories. Alison described the special feeling she had when writing *A Traveller in Time* and went on to explain that in *The Country Child* there was 'a lot of sadness if you read it thoroughly, little tinkles of sadness in the background'. She regretted that the pattern of the English fields was changing more in the second half of the twentieth century than she could ever have imagined, and regretted also the passing of the small field with its trees, which was often a meeting place. She also expressed her pessimism, asking who cared for flowers any more? Human beings were not getting better in a moral way and, she believed, were discovering things that were 'almost evil'. Alison then spoke about her optimism. She felt that people were more conscious of beauty than at any time since the Elizabethan age. This beauty was spread out for all to see and, because it had 'nothing to do with money', was equally available to the poorer members of society. She claimed that she was trying to preach this message in her books, to promote the idea of beauty as a medium for healing.

For all her idealism, Alison remained as hard-headed as ever when it came to business matters. Although she was needlessly worried during 1967 that she would have to appear before an income tax tribunal, her income from writing continued to be a source of great gratification and security. She received several half-yearly cheques from Faber for more than nine hundred pounds and in May 1969 received £1119. 5s. 3d. After royalty payments, this total was achieved with the help of £40 for a Japanese translation of Tim Rabbit stories, over £75 from Viking Press in America for their publication of *A Traveller in Time*, and nearly £100 from Penguin for their edition of *Magic in my Pocket*.[22]

Her half-yearly payments from Collins averaged out at over £300. She received somewhat smaller payments from Heinemann and trifling sums from Hale. She transferred £1000 pounds from various sources into National Savings in April 1968 and again in July 1969. Even if she had not had such a handsome income and substantial savings, she possessed a large number of valuable capital assets. Her paintings were chief among these and in the summer of 1969 she was offered £2500 for her painting by Ambrose Breughel, an offer she refused.

In enjoying such affluence, it is perhaps inevitable that she should have remained a steadfast supporter of the Conservative party. She accepted the Labour party's landslide victory in the general election of spring 1966, on the grounds that the government had made a good beginning and should be allowed to build on it. She continued, however, to vote Conservative and even likened Enoch Powell to Winston Churchill for his capacity to warn the nation of the dangers that lay in store for it. She grumbled that her newspapers seemed to be full of troubles and was particularly alarmed by the disturbances in Paris during the spring of 1968, wondering whether they would produce a French revolution in her time. Although she was excited by the moon landings of 1968, not all scientific developments pleased her and she was horrified to learn of the siting of a nuclear power station on the island of Anglesey, thinking of Charles Tunnicliffe 'and his birds and his world of peace'. She communicated these feelings to Tunnicliffe who replied, 'Poor old Anglesey! It is no longer the fresh unsophisticated island it used to be. Jet planes scream across the sky . . . atomic power stations shatter the skyline and great pylons are striding over the land!'

Alison commiserated with Tunnicliffe again on the death of his wife, writing him a letter of support and explaining her own faith to him. For his part, Tunnicliffe assured her that he would continue to illustrate her books as long as she wrote them. In Peter du Sautoy's opinion, however, he was performing this task largely as a personal favour, as her inspiration began to fade toward the end of her life.[23] Alison herself was conscious that she could no longer write as productively and as efficiently as before. Although she bought herself a new typewriter in October 1966, she was not pleased with what she produced on it. It is a measure of her desperation, perhaps, that in May 1967 she sent off two stories to Kaye and Ward – bypassing her established publishers and their concern for her reputation – in full knowledge of the fact that one, 'The Explorers', was 'a rotten tale'. A year later she was rather fitfully writing a ghost story and various fairy tales. In November 1969 she was working on a 'Commonplace Book'. Although she considered it 'so good', Faber did not share her view and rejected the rather scrappy offering. A little before this Alison had sent Peter du Sautoy a typescript which seems to have been embarrassingly similar to some earlier stories, having 'a faint connection with Heinemann, I could alter the names of the two Snug and Serena tales, that is all that is needed to cut them off from their origins'.[24]

More fruitful were Alison's efforts for Collins. Early in 1969 she wrote *Hare and the Rainbow* in under three weeks. Later that year she produced the typescript of *Fuzzypeg's Brother*. Considering her other failures, she must have been delighted that William Collins told her editor, Roger Benedictus, that it was her best ever. Benedictus, however, aroused Alison's wrath by 'not liking the green door and brass handle'. Alison's response to this criticism was extraordinary and an indication of her increasing tendency to confuse fact with fiction: 'I *know* a gorse bush with a door and a brass knocker . . . but I saw this place in childhood – a patch in our Top Pasture, where I once crept.'[25]

Many of Alison's previous books continued to earn well during these years, some finding their way into paperback or foreign editions. She was gratified when Faber reprinted her novel *High Meadows*, although she found it 'difficult' writing a new foreword to the book. But Faber turned down her suggestion that they reprint *Cuckoo in June* and *A Year in the Country*. She expressed her deep disappointment when Hale refused to reprint her book *Buckinghamshire*, which she considered one of her best and the product of a great deal of research.[26] She was further disappointed when an American publisher, Four Winds Press, declined *The Country Child* in December 1967, which had been published in New York in 1931.

Alison produced hardly anything for journals during this period, the exceptions being an essay published in *Homes and Gardens* and a solitary review. In contrast, the by-products of her phenomenal output were being marketed with great success. She received five per cent royalites on three Grey Rabbit jigsaw games during 1966. There was a Grey Rabbit domino game, and Peggy Foye continued to produce models of the Grey Rabbit series, including a carousel which played the theme music from Dr Zhivago. Delysé turned out records based on the Grey Rabbit books in considerable numbers, and in the summer of 1970 Alison wrote the blurb for the jacket of an LP for them. Sam Pig also appeared in record form. In anticipation of a Grey Rabbit TV series in May 1969 Collins wanted to rationalise Alison's various merchandising agreements and asked her to cancel her existing contracts with David Davis for music, Kenneth Collins for toys, Peggy Foye for models and Ann Hogarth for puppets. A fresh arrangement was offered. Alison felt 'most indignant. I rang up R[oger] B[enedictus], he just recited excuses, calling them Merchandize for the future.'[27] In the end, after Alison had consulted Peter du Sautoy, no new contractual arrangements were agreed.

Broadcasts and television adaptations of her books continued. BBC television's 'Jackanory' was a regular customer, presenting a Sam Pig story read by Dandy Nichols in October 1967, some Grey Rabbit tales and several stories, including 'The Red Hen' in the spring of 1969. BBC radio bought rights in perpetuity to her popular story 'Hedgehog and Mole Go Ballooning' and there were also five readings from *A Traveller in Time*. By far the most exciting prospect for Alison, however, was the proposal by a film company, Leopard Productions, to produce a series of Grey Rabbit programmes for television. Alison was immediately attracted by the large financial gain she stood to make – an advance of a thousand pounds was mentioned in August 1968, to be followed by a possible total income of sixty thousand pounds. The idea ran into immediate difficulties when Margaret Tempest raised objections on financial and artistic grounds. When she criticised some trial versions of the Grey Rabbit cartoon characters sent to her by the producer, she provoked this weary and depressed response from Alison: 'Letter from MT. My heart sank as I saw the postmark Ipswich. Of course she doesn't like the rabbit, a Walt Disney one, says she. Head too large. Colour all wrong.'[28] Eventually a trial film, *Grey Rabbit and the Weasels*, was ready for viewing by November 1969. Alison pronounced it 'delightful, such fun, so gay. I felt quite happy!!' The series, however, was never made.

The conflict with Margaret Tempest over the proposed television series was part, and perhaps a symptom, of a far larger upheaval that was taking place. From 1966 onwards it is clear that Alison was trying to replace Margaret with another illustrator. In May of that year Heinemann proposed to reissue the first four Grey Rabbit books in a special Cowslip series with pictures by Jennie Corbett. It appears that Jennie Corbett had been brought in chiefly because Margaret Tempest had told the publishers she was too ill to undertake any more work at that point. The proposal was for Corbett to illustrate all the books in the series – each one of which was by Alison. In the end Margaret's position as the illustrator of the first four Grey Rabbit books, reissued by Heinemann in the original format, was confirmed – but not before a bitter exchange of letters had taken place. Alison represented herself as the virtuous one in this correspondence, denying that she had broken her word to Margaret Tempest, often vowing not to open her letters and sometimes tossing them aside when she had read them.

As it happened, Margaret Tempest was only to illustrate one more of the Grey Rabbit books, *Little Grey Rabbit's Pancake Day*, published in 1967. Alison had objected to the first versions of the illustrations in November 1966, and Collins had promised that they would be 'freshened up', but in such a fashion that Margaret Tempest would never know. Although Alison felt that most of the illustrations were in the end perfectly satisfactory, when advance copies of the book arrived in September 1967, she wrote, 'Is this the last I shall do? I don't think MT can paint any more, her colours very poor and faint. I would go on with the series.'[29] The series did indeed continue, but with another illustrator. From the end of 1968 Alison was pressing the services of Katherine Wigglesworth upon Collins. She made the proposal formally to Roger Benedictus in November and by 17 January 1969 the drafts of Katherine's illustrations for *Little Grey Rabbit Goes to the North Pole* arrived at Thackers. Alison thought 'they are good, and very much like MT's. Children will not notice. MT will be infuriated. I'm fed up with the whole thing.'[30]

Early in 1969 Collins went through the process of comparing Margaret Tempest's work for the next Grey Rabbit book with that of Katherine Wigglesworth, which they liked 'very much'. Alison was alarmed that somehow her friend Katherine would be by-passed by Margaret Tempest even at this stage. In March she was angry when Roger Benedictus rejected some of Katherine's illustrations, saying he did not like the way the human beings were drawn. She expressed her anxieties in a letter to Peter du Sautoy: 'I feel under a spell just now, caught in a web with the Grey Rabbit books. . . . I have been worried about the illustrations for the GR books, and MT is difficult, she won't give up, but she can no longer do them.'[31]

On 17 April Alison was relieved to learn that Katherine had been commissioned for the new book, but she disliked Collins's proposal to write two separate copyrights into the contracts, one for the author and one for the new illustrator. She felt the proposed arrangement was too complicated and that somehow she would receive less money from royalties. Katherine Wigglesworth also objected, suspecting that all Roger Benedictus wished to do was make an excessive profit for Collins. The two women were eventually allotted a 2½% royalty each. This was a considerable improvement on the previous arrangement whereby Alison and Margaret Tempest had each been paid a modest sum of money per book.

Whatever resentment Margaret Tempest may have harboured over her usurpation by Katherine Wigglesworth, a meeting between the two women at this time apparently went off very well. According to Katherine, William Collins urged her to undertake this diplomatic mission: 'It will not be easy, Alison and Margaret are both determined ladies and they are at loggerheads. They both feel the popularity of the series is due to *their* work, however, if you can please both it will be splendid.'[32]

Alison and Katherine have each left their own version of this famous meeting. Alison claimed that Margaret Tempest approved of the new illustrations, but added 'what would you do if I did not approve?' Katherine Wigglesworth, sensitive to the fact that Margaret Tempest was suffering from Parkinson's Disease, found her 'to be a very gentle elderly lady. She was certainly strong minded, but so very reasonable. We got on very well. I had to copy her style. Send or take all my rough drawings to her. Then send them to Alison, and then do the colour and finish them! . . . Grey Rabbit had been her hobby and delight for years – it was very sad she had to give up doing the pictures.'[33] Katherine Wigglesworth was to illustrate the last five Little Grey Rabbit books.

Alison's first publication during these years was *The Mouse, The Rabbit, and the Little White Hen*. As we have seen, this story represented a new departure for her and was planned as the first of the new Cowslip series – a remarkable indication of the urge to write which still possessed her in her early eighties. The *Observer* described it as a 'stylish new miniature story, in a new format, for five to three year olds'. The reviewer thought that 'the delicious pictures (by Jennie Corbett) could hardly be bettered'.[34] The book, like its fellows in the series, was priced at six shillings. Among the others published at the same time was *Enchantment*. One reviewer quoted approvingly from this book: 'Have you ever been caught up in a web of fancy, and kept there while the clock ticks on and time seems to disappear?' He added, 'It's enthralling reading not only for the little ones but for their parents, too.'[35]

Despite its troubled conception the Cowslip series, once launched, was enthusiastically received. It included, as well as *Enchantment, The Mouse, The Rabbit, and the Little White Hen, How Little Grey Rabbit Got Back Her Tail* and *The Great Adventure of Hare*. The *Birmingham Post* welcomed these 'charming books' and the 'return to the world of whimsy, where birds and wood creatures talk and behave like human beings, but they are written with such skill and charm that they cannot fail to please'.[36] Diana Norman delved a little deeper into the secret of their charm: 'Perhaps one of the reasons why, as a child, I liked Alison Uttley is because she had a sort of reality in her books. Her animals are not quite humanised – they retain the characteristics of animals. She conveys the haunting strangeness of the countryside, something of its fear and a great deal of its beauty.'

Two books with their roots deep in the Derbyshire soil of Alison's childhood also appeared in 1966. The first of these was a book of essays 'mixed with some short episodes which have been important at times of [my] Life'. As was the case with so many of her books, she could not make up her mind what it should be called. She tried out a variety of titles on Peter du Sautoy, including 'When that I Was', 'There are More Things', 'A Peck of Gold', and 'Country Heritage'. She disliked the latter title, chiefly because 'I detest the word heritage.' On balance, she preferred 'There are More Things'. As so often happened, Peter du Sautoy made up her mind for her, telling her in January 1966 that he preferred *A Peck of Gold* – which was a quotation from a Robert Frost poem.[37] The book sold out its first edition within a year. The *Higher Education Journal* enjoyed the 'nostalgia tempered with the practical delights of quiet living'.[38] *Homes and Gardens* called it a 'charming little book' and continued, 'her style is as simple and evocative as her subject, and will bear re-reading many times'.[39] More weightily, *The Times Literary Supplement* wrote:

> Somebody suggested to Mrs Uttley that one virtue of television was that 'it saves using the imagination'. If, as she suspects, the imaginative gift is on the wane, she at least remains well endowed. These remembered impressions of a country childhood show a child sometimes merely fanciful but at the same time imaginative and observant. . . . For her, the environment of childhood is an integral part of a writer's books, an opinion which in her own case is fully borne out.[40]

Recipes from An Old Farmhouse was published in the autumn of 1966. The idea, which had apparently been originally suggested to Alison by Peter du Sautoy, very much attracted her and she had set about the project with zest. The text needed the attention of some of Faber's cookery experts, since Alison absentmindedly tended to leave out certain vital ingredients. Although earlier in 1966 Faber feared they had lost two chapters of the typescript, they were later found and in August Alison received a parcel containing the advance copies: 'I was thrilled to open it, and I love it. So charming and so simple, yet so fairy-like in its pictures and memories.'[41] The book is one of the most appealing of Alison's later years, combining nostalgia with practicality, and illustrated by Pauline Baynes with great feeling and poise.

Alison captured the book's special significance for herself in an introduction:

> Cookery in our old farmhouse was an important part of life, and I was a wide-eyed witness of baking and brewing, of boiling and stewing, as I played with a doll or sat on a stool close to the big table, and

watched while I waited to scrape the big yellow bowls with a little tea-spoon to get the fragments left. . . . So cooking was a time of happiness for us, as we dipped and tasted and smelled the good odours, but for my mother and the maid it was hard work.[42]

Reviewers responded enthusiastically. *The Times*, noticing that Alison had based her text on her mother's old cookery book written in delicate and sloping handwriting, said 'There is a charming simplicity about her chosen recipes.'[43] The *Daily Sketch* dwelt appetisingly on 'mouthwatering things like lemon cream tartlets and gingerbread fingers'; it also considered the book to be 'beautifully illustrated'.[44] The *Observer* noted astutely that the book was 'designed to appeal to the nostalgia for hot, June days in the hay fields and high teas in a cool, stone-flagged kitchen', but added 'Whimiscal though some of them are, many of the recipes deserve resuscitating.' The *Yorkshire Post* wrote 'Alison Uttley never fails to produce books which are full of warmth and comfort.'[45] The *Daily Telegraph* reviewer confessed to having 'fallen under the spell of that fairy godmother of the old-time countryside, Alison Uttley'. The book sold very well and was eventually reissued as a paperback by Faber in 1973. On this occasion, the *Guardian's* reviewer wrote: 'In principle I am against anything which hints at sentimentality or nostalgia for the Good Old Days, but I dare anyone to pick up this book and not be enchanted by its cool, sparse writing and by Pauline Baynes' delicate black and white decorations.'[46]

Another Uttley caught the attention of reviewers during 1966, when John's *The Story of the Channel Islands* was published by Faber on 1 September. In the advance copy he sent Alison on 8 August, John had written in his neat but rather cramped hand: 'My Dear Mother, My 6 gratis copies of the Book have just come. So it gives me great pleasure to send one on to you. What a change for the 'traffic' to be this way round. With much love, John.' Alison felt 'a great thrill to see it . . . a great work and a struggle, and I'm so thankful.' The book received its best notice in *The Times*: 'The story moves briskly, and always engagingly, through a thousand years and more. The Channel Islands take on an interest for others besides tourists.'

During 1967 Alison published two books for children. The first of these, *Little Grey Rabbit's Pancake Day*, had the added significance, as we have seen, of being the last in the series to be illustrated by Margaret Tempest. It also coincided with Collins's celebrations of the 150th year of the founding of the firm. In Collins's advertising campaign, emphasis was laid upon the fact that the Queen regularly bought Grey Rabbit books for her children, that each reprint ran to ten thousand copies and that since their first appearance on the Collins list in 1934, more than six million of the little books had been sold. Heinemann published Alison's second title during 1967, *The Little Red Fox and The Big Tree*.

Remarkably for her, Alison only published one book during 1968. She sent the typescript to Faber in November 1967, describing it as a book of essays about ghosts, the supernatural and earthly objects, and adding apologetically 'I have been a long time working at it, and for weeks I did nothing, no ideas. It has rather a mixed lot of subjects, rather disconnected I fear.'[47] Having submitted the typescript, Alison almost immediately fell ill with a serious attack of bronchitis. From her sickbed she wrote a letter, misdating it with the wrong year in her confusion, telling du Sautoy of her relief at his favourable response to the typescript. By the end of 1967, on du Sautoy's suggestion, the original title of 'Magic Casements', which Alison recognised as 'not very original', had been abandoned and the book was published on 15 October 1968 as *The Button Box*. One problem that arose during the production process was that Tunnicliffe was slow in delivering the illustrations and du Sautoy asked Alison if she could discreetly get him to hurry up. As it happened, the news of her serious illness pricked Tunnicliffe's conscience and spurred him on. Publication day provoked the now familiar responses of those reviewers who were particularly attuned to the 'great charm' of her country essays. Ronald Blythe found it an opportunity to develop his intelligent and perceptive appraisal of Alison's art:

> It is hard to convey the peculiar quality of *Alison Uttley*. To say that she is a quiet exact country essayist, the philosopher of small things, is to suggest a familiar type of rural miniaturist. Whereas, as anyone who has had the good fortune to discover her knows, she chooses diminutive pegs and an almost reckless simplicity to display her great visions and certainties. *The Button Box* . . . contains an important confession: the author was trained to be a physicist. Now we know why her minutiae add up to profundity; they are molecular.[48]

The Times Literary Supplement, on the other hand, produced one of the most devastating criticisms of Alison's work to date: 'Her essays grope back always to the things that were – the "romantic" view over windswept mowing grass and the far hill crowned with beech trees. . . . Mrs Uttley's outdoor vision tends to be coloured up by fancy. There is a wood wherein "a host of spirits . . . dance among primroses and blue-bells."'[49]

The reviewer added that, despite Alison's account of her scientific education, 'She can still slip up on a "true" description of a long drive straight into the setting sun, with the slip of a new moon persistently visible on the *right*. Unless the solar system has been re-aligned this is impossible.' The review ended, rather grudgingly: 'But the essays bask in heaven-lit nostalgia, and it is perhaps unjust to come with a little pin and prick their charm.'[50]

Little Grey Rabbit Goes to the North Pole was published in 1970; a disappointing debut in the series for Katherine Wigglesworth, since it seems to have provoked little reaction. *Lavender Shoes, Eight Tales of Enchantment* was also published during this year. Considerable difficulty surrounded the birth of this book. It centred chiefly on Alison's understandable, though by now embarrassing, tendency to rework earlier material and even to present 'new' stories that were heavily dependent upon previously published tales. At Faber, Phyllis Hunt had to undertake considerable detective work, with the aid of Heinemann, to discover whether the first story in *Lavender Shoes* was the same as one that had already appeared under the Heinemann imprint. In the end, the mystery was unravelled by the discovery that the Heinemann book in question was *The Mouse, the Rabbit, and the Little White Hen* – the tale which Alison now offered to Faber being entitled 'The Fox and the Little White Hen'.[51] A month later alarm bells were ringing again at the discovery that the story 'A Christmas Surprise', which appeared in *Lavender Shoes*, had been originally published in an anthology, *The Tall Book of Christmas*. Kaye and Ward granted Faber the right to reprint the story for a payment of five guineas, but not without some wrangling over whether the latter had acted hastily in pushing ahead with publication before clearing the question of a possible infringement of rights.[52] Alison eventually, and rather oddly, expressed her relief that the tale in dispute was to be illustrated afresh by Janina Ede, and not by 'that awful Jennie Corbett'.[53]

The production of Alison's third book to be published during 1970, *A Ten O'Clock Scholar*, was another to provoke anxieties over the illustrations. This time, and very untypically, Alison's criticism were directed at Tunnicliffe. In March 1970 Peter du Sautoy agreed with her that the second Tunnicliffe illustration was 'not all that wonderful'. He added that perhaps the explanation was that 'he was somewhat upset by our comments on the first Walter de la Mare illustration'.[54] Tunnicliffe's discontent obviously stirred up a hornet's nest and Faber were soon evaluating their financial arrangements with him; though eventually they decided to stick to their policy of not issuing him with a contract because it was not necessary: 'We have paid him, and that is really that.'[55]

On its appearance, towards the end of 1970, *A Ten O'Clock Scholar* harvested a small sheaf of complimentary reviews. There is no mistaking the fact, though, that certain journals with an interest in country lives, and particular reviewers who had already paid Alison great attention, dominated the chorus of praise. *Country Life* wrote that for Alison the discovery of 'folk unanimity' . . . is a glowing mystery which illuminates her prose with a singular candour which is likely to remain alight', just as it did in Flora Thompson's *Lark Rise to Candleford*.[56] The *Dalesman* said, 'May there be many more such annual volumes as this',[57] while the *Countryman* felt that in the book 'There is edge but never bitterness; she neither magnifies nor reduces a lifetime's varied experiences. Everything is given its true value, and there is continued movement between what is significant and what is delightful.'[58] One of the few reservations about the book was expressed in the *Church Times*, which thought that 'if her work has a fault, it could be said to err on the side of cosiness'. The reviewer added, 'But it is most captivating for an hour, and what she offers here is the sweetly sad flavour of old photograph albums.'[59] *The Times Literary Supplement* judged the book to be 'Nostalgic, sentimental, sometimes whimsical . . . a miscellany in which the writer's many admirers will enjoy browsing.'[60] It was a neat summary of Alison's continuing appeal.

CHAPTER 22

Last Years, 1971–76

Alison Uttley was a born storyteller.
Daily Telegraph, 8 May 1976

In the autumn of 1971 Alison wrote 'I am a bad writer of a diary, – days go too fast to write.' At the end of the year she stopped keeping a diary altogether, writing on a final page 'Well goodbye old year, lots of happiness and beauty and fun. I hope 1972 will be as good.'[1] Despite her memories of much happiness, she also endured great loneliness and as a result sometimes tried to monopolise the attention of her visitors and friends. Until she approached death, however, the last years of her life were as active as her advanced age allowed. Seven of her books were published, two of them within a year of her death, and she continued to send ideas to her publishers. It is perhaps not surprising that, as she grew frailer and had more difficulty in organising her thoughts, she submitted fewer typescripts and that those she did produce were rejected. In August 1973 Faber turned down a story entitled 'Sam Pig Goes to the Moon' on the grounds that 'the mixture of science and fantasy doesn't really come off . . . the story can't stand on its own. It is too slight.'[2] A couple of months later two short country tales were rejected as being 'both a bit flat . . . they are not exciting in any way. The farming scene goes back to the author's youth and for adults it has a certain nostalgic charm, but I don't think there is much here to hold children's interest.'[3] A year afterwards Peter du Sautoy confessed himself rather puzzled over a typescript that Alison sent him, telling her that he was not at all sure whether it could be made into a book. Alison gave a poignant description of her failure to follow through her creative ideas in an interview shown on BBC television's 'The Book Programme' in December 1975. She explained that she had half-written a Grey Rabbit book but that her mind had 'clouded up'. She refused to reveal what the title was, on the grounds that she would be badgered to finish the book, although she added that she could easily finish it.[4]

As it happened, she had enough typescripts proceeding towards publication to satisfy many authors for a lifetime. Heinemann published *The Brown Mouse Book* in the autumn of 1971. The book was a collection of five tales about Snug and Serena, which had been out of print for some time. One reviewer noticed that 'Katherine Wigglesworth has skilfully filled the pages with lively little animals.'[5] Katherine's illustrations were a vital element in the success of four more books: *Fuzzypeg's Brother*, published in 1971, *Little Grey Rabbit's Spring Cleaning Party*, which appeared a year later, *Little Grey Rabbit and the Snow-Baby*, 1973, and *Hare and the Rainbow*, 1975. If the illustrations in these books generally maintained the high standards set by Margaret Tempest, the power of Alison's imagination and the supreme skill of her writing were also undiminished. A child of the early 1970s, coming fresh to these books, would have found as subtle a mixture of homely, magical and fantastical imagery as in the first few of the series, published forty years before.

Alison produced a final collection of *Fairy Tales*, edited by Kathleen Lines, which was published in 1975. One more book of essays, *Secret Places*, was published in 1972. She had finished the book on 11 February 1971 and celebrated the fact in her diary by writing, quite inappropriately, 'Eureka!' The typescript was sent off to Faber, bearing the provisional title of 'Over Hill, Over Dale', and Peter du Sautoy accepted it towards the end of March. *Secret Places* was the last book of Alison's to be illustrated by Charles Tunnicliffe, who was paid £180 for his work. A problem arose over the need to provide a portrait of Margaret MacDonald. Tunnicliffe, remembering Alison's earlier criticisms of his representation of Walter de la Mare, refused to attempt a likeness. Instead, he produced an illustration of the Margaret MacDonald memorial which shows the Prime Minister's wife surrounded by the statues of eight children, remarking, 'it looks a little like an illustration of a population explosion, but don't mention this to Mrs Uttley'.[6]

The twelve chapters in the book might act as their own memorial to Alison's extraordinary powers of observation and recollection. In her essay on 'The Poetry of Walter de la Mare', she produced a moving analysis of her old friend's qualities, one which might also serve as her own epitaph:

> It is this interest in every facet of life, and the power of communicating the excitement of it, that is the abiding charm and strength of Walter de la Mare. He is *tremendously interested*. He holds a torch and flashes an illumination on even the most prosaic object, endowing it with beauty – or rather, showing us its beauty, pointing out all the delicate intricacies we had never noticed before. We see it for the first time, as Adam might have seen the flowers and beasts in the Garden of Eden. And the flash of light which he sheds on these things is gentle yellow candlelight, or the brilliant spectrum of the rainbow, or the cold light of the moon and the far-away stars.[7]

Alison's backlist of titles sold in respectable quantities, providing a very satisfactory income together with the proceeds from television, radio and merchandising. There were some casualties, though, with the hardback of *The Country Child* going out of print in November 1973. Peter du Sautoy, while pointing out that the book was available in a Puffin edition and also from Nelson in their School edition, explained to Alison apologetically that 'The sale has not been quite big enough in recent years to justify a normal reprint, but perhaps if we wait a while, we could manage it.'[8] In the meantime, Faber were able to produce *The Sam Pig Story Book* which came out in paperback in September 1971, and in the same month Puffin offered a three hundred pound advance for another collection of the Little Red Fox tales. Alison was gratified by this proposal, but not overpleased that her book would appear in the same series as 'Chitty Chitty Bongo (?) [an] ugly book and pictures'.[9] Early in 1972 she greeted the news that her *Recipes from an Old Farmhouse* was going into paperback by calling it a gleam of sunshine in the gloom created by the power cuts which were then occurring. She promptly asked Faber about reprints of two of her favourite books, *Macduff* and *A Year in the Country*, but they could not oblige her. She was delighted when the publisher George Mann decided to reprint *Carts and Candlesticks* and *The Farm on the Hill* for the modest fee of twenty-five pounds each. The firm brought out *Ambush of Young Days* a little later. The success of Kathleen Lines's selection of *Fairy Tales* led to a proposal to produce another volume of Alison's Christmas stories in paperback.

She kept a wary eye on her public image. Her extraordinary, almost neurotic defensiveness over what she saw as difficult or shameful episodes in her life never wavered and she was quick to denounce any enquiries that seemed to her to be probing 'by ignorant strangers'. On rare occasions, however, she dropped her guard. The BBC television profile of her for 'The Book Programme' was welcomed, as was an interview published in the *Daily Mail* early in 1975, entitled 'Alice in Wonderland'. She co-operated with the Kerlan collection in the University of Minnesota, and with a freelance American researcher who wanted to compile a bibliography of her work, finding herself 'amazed to see the number of books'.[10]

She also responded warmly to the admiration of her child readers. She sent on to Peter du Sautoy a quotation from a letter she received from a little girl of eight: 'I think your books about Sam Pig are really wonderful. When I ever get unhappy, I just open a book about Sam Pig, and there I am, changed again.'[11] In the 1975 television programme, 'Alison Uttley and Little Grey Rabbit', she was shown receiving a group of visiting school children, and saying, as she reached out to greet one of the little girls, 'Hello, what's your name? Oh, what a hot little hand!' She took pains to admire the children's pictures of the characters she had created and in response to one child observing how much he liked her garden, replied 'I used to have a little dog who liked it, and we played so much.'[12] She once recorded in her diary how much she had enjoyed watching the du Sautoy grandchildren playing 'Cowboys and Indians in the wood and [on the] lawn – such abandon as they flung themselves down on the grass! I love to see their joy!'[13]

Another vital contact, though at a distance, was with her friend Tatiana Tess. She asked Faber if they could fit a story by Tatiana into one of her own books, and she was touched to receive a translation of *Journey Without Companions*, which contained a section on Tatiana's relationship with Alison. She was even glad to receive a visit from Roger Benedictus, his wife and six-month-old baby in the spring of 1971. The visit perhaps purged the memories of some of their early disagreements, for the Benedictus baby, Philip, 'smiled all over his face when he saw me, and held out his arms to me. All afternoon he was angelic and laughing. The loveliest baby I have ever seen.'[14] In a subsequent 'thank-you' letter, Benedictus's wife, Tanya, gave an indication of how unnerving a first meeting with Alison could be, confessing that she had 'been more than a little nervous of the visit, expecting someone of your fame to be overawing – but while, if you will forgive me, the awesomeness is there, it was wonderful to be received with such warmth and interest'.[15]

The interest was genuine, for Alison's lively curiosity remained undimmed. But she was undeniably more absent-minded than ever before. She tended, perhaps understandably, to mix up the new decimal coinage and, less understandably, made such mistakes as pouring water rather than paraffin into a lamp on her porch. Martin Byers recalls visiting her during the early 1970s when he was puzzled to find various-sized portions of the same iced cake distributed in several tins; as he was about to eat a slice, the grocer arrived with the weekly standing order which included another iced cake identical to the one scattered throughout the kitchen. More worrying was the evidence that his aunt was finding it increasingly difficult to cope with basic tasks like the cooking and keeping the kitchen clean. She discovered the joys of tinned curry during the autumn of 1971, but a reorganisation of her work surfaces might have helped more. According to Martin Byers, 'her kitchen at Thackers was always the most inconvenient and untidy that I had ever seen. Completely unmodernised in those days in its equipment, the table and other surfaces were covered in ornamental jugs and plates, trays, pots and pans, plants, tins of cooking ingredients, etc., so that there was no place to put down anything else.'[16]

As she became more muddled and less physically competent, Alison found she could not venture as far afield as she would have liked. She did, however, pass her driving test in November 1971, taking a wry pleasure in the judgement that she was 'in full possession of her faculties'. But a collison with a gatepost decided her against driving as much as she had been used to, and when she went in the summer of 1971 to visit Miss Wood at Ellesborough to talk about her vision of fairies, she allowed John to do the driving. It was now that she made one of her last trips to London, calling on Sir William Collins and then going to see Faber's new offices in Queen Square. Otherwise, she increasingly relied on local friends to take her on excursions.

At the end of March 1971 she passively accepted John's telling her that 'they cannot have me in Guernsey, too much work. I agree, John gets tired and Helen irritable. They have Mrs Paine on their hands. So be it. John will come here and take me out, he says!'[17] This untypical fatalism was symptomatic of her waning powers. In the spring of 1971 Alison was forced to recognise that she could no longer kneel in church. A little later she tumbled down her stairs, crushing her foot in the process, and early in 1972 tripped over a lead from an electric fire and fell so heavily that she limped badly for some time. She complained on various occasions of severe pains in her bowels and in the spring of 1971 entered St Joseph's Nursing Home in Beaconsfield for a minor operation to help the problem. In October of that year she returned to the nursing home for further treatment, although shortly after her discharge she recorded 'Eating very little and feeling weak as water. Oh life!!'

In October 1974 Peter du Sautoy wrote to Alison's solicitors about her will, but also expressed his anxiety about how best to help her as her health failed and her son remained in Guernsey: 'Mrs Uttley has a daily help and a gardener, I believe, and I think she lets a bedroom to a schoolmaster, so she is not entirely alone at night. But, inevitably, she does spend a good deal of time on her own, and this causes us considerable concern.'[18]

Fortunately, for the last year or so of her life Alison was cared for by Stan and Joy Sheller. The Shellers were described by one of Alison's friends as 'a wonderful couple'[19] and after Alison's death Peter du Sautoy told them, 'I know very well that she could not have survived at all without your support and I think you are absolutely wonderful in the care and affection you gave her. I do understand that it must have been trying at times but your patience seems to have overcome everything. . . at least we didn't have to face the calamity that I always greatly feared, a fire resulting from the dangerous use of electricity.'[20]

In the spring of 1976 Alison suffered a bad fall. She lay all night in the hall in considerable pain. The next morning she was discovered and taken to High Wycombe General Hospital, where a fractured femur was diagnosed. The final act in the tragic and ultimately destructive relationship between Alison and her son was now played out. Neither John nor Helen immediately came to visit Alison, on the grounds that Dr Milner had told them, 'She is not going to die . . . and there will be more demands and orders once she is allowed out of sedation. Leave it to me, and I will tell you when to come.'[21] Helen asked Peter du Sautoy, 'what ARE they saving the poor old girl FOR?'

It is not difficult to understand why Helen in particular reacted so callously to Alison's final illness. Quite apart from the battle she had been forced to fight in order to assert a prime claim to John's love, she felt she had absorbed a tremendous amount of unpleasantness at her mother-in-law's hands. In her view, Alison had snubbed her, condescended towards her and quarrelled with her. Disinclined to play the sacrificial lamb, Helen had been no innocent party in these confrontations, but she may well have felt permanently aggrieved as a result of them. It is also important to appreciate that she held Alison responsible for John's continuing psychological problems. While Alison lay dying, he was still on 'daily doses of the pills' and Helen must have experienced some resentment at the burden which his emotional frailty imposed on her patience and strength. She later expressed herself on the subject in a letter to Peter du Sautoy: 'I don't know if it's possible to understand, standing on the touchline, what her effect on him is? I'm sure I couldn't, in fact. It has taken me years to get as far into it as I now feel I am – he is fundamentally *frightened* of her, also rejected, hence his . . . complete lack of confidence in himself.'[22]

For his part, John's unease in his mother's presence, perhaps arising from his feeling that he had always fundamentally disappointed her, was enough to prevent him from flying to her bedside. He may also have remembered, and resented, Alison's extraordinary demand in November 1971 that he should come over from Guernsey to take her back to Thackers from the St Joseph's Nursing Home after her illness. Now he did eventually come and visit his mother later in April in hospital at High Wycombe, but only saw her a couple of times.

Towards the end of April, a decision was made to move Alison to a nursing home in Berkshire. Peter du Sautoy thought that Alison would never now go back to Thackers, but that 'contrary to what one might have thought a few weeks ago I don't believe she would mind being moved to a home, as she is not likely to understand fully what is happening to her'.[23] Certainly, Alison seems hardly to have been in touch with reality during this period, and once became so distraught that she tried in her desperation and confusion to bite one of the nurses – news which prompted Helen to remark 'did you hear about her BITING the nurse? I nearly fell off my chair with laughing when I was told.'[24]

By 5 May it had become apparent that Alison was dying and the plan of taking her to a nursing home was abandoned. For two weeks previously she had refused to eat or drink, and had been put on a saline drip and heavily sedated. John and Helen left for a holiday in Spain on 5 May. It was yet another illustration of their tangled and uncharitable feelings towards her. During Alison's last days, her part-time secretary, Kathleen Day, wrote indignantly to Peter du Sautoy, 'I do feel very strongly that Mrs Uttley, although not altogether aware of what was happening, did long to see her son, but she has given up now.'[25]

On Wednesday 5 May Stan and Joy Sheller visited Alison, but 'she couldn't speak and her eyes were closed, as we held her hand and talked to her, we both felt her squeeze our hands and at one time a smile came to her face'.[26] Peter du Sautoy was the last of her friends to see her, visiting her on 6 May, 'hoping I might give her the feeling that she was not abandoned, but I wasn't able to make any contact at all'.[27]

A little later on 7 May Alison died. Her obituary in *The Times* was a substantial one and observed that of all her great output of books for children, 'some of the Grey Rabbit books . . . and some of the Sam Pig tales – will surely live for many years, though they may be among the last of the old style of children's stories. They have certainly been much loved.'[28] The *Daily Telegraph* obituary reminded its readers that 'Love of the countryside was always an important strand in her writing and besides her innumerable children's books she wrote evocative books for adults in a delightfully leisurely style. . . . Alison Uttley was a born storyteller.'[29]

Because she had for some months been unable to cope with everyday matters, Alison left her financial affairs in much disarray. She had not paid income tax for two years and owed the Inland Revenue £1040; in 1973 she had sold a valuable picture and failed to declare the proceeds for the purposes of Capital Gains Tax; there was a bill for electricity of over £280, a rates bill of more than £124 and various miscellaneous expenses for newspapers, laundry, wine and spirits and several other items, amounting to a little over £180. Thackers was crammed with belongings of widely varying values and it was later discovered that Alison had hidden some choice pieces of silver in a number of unlikely places, much of it in the tallboy. Most of the contents were sold. Among her most valuable pieces of furniture were a William and Mary escritoire which fetched £600, a George III oak chest which sold at £270, a £520 kneehole chest of drawers, a £420 Breton carved cupboard and an Eastern runner which went at £500. There were some costly paintings, including a harbour scene by M. Schoevaerts which had been valued at £4000 some years before. There were scores of smaller items, including a large amount of pottery, various ornaments and a good deal of silver, brass and pewter. The house was eventually sold for £28,000 and the net value of her estate was £109,316.06. The first instalment of Capital Transfer Tax amounted to almost £24,500, but fortunately Alison had left £22,000 in her bank account.[30]

At least the provisions of her will were clear. John and Peter du Sautoy were her executors and trustees. Apart from a few particular bequests, her estate and all the income from her literary property were to go to John. After his death, the income from her literary property was to be administered by du Sautoy as trustee and bestowed in three equal parts upon Sedbergh school, Ashburne Hall and any offspring of John's. In the event of there being no such offspring, this third was to pass to the National Trust. Although Helen was to inherit the residue of the non-literary estate in the event of John predeceasing her, this did not amount to a fortune. By ensuring that the income from her literary property would never go to her daughter-in-law, Alison exacted her planned posthumous revenge upon her. She did, however, leave her a solitaire diamond ring that had originally belonged to the Uttley family, but somehow the ring was never found.[31]

Alison's books and papers were to go to Manchester University, but there was some delay before a van was sent to collect them. Meanwhile, John was in the process of clearing his mother's house of all its effects. He seemed, according to his wife, to be in a frenzy, 'set on getting rid of anything he could; all pictures of Alison, any letters (all from the time he left home, certainly Cambridge)'.[32] He had just found a drawerful of unfinished typescripts and had begun to cast them upon the bonfire, when 'the chap from Manchester University called at Thackers. He ticked off John for doing such a thing.' Helen prudently pocketed a few mementoes, including 'a pocket-sized likeness of his father, in uniform, which I took unknown to him, to show to the doctor who was treating him then'.[33] Helen also saved from the holocaust Alison's diaries covering the years from 1932 to 1971. These were left to Peter du Sautoy as the basis for a future biography. When John had finally purged Thackers of all that he found offensive or troublesome and locked the door for the last time, according to Helen he 'breathed a sigh of relief, and murmured a thankful "never again" sort of remark – I can't quote exactly what he said, but it meant everything'.[34] Some of Alison's Beaconsfield friends also felt a burden lifted from them now that the demands that she had made on them during her last months had come to an end. One of them later wrote, 'I have never buried anyone . . . with more relief than I helped to bury Alison!'[35]

Alison's funeral took place at Penn church on Friday 21 May. One of the mourners remembers John standing at the graveside, a sombre and silent man in a mackintosh.[36] His wife felt that Alison's death, and the dispersal and destruction of so many mementoes that bound them together, was at first a great relief to him. But the feelings of guilt and despair, from which his relationship with his mother had never been entirely free, soon reasserted themselves. On 19 July 1978 he drove his car over a cliff in Guernsey and killed himself. Helen died in April 1984. As for Alison, she lies in the pretty churchyard in Penn under a simple headstone which bears the inscription 'Alison Uttley, Writer, a Spinner of Tales'. Perhaps in the grave her questing, dominating, brilliant and relentless spirit has found peace.

ENDNOTES

Chapter 1

1 Alison Uttley, diary, 16 December 1961
2 *A Peck of Gold*, p. 26
3 *Ibid.*, p. 28
4 *Ibid.*
5 *Ibid.*, p. 29
6 Diary, 30 June 1957
7 *Wild Honey*, p. 32
8 Diary, 13 March 1943
9 *Country Hoard*, p. 16
10 *Ambush of Young Days*, p. 215
11 *Ibid.*, pp. 215–16
12 BBC TV, 'The Book Programme', 'Alison Uttley and Little Grey Rabbit', 23 December 1975
13 *The Country Child* (Puffin edition), p. 115
14 *Wild Honey*, p. 85
15 Diary, 28 September 1941
16 Diary, 2 October 1964
17 Diary, 21 December 1944
18 Mrs Clay of Castle Top Farm to the author, 28 May 1985
19 Diary, 8 April 1964
20 Diary, 13 February 1937
21 Diary, 1 December 1934
22 Diary, 21 September 1932
23 Diary, 8 November 1944
24 Diary, 10 February 1936
25 Diary, 3 February 1941
26 *Ambush of Young Days*, p. 17
27 *Ibid.*, p. 31
28 *Country Hoard*, p. 38
29 *Ambush of Young Days*, p. 29
30 *Ibid.*, p. 38
31 *Ibid.*, p. 39
32 *Ibid.*, p. 40
33 Interview between the author and Mrs Lilian King, February 1984

Chapter 2

1 Rylands, R.142040.2, Elizabeth to Alison Uttley, 9 January 1968
2 Alison Uttley, interviewed on BBC TV, 'Line-Up', 14 May 1970
3 Diary, 25 February 1948
4 Diary, 5 September 1948
5 Diary, 30 June 1933
6 Diary, 23 April 1936
7 Diary, 9 March 1937
8 Diary, 8 September 1938
9 Diary, 19 April 1938
10 Diary, 13 December 1954
11 Diary, 14 October 1968
12 Diary, 4 April 1961
13 *Ambush of Young Days*, p. 11
14 *Ibid.*, p. 10
15 *Ibid.*, pp. 10–11
16 *The Country Child*, p. 18
17 *Ambush of Young Days*, p. 13
18 *Ibid.*, p. 14
19 *Ibid.*, p. 15
20 *Ibid.*, p. 18
21 Alison Uttley, BBC TV, 'The Book Programme', 23 December 1975
22 *Ibid.*
23 *A Peck of Gold*, p. 44
24 *Ibid.*
25 Alison Uttley, BBC TV, 'Line-Up', 1970
26 *Ambush of Young Days*, p. 31
27 *The Country Child*, p. 80
28 *A Peck of Gold*, p. 47
29 *The Swans Fly Over*, p. 9
30 *Ibid.*, p. 12
31 *Ibid.*
32 *Ibid.*, p. 13
33 *A Peck of Gold*, p. 46
34 *The Country Child*, pp. 77–8
35 *Ambush of Young Days*, p. 32
36 *Ibid.*, p. 53
37 *Ibid.*, p. 56
38 Diary, 11 February 1932
39 *The Country Child*, pp. 206–07
40 *Ibid.*, p. 222
41 Du Sautoy papers, Alison Uttley to Peter du Sautoy, 17 June 1968

42 *Ambush of Young Days*, p. 126
43 *Here's a New Day*, p. 60
44 *The Country Child*, pp. 107–08
45 *Ibid.*
46 *Ibid.*
47 Alison Uttley, BBC TV, 'The Book Programme', 1975
48 *The Country Child*, p. 132
49 *Ibid.*, p. 131
50 Diary, 8 March 1966
51 Diary, 7 April 1963
52 *Ibid.*

Chapter 3
1 *Ambush of Young Days*, p. 190
2 Diary, 23 January 1964
3 Diary, 22 February 1954
4 Rylands, R.142025, Annie Stevenson to Alison Uttley, 10 April 1974
5 *Here's a New Day*, pp. 64–6, p. 69
6 *Ambush*, p. 192
7 *Ibid.*
8 *Ibid.*, p. 194
9 *Ibid.*
10 *Ibid.*, p. 192
11 *Ibid.*, p. 198
12 *Ibid.*, p. 200
13 *Ibid.*, p. 201
14 *A Peck of Gold*, p. 104
15 *Ibid.*, p. 111
16 *Ibid.*, p. 114
17 Diary, 17 April 1960
18 *Ambush of Young Days*, p. 129
19 *Ibid.*, p. 131
20 *Ibid.*
21 *Ibid.*, p. 132
22 *Ibid.*, pp. 132–3
23 *Ibid.*, p. 133
24 *Here's a New Day*, p. 136
25 *Ibid.*, p. 142
26 *A Peck of Gold*, p. 127
27 *Ambush of Young Days*, p. 209
28 *Ibid.*, p. 206
29 Diary, 19 April 1954
30 *Ambush of Young Days*, p. 208
31 *Ibid.*, 214
32 *Ibid.*, p. 222
33 *Cuckoo in June*, p. 88
34 Diary, 28 August 1962
35 Diary, 17 May 1964
36 *The Country Child*, pp. 128–9
37 Katherine Wigglesworth to the author, 3 January 1984

Chapter 4
1 *Ambush of Young Days*, p. 175
2 *Ibid.*, p. 176
3 *Ibid.*
4 *A Ten O'Clock Scholar*, p. 14
5 *Ambush of Young Days*, p. 177
6 *The Country Child*, p. 43
7 *Ibid.*, p. 44
8 *Ambush of Young Days*, pp. 177–8
9 *Ibid.*
10 *A Ten O'Clock Scholar*, p. 16
11 *Ibid.*, p. 14 and *Ambush of Young Days*, p. 181
12 *A Ten O'Clock Scholar*, p. 23
13 BBC TV, 'The Book Programme', 23 December 1975
14 BBC TV, 'Line-Up', 1970
15 *A Ten O'Clock Scholar*, p. 16
16 *Ambush of Young Days*, pp. 180–1
17 *A Ten O'Clock Scholar*, p. 17 and *Ambush of Young Days*, p. 184
18 *A Ten O'Clock Scholar*, p. 17
19 *Ibid.*, p. 25
20 Diary, 14 October 1944 and 16 March 1956
21 Diary, 14 October 1963
22 Diary, 15 August 1963
23 *Wild Honey*, p. 23
24 *Ambush of Young Days*, p. 165
25 Du Sautoy papers, Alison Uttley to Peter du Sautoy, 4 October 1961
26 *Ibid.*

Chapter 5
1 *Plowmen's Clocks*, p. 30
2 *The Country Child*, p. 158
3 *Cuckoo in June*, p. 91
4 *Ibid.*
5 *Ibid.*, pp. 94–5
6 *Ibid.*, p. 96
7 *Ibid.*, p. 98
8 Diary, 9 January 1967
9 *Cuckoo in June*, p. 97
10 Diary, 15 May 1970
11 Diary, 1 June 1970
12 Interview with Joyce Kann, 27 January 1984
13 Elizabeth Saintsbury, *The World of Alison Uttley*, pp. 94–5
14 Diary, 1 May 1965
15 *Wild Honey*, pp. 15–16
16 *Ibid.*, pp. 14–15
17 Rylands, G.29818, 'Short Autobiography for Messrs. Collins'

18 *Wild Honey*, p. 10
19 *Ibid.*, pp. 10–11
20 *Ibid.*, p. 12
21 *Ibid.*
22 *Ibid.*, pp. 13–14
23 *Ibid.*, p. 14
24 *The Swans Fly Over*, p. 39
25 *Wild Honey*, p. 11
26 *Something For Nothing*, p. 123
27 *Ibid.*
28 *Ibid.*, p. 117
29 'The Book Programme', BBC TV, 23 December 1975
30 *The Times*, 'Poetic Scientist', 29 December 1959
31 'Line-Up', BBC TV, 1970
32 *The Button Box*, p. 41

Chapter 6
1 Letter from the Secretary to the Registrar, Manchester University, 27 July 1982
2 Du Sautoy papers, Alison Uttley to Peter du Sautoy, 4 October 1961
3 *Ashburne Hall; the First Fifty Years, 1899–1949* (a pamphlet, 1949)
4 *Ibid.*
5 Letter from Dr Elizabeth French, Warden of Ashburne Hall, to the author, 27 September 1984
6 Mrs Barbara Lees to the author, 11 April 1984
7 Du Sautoy papers, Alison Uttley to Peter du Sautoy, 4 October 1961
8 *Here's A New Day*, p. 59
9 Interview with Dr F. Ratcliffe, Librarian, Cambridge University, 11 July 1984
10 Alison Uttley bequest, 1979
11 Alison Uttley to Mrs Barbara Lees, 14 May 1970 (letter in author's possession)
12 Dr Hilda Oakeley to Alison Uttley, 17 April 1943 (letter in author's possession)
13 Diary, 19 December 1947
14 Diary, 21 July 1938
15 Diary, 12 February 1937
16 *Ibid.*
17 Diary, 8 April 1970
18 Rylands, letter to Alison Uttley, 26 January 1949
19 *Yggdrasill*, Michaelmas term, 1903
20 *Ibid.*, Lent term, 1906

21 *Ibid.*
22 Diary, 1 January 1947
23 Diary, 3 February 1953
24 Rylands, letter to Alison Uttley, 26 January 1949
25 *Secret Places*, p. 12
26 Diary, 26 April 1932
27 Diary, 6 February 1966
28 *Secret Places*, p. 12
29 Du Sautoy papers, Alison Uttley to Peter du Sautoy, 4 October 1961
30 Alison Uttley, 'The Book Programme', 23 December 1975
31 Diary, 5 November 1932
32 Diary, 5 January 1965
33 *Something For Nothing*, p. 85
34 *Ibid.*, p. 86
35 Interview with Dr F. Ratcliffe, Librarian, Cambridge University
36 BBC TV 'Line-Up', 1970
37 Du Sautoy papers, Alison Uttley to Peter du Sautoy, 4 October 1961
38 *Wild Honey*, p. 18
39 *Something For Nothing*, p. 124
40 *The Stuff of Dreams*, pp. 23–4
41 *Ibid.*, p. 48
42 *Ibid.*, pp. 48–9
43 *Ibid.*, p. 50
44 *Ibid.*, p. 52
45 *Ibid.*, p. 51
46 *Ibid.*, pp. 53–4
47 *Ibid.*, p. 54
48 Du Sautoy papers, Alison Uttley to Peter du Sautoy, 4 October 1961

Chapter 7
1 Du Sautoy papers, Alison Uttley to Peter du Sautoy, 11 October 1961
2 *Ibid.*
3 *Ibid* and *The Button Box*, p. 14
4 *The Button Box*, p. 14
5 Du Sautoy papers, Alison Uttley to Peter du Sautoy, 4 October 1961
6 *Here's a New Day*, p. 78
7 Diary, 23 July 1966
8 Diary, 26 March 1967
9 Du Sautoy papers, Alison Uttley to Peter du Sautoy, 4 October 1961

10 Diary, 14 September 1969
11 *Wild Honey*, p. 18
12 Du Sautoy papers, Alison Uttley to Peter du Sautoy, 4 October 1961
13 *Wild Honey*, pp. 18–19
14 Du Sautoy papers, Alison Uttley to Peter du Sautoy, 4 October 1961
15 *Ibid.*
16 *Wild Honey*, p. 122
17 Du Sautoy papers, Alison Uttley to Peter du Sautoy, 4 October 1961
18 Rylands, 142059, interview with Sally Button prior to the publication of *Little Grey Rabbit's Valentine* (1953).
19 Diary, 16 November 1968
20 Diary, 23 January 1967
21 *Ibid.*
22 *The Button Box*, p. 25
23 *Ibid.*, p. 16
24 *Ibid.*
25 *Secret Places*, pp. 14–15
26 *Ibid.*, p. 15
27 *Ibid.*, p. 13
28 *Plowmen's Clocks*, p. 96
29 *Secret Places*, p. 16
30 Diary, 30 November 1964
31 *Secret Places*, pp. 17–18
32 *Ibid.*, p. 19
33 *Ibid.*
34 *Ibid.*, p. 20
35 Du Sautoy papers, Alison Uttley to Peter du Sautoy, 17 June 1968
36 *Secret Places*, p. 21
37 *Ibid.*, p. 23
38 Du Sautoy papers, Alison Uttley to Peter du Sautoy, 17 June 1968
39 *Secret Places*, p. 20
40 *Ibid.*, pp. 22–3
41 *Wild Honey*, p. 43
42 *Secret Places*, p. 21
43 *Ibid.*, p. 23
44 Du Sautoy papers, Alison Uttley to Peter du Sautoy, 17 June 1968
45 *Ibid.*
46 *Ibid.*
47 *Ibid.*, Peter du Sautoy to Malcolm MacDonald, 20 July 1971
48 Diary, 9 November 1934
49 *Secret Places*, p. 24
50 Diary, 18 August 1969
51 *Secret Places*, p. 24

Chapter 8
1 'Some Recollections of Alison Uttley', letter from Martin Byers to the author, 22 September 1984
2 Du Sautoy papers, Alison Uttley to Peter du Sautoy, 4 October 1961
3 Diary, 21 August 1959
4 Diary, 21 January 1939
5 Du Sautoy papers, Alison Uttley to Peter du Sautoy, 4 October 1961
6 Dr Katherine Watson (daughter of Gertrude Armfield, née Uttley) to the author, 30 October 1984
7 Du Sautoy papers, Alison Uttley to Peter du Sautoy, 4 October 1961
8 *Ibid.*
9 Diary, 14 May 1938
10 Diary, 3 September 1936
11 Du Sautoy papers, Alison Uttley to Peter du Sautoy, 4 October 1961
12 Interview with Mr A. Tolson, October 1984
13 Interview with Dr Katherine Watson (daughter of Gertrude Armfield, née Uttley), 30 October 1984
14 Diary, 25 December 1943
15 *Ibid.*
16 Helen Uttley to the author (quoting Martin Byers), 13 March 1984
17 Martin Byers, 'Some Recollections of Alison Uttley', 22 September 1984
18 Diary, 2 May 1956
19 Interview with Dr K. Watson and Diary, 29 July 1970
20 *Ibid.*
21 Diary, 3 February 1959
22 Helen Uttley to the author, 13 March 1984
23 Diary, 1 January 1935
24 Interview with Mr A. Tolson
25 *Ibid.*, and interview with Dr K. Watson. Also Helen Uttley to the author, 13 March 1984
26 Diary, 23 September 1954
27 *Plowmen's Clocks*, pp. 102–3
28 Diary, 26 February 1932
29 *Plowmen's Clocks*, p. 103
30 *Wild Honey*, pp. 128–9
31 Diary, 26 February 1932

32 *Ibid.*
33 *Ibid.*
34 Diary, 11 October 1932
35 Peter du Sautoy interviewed in
    'The Snow-Baby', by Denis Judd,
    BBC Radio 4, 16 December 1984
36 Diary, 4 February 1947
37 Diary, 13 February 1933
38 Diary, 18 January 1964
39 Du Sautoy papers, Alison Uttley to
    Peter du Sautoy, 4 October 1961
40 Interview with Mr A. Tolson
41 Interview with Dr K. Watson
42 Diary, 25 October 1932
43 Diary, 12 September 1964
44 Diary, 12 September 1945

Chapter 9
1   Diary, 4 February 1935, 13 April
    1940, 26 August 1938
2   Diary, 8 December 1932
3   *Here's A New Day*, p. 75
4   Diary, 30 November 1964
5   Diary, 29 June 1933
6   *Secret Places*, pp. 116–17
7   Diary, 24 May 1942
8   Diary, 10 February 1933
9   Katherine Wigglesworth, interview
    with the author, 8 February 1984
10 *Plowmen's Clocks*, pp. 103–4
11 *Wild Honey*, pp. 130–1
12 Notes taken by the author at
    Downs House, 10–11 April 1984
13 Du Sautoy papers, Alison Uttley to
    Peter du Sautoy, 4 October 1961
14 *Plowmen's Clocks*, p. 104
15 *Wild Honey*, p. 130
16 Diary, 26 November 1932
17 Diary, 3 September 1936
18 Du Sautoy papers, Alison Uttley to
    Peter du Sautoy, 4 October 1961
19 *Ambush of Young Days*, p. 44
20 Diary, 22 September 1954
21 Martin Byers to the author, 22
    September 1984
22 Diary, 3 January 1945
23 Diary, 14 August 1957
24 Diary, 18 May 1943
25 Diary, 5 December 1934 and 23
    November 1936
26 Diary, 23 September 1954
27 Author's interview with Dr F. W.
    Ratcliffe, 11 July 1984
28 Author's interview with Mrs Lilian

King, 16 March 1984, and Mrs
Joyce Kann, 27 January 1984
29 Mrs K. Luscombe (Helen Uttley's
    sister) to the author
30 Martin Byers, 22 September 1984
31 Interview with Katherine
    Wigglesworth, 8 February 1984
32 Interview with Anthony Tolson,
    October 1984
33 Diary, 30 January 1970
34 Diary, 25 September 1953
35 Diary, 22 January 1932
36 Du Sautoy papers, Alison Uttley
    to Peter du Sautoy, 1 September
    1961
37 *A Peck of Gold*, p. 87
38 Diary, 13 February 1960
39 *The Button Box*, p. 16
40 *Wild Honey*, p. 19
41 *Homes and Gardens*, August 1928
42 Diary, 16 May 1965

Chapter 10
1   *The Button Box*, pp. 9–10
2   *Ibid.*, p. 10
3   *Ibid.*
4   *Ibid.*, p. 11
5   *Ibid.*, p. 17
6   *Ibid.*, p. 15
7   Alison Uttley interviewed in
    'Line-Up', BBC TV, 1970
8   *Something For Nothing*, p. 86
9   *Ibid.*, pp. 86–7
10 Rylands, R.141974, Box 22,
    Samuel Alexander to Alison
    Uttley, 7 December 1928
11 *The Button Box*, p. 17
12 Diary, 10 April 1969
13 *The Button Box*, p. 17
14 *Wild Honey*, p. 20
15 *Ibid.*, p. 21
16 Diary, 21 July 1932
17 *The Button Box*, p. 17
18 *Ambush of Young Days*, pp. 26–7
19 BBC TV, 'Line-Up', 1970
20 *A Peck of Gold*, p. 34
21 *Wild Honey*, p. 21
22 *Ibid.*, p. 24
23 Betty Fairbairn, interview, 27
    January 1984
24 Diary, 8 February 1960
25 *Wild Honey*, p. 21
26 *The Button Box*, p. 17
27 Rylands, G.29818, Alison Uttley,

'Short Autobiography for Messrs Collins, Publishers', 21 October 1957

28 Du Sautoy papers, *Mrs Nimble and Mr Bumble*

29 Rylands, G.29818, Alison Uttley, 'Short Autobiography'

30 Letters at Heinemann: Alison Uttley to Katherine Munro, 28 January 1929, and Heinemann to Alison Uttley, 18 February 1929

31 Diary, 23 April 1971

32 Diary, 3 September 1938

33 Rylands, G.27069, original ms. of *The Squirrel, the Hare and the Little Grey Rabbit*

34 *The Squirrel, the Hare and the Little Grey Rabbit* (1929 edition)

35 BBC TV, 'Line-Up', 1970

36 Foreword to later Grey Rabbit books

37 Diary, 8 January 1964

38 Dairy, 10 April 1969

39 *A Ten O'Clock Scholar*, p. 111

40 *Ibid.*, pp. 116–17

41 Interview in *The Times*, 29 December 1959

42 Interview with Katherine Wigglesworth, 8 February 1984

43 Diary, 28 May 1969

44 Diary, 25 August 1968

45 Diary, 25 March 1964

46 Rylands, G.27069, original ms. of *How Little Grey Rabbit Got Back Her Tail*

47 Susan Dickinson, interviewed in 'The Snow-Baby' by Denis Judd, BBC Radio 4, 16 December 1984

48 Du Sautoy papers, Alison Uttley writing in *Something About the Author: Facts and Pictures about Contemporary Authors and Illustrators of Books for Young People*, edited by Anne Commire, Gale Research Book Tower, Detroit, Michigan (an off-print)

Chapter 11
1 *Altrincham Guardian*, 3 October 1930
2 *Ibid.*
3 *Ibid.*
4 *Ibid.*
5 Diary, 5 February 1933

6 Diary, 28 January 1936

7 *Altrincham Guardian*, 3 October 1930

8 Dick Frost to the author, 13 May 1984

9 Letter given to the author by Helen Uttley, James Uttley to John, 1 June 1930

10 *Ibid.*

11 *Ibid.*

12 *Ibid.*

13 *Altrincham Guardian*, 3 October 1930

14 Diary, 29 July 1938

15 Diary, 27 July 1968

16 Diary, 24 May 1941 and 18 September 1940

17 Dick Frost to the author, 13 May 1984

18 Martin Byers to the author, 22 September 1984

19 *Ibid.*

20 *Ibid.*

21 Diary, 5 October 1940

22 Papers given to the author by Dr Katherine Watson (née Armfield) Last Will and Testament of James Arthur Uttley, 12 November 1926

23 Katherine Watson papers, 'Valuation of the Estate of James Uttley deceased'.

24 *Ibid.*, Alison Uttley to Harold Armfield, 4 May 1931

25 *Ibid.*, George Uttley to Harold Armfield, 1 November 1930

26 *Ibid.*

27 *Ibid.*

28 *Ibid.*, Alison Uttley to Harold Armfield, 8 June 1931

29 *Ibid.*, 27 April 1935

30 *Something For Nothing*, p. 87

31 Rylands, R.141974, Box 22, Samuel Alexander to Alison Uttley, 30 September 1930

32 *Something For Nothing*, p. 87

Chapter 12
1 Diary, 5 February 1932
2 Diary, 9 June 1932
3 Diary, 18 October 1932
4 Diary, 15 May 1932
5 Diary, 4 October 1932
6 Diary, 23 April 1932 and 3 May 1932

7 Diary, 12 May 1932
8 Diary, 15 March 1932
9 Diary, 30 April 1933
10 Diary, 29 January 1932
11 *Ibid.*
12 Diary, 8 May 1932
13 Diary, 17 July 1932
14 Diary, 5 November 1932
15 Diary, 15 December 1932
16 Diary, 30 December 1932
17 Diary, 10 February 1933
18 Diary, 20 May 1932
19 Diary, 6 August 1933
20 Diary, 12 January 1933
21 Diary, 22 October 1933
22 Diary, 10 March 1932
23 Diary, 1 December 1932
24 Diary, 2 April 1933
25 Diary, 1 June 1932
26 Diary, 10 February 1932
27 Diary, 26 January 1933
28 Diary, 17 December 1933
29 Diary, 14 October 1932
30 Diary, 1 March 1933
31 Diary, 21 August 1932
32 Diary, 21 January 1932
33 Diary, 22 January 1932
34 Diary, 20 September 1932
35 Diary, 13 November 1932
36 Diary, 5 May 1933
37 Diary, 7 December 1933
38 Diary, 6 October 1933
39 Diary, 17 July 1965
40 Diary, 4 February 1933
41 Diary, 3 March 1933
42 Diary, 7 August 1934
43 Diary, 21 February 1933
44 *The Times Literary Supplement*, 17 September 1931
45 *Manchester Guardian*, 18 October 1931
46 *Evening News*, 15 September 1931
47 *Time and Tide*, 19 September 1931
48 Diary, 15 September 1932
49 Diary, 17 September 1932
50 *Everyman*, 10 December 1932
51 The *Listener*, 9 November 1932
52 *Manchester Guardian*, 1 December 1932
53 *New Statesman*, 10 December 1932
54 *Spectator*, 2 December 1932
55 Diary, 28 October 1932
56 The *Bookman*, Christmas 1932
57 Rylands, III A 4 (G.7073)
58 Rylands, III A 3 (G.27072)
59 Information supplied by Heinemann, via Peter Carter-Ruck, 27 November 1984
60 Diary, 3 May 1966
61 Du Sautoy papers, Alison Uttley to Peter du Sautoy, 15 May 1969
62 Diary, 9 December 1932
63 *Ibid.*
64 Diary, 20 January 1933
65 Du Sautoy papers, offprint of Alison Uttley writing in *Something About the Author* (ed. Anne Commire)
66 Diary, 17 June 1933
67 Diary, 11 August 1933
68 Diary, 1 November 1933
69 Diary, 28 November 1933

Chapter 13
1 Diary, 14 February 1934
2 Diary, 4 March 1935
3 Diary, 1 August 1934
4 Diary, 2 January 1935
5 Diary, 13 March 1934
6 Diary, 10 August 1936
7 Diary, 10 September 1936
8 Diary, 3 January 1936
9 Diary, 24 June 1935
10 BBC TV, 'The Book Programme', 'Alison Uttley and Little Grey Rabbit', 23 December 1975
11 Diary, 2 October 1934
12 Diary, 2 January 1935
13 Diary, 25 December 1935
14 Diary, 8 October 1934
15 Diary, 17 December 1934
16 Diary, 2 August 1935
17 Dick Frost to the author, 13 May 1984
18 Mrs K. Luscombe (Helen Uttley's sister) to the author, 10 May 1984
19 Diary, 10 June 1936
20 Diary, 25 February 1934
21 Diary, 25 October 1934
22 Diary, 9 February 1936
23 Diary, 24 January 1935
24 Diary, 20 December 1935
25 Diary, 8 August 1935
26 Diary, 2 March 1936
27 Diary, 31 January 1936
28 Diary, 30 October 1935
29 Diary, 24 December 1935
30 Diary, 31 December 1936

31 Diary, 21 June 1936
32 Diary, 13 February 1936
33 *Ibid*.
34 Diary, 25 September 1936
35 Diary, 26 April 1936
36 Diary, 19 February 1934
37 Diary, 31 December 1936
38 Diary, 13 November 1935
39 Diary, 24 May 1934
40 Diary, 20 January 1936
41 Diary, 21 January 1936
42 Diary, 3 December 1936
43 Diary, 11 December 1936
44 *Ibid*.
45 Diary, 19 October 1934
46 Diary, 15 January 1935
47 Diary, 23 August 1934
48 Diary, 18 December 1936
49 Diary, 10 February 1934
50 Diary, 28 October 1932
51 Diary, 7 August 1934
52 Diary, 17 December 1935
53 Diary, 30 August 1936
54 Diary, 25 April 1934
55 Diary, 12 December 1934
56 Diary, 15 August 1936
57 Diary, 11 June 1934
58 Diary, 1 October 1936
59 *Vogue*, November 1936, and *Time and Tide*, December 1936
60 The *Lady*, December 1936
61 *John O'London's Weekly*, December 1936
62 Diary, 29 February 1936
63 Diary, 16 August 1935
64 Diary, 6 December 1934
65 Diary, 22 April 1936
66 Diary, 11 May 1936
67 Diary, 30 October 1936
68 Diary, 28 October 1936

Chapter 14
1 Diary, 29 January 1937
2 Diary, 11 January 1938
3 Diary, 9 July 1938
4 Diary, 23 July 1937
5 Diary, 17 December 1937
6 Diary, 18 February 1937
7 Diary, 30 September 1937
8 Diary, 19 October 1938
9 Diary, 24 July 1937
10 Diary, 14 February 1937
11 Diary, 31 July 1937
12 *Ibid*.
13 Diary, 29 August 1937
14 Diary, 5 February 1938
15 Diary, 22 July 1938
16 Diary, 18 July 1937
17 Diary, 26 September 1937
18 Diary, 3 February 1937
19 Diary, 20 January 1938
20 Diary, 31 January 1938
21 Diary, 9 August 1937
22 Diary, 24 January 1937
23 Diary, 28 November 1938
24 Diary, 8 August 1937
25 Diary, 2 November 1936
26 Diary, 19 May 1937
27 Rylands, R.141974, Box 22, Samuel Alexander to Alison Uttley, 7 September 1938
28 Diary, 8 November 1937
29 Diary, 10 March 1937
30 Diary, 26 April 1938
31 Diary, 23 September 1938
32 Diary, 30 September 1938
33 Diary, 7 January 1937
34 Diary, 29 April 1938
35 Diary, 12 January 1938
36 Diary, 28 January 1937
37 *Ambush of Young Days*, p. 96
38 The *Listener*, February 1937
39 *Woman's Magazine*, June 1937
40 Diary, 1 August 1937
41 *Education*, 19 March 1937
42 *The Sunday Times*, 7 February 1937
43 Diary, 8 February 1937
44 Diary, 10 February 1937
45 Diary, 7 September 1937
46 Diary, 30 April 1937
47 *The Times Literary Supplement*, 25 December 1937
48 The *Observer*, 28 November 1937
49 Diary, 16 March 1937
50 Diary, 2 April 1937
51 Diary, 20 June 1937
52 Diary, 24 February 1938
53 *High Meadows*, p. 187
54 Diary, 24 May 1938
55 Diary, 18 October 1938
56 Diary, 5 March 1937
57 Diary, 13 August 1937
58 Diary, 21 September 1937
59 Peter du Sautoy to the author, various conversations
60 Diary, 15 December 1937
61 Diary, 28 March 1938
62 Diary, 14 May 1938

63 Diary, 19 October 1938
64 Diary, 23 August 1937
65 Diary, 4 January 1938
66 Diary, 20 July 1938
67 *Ibid.*

Chapter 15
1 Peter du Sautoy, interviewed in
   'The Snow-baby' by Denis Judd,
   BBC Radio 4, 16 December 1984
2 *Ibid.*
3 Susan Dickinson, interviewed in
   'The Snow-baby'.
4 Diary, 12 September 1967
5 Peter du Sautoy, 'The Snow-baby'
6 Interview with Mrs Ethel Stewart
   and Frances Stewart, 10 February
   1984
7 Sir Oliver Millar to the author, 14
   May 1984
8 Diary, 11 November 1938
9 Katherine Wigglesworth to the
   author, 13 February 1984
10 Diary, 14 October 1939
11 Diary, 31 July 1941
12 Diary, 11 September 1941
13 Interview with Mrs Lilian King, 16
   March 1984
14 Diary, 25 October 1940
15 Diary, 27 August 1941
16 Diary, 10 April 1941
17 Diary, 25 February 1940
18 Diary, 14 January 1941
19 Diary, 23 May 1940
20 Diary, 27 December 1940
21 Diary, 15 October 1939
22 Diary, 4 July 1941
23 Diary, 22 January 1939
24 Diary, 9 November 1940
25 Diary, 17 December 1939
26 Diary, 17 January 1941
27 Diary, 19 January 1941
28 Diary, 1 December 1939
29 Diary, 3 September 1939
30 Diary, 21 October 1939
31 Diary, 21 May 1940
32 Diary, 1 September 1940
33 Diary, 4 October 1939
34 Diary, 30 October 1939
35 Diary, 19 September 1940
36 Diary, 3 January 1941
37 Diary, 31 January 1941
38 Diary, 26 January 1940
39 Diary, 3 January 1940

40 Diary, 15 March 1940
41 Diary, 4 April 1940 and 26 June 1940
42 Diary, 28 March 1940
43 Diary, 4 December 1940
44 Diary, 11 June 1941
45 Diary, 27 May 1941
46 Diary, 3 December 1968
47 Katherine Wigglesworth to the
   author, 3 January 1984
48 Diary, 21 April 1943
49 Dr Frederick Ratcliffe, interviewed
   by the author, 11 July 1984
50 'The Snow-baby', 16 December 1984
51 *Ibid.*
52 Diary, 12 June 1940
53 Diary, 16 June 1940
54 Diary, 18 March 1940
55 Rylands, III A 8 (G.27077)
56 The *Observer*, 4 December 1939
57 *The Sunday Times*, December 1939
58 *The Times Educational Supplement*,
   Christmas edition 1941
59 Diary, 22 August 1939
60 Diary, 22 July 1939
61 Diary, 9 November 1939
62 The *Observer*, 14 November 1939
63 Diary, 14 November 1939
64 Diary, 21 November 1939
65 Diary, 13 January 1940
66 Diary, 18 July 1940
67 Diary, 23 April 1941
68 The *Spectator*, May 1941
69 Diary, 11 December 1940
70 Angus Calder, *The People's War:
   Britain 1939–45*, Granada, 1971, p. 591
71 Peter du Sautoy in conversation with
   the author, 20 July 1984
72 Diary, 2 December 1940

Chapter 16
1 Diary, 1 January 1942
2 Diary, 19 April 1942
3 Diary, 20 April 1942
4 Diary, 21 April 1942
5 Diary, 2 July 1942
6 *Ibid.*
7 *Ibid.*
8 Dick Frost to the author, quoting
   Helen Uttley (John's wife), 22 May
   1984
9 Diary, 2 July 1942, and Katherine
   Wigglesworth to the author, 8
   February 1984
10 Diary, 24 June 1943

11 *Ibid.*
12 Diary, 22 September 1942
13 Diary, 8 May 1943
14 Diary, 18 May 1943
15 Diary, 7 June 1943
16 Diary, 28 November 1943
17 Diary, 4 April 1942
18 Diary, 4 March 1944
19 Rylands, R.141974, Walter de la Mare to Alison Uttley, 28 September 1943
20 Diary, 12 July 1943
21 Diary, 13 October 1944
22 Diary, 30 July 1945
23 Diary, 13 March 1943
24 Diary, 2 July 1944
25 Diary, 20 February 1943
26 Diary, 13 January 1943
27 Diary, 12 January 1944
28 Diary, 15 March 1942
29 Diary, 19 June 1944
30 Diary, 27 March 1942
31 Diary, 13 April 1943
32 *Manchester Guardian*, 24 March 1943
33 The *Listener*, 20 May 1943
34 *Home Chat*, 3 July 1943
35 Diary, 5 December 1945
36 Diary, 12 February 1946

Chapter 17
1 Diary, 23 October 1948
2 Sir Oliver Millar to the author, 14 May 1984
3 Diary, 19 February 1949
4 Diary, 6 January 1946
5 Interview with Mrs Betty Fairbairn, 27 January 1984
6 Diary, 30 November 1947
7 Diary, 5 December 1947
8 Diary, 17 and 18 October 1945
9 Diary, 13 July 1946
10 Diary, 24 August 1946
11 Diary, 27 August 1946
12 Diary, 29 August 1946
13 Mrs Kathleen Luscombe (Helen Uttley's sister) to the author, 10 May 1984
14 Helen Uttley to the author, 2 January 1984
15 *Ibid.*, 13 March 1984
16 Dick Frost to the author, 22 May 1984
17 Kathleen Luscombe to the author, 10 May 1984
18 *Ibid.*, 23 May 1984

19 Diary, 23 November 1946
20 Diary, 12 December 1946
21 Diary, 14 December 1946
22 Diary, 21 September 1947
23 Diary, 31 December 1947
24 Diary, 20 June 1948
25 Diary, 18 June 1949
26 Opening page of Diary for 1949
27 Diary, 7 August 1949
28 Diary, 20 March 1947
29 Susan Dickinson, 'The Snow-baby', 16 December 1984
30 Diary, 21 April 1950
31 Diary, 18 March 1950
32 Diary, 14 April 1950
33 *The Sunday Times*, 23 January 1949
34 Diary, 25 March 1950

Chapter 18
1 Diary, 17 December 1954
2 Diary, 11 January 1953
3 Diary, 6 January 1951
4 Diary, 7 November 1953
5 Diary, 25 January 1955
6 Poem by John Uttley to Helen, 12 April 1967, in author's possession
7 Diary, 23 November 1954
8 Diary, 22 February 1954
9 Diary, 16 December 1955
10 Diary, 6 May 1951
11 Diary, 1 November 1954
12 Diary, 31 October 1955
13 Diary, 5 April 1954
14 Diary, 2 April 1955
15 *Irish Independent*, 15 November 1952
16 Diary, 28 January 1953
17 Diary, 3 January 1953
18 Diary, 24 January 1953
19 *The Stuff of Dreams*, pp. 9–10
20 *The Sunday Times*, 29 November 1953
21 *The Times*, 18 December 1953
22 Diary, 23 February 1954

Chapter 19
1 Diary, 1 January 1956
2 Diary, 1 January 1957
3 Diary, 17 June 1957
4 Diary, 17 December 1959
5 Diary, 31 December 1959
6 Diary, 19 November 1957
7 Diary, 10 January 1958
8 Diary, 9 January 1958

9 Diary, 21 February 1957
10 Diary, 21 October 1958
11 Du Sautoy papers, Alison Uttley to Peter du Sautoy, 29 December 1960
12 Diary, 1 July 1957
13 Tony Tolson to the author, October 1984, and Martin Byers to the author, 30 September 1984
14 Diary, 20 August 1957
15 Diary, 16 December 1957
16 Diary, 22 June 1956
17 Rylands, Gwladys Llewellyn to Alison Uttley, 20 December 1957
18 Diary, 23 March 1959
19 Diary, 8 February 1960
20 Diary, 30 June 1956
21 Diary, 31 October 1956
22 Diary, 3 November 1956
23 Diary, 4 November 1956
24 Diary, 19 March 1960
25 Diary, 17 January 1957
26 *The Times* obituary for Dr Kerlan, 15 January 1964
27 *The Times*, 29 December 1959
28 Du Sautoy papers, Alison Uttley to Peter du Sautoy, 11 August 1961. Note: Alison produced some brief autobiographical notes for Peter du Sautoy, some of which have been used in this book.
29 Ibid., Alison Uttley to Peter du Sautoy, 12 December 1962
30 Diary, 28 May 1958
31 Diary, 29 June 1958
32 Diary, 5 February 1958
33 Diary, 6 August 1958
34 Diary, 1 May 1956
35 The *Observer*, 23 November 1958
36 *The Times Literary Supplement*, 21 November 1958
37 *Daily Worker*, 18 December 1957
38 Du Sautoy papers, Alison Uttley to Peter du Sautoy, 18 February 1960
39 The *Scotsman*, 26 November 1960
40 *The Times Literary Supplement*, 15 November 1957
41 Kathleen Lines, Foreword to *Fairy Tales* (1979)
42 The *Scotsman*, 12 December 1957
43 *Country Life*, 31 December 1959
44 *The Times Literary Supplement*, 25 December 1959
45 Du Sautoy papers, Peter du Sautoy to Alison Uttley, 1 December 1959

46 *The Times Literary Supplement*, 23 December 1960
47 The *Countryman*, Spring 1961
48 Du Sautoy papers, Faber report, 24 March 1959
49 Diary, 14 April 1959
50 *John O'London's Weekly*, 25 August 1960

Chapter 20
1 Du Sautoy papers, Alison Uttley to Peter du Sautoy, 22 November 1962
2 Diary, 1 January 1961
3 Diary, 14 June 1962
4 Diary, 17 January 1965
5 Diary, 13 August 1961
6 Diary, 1 July 1965
7 Diary, 24 July 1964
8 Du Sautoy papers, Alison Uttley to Peter du Sautoy, 12 February 1963
9 Diary, 31 January 1961. Memorandum
10 Diary, 1 April 1964
11 Diary, 12 April 1961
12 Diary, 19 June 1963
13 Diary, 1 August 1964
14 Diary, 16 October 1964
15 *The Sunday Times*, 'Mrs Uttley and Dr Seuss', 21 November 1965
16 Diary, 22 November 1965
17 Diary, 27 November 1963
18 Diary, 11 October 1963
19 Diary, 14 July 1961
20 Diary, 13 November 1964
21 Du Sautoy papers, Alison Uttley to Peter du Sautoy, 5 August 1964
22 Ibid., Phyllis Hunt to Peter du Sautoy, 10 August 1964
23 Diary, 18 August 1964
24 Diary, 2 September 1964
25 Du Sautoy papers, Margaret McElderry to Peter du Sautoy, 27 December 1962
26 Ibid., Walter J. Minton to Peter du Sautoy, 13 February 1964
27 Ibid., Peter du Sautoy to W.J. Crawley, 12 November 1962
28 Diary, 10 March 1962
29 Rylands, R.142124, A.E. Kennedy to Alison Uttley, 16 December 1962
30 Diary, 18 January 1963
31 *Teacher's World*, 2 February 1962

32 Du Sautoy papers, Faber
    memorandum by Phyllis Hunt, 24
    April 1961
33 *Guardian*, 5 April 1963
34 *The Times Literary Supplement*, 23
    November 1962
35 *Guardian*, 14 December 1962
36 The *Countryman*, Spring 1963
37 The *Friend*, 4 December 1964
38 *Country Life*, 14 January 1965
39 The *Tablet*, 30 January 1965
40 The *Countryman*, Spring 1965
41 The *Queen*, 17 November 1965
42 *Punch*, 15 December 1965
43 *Children's Book News*, November/
    December 1965
44 *Daily Worker*, 2 December 1965

Chapter 21
1   Diary, 4 November 1968
2   Diary, 17 December 1968
3   Diary, 1 November 1969
4   Du Sautoy papers, Alison Uttley to
    Peter du Sautoy, 12 November
    1968
5   *Ibid.*, Alison Uttley to Peter du
    Sautoy, 2 March 1967
6   Diary, 27 June 1970
7   Diary, 31 July 1969
8   Diary, 3 July 1970
9   Diary, 30 November 1967
10 Diary, 6 June 1969
11 Diary, 12 March 1970
12 Du Sautoy papers, Alison Uttley to
    Peter du Sautoy, 2 April 1970
13 *Ibid.* and memo by Peter du Sautoy,
    8 May 1970
14 Diary, 8 April 1970
15 Diary, 14 May 1970
16 Diary, 13 May 1970
17 Manchester University, Founder's
    Day, 13 May 1970, address by
    Professor W.I.C. Morris
18 Diary, 14 March 1969
19 Diary, 11 March 1970
20 Diary, 9 July 1970
21 BBC TV, 'Line-Up', 14 May 1970
22 Diary, 21 May 1969
23 Peter du Sautoy to the author, 1983
24 Du Sautoy papers, Alison Uttley to
    Peter du Sautoy, 18 March 1969
25 Diary, 19 January 1970
26 Diary, 13 October 1970
27 Diary, 9 May 1969

28 Diary, 3 September 1968
29 Diary, 13 September 1967
30 Diary, 17 January 1969
31 Du Sautoy papers, Alison Uttley to
    Peter du Sautoy, 3 April 1969
32 Katherine Wigglesworth to the
    author, February 1984
33 *Ibid.*
34 The *Observer*, 10 April 1966
35 *Shields Gazette*, 7 May 1966
36 *Birmingham Post*, 5 May 1966
37 Du Sautoy papers, Peter du Sautoy
    to Alison Uttley, 24 January 1966
38 *Higher Education Journal*, Spring
    Term 1967
39 *Homes and Gardens*, April 1967
40 *The Times Literary Supplement*, 23
    February 1967
41 Diary, 31 August 1966
42 *Recipes from an Old Farm House*
    (1966) p. 9
43 *The Times*, 19 September 1966
44 *Daily Sketch*, 22 September 1966
45 *Yorkshire Post*, 29 December 1966
46 *Guardian*, 12 April 1973
47 Du Sautoy papers, Alison Uttley to
    Peter du Sautoy, 9 November 1967
48 The *Countryman*, Spring 1969
49 *The Times Literary Supplement*, 7
    November 1968
50 *Ibid.*
51 Du Sautoy papers, 2 January 1970
52 Du Sautoy papers, Mr Pickard to
    Peter du Sautoy, 20 March, 1 April
    and 6 May 1970
53 Diary, 6 May 1970
54 Du Sautoy papers, Peter du Sautoy
    to Alison Uttley, 9 March 1970
55 *Ibid.*, Faber memo, 11 March 1970
56 *Country Life*, 28 January 1971
57 The *Dalesman*, April 1971
58 The *Countryman*, Spring 1971
59 *The Church Times*, 15 January 1971
60 *The Times Literary Supplement*, 26
    February 1971

Chapter 22
1   Diary, 31 December 1971
2   Du Sautoy papers, Faber memo, 8
    August 1973
3   *Ibid.*, Faber memo, 11 October 1973
4   BBC TV, 'The Book Programme',
    'Alison Uttley and Little Grey
    Rabbit', 23 December 1975

5 *Birmingham Post*, 18 December 1971
6 *Ibid.*, Tunnicliffe to Peter du Sautoy, 5 October 1971
7 *Secret Places* (1972), p. 115
8 Du Sautoy papers, Peter du Sautoy to Alison Uttley, 13 November 1973
9 Diary, 3 September 1971
10 Du Sautoy papers, Alison Uttley to Peter du Sautoy, 6 November 1971
11 *Ibid.*, Alison Uttley to Peter du Sautoy, September 1976
12 BBC TV, 'The Book Programme', 23 December 1975
13 Diary, 14 February 1971
14 Diary, 9 May 1971 (relating to visit of 2 May 1971)
15 Letter from Tanya Benedictus, in Diary for 1971, 8 May 1971
16 Martin Byers to the author, 22 September 1984
17 Diary, 31 March 1971
18 Du Sautoy papers, Peter du Sautoy to R.J.B. Marsden, 21 October 1974
19 Mrs Lilian King to the author
20 Du Sautoy papers, Peter du Sautoy to Mrs Joy Sheller, 7 May 1976
21 *Ibid.*, Helen Uttley to Peter du Sautoy, 4 April 1976
22 *Ibid.*
23 *Ibid.*, Peter du Sautoy to Kathleen Day, 27 April 1976
24 *Ibid.* and Helen Uttley to Peter du Sautoy, 4 April 1976
25 *Ibid.*, Kathleen Day to Peter du Sautoy, 5 May 1976
26 *Ibid.*, Joy Sheller to Peter du Sautoy, 11 May 1976
27 *Ibid.*, Peter du Sautoy, 7 May 1976
28 *The Times*, 8 May 1976
29 *Daily Telegraph*, 8 May 1976
30 Du Sautoy papers, R.J.B. Marsden to Peter du Sautoy, 23 August 1976
31 *Ibid.*, Last Will and Testament of Alice Jane Uttley
32 *Ibid.*, Helen Uttley to Peter du Sautoy, 7 December 1982
33 *Ibid.*
34 *Ibid.*
35 Betty Fairbairn to Helen Uttley, 24 January 1984. Letter in author's possession
36 Susan Dickinson in conversation with the author

BIBLIOGRAPHY

MANUSCRIPT SOURCES

Alison Uttley's diaries, 1932–71

Alison Uttley papers, John Rylands University Library of Manchester.

Peter du Sautoy papers

Dr Katherine Watson papers

Alison Uttley papers at Faber, Collins and Heinemann

Letters given to the author by Helen Uttley, Kathleen Luscombe, Barbara Lees and Agnes Stewart

Papers and documents in the possession of Ashburne Hall, University of Manchester

NEWSPAPERS AND JOURNALS

Manchester Guardian; Guardian; Yggdrasill; Altrincham Guardian; The Times; The Times Literary Supplement; Evening News; Time and Tide; Everyman; Listener; New Statesman; Bookman; Vogue; Lady; John O'London Weekly; Woman; Observer; The Sunday Times; The Times Educational Supplement; Spectator; Irish Independent; Daily Worker; Scotsman; Country Life; Countryman; Teacher's World; Friend; Tablet; Queen; Punch; Children's Book News; Saturday Book; Birmingham Post; Daily Telegraph; Home Chat; Farmer's Weekly; Good Housekeeping; Housewife; Merry-Go-Round; New World; Manchester Evening News; My Magazine; Radio Times; Shields Gazette; Bookseller; Northern Dispatch; St Martin's Review; My Home; Chichester Observer; Stroud News and Journal; Oxford Times; Northern Echo; Bath Chronicle and Herald; Scottish Field; Higher Education Journal; British Book News; Saturday Review; Methodist Times; Education; Methodist Recorder; Books of Today; Catholic Herald; Homes and Gardens; Hindusthan Standard; Morning Star; Yorkshire Post; Junior Bookshelf; Good Parents; Dalesman; Burton Daily Mail; Ideal Home; Bucks Free Press; Bucks Advertiser

BOOKS, ARTICLES, TELEVISION AND RADIO PROGRAMMES ON ALISON UTTLEY

Elizabeth Saintsbury, *The World of Alison Uttley*, Howard Baker, London, 1980 (Despite the author's best efforts, this book is inevitably and grievously handicapped by its complete dependence for evidence upon Alison's published work and a few interviews.)

Barbara Brill, 'Artist and Writer: a Country Partnership' (Alison Uttley and C.F. Tunnicliffe), in *Countryman*, vol.84, no.4, winter, 1979–80

A profile of Alison Uttley, in 'Line-up', BBC TV, 14 May 1970

'Alison Uttley and Little Grey Rabbit', 'The Book Programme', BBC TV, 23 December 1975

'The Snow-baby', an appreciation of Alison Uttley on the centenary of her birth, by Denis Judd, BBC Radio 4, 16 December 1984

BOOKS BY ALISON UTTLEY
PUBLICATIONS FOR CHILDREN
Fiction

The Squirrel, The Hare and the Little Grey Rabbit, illustrated by Margaret Tempest, Heinemann, London, 1929

How Little Grey Rabbit Got Back Her Tail, illustrated by Margaret Tempest, Heinemann, London, 1930

The Great Adventure of Hare, illustrated by Margaret Tempest, Heinemann, London, 1931

Moonshine and Magic, illustrated by Will Townsend, Faber, London, 1932

The Story of Fuzzypeg the Hedgehog, illustrated by Margaret Tempest, Heinemann, London, 1932

Squirrel Goes Skating, illustrated by Margaret Tempest, Collins, London, 1934

Wise Owl's Story, illustrated by Margaret Tempest, Collins, London, 1935

The Adventures of Peter and Judy in Bunnyland, illustrated by L. Young, Collins, London, 1935

Candelight Tales, illustrated by Elinor Bellingham-Smith, Faber, London, 1936

Little Grey Rabbit's Party, illustrated by Margaret Tempest, Collins, London, 1936

The Knot Squirrel Tied, illustrated by Margaret Tempest, Collins, London, 1937

The Adventures of No Ordinary Rabbit, illustrated by Alec Buckels, Faber, London, 1937

Mustard, Pepper, and Salt, illustrated by Gwen Raverat, Faber, London, 1938

Fuzzypeg Goes To School, illustrated by Margaret Tempest, Collins, London, 1938

A Traveller in Time, Faber, London, 1939; Putnam, New York, 1940; Viking, New York, 1964; Puffin, Harmondsworth, 1977

Tales of the Four Pigs and Brock the Badger, illustrated by Alec Buckels, Faber, London, 1939

Little Grey Rabbit's Christmas, illustrated by Margaret Tempest, Collins, London, 1939

Moldy Warp, The Mole, illustrated by Margaret Tempest, Collins, London, 1940

The Adventures of Sam Pig, illustrated by Francis Gower, Faber, London, 1940; Puffin, Harmondsworth, 1976

Sam Pig Goes to Market, illustrated by A.E. Kennedy, Faber, London, 1941; Puffin, Harmondsworth, 1979

Six Tales of Brock the Badger, illustrated by Alec Buckels and Francis Gower, Faber, London, 1941

Six Tales of Sam Pig, illustrated by Alec Buckels and Francis Gower, Faber, London, 1941

Six Tales of the Four Pigs, illustrated by Alec Buckels, Faber, London, 1941

Ten Tales of Tim Rabbit, illustrated by Alec Buckels and Francis Gower, Faber, London, 1941

Hare Joins the Home Guard, illustrated by Margaret Tempest, Collins, London, 1942

Little Grey Rabbit's Washing-Day, illustrated by Margaret Tempest, Collins, London, 1942

Nine Starlight Tales, illustrated by Irene Hawkins, Faber, London, 1942

Sam Pig and Sally, illustrated by A.E. Kennedy, Faber, London, 1942; Puffin, Harmondsworth, 1979

Cuckoo Cherry-Tree, illustrated by Irene Hawkins, Faber, London, 1943

Sam Pig at the Circus, illustrated by A.E. Kennedy, Faber, London, 1943; Puffin, Harmondsworth, 1982

Water-Rat's Picnic, illustrated by Margaret Tempest, Collins, London, 1943

Little Grey Rabbit's Birthday, illustrated by Margaret Tempest, Collins, London, 1944

Mrs. Nimble and Mr. Bumble, illustrated by Horace Knowles, with *This Duck and That Duck*, by Herbert McKay, Francis James, London, 1944

The Spice Woman's Basket and Other Tales, illustrated by Irene Hawkins, Faber, London, 1944

The Adventures of Tim Rabbit, illustrated by A.E. Kennedy, Faber, London, 1945; Puffin, Harmondsworth, 1978

The Weather Cock and Other Stories, illustrated by Nancy Innes, Faber, London, 1945

The Speckledy Hen, illustrated by Margaret Tempest, Collins, London, 1946

Some Moonshine Tales, drawings by Sarah Nechamkin, Faber, London, 1945

Little Grey Rabbit and the Weasels, illustrated by Margaret Tempest, Collins, London, 1947

Grey Rabbit and the Wandering Hedgehog, illustrated by Margaret Tempest, Collins, London, 1948

John Barleycorn: Twelve Tales of Fairy and Magic, illustrated by Philip Hepworth, Faber, London, 1948

Sam Pig in Trouble, illustrated by A.E. Kennedy, Faber, London, 1948

The Cobbler's Shop and Other Tales, illustrated by Irene Hawkins, Faber, London, 1950

Macduff, illustrated by A.E. Kennedy, Faber, London, 1950

Little Grey Rabbit Makes Lace, illustrated by Margaret Tempest, Collins, London, 1950

The Little Brown Mouse Books (Snug and Serena Meet a Queen; Snug and Serena Pick Cowslips; Going to the Fair; Toad's Castle; Mrs. Mouse Spring-Cleans; Christmas at the Rose and Crown; The Gypsy Hedgehogs; Snug and the Chimney-Sweeper; The Mouse Telegrams; The Flower Show; Snug and the Silver Spoon; Mr. Stoat Walks In), illustrated by Katherine Wigglesworth, Heinemann, London, 1950–57

Yours Ever, Sam Pig, illustrated by A.E. Kennedy, Faber, London, 1951; Puffin, Harmondsworth, 1977

Hare and the Easter Eggs, illustrated by Margaret Tempest, Collins, London, 1952

Little Grey Rabbit's Valentine, illustrated by Margaret Tempest, Collins, London, 1953

Little Grey Rabbit Goes to Sea, illustrated by Margaret Tempest, Collins, London, 1954

Little Red Fox and the Wicked Uncle, illustrated by Katherine Wigglesworth, Heinemann, London, 1954; Bobbs Merrill, Indianapolis, 1962

Sam Pig and the Singing Gate, illustrated by A.E. Kennedy, Faber, London, 1955

Hare and Guy Fawkes, illustrated by Margaret Tempest, Collins, London, 1956

Little Red Fox and Cinderella, illustrated by Katherine Wigglesworth, Heinemann, London, 1956

Magic in My Pocket: A Selection of Tales, illustrated by Judith Brook, Penguin, London, 1957

Little Grey Rabbit's Paint-Box, illustrated by Margaret Tempest, Collins, London, 1958

Little Red Fox and the Magic Moon, illustrated by Katherine Wigglesworth, Heinemann, London, 1958

Snug and Serena Count Twelve, illustrated by Katherine Wigglesworth, Heinemann, London, 1959; Bobbs Merrill, Indianapolis, 1962

Tim Rabbit and Company, illustrated by A.E. Kennedy, Faber, London, 1959

Sam Pig Goes to the Seaside: Sixteen Stories, illustrated by A.E. Kennedy, Faber, London, 1960; Puffin, Harmondsworth, 1978

Grey Rabbit Finds a Shoe, illustrated by Margaret Tempest, Collins, London, 1960

John at the Old Farm, illustrated by Jennifer Miles, Heinemann, London, 1960

Grey Rabbit and the Circus, illustrated by Margaret Tempest, Collins, London, 1961

Snug and Serena Go to Town, illustrated by Katherine Wigglesworth, Heinemann, London, 1961; Bobbs Merrill, Indianapolis, 1963

Little Red Fox and the Unicorn, illustrated by Katherine Wigglesworth, Heinemann, London, 1962

The Little Knife Who Did All the Work: Twelve Tales of Magic, illustrated by Pauline Baynes, Faber, London, 1962; Puffin, Harmondsworth, 1978

Grey Rabbit's May Day, illustrated by Margaret Tempest, Collins, London, 1963

Tim Rabbit's Dozen, illustrated by Shirley Hughes, Faber, London, 1964

Hare Goes Shopping, illustrated by Margaret Tempest, Collins, London, 1965

The Sam Pig Storybook, illustrated by Cecil Leslie, Faber, London, 1965

The Mouse, The Rabbit, and the Little White Hen, illustrated by Jennie Corbett, Heinemann, London, 1966

Enchantment, illustrated by Jennie Corbett, Heinemann, London, 1966

Little Grey Rabbit's Pancake Day, illustrated by Margaret Tempest, Collins, London, 1967

Little Red Fox, illustrated by Katherine Wigglesworth, Puffin, Harmondsworth, 1967

The Little Red Fox and the Big Big Tree, illustrated by Jennie Corbett, Heinemann, London, 1968

Little Grey Rabbit Goes to the North Pole, illustrated by Katherine Wigglesworth, Collins, London, 1970

Lavender Shoes: Eight Tales of Enchantment, illustrated by Janina Ede, Faber, London, 1970

The Brown Mouse Book: Magical Tales of Two Little Mice, illustrated by Katherine Wigglesworth, Heinemann, London, 1971

Fuzzypeg's Brother, illustrated by Katherine Wigglesworth, Collins, London, 1971

Little Grey Rabbit's Spring Cleaning Party, illustrated by Katherine Wigglesworth, Collins, London, 1972

Little Grey Rabbit and the Snow-Baby, illustrated by Katherine Wigglesworth, Collins, London, 1973

Fairy Tales, edited by Kathleen Lines, illustrated by Ann Strugnell, Faber, London, 1975

Hare and the Rainbow, pictures by Katherine Wigglesworth, Collins, London, 1975; Puffin, Harmondsworth, 1979

Little Grey Rabbit's Storybook, illustrated by Margaret Tempest, Collins, London, 1977

From Spring to Spring, chosen by Kathleen Lines, illustrated by Shirley Hughes, Faber, London, 1978

Tales of Grey Rabbit, illustrated by Faith Jaques, Heinemann, London, 1980; Piccolo Books, London, 1982

Little Grey Rabbit's Second Storybook, pictures by Margaret Tempest, Collins, London, 1981

Tales of Little Brown Mouse, illustrated by Faith Jaques, Heinemann, London, 1984

Foxglove Tales, chosen by Lucy Meredith, illustrated by Shirley Felts, Faber, London, 1984

Little Grey Rabbit's Alphabet Book, pictures by Margaret Tempest, Collins, London, 1985

Plays

Little Grey Rabbit to the Rescue, illustrated by Margaret Tempest, Collins, London, 1945

The Washerwoman's Child: A Play on the Life and Stories of Hans Christian Andersen, illustrated by Irene Hawkins, Faber, London, 1946

Three Little Grey Rabbit Plays (includes *Grey Rabbit's Hospital, The Robber, A Christmas Story*), Heinemann, London, 1961

PUBLICATIONS FOR ADULTS

Novels

High Meadows, Faber, London, 1938

When All Is Done, Faber, London, 1945

Other

The Country Child, Faber, London, and Macmillan, New York, 1931; Peacock Books, Harmondsworth, 1963, reissued in Puffin Books, 1969

Ambush of Young Days, Faber, London, 1937

The Farm on the Hill, Faber, London, 1941

Country Hoard, Faber, London, 1943; Howard Baker, London, 1976

Country Things, Faber, London, 1946

Carts and Candlesticks, Faber, London, 1948

Buckinghamshire, Hale, London, 1950

Plowmen's Clocks, Faber, London, 1952

The Stuff of Dreams, Faber, London, 1953

Here's a New Day, Faber, London, 1956

A Year in the Country, Faber, London, 1957; Howard Baker, London, 1976

The Swans Fly Over, Faber, London, 1959

Something for Nothing, Faber, London, 1960

Wild Honey, Faber, London, 1962; Howard Baker, London, 1978

Cuckoo in June, Faber, London, 1964; Howard Baker, London, 1978

A Peck of Gold, Faber, London, 1966

Recipes from an Old Farmhouse, Faber, London, 1966

The Button Box and Other Essays, Faber, London, 1968

The Ten O'Clock Scholar and Other Essays, Faber, London, 1970

Secret Places and Other Essays, Faber, London, 1972

Editor, *In Praise of Country Life: An Anthology*, Muller, London, 1949

Stories for Christmas, chosen by Kathleen Lines, illustrated by Gavin Rowe, Puffin, Harmondsworth, 1977

Our Village: Alison Uttley's Cromford, illustrated by C.F. Tunnicliffe, selected by Jacqueline Mitchell, Scarthin, Cromford, 1984

Country World, chosen by Lucy Meredith, illustrated by C.F. Tunnicliffe, Faber, London, 1984

INDEX